Duras, Writing, and the Ethical

Making the Broken Whole

MARTIN CROWLEY

CLARENDON PRESS · OXFORD

OXFORD
UNIVERSITY PRESS

Great Clarendon Street, Oxford OX2 6DP

Oxford University Press is a department of the University of Oxford.
It furthers the University's objective of excellence in research, scholarship,
and education by publishing worldwide in

Oxford New York

Athens Auckland Bangkok Bogotá Buenos Aires Calcutta
Cape Town Chennai Dar es Salaam Delhi Florence Hong Kong Istanbul
Karachi Kuala Lumpur Madrid Melbourne Mexico City Mumbai
Nairobi Paris São Paulo Shanghai Singapore Taipei Tokyo Toronto Warsaw

and associated companies in Berlin Ibadan

Oxford is a registered trade mark of Oxford University Press
in the UK and certain other countries

Published in the United States
by Oxford University Press Inc., New York

© Martin Crowley 2000

British Library Cataloguing in Publication Data

Data available

Library of Congress Cataloging in Publication Data

Data available

ISBN 0-19-816013-5

1 3 5 7 9 10 8 6 4 2

Typeset by Jayvee, Trivandrum, India
Printed in Great Britain
on acid-free paper by
Biddles Ltd.,
Guildford and King's Lynn

In Memory of

ELEANOR MARGARET WOOLLER

(1931–1993)

ACKNOWLEDGEMENTS

An earlier version of part of Chapter 4 appeared as ' "Il n'y a qu'une espèce humaine": Between Duras and Antelme', in Andrew Leak and George Paizis (eds.), *The Holocaust and the Text: Speaking the Unspeakable* (London: Macmillan, 2000), 174–92. Part of Chapter 5 appeared as ' "C'est curieux un mort": Duras on Homosexuality', in *Modern Language Review*, 93/3 (July 1998), 659–77; I am grateful to the Modern Humanities Research Association for permission to reproduce it here. Part of Chapter 6 appears in ' "Like the French of France"?: Immigration and Translation in the Later Novels of Marguerite Duras', in James Williams (ed.), *Revisioning Duras* (Liverpool: Liverpool University Press, forthcoming).

For help with this project, I would like first to express my great gratitude to Ann Jefferson for her committed, generous, and enthusiastic supervision of the D.Phil. on which this book is based. Malcolm Bowie, Colin Davis, and Emma Wilson read and commented expertly on earlier versions of what follows, as did Leslie Hill, who has consistently been generous with time, information, and ceaselessly provocative discussion; I greatly appreciate all their help, as well as that of Michael Holland, who kindly provided early evidence of the intellectual relationship between Duras and Blanchot. I am also grateful to Sophie Goldsworthy, at Oxford University Press, for seeing this book through to publication; and to Adrian Armstrong, Daron Burrows, and especially, Henry Phillips for considerable support during this process. Many of the ideas developed here have been sustained by the friendship and unfailing intellectual companionship of Nicola Luckhurst and Ingrid Wassenaar, and it is a pleasure to thank them for this. Finally, I would like to thank beyond all measure Rachel Wooller, who has tirelessly discussed and encouraged this project, and whose extraordinary support has been both a blessing and an inspiration.

CONTENTS

ABBREVIATIONS

The following abbreviations are used for references to major texts by Duras. Full information for all texts may be found in the bibliography.

AA	*L'Amante anglaise*
ACN	*L'Amant de la Chine du Nord*
AMA	*L'Après-midi de Monsieur Andesmas*
Ar	*L'Amour*
ASD	*Abahn Sabana David*
'ASM'	'Aurélia Steiner Melbourne'
'ASP'	'Aurélia Steiner Paris'
'ASV'	'Aurélia Steiner Vancouver'
At	*L'Amant*
BCP	*Un Barrage contre le Pacifique*
C	*Le Camion*
CT	*C'est tout*
D	*La Douleur*
Dd	*Détruire dit-elle*
DH	*Dix heures et demie du soir en été*
DJ	*Des Journées entières dans les arbres*
É	*Écrire*
EL	*Emily L.*
É80	*L'Été 80*
HAC	*L'Homme assis dans le couloir*
'HACa'	'L'Homme assis dans le couloir'
HMA	*Hiroshima mon amour*
I	*Les Impudents*
IS	*India Song*
L	*Les Lieux de Marguerite Duras*
MC	*Moderato cantabile*
ME	*Le Monde extérieur*
MG	*Le Marin de Gibraltar*
MM	*La Maladie de la mort*
NG	*Nathalie Granger, suivie de: La Femme du Gange*
NN	*Le Navire Night et autres textes*
O	*Outside*
P	*Les Parleuses*
PC	*Les Petits Chevaux de Tarquinia*
PE	*La Pluie d'été*
RCT	*Romans, Cinéma, Théâtre: Un Parcours*

xi

RLVS	*Le Ravissement de Lol V. Stein*
S	*Le Square*
VC	*Le Vice-Consul*
VM	*La Vie matérielle*
VSO	*Les Viaducs de la Seine-et-Oise*
VT	*La Vie tranquille*
YAS	*Yann Andréa Steiner*
YB	*Les Yeux bleus cheveux noirs*
YV	*Les Yeux verts*

Nothing will come of nothing: speak again.
King Lear

INTRODUCTION

Ç'aurait été un mot-absence, un mot-trou, creusé en son centre d'un
trou, de ce trou où tous les autres mots auraient été enterrés. On
n'aurait pas pu le dire mais on aurait pu le faire résonner.

Le Ravissement de Lol V. Stein

Duras is not an ethical writer. She neither shows nor tells us how to
lead the good life, nor does she tease out the complications of our
moral decisions in such a way as to suggest their baffling complexity. The lyrical combination of paroxysm and debris that might
characterize the quintessentially Durassian is hardly the space of a
meaningful discussion of right and wrong. Everything that follows
here, then, is highly unlikely.

And yet: it will be the argument of this study that, while Duras's
writing is hardly 'ethical' in any such ready sense, this writing is both
misrecognized and undervalued if it is not read as a sustained,
uncomfortable, and important encounter with ethical questions
and dilemmas. It is my contention that Duras's extraordinary work
is shot through with an address to concerns which are those of the
ethical; and that the drama and the pathos of her writing are to
be traced in large part to the particular—awkward—form of this
address. Over the following chapters, I will attempt to demonstrate
that ethical questions have consistently been at stake in the key
inflections of Duras's writing; such a demonstration will, I hope,
bring to Duras criticism a dimension without which it cannot hope
to respond to the enormity of its inspiring object.

By way of a brief introduction to my reading of Duras, I propose
over the following pages to indicate some of the contexts within
which this reading is situated, and to suggest its possible significance
for these contexts. Outlining the approach to be found in the coming chapters, this sketch will take us from the intricacies of Duras's
textual practice to some of the most pressing concerns of our day
(which is still, in a sense, also Duras's). And it is, I will be arguing,
precisely at this exacting juncture that Duras demands to be read.
Duras's writing is of a complexity and a subtlety that are seriously
neglected if she is not read, as I shall endeavour to do, at the level of
the tiniest textual details. Such reading also suggests, as I shall

argue, that Duras's work has much to offer to both our literary and our ethical understanding.[1]

Writing Beyond Excess

That Duras's writing has become such a dazzling success ought not to blind us to its constant atmosphere of crisis. Indeed, her entire *œuvre* may be seen as a sustained attempt to catch up in writing the inexpressible drama of all manner of extreme experiences. In fact, it is in part the intensity of this effort that has helped Duras's writing to achieve its current pre-eminence: for her growing popularity has coincided with the ascendancy of a critical discourse fascinated by notions of excess and transgression, notions which this discourse has been able to find dramatized to perfection in Duras's texts. From Bataille *via* Blanchot and *Tel Quel*, this discourse has passed into general critical usage, to the point where references to violence, excess, and transgression have become all but a critical commonplace. The limit experiences with which Duras's work is overwhelmingly concerned make this work enormously appealing to such a critical vocabulary, and rightly so: thère is much in her writing that can hardly be discussed without recourse to its terms. It is one of my contentions here, however, that a close reading of Duras's texts reveals just what is lost of the awful truths of excess and transgression when these terms become common critical coin. The implication of Duras's textual practice for current critical thinking about writing as excessive may, indeed, be that such thinking is, properly speaking, impossible.

---

[1] Key examples of close reading of Duras's work have been provided by Dominique Noguez, 'La Gloire des mots', *L'Arc*, 98 (1985), 25–39; Danielle Bajomée, *Duras ou la douleur* (Brussels: De Boeck-Wesmael, 1989); Christiane P. Makward, 'For a Stylistics of Marguerite Duras', *L'Esprit Créateur*, 30/1 (Spring 1990), 28–39; and Susan D. Cohen, who discusses Duras's style towards the end of her *Women and Discourse in the Fiction of Marguerite Duras* (Basingstoke: Macmillan, 1993). See also, for example, Leslie Hill's attentiveness to the shifts produced in the genesis of certain of Duras's texts (particularly *Le Square* and *L'Homme assis dans le couloir*) in his *Marguerite Duras: Apocalyptic Desires* (London: Routledge, 1993), and James S. Williams, *The Erotics of Passage: Pleasure, Politics and Form in the Later Work of Marguerite Duras* (Liverpool: Liverpool University Press, 1997). A crucial reading of Duras, which will be of major importance to the notions explored both in this introduction and throughout this study, is Julia Kristeva's 'La Maladie de la douleur', in *Soleil noir: Dépression et mélancolie* (Paris: Gallimard, 1987), 227–65.

INTRODUCTION 3

There can be no doubt that Duras associates writing and extremity of experience, aligning writing (in a familiar Romantic constellation) with passion, death, crime, mental alienation, mystery, and so on. Two examples (of many): in 1983, she declares that 'Un écrivain se tue à chaque ligne de sa vie ou bien il n'écrit pas';[2] in *Les Yeux verts*, we may read: 'C'est comme le crime d'écrire, après on ne sait pas. Les criminels disent: "Je ne sais pas ce qui m'est arrivé"'. (*YV*, 158) And this analogy is one that Duras criticism has been happy to pick up, giving rise to frequent assertions that texts which address themselves to extreme subject matter in some sense enact, perform, or realize this extremity in their own fabric or mode of existence, a notion often symbolized in chiastic formulations along the lines of 'writing of x, x of writing' (where 'x' represents, precisely, some or other instance of the unknown, the excessive, the overwhelming).[3] In this respect, this criticism remains within an honourable modernist tradition, which enhances its fetishization of the textual object by transferring metaphorically to that object the qualities of its referent.[4] The equation of writing with excess in this manner is, moreover, sustained by (implicit) adherence to what we might see as a heroic, active notion of transgression, in which a transgressive moment is presented as a valuable strategy within an overall programme of subversion.[5] If transgression, violence, excess, and so on,

<hr />

[2] Yann Andréa, 'C'est fou c'que j'peux t'aimer', *Libération*, 4 janvier 1983 (supplément 'livres', unpaginated).

[3] See, for example: Carol Hofmann's *Forgetting and Marguerite Duras* (Niwot: University Press of Colorado, 1991), which concludes with the assertion that 'through its own self-questioning and elusiveness', Duras's language 'becomes forgetting itself' (153); or Janine Ricouart's *Écriture féminine et violence: Une Étude de Marguerite Duras* (Birmingham, Alabama: Summa, 1991), of which the fourth chapter is entitled 'Violence de l'écriture/Écriture de la violence', and which claims, for instance, that 'les différents types de violence que j'ai introduits tout au long de mon étude se retrouvent au niveau de l'écriture même' (109); or the title of Catherine Rodgers's 'Lectures de la sorcière, ensorcellement de l'écriture', in Rodgers and Raynalle Udris (eds.), *Marguerite Duras: Lectures plurielles* (Amsterdam: Rodopi, 1998), 17–34. Dramatically, Najet Limam-Tnami goes so far as to claim that 'l'adéquation du contenu et de l'expression s'affirme explicitement comme la visée de l'écriture spéculaire de l'auteur'. (*Roman et cinéma chez Marguerite Duras: Une Poétique de la spécularité* (Tunis: Faculté des sciences humaines et sociales/Alif-Les Éditions de la Méditerranée, 1996), 199.) Further examples of this belief in an equivalence or analogy between text and subject matter (and there are many) will be discussed in the course of my readings of particular texts in the following chapters.

[4] With reference to *Tel Quel* readings of Bataille, this is argued by Susan Rubin Suleiman, in her 'Transgression and the Avant-Garde', in *Subversive Intent* (Cambridge, Mass.: Harvard University Press, 1990), 72–87.

[5] Bronwen Martin, for example, claims that Duras's 'challenge to the Cartesian or

are in fact recuperable in this fashion (itself perhaps sustained by a quasi-Bakhtinian idea of transgression as carnivalesque subversion, the world turned joyfully upside down), then they may indeed be thought to be instantiated in the literary text, since they have already been domesticated, brought within the happy home of all that is constructive, productive, useful.

There are, however, two problems with the use of this understanding of transgression in relation to Duras. In the first place, it entails a kind of logical inconsistency: while the transgressive may perhaps be thought along these positive lines, its various critical avatars (principally, excess and violence) cannot. If the excessive becomes part of a useful campaign of subversion, it is, quite simply, no longer excessive. The criticism that would tame this excess by seeing it enacted in the literary text thus loses precisely what it thinks to celebrate in the very gesture of its celebration, attempting to hitch itself up (in an extremely dilute kind of Hegelian dialectic) to the negativity which is, precisely, beyond all useful recuperation. For these are the terms—and they are, primarily, Bataille's—in which Duras understands the extremity by which she is fascinated: not as constructive negativity on the way to a greater good, but as dereliction, waste, exorbitance.[6]

conventional patterns of reason' is achieved in part 'through the setting-up of the transgression of boundaries', and that this process 'seeks to dismantle the barriers of Western reason and logic, to eradicate all forms of exclusion, thereby gaining access to the realm of the Absolute'. (Martin, 'Spatial Figurativity in Marguerite Duras', in Rodgers and Udris (eds.), *Marguerite Duras: Lectures plurielles*, 95–113 (111–12)).

[6] For instances of thinking about transgression in these terms, see for example Georges Bataille, *L'Érotisme* (Paris: Minuit, 1957; coll. 'Arguments', 1970); Maurice Blanchot, *Le Pas au-delà* (Paris: Gallimard, 1973); and Michel Foucault, 'Préface à la transgression', in *Dits et écrits, 1954–1988*, i (1954–1969) (Paris: Gallimard, 1994), 233–50. An excellent account of the problem I am addressing here may be found in Benjamin Noys, 'Transgressing Transgression: The Limits of Bataille's Fiction', in Larry Duffy and Adrian Tudor (eds.), *Les Lieux interdits: Transgression and French Literature* (Hull: University of Hull Press, 1998), 307–21. The notion of a negativity beyond dialectical utility ('négativité sans emploi') may be found in Bataille's *Le Coupable*: see Georges Bataille, *Œuvres complètes*, v (Paris: Gallimard, 1973); 289; see also 369 and 564. (I owe the details of this reference to Leslie Hill's *Blanchot: Extreme Contemporary* (London: Routledge, 1997)). The importance of this notion to Duras may be judged from her use, in the synopsis to her screenplay for *Hiroshima mon amour*, of the phrase 'amour sans emploi' (*HMA* 16). The late 1950s see more than one intersection between Duras and Bataille: see the pieces 'Bataille, Feydeau et Dieu' (1957) and 'A propos de Georges Bataille' (1958) (*O*, 27–33 and 34–6, respectively); and, with reference to *Hiroshima*, note Duras's decision to pass on money from the film's profits to Bataille, and Bataille's stated intention to write on the film. (See Michel Surya (ed.), *Georges Bataille: Choix de lettres, 1917–1962* (Paris: Gallimard, 1997), 524, 529 (editor's note); and Leslie Hill, *Marguerite Duras: Apocalyptic Desires*, 165 n. 2.) Marcelle Marini gives an excellent account of Duras's relation to Bataillean notions of

It is not a matter, then, of the happy arrival in a realized beyond, itself a step towards a positive goal; rather, for Duras, an encounter with the transgressive is understood as an anguished fretting at the limits of experience, of language. When she does associate writing and transgression, then, it will be in a reference to 'Cette transgression innommable—au sens propre du terme—, indéfinissable que l'on appelle l'écrit'.[7] Not subversive, not available for conscription into any positive programme: transgression, writing are linked as empty, ungraspable, unknowable. And here we meet the second problem for a critical rhetoric which would like to see Duras's texts as enacting their excessive concerns: while this rhetoric may think of itself as following Duras's own, outlandish pronouncements, she frequently, in fact, indicates that any equivalence between writing and extremity may be posited only to the precise extent that it is also understood as impossible.

Two moments from *Les Yeux verts* are crucial here. In the first, Duras removes writing from the realm of work (and hence from the labour of the negative, the usefully subversive); and she does so in importantly paradoxical terms, defining writing as 'un non-travail. C'est atteindre le non-travail' (*YV*, 17; original emphasis). Vital here is the twist Duras herself chooses to emphasize: what is attained in writing is intransitivity, unworking: nothing that could be thought of as attainment.[8] Thus, when, later in the same text, Duras does compare writing and extreme experience, she does so in terms which indicate that this analogy may be thought to the precise extent that it is also impossible. Referring to the solitary *expérience intérieure* that is the business of writing, she states that:

---

transgression—from which she wishes to distinguish Duras—in 'Transgressions', in Vircondelet (ed.), *Duras, Dieu et l'écrit* (Monaco: Éditions du Rocher, 1998), 71–84; Bernard Alazet, in *Le Navire Night de Marguerite Duras: Écrire l'effacement* (Paris: Presses Universitaires de Lille, 1992), argues for the rejection of all affirmatively transgressive readings of Duras, and thus of 'toute forme de positivité' (177).

[7] Suzanne Lamy and André Roy (eds.), *Marguerite Duras à Montréal* (Montreal: Éditions Spirale, 1981), 45.

[8] We might think of Beckett, perhaps, from his 1931 piece on Proust: 'We are disappointed at the nullity of what we are pleased to call attainment.' (Samuel Beckett and Georges Duthuit, *Proust* and *Three Dialogues* (London: John Calder, 1965), 13–14.) On the term 'unworking', and its relatives, which I will occasionally invoke to suggest the Blanchotian dimension to these questions, see Simon Critchley, *Very Little . . . Almost Nothing* (London: Routledge, 1997), 31 ff. and 85 ff.

On est là au bout du monde, au bout de soi, dans un dépaysement incessant, dans une approche constante qui n'atteint pas. Car là on n'atteint rien de même que dans l'invivable du désir et de la passion.

$(YV, 166)^9$

Nothing is achieved, nothing attained in writing: except for nothing, compared in an analogy which declares its own impossibility to the ungraspable excess of passion. The equivalence between writing and extremity, then, is for Duras an equivalence which ruins itself as soon as it is posited, an equivalence between two punctures, through which the supposed substance of this comparison inevitably drains away.

None of which should be seen as fetishizing writing, maintaining it in the purity of an unreachable beyond: as Duras stresses by her use of paradox and impossible analogy, writing is a work which is its own unworking, a labour whose achievement is the ruination of all achievement. (Or, as Blanchot puts it, 'œuvre de l'absence de l'œuvre', and thus—impossibly—akin to transgression, 'accomplissement inévitable de ce qu'il est *impossible* d'accomplir' (Blanchot, *Le Pas au-delà*, 79/147; original emphasis)).[10] Which means that writing hovers on the edge of the world, neither usefully present nor successfully transcendent—a ghost come to haunt the thinking which would like to tidy it away by making it simultaneously excessive and productive. This model of haunting is, in fact, one of Duras's favourites in her accounts of her own experience of writing, often described as a kind of visitation:

Quand j'écris, j'ai le sentiment d'être dans l'extrême déconcentration, je ne me possède plus du tout, je suis moi-même une passoire, j'ai la tête trouée ... je ne suis pas seule à écrire quand j'écris.

$(L, 98)$

For all that the vision of writing as a haunting works to shore up its mystical association with the beyond, at least two points work to unsettle this happy equivalence. First, this model of dispossession,

---

[9] This passage is highlighted by Danielle Bajomée, as part of a careful and thorough discussion of Duras's understanding of the nature of writing. See Danielle Bajomée, *Duras ou la douleur*, 157–8.

[10] For extended discussion of Blanchot's treatment of writing and transgression in the context of an account of his work in general, see Hill, *Blanchot: Extreme Contemporary*. See also John Gregg, *Maurice Blanchot and the Literature of Transgression* (Princeton: Princeton University Press, 1994).

emptiness, internal rupture disallows the notion of a coincidence between excessive experience and what is generally referred to as 'writing itself', 'the text itself', and so on: if writing is thought according to this kind of extremity, then it has, as Duras's image of haunting strongly suggests, no 'self', no stability, no proper place which might serve as the locus of this kind of coincidence. (The Blanchotian dimensions of Duras's thinking about the business of writing are again apparent here). Secondly, the substance of this Durassian model of visitation suggests that writing, far from achieving some sort of communion with a realized beyond of utter excess, also in fact remains hooked into the banal contingencies of lived experience:

> Ce qui vous arrive dessus dans l'écrit, c'est sans doute tout simplement la masse du vécu, si on peut dire, très simplement . . . Mais, cette masse du vécu, non inventoriée, non rationalisée, est dans une sorte de désordre originel. On est hanté par son vécu.

> (*L*, 99)

The very figure that takes writing out of the world also keeps it earthed, composed of the crazy, contingent, residual mess of lived experience: 'Il y a un choix qui s'opère, un choix organique qui s'opère et qui fait qu'il ne reste presque rien de la totalité des choses, du vécu, mais que ce presque rien devient l'irremplaçable, quand on écrit.'[11]

Writing is thus positioned as Romantically wild and unknowable through the operation of an uncertain something, which keeps it— awkwardly and essentially—caught up in the world, excessive inasmuch as it is *between* excess and 'la totalité des choses'. Which suggests, again, that the enthusiastic critical assertion of a useful equivalence between Duras's writing and its extreme subject matter should be treated with some caution. And this is, moreover, precisely what is suggested by the operation of Duras's texts. Throughout this study, I will endeavour to bring out the various ways in which the patterns and strategies of Duras's writing implicate themselves in the very heart of their excessive concerns, even at times hinting at a formal enactment of these concerns—before slipping away, demonstrating in their quiet complication the impossibility of such a coincidence, and indicating, incidentally, an entirely

---

[11] Marguerite Duras, 'Écrire', *L'Esprit Créateur*, 30/1 (Spring 1990), 6–7 (6).

different (and compelling) way of thinking this relation. Before we can get to the nature of this alternative, however, we will have to take a brief detour: through the nature of the ethical as Duras configures it.

Duras and the Ethical

If one considers the limit experiences with which Duras's work is everywhere concerned, their fascinating duality soon becomes apparent. Typically, Duras is obsessed with such phenomena as passion, murder, violence, madness, death, loss. As it ravishes its subject, this type of experience exceeds comprehension and expression; to this extent, it is of interest to Duras inasmuch as it takes its subject out of the world, beyond the realm of that which may be symbolized, understood, evaluated. And yet evaluation is never far removed from the scene of its dramatic incursion, since the quintessentially Durassian excessive experience also suggests a continuing relationship with the world, in the shape of the ethical questions from which it cannot be separated. Duras's fascination is with phenomena which, though they tear asunder in the extraordinary moment of their arrival the categories by which we make sense of and judge the world, are also characterized by their inevitable, continuing relationship with these categories. And this, I would argue, represents the source of the fascination of such subject matter for Duras: as limit experiences, these phenomena are poised absorbingly at the very edge of the world, where our understanding just begins to slip, but has not yet entirely given way.

We might note, here, a resemblance between this Durassian ethical and Levinas's conception of the ethical relation (which has, of course, had an immense impact on recent literary critical work on the ethical).[12] In both cases, 'the ethical' represents a term which

---

[12] The importance of Levinas to recent thinking about the ethical cannot be overstated. It is well described in Geoffrey Galt Harpham, *Getting It Right: Language, Literature, and Ethics* (London: University Press of Chicago, 1992), 7; and Norman Ravvin, 'Have You Reread Levinas Lately? Transformations of the Face in Post-Holocaust Fiction', in Andrew Hadfield, Dominic Rainsford, and Tim Woods (eds.), *The Ethics in Literature* (Basingstoke: Macmillan, 1999), 52–69. I do not propose to provide here a systematic account of Levinas's thought, as I am far from qualified to do so. See, instead, Simon Critchley, *The Ethics of Deconstruction* (Oxford: Blackwell, 1992); Colin Davis, *Levinas* (Cambridge: Polity, 1996); and Seán Hand (ed.), *The Levinas Reader* (Oxford: Blackwell, 1989). One of the clearest accounts to be had of

also names its own insufficiency; in which the gesture out of the ethical world (for Kierkegaard, in *Fear and Trembling* and *Either/Or*, the gesture of faith) also takes place within the world, within the actual—within the ethical. Levinas's understanding of the nature of my ethical responsibility for the other person introduces a view of the ethical as both irreducibly actual and simultaneously excessive, gesturing towards the beyond. I am never done with my responsibility for the other; to this extent, it is excessive, infinitely beyond comprehension, and so disruptive of the world (understood as the world of ontology, of phenomenology, that which is). Nonetheless, this encounter is also, paradoxically, an actual event within this world—while at the same time also being thought as the rupturing of the world by the divine nakedness of the face of the other.[13] The ethical relation would, therefore, be located on the very edge of the world, resolutely concrete, but also radically irruptive. Thus it is, then, that this relation comes to be seen as an actual encounter with an otherness which cannot be conceptualized, which cannot be *thought* as such: the actualization, in our lived experience, of the encounter with that with which there can be no encounter.[14] (Both the necessity and the effect of this kind of paradoxical formulation will be vital here, and will be described shortly.) Neither merely that which is, nor merely that which exceeds that which is, the ethical

the structure and key problems of the Levinasian ethical is still that to be found in Blanchot's discussion of Levinas's *Totalité et infini*, in his *L'Entretien infini* (Paris: Gallimard, 1969), 70ff. Useful interviews with Levinas, in which he discusses important aspects of his thought, may be found in his *Éthique et infini* (Paris: Fayard, 1982), and in Richard Kearney, *Dialogues with Contemporary Thinkers* (Manchester: Manchester University Press, 1984). The link between Duras and Levinas is also made by James Williams—although Williams is rather more critical of Duras from this perspective than I will be. See Williams, *The Erotics of Passage*, 8; and 'The Point of No Return: Chiastic Adventures Between Self and Other in *Les Mains négatives* and *Au-delà des pages*', in Rodgers and Udris (eds.), *Marguerite Duras: Lectures plurielles*, 77–94 (78).

[13] For Levinas, it is a matter of a 'responsabilité dont il est impossible de fixer les limites, ni de mesurer l'urgence extrême' (*De Dieu qui vient à l'idée* (Paris: Vrin, 1982), 116); accordingly, it is a responsibility to which I will never be equal, 'C'est une responsabilité qui va au-delà de ce que je fais' (*Éthique et infini*, 92). That this way of conceiving of the ethical also implies what one might describe as the opening onto the beyond from the face of the other is summarized in such statements as 'Dans l'accès au visage, il y a certainement aussi un accès à l'idée de Dieu' (*Éthique et infini*, 86). It is by means of this acute, urgent teetering on the edge of the beyond that Levinas's model makes Kierkegaard's leap of faith a leap *within and beyond* the world, perhaps better figured as the divine spark of responsibility which arcs from the other person's face. Blanchot, on the other hand, demurs at this introduction of a theological referent: 'Laissons Dieu de côté, nom trop imposant' (*L'Entretien infini*, 71). On this, see Critchley, *Very Little . . . Almost Nothing*, 80–2.

[14] I refer here to Blanchot's interrogative formulation from *L'Entretien infini*: 'Étrange rapport qui consiste en ce qu'il n'y a pas de rapport' (73).

on this account is situated at that very edge between the world and its beyond with which Duras is so fascinated. This comparison between two enormously dissimilar thinkers is not meant to imply that Duras's writings actualize Levinas's philosophical model (for reasons which will be discussed below), nor that the two are in some secret way connected (although Blanchot does serve as an intriguing link here): rather, I am hoping to suggest that Duras's thought resonates within a wider intellectual context than is often acknowledged. As Duras indicates, and as Levinas in a vastly different idiom strangely also suggests, the ethical is located in some sense at its own elastic limit, where, as a realm of lived experience emphatically within the world, it is stretched beyond endurance by the dilemmas which irrupt within it, without for all that quite giving way. In talking of 'the ethical' in relation to Duras, it will be this ruptured but persistent limit that I will attempt to trace.

In her presentation of absolute moments of extremity, then, Duras also takes us to the limits of our ethical experience; and the nature of this presentation may, I will suggest, hold important implications for our understanding both of this experience, and of its relationship to writing. The ethical dimension of Duras's work may be said to reside both in the particular issues it addresses—violence, pain, passion, judgement, and so on—and, further, in the characteristic structure of this address. There is, I will argue, a close relationship between the address to the beyond so readily identified with Duras's work and her interrogation of the intersection of writing and the ethical. As Duras's early writing confronts the beyond (of language, law, the social), its patterns suggest both an identification with this beyond and the impossibility of such identification; thus, a line is uncertainly traced between the world (of which the text is a part) and that which exceeds the world (towards which the text gestures). In Duras's later work, this model (which I will call *impossible enactment*, defined by a constant textual exploration of the limits of an adequation between writing and excess) is replaced by a more *ad hoc* series of encounters between writing and extremity whose ambiguities map the line of uncertainty by which this encounter is characterized. Since, as I have indicated, the extremity which constitutes the appearance of the beyond in Duras's texts consistently bears an ethical inflection, this line also marks the location of the ethical in Duras's writing: at the limit of the world (of understanding and expression, for example), but insistently (if uncertainly) making its presence felt within this world. Demonstrating the impossibility of instantiating excess, Duras's texts offer instead an uncertain sketch of the limit between the world and its beyond, where they also locate the ethical. With which, therefore, they coincide—impossibly.

There is in operation here, then, the exacting structure of a relation which cannot be thought to take place other than in its own impossibility; what Blanchot—describing the Levinasian ethical—terms a 'rapport sans rapport', a connection which also separates.[15] Which means that, in Duras, the meeting of writing and the ethical is in no sense graspable as coincidence, equivalence, enactment, and so on: it is, rather, an impossible encounter on a shared edge. This—baffling, exhausting, compelling—is how Duras configures the strange meeting between writing and the ethical. While she may not be an ethical writer, then, the question of how we read Duras may well, nonetheless, be an ethical question.

Reading and the Ethical

The return of the ethical within the literary criticism of the last two decades is well established, and well documented.[16] In order to get closer to the essential contribution Duras may have to make to questions at the heart of such criticism, I would like now briefly to outline the kind of contribution her writing might make to what we now know as 'ethical criticism'. As I have already suggested, the characteristic feature of Duras's address to the ethical is her fascination with that limit point at which ethical categories no longer

[15] The notion of the 'rapport sans rapport' forms the core of Blanchot's discussion of Levinas in *L'Entretien infini*, where it appears for example as 'un rapport qui me rapporte à ce qui me dépasse et m'échappe dans la mesure même où, dans ce rapport, je suis et reste séparé' (75). (The phrase 'rapport sans rapport' may be found on 104). On Blanchot's reading of *Totalité et infini*, see Critchley, *Very Little . . . Almost Nothing*, 81–2.

[16] Discussions of this point now habitually take as their opening topos a quotation from Steven Connor, to the effect that 'the word "ethics" seems to have replaced "textuality" as the most charged term in the vocabulary of contemporary literary and cultural theory'. (Connor, 'Honour Bound?', *Times Literary Supplement*, 5 January 1996, 24–6 (25).) Compare also Tobin Siebers's claim that 'only ethics effectively reveals the coherence implicit in the diversity of critical approaches today' (Siebers, *The Ethics of Criticism* (London: Cornell University Press, 1988), 13). For a good account of this return to/of the ethical, see Hadfield, Rainsford, and Woods, 'Introduction: Literature and the Return to Ethics', in their *The Ethics in Literature*, 1–14 (1–4).

have any purchase, but are not yet for all that suspended. At work here is, then, the odd edge between ravishment and residual judgement. It is, crucially, in the tiny details of Duras's writing, which negotiate its ceaselessly uncertain encounter with the extremity of its material, that her vision of the ethical as located at the limit of its own possibility is elaborated. These details invite a way of reading which, overwhelmed and intricate, excessive and detailed, responds to this work by tracing the line (the edge of the ethical) which they sketch.

As I shall be demonstrating, Duras's texts suggest a model of reading in which the reader is overcome by their dizzying force, while clinging to their subtle details. In so doing, the reader follows their elaboration of the ethical, while failing quite to enact in the experience of reading a thematic proposition (since both this proposition and the work of the texts question the possibility of stable enactment, concerned as they are with the oscillation at the edge of the ethical). The awkwardness which characterizes this model thus keeps the reader in a precarious position between ravishment and its rationalization which both is and is not the reproduction of the Durassian ethical. And this combination of excess and detail, which I am presenting as the structure of a possible critical model at least in relation to Duras's work, offers, as a form of ethical criticism, two principal advantages.

First, its valorization of a critical passion, of the critical experience of being overwhelmed by the impertinent text, as impossibly analogous to extreme ethical experience, holds open the possibility of an encounter with the kind of swirling, elliptical, oblique writing all too often neglected even in much of the best of recent ethical criticism, which seems frequently too happy to restrict its scope to the novel, and to a certain type of novel at that. The recognition that less extensively sinuous, more explosive, but no less subtle works, if read in a manner similar to that which I am here proposing as appropriate for Duras, might also have valuable contributions to make to our ethical conversation, should surely broaden the range of current ethical criticism—which can be no bad thing. We might, indeed, wish to add to (for example) Martha Nussbaum's valorization of the capacity of literature to stimulate our important affective investment in the twists of the particular a way of reading ethically texts which render us dizzy, bewildered, ecstatic, as well as reflectively—if passionately—attuned to the moral truths of our emotional life.[17] Moreover, while the reading of texts whose relation to our ethical life seems perhaps more oblique, or more explosive, is indeed under way (generally in the branch of ethical criticism more indebted to Levinas and/or Derrida), it seems frequently—for all that rejection of any notion of the literary text as a mere illustration of conceptual content is a contemporary critical article of faith— that such reading remains dependent on a critical model according to which the supposedly elusive, or fragmentary, or shattering text (or experience of reading) would find its disruptive operation recuperated as the allegorization of a philosophical or ethical proposition.[18] Failing to think this analogy according to its necessary impossibility, as I have outlined this above, such criticism enacts the effacement—by the stability of its own critical model—of the excessive qualities supposedly being allegorized. Against this critical context, the intricacies of Duras's overwhelming texts—as I will attempt to show throughout this study—may thus be seen as working both to signal the impossibility of their reduction to the mere enactment of a prior proposition, and simultaneously to bind these texts (exorbitantly, ungraspably) into exactly the kind of substantive ethical debate contained in such propositions.

Secondly, the insistence on detail in this model ensures that such texts are read with full attention to their intricacies, thereby actualizing the stress on close reading which, in much ethical criticism, can remain at the level of lip service. I hope to provide in my readings of Duras some indication of how a criticism interested in the encounter between writing and the ethical can pursue this interest—even in the face of bewildering, distressing texts—at the level of the most delicate textual twists. Those familiar with Duras only via received wisdom, or the extravagant interventions of Marguerite Duras, public figure, might be surprised by this suggestion that the

---

[17] Nussbaum is quite explicit about the restriction of her critical approach to a certain type of work, whose principal defining features are that it be 'written in a style that gives sufficient attention to particularity and emotion', and that it engage its readers 'in relevant activities of searching and feeling, especially feeling concerning their own possibilities as well as those of the characters' (Martha C. Nussbaum, *Love's Knowledge* (Oxford: Oxford University Press, 1990), 46).

[18] See, for example, Chris McNab, 'Derrida, Rushdie, and the Ethics of Mortality', in Hadfield, Rainsford, and Woods (eds.), *The Ethics in Literature*, 136–51; Robert Eaglestone, 'Flaws: James, Nussbaum, Miller, Levinas', in Dominic Rainsford and Tim Woods (eds.), *Critical Ethics: Text, Theory, Responsibility* (Basingstoke: Macmillan, 1999), 77–87; Lori Branch West, 'The Benefit of Doubt: The Ethics of Reading', in Rainsford and Woods (eds.), *Critical Ethics*, 187–202.

high priestess of absolute passion, whose egotistical juggernaut is fuelled by relentless manipulation and self-mythologization, and whose writings (when not derisory or derivative) constitute endless hymns to dark desire, in fact signs texts marked throughout her career by delicate, minute formal intricacies which propose exacting interrogations of the intractable material they nonetheless, stubbornly, treat. The Duras cliché has its truth, of course; and this truth is indeed in part comprised of the exaggerated picture I have just painted. More interestingly, however, it is also both possible and important to argue that Duras's exorbitance is not just limited to this journalistic snapshot; that it is also, and crucially, located in the subtle operations of her texts at their most intimate level. For the details of Duras's writing, as I will try to show, function both to tie this writing into the ethical knots with which it also engages at more sweeping levels of thematization; and, at the same time, to keep this bond in a state of indeterminacy, held open—as possibility and vacancy—by the wild Durassian particular.

Hovering around the borders of Duras's texts, then, there is a figure which begins to seem richly suggestive in terms of a possible ethical criticism, offering in its image of a ruptured but persistent contact an impossible analogy to—as well as a key part of—the business of reading Duras. For, if we now recall Duras's positioning of writing as excessive precisely inasmuch as it accompanies everyday life uncertainly, as an obscure haunting, we might perhaps envisage a possible response (with reference to Duras's texts) to the question of the relationship between writing and our ethical life. As I argued above, Duras's writing meets its ethical concerns impossibly, on a shared edge. We are now in a position to add to this image the strange combination of excess and detail which characterizes the experience of reading Duras. This aspect presents, of course, this same structure, an encounter with the line between the world and its beyond—and again, necessarily, this coincidence is unthinkable as such. And it is here, in this dispersed network of articulated relationships, that we may find the fundamental importance of the address offered by Duras's writing to our ethical life. For it is as a result of this accumulation of impossible meetings (between writing, reading, and the ethical), and the structure of suspended but persistent contact that this suggests, that Duras's writing establishes its characteristic relation to this ethical life: as an *uncertain accompaniment*, touching insistently on its extreme dilemmas, tracing their urgency largely by the indeterminacy (between exorbitancy and hesitancy) of its presence. The various aspects of this writing which I will be discussing here bind it resolutely and intricately into our ethical experience, while also constantly undoing this bond, leaving Duras and her writing simply—doggedly, obscurely—*there*, alongside.

Writing and the Ethical

Shortly, I will sketch out the potential of this model as a contribution to current thinking on the relation between writing and our ethical life. First, however, I propose to set this sketch in the context of my argument as a whole, by outlining the structure of the following study.

Run through by the figure of Duras, what follows is organized chronologically, with a shape which seeks to respond to the fluctuations of Duras's writing career, and to demonstrate how these fluctuations express the persistent working-through of certain recurrent concerns. A view of Duras as having consistently been engaged with ethical questions allows a particular developmental narrative to become apparent; it is this narrative which will dictate the structure of this study. Part I maps Duras's writing from 1943 to 1971, and, divided into three chronologically consecutive chapters (which mark phases in the development of Duras's writing in its encounter with the ethical), follows the gestures made during this period of Duras's work towards the impossible enactment in writing of the irruption of extremity. Chapter 1 considers the attempt already apparent in Duras's early texts (from 1943 to 1955) to provide a writing which grasps after that which lies beyond the world, and so describes the birth of the structure (writing on the edge of beyond) which will subtend the rest of Duras's career. Chapters 2 and 3 trace prominent examples of Duras's evolving ethical concerns—respectively, the traumatic, irruptive event (in the texts of 1958 to 1967) and aspects of the events of May 1968 (in those of 1969 to 1971)—and explore the encounter produced by Duras during these periods between their area of ethical interest and the business of writing. The first part of the study thus traces the figure which winds through this part of Duras's career, produced by the gesture towards textual enactment of the encounter with the beyond, namely: *the spiral of impossible enactment*. By 1971, this spiral has wound itself to an extraordinary degree of tension, as Duras confronts the paradox of expressing her valorization of incomprehension. As her writing becomes ever more devastated, both lyrical and ruined, there is a sense in which the exploration of this spiral of impossible enactment can go no further, that it has reached an ultimate point of exacerbation. At which point, Duras as it were draws breath, and moves from working primarily in prose, with some work in film and in the theatre, to working primarily in film, with some accompanying prose. To map this sabbatical from prose writing in the 1970s, the study provides a brief Interlude, during which I discuss the issues motivating Duras's move into work primarily for the cinema, and suggest why the fate of these issues leads to a return to writing at the end of this decade.[19] Part II of the study picks up Duras's writing with its full-scale return in 1979, after which the chronological schema of the study shifts. The three chapters of this second section are no longer sequential, but rather contemporaneous. For when Duras returns to prose writing, it will no longer be a developing writerly voice (divisible into a series of phases, interlinked by a shared structural gesture), but rather writing *per se* that is brought into an encounter with the dilemmas of ethical experience, picked up from the first section of her writing career, but now addressed on a grander scale. Moreover, this writing now confidently rejects the exploration of the drive to produce a rigorous but impossible homology between writing and its excessive subject matter, and instead explores its encounter with intractable material by concentrating on the uncertain edges of this encounter, produced in part by the increased contentiousness of Duras's work. The departure from writing during the 1970s appears to give Duras a triple sense of heightened significance. First, writing, glossed repeatedly as an extraordinary and pre-eminent phenomenon, appears as big enough to tackle overwhelming questions without worrying about

[19] Clearly, the chronology of this sabbatical is somewhat blurred: its borders display not neat periodization, but rather imbrication. Thus, for example, *India Song* (1973) bears the generic 'Texte théâtre film': still a piece of written work, but inseparable from the film it accompanies. To this extent, I will be considering it as belonging to Duras's filmic sabbatical of the 1970s. Similarly *L'Amour*, which is the last Duras text until 1979 not effectively to represent either a play or the screenplay of a film, is nonetheless re-elaborated in the 1972 film *La Femme du Gange*. And when Duras returns to writing, this return will piggyback on her cinematic output: the first text after 1971 which lacks an accompanying film is the third *Aurélia Steiner* text, *Aurélia Steiner Paris*—although this is also plainly the third part of a trilogy, the first two parts of which do accompany films. So, while the edges of this Interlude are rather hazy, the general movement (from writing to film and back again) remains.

dealing with the problems they raise by means of a possible formal enactment of their structures. Secondly, these problems (which generally respond to questions already addressed by Duras in the first half of her writing career) are explored at the elevated level of their broader historical and social significance. Thirdly, the figure of Duras is raised to a point at which she too is implicated in the encounter between her work and its excessive subject matter. It is as a response to the force of this triple elevation that Part II abandons periodization, and adopts a synchronic presentation of three key areas of ethical concern which run through Duras's later work, namely, historical trauma, sexuality, and the status of the self.

Throughout this account, then, I will be attempting to bring out the importance of the ethical as a constant presence in Duras's work. I will also attempt to suggest something of the ways in which this work contributes to our understanding of the relationship between the literary text and its excessive concerns. The question, then, would be the question of 'writing and the ethical', of this 'and'. What relation is at stake here? Answering this question will begin, I hope, to show why Duras is indeed a writer of crucial importance. I have argued, over the course of this introduction, that Duras's writing presents itself as an uncertain accompaniment to our attempts to negotiate the demands of our ethical life. This claim will, I hope, be borne out by the detailed readings offered over the following chapters. I will not necessarily be pushing this model to the fore in and around every reading, since I would like the focus of these sections to be on the detailed operation of Duras's writing. I will, however, invoke it in order to summarize key aspects where appropriate, and will attempt in my conclusion to draw together under its sign the various particular strands explored throughout the study. Despite its necessary discretion, this figure of accompaniment has, I believe, much to recommend it; this may become clear if we spend a little longer on the uncomfortable topos of the edge.

It would seem that the encounter with the other (the ethical, as this is currently configured, after Levinas) may be thought of as structured around a line of minimal contact: just enough to ensure that there is indeed an encounter, but not so much that this encounter with the wholly other turns into assimilation.[20] This is

[20] On this, see Derrida's criticism of Levinas's criticism of Husserl, in 'Violence et métaphysique' (in *L'Écriture et la différence* (Paris: Seuil, 1967; coll. 'Points', 1979), 117–228): 'On ne pourrait ni parler, ni avoir quelque sens que ce soit du tout-autre s'il n'y avait un phénomène

why, consequently, this encounter finds itself frequently expressed in such paradoxical formulations as the 'encounter with that with which there can be no encounter', and so on: the twists of paradox erode all but the line of uncertainty on which this impossible conceptualization must remain caught if it is to exist at all. Which would, in one sense, be the only way for it to remain ethical.[21] Now, this line (of the encounter with the wholly other, of the attempt to address this encounter in language) is the line which runs through Duras's texts. Which might, perhaps, make them exemplarily ethical texts, were it not for the ruination of this status by its confident (premature, redemptive) formulation. Duras's are indeed ethical texts, then, to the extent that they implicate themselves, by their shaky tracing of this line, in the demands of the ethical, while refusing to allow us to efface this line by thinking of them in such congratulatory or accomplished terms. That is to say, they just keep on asking the question of their relation to the ethical extremity they present, without allowing even this interrogation to achieve redemptively positive status. Thus it is that they constitute themselves as an uncertain accompaniment to our ethical life, maintaining this fragile status, as I have suggested, by drawing together in a kind of (dis)assembly the various relations of non-relation which articulate their contact with this domain. This accompaniment, moreover, is not merely abstract or formal. For these texts also thematize the dilemmas of this ethical life. Which means that they retain enough (minimal, again) referential purchase on these dilemmas for their cherished, radical intransitivity to become caught up in the particular, live dramas of the ethical. And yet they also

du tout-autre, une évidence du tout-autre comme tel' (181). On the other side of this (non-reciprocal) encounter, Simon Critchley has recently argued that the ethical relation is in fact opened by a minimal fissure within the subject: 'it is only because there is a *certain disposition towards alterity within the subject, as the structure or pattern of subjectivity*, that there can be an ethical relation' (Critchley, 'The Original Traumatism: Levinas and Psychoanalysis', in Rainsford and Woods (eds.), *Critical Ethics*, 88–104 (90); original emphasis). Which two comments, between them, figure the encounter (and thus the ethical relation) as the most delicate imaginable: minimally opened from within towards the other, I have of this other only the minimal grasp necessary for the other to appear to me at all.

[21] See, again, Critchley: 'The *paradox* is here that what this ethical language seeks to thematize is by definition unthematizable, it is a conception of the subject constituted in a relation to alterity that is irreducible to ontology, that is, irreducible to thematization or conceptuality. Levinas's work is a *phenomenology of the unphenomenologizable*, or what he calls the order of the enigma in distinction from that of the phenomenon' ('The Original Traumatism', 91); and 'As Wittgenstein might have said, the ethicality of thought is revealed in its persistent attempt to run up or bump up against the limits of language' (91).

place this apparent purchase in question. Drawing the reader into the arc of their flight, they touch on our ethical life, without ever allowing us to be sure of the status of this gossamer contact.

Duras's texts refuse to give up on the notion that they might have something to offer to our exhausted attempts to negotiate the extreme experiences with which they engage—this is the inescapable sense of their insistent address to these experiences. At the same time, they also refuse to allow us any confidence in the redemptive status this engagement might seem to promise—this is the consequence of their endless worrying at the question of this relation. Just what kind of response, then, do they in fact offer to the shattered world they confront? Is Kristeva right to see Duras's as a 'littérature non cathartique' ('La Maladie de la douleur', 233), as one with this devastation—or does Duras indeed, as has been suggested, surpass the negativity by which she is fascinated, to provide us with some sort of aesthetic support, or even salvation?[22] I will return to this issue at various times throughout this study, and especially in my Conclusion; for now, perhaps I might just indicate that Duras's texts will indeed here frequently be considered in relation to the question of their supposedly redemptive qualities; and that it is, even, within the space of this trembling question that I would want to locate their extraordinary significance.

Over the course of Duras's writing career, the question of the relation between text and world underwent regular upheavals. From Sartrean commitment to Blanchotian 'désœuvrement', from

---

[22] See, for example, Michael Sheringham, '"Là où se fait notre histoire . . .": l'autobiographique et la quotidienneté chez Marguerite Duras', in Rodgers and Udris (eds.), *Marguerite Duras: Lectures plurielles*, 115–32, esp. 122; and, especially, Madeleine Borgomano, 'Que sont les oiseaux devenus . . .?: Étude sémio-analytique des écrits de Marguerite Duras depuis *L'Amant*', in Rodgers and Udris (eds.), *Marguerite Duras: Lectures plurielles*, 151–67, esp. 165, n. 3: 'L'interprétation négative que fait Kristeva de l'œuvre de Duras . . . me paraît si défectueuse, par oubli de la dimension énonciative, qu'elle en devient fausse . . . Kristeva dénonce le poison sans voir que Duras offre en même temps le contre-poison.' Kristeva defends herself against those whom she terms 'les groupies de Duras' in 'Une Étrangère', *Nouvelle Revue Française*, 542 (mars 1998), 3–9, claiming that '[Duras] voyait dans mon diagnostic plutôt un hommage' (3). A particularly provocative take on Kristeva's position is offered by Emma Wilson: 'Is it possible, indeed, that Duras's texts work to undermine the reader's certainty and sanity, forming, rather than reflecting, the trauma of non-cathartic identification Kristeva has sought to analyse? And might this be understood in positive rather than negative terms?' (Wilson, '"Mon histoire de Lol V. Stein": Duras, Reading, and Amnesia', in *Sexuality and the Reading Encounter: Identity and Desire in Proust, Duras, Tournier, and Cixous* (Oxford: Clarendon, 1996), 163–91 (163).) Kristeva's argument, and subsequent responses to it from within Duras criticism, are well presented in Williams, *The Erotics of Passage*, 4–6.

the supposed abolition of both author and referential relation to the
return of these notions in other, stranger guises, her critical context
has consistently worried at the question of how writing is in fact to
be related to lived experience. Duras's ability to maintain her writing in a state of what we might call tangential referentiality, touching on 'la masse du vécu' in a gesture of minimal but irreducible
contact, offers a considerable, and potentially rich approach to this
fundamental question.[23] In our current context of notions such as
autofiction and life writing, or of an ever-increasing interest in testimonial literature of all kinds, the delicate tracing of the line of referential contact in Duras's work would already be of considerable
interest; beyond this, however, is Duras's suggestion that this line
has also to bear the weight of our most exacting dilemmas, as her
writing situates its ever uncertain encounter with our lived experience principally in relation to the ethical. This encounter, moreover, draws in some of the most vital, and devastating, questions of
Duras's time (which is still, for a while perhaps, ours): it is a matter,
repeatedly, of testimony, of racial or sexual identity, of violent crimes
against individuals and against humanity, of impoverishment and
utter destitution. The constant stretching of the limit of the ethical
produced by the details of Duras's writing on the edge of the beyond
argues for the refusal to accept that our ethical responsibilities in
these and other areas, and the demands made by these responsibilities on the business of writing, might ever be finally grasped—while
also insisting both that the attempt to get to grips with these questions may not be abandoned, and that this ceaseless questioning
may itself not be smugly counted as necessarily positive or redemptive. To this extent, and in the light of the extreme experiences with
which her work is concerned, the case for reading Duras, and for
reading her closely, awkwardly, and uncertainly, is surely irresistible.
'Faut pas dire les choses comme ça, vaut mieux dérailler comme je
le fais, faut pas faire la morale. C'est pas beau c'est pas bien puis il
faut continuer à me lire absolument.'[24]

[23] Although she develops this insight into a dramatically redemptive vision of Duras's
writing, Ingrid Safranek is, I believe, absolutely right to claim that Duras's 'projet global' is
to 'figurer le problème même de la relation entre vie et littérature' (Safranek, 'L'Écriture
absolue ou la dernière des romantiques', in Vircondelet (ed.), *Duras, Dieu et l'écrit*, 243–76
(246)).
[24] Marguerite Duras, 'Avec ou sans les amitiés de M.D.', *Libération*, 23 juillet 1985, 33.

PART I

Impossible Enactment

I

THE WRITING OF THE BEYOND

Il faut se faire à cette idée que peut-être c'est inexprimable.
Les Petits Chevaux de Tarquinia

According to one version, the story of Duras's career begins as follows. Robert Antelme, the manuscript of *Les Impudents* under his arm, trails round various of his influential friends in search of a publisher. 'Je vous préviens', he tells them, 'si vous ne lui dites pas qu'elle est un écrivain, elle se tuera.'[1]

Duras's writing thus begins in crisis, in an atmosphere of extremity that her work will never abandon. In the words of Dionys Mascolo, 'elle a été, au moins pendant douze ou quinze ans, dans la plus grande angoisse devant l'acte d'écrire, d'un scrupule extraordinaire'.[2] And right from the start, already from *Les Impudents*, her texts are concerned with 'la plus grande angoisse': the anguish produced by the appearance of the uncontrollable beyond into the obscure platitudes of the everyday. By the end of her first decade as an author, Duras's *œuvre* already includes two suicides, one fatal car accident, two lost virginities, a young man blown up by a mine he was attempting to clear, an opportunistic murder, an uncle killed by his nephew, as well as countless passionate entanglements, betrayals, revelations, abandonments . . .

Duras announces her arrival on the literary scene with a series of works which would be remarkable for their body count alone. More significant than this preoccupation with sex and violence, however, is the fact that the early years of her writing career also allow Duras

---

[1] Antelme's words are recalled by Dominique Arban, at the time a lectrice for Plon (who published *Les Impudents*). (Arban, *Je me retournerai souvent* . . . (Paris: Flammarion, 1990), cited in Claire Devarrieux, 'Morte, je peux encore écrire', *Libération*, 4 mars 1996, 31–4 (32).)

[2] Aliette Armel, 'Un Itinéraire politique' (interview with Dionys Mascolo), *Le Magazine littéraire*, 278 (juin 1990), 36–40; cited in Marie-Thérèse Ligot, *Marguerite Duras: Un Barrage contre le Pacifique* (Paris: Gallimard, coll. 'Foliothèque', 1992), 171. Michèle Manceaux describes the suicidal atmosphere of Duras's literary début as already containing in kernel 'le chantage mortel de la passion qui fonde l'œuvre de l'écrivain et les menaces, les excès, les condamnations qui parsèment sa vie' (Manceaux, 'Tuer, dit-elle', *Nouvelle Revue Française*, 542 (mars 1998), 101–6 (101)).

to establish the terms for the exploration of the relationship between writing and extremity which will characterize her work as a whole. Specifically, this means an investigation of the possibility of moving beyond the thematization of extremity, to embrace the textual enactment of the incursions of the beyond into the everyday. Duras's texts of 1943 to 1971 (with which Part I of this study will be concerned) repeatedly explore the possibility of such enactment; her writing of 1943 to 1955 shows her first engagements with this question, as the irruptions of extremity presented thematically are also investigated stylistically, syntactically, and structurally. These irruptions, while already raising ethical questions (we have here, as we have just seen, suicide, manslaughter, and infidelity, for example), do not quite constitute one sustained overall ethical concern; such coherence will come in 1958, as *Moderato cantabile* signals the beginning of a ten-year-long exploration of the relationship between narrative and judgement after the excessive event. Until 1955, we may say, Duras is producing a range of encounters between writing and varieties of extreme ethical experience, and mapping the problematic textual enactment of this encounter.

This extreme experience already exhibits the limit status which fascinates Duras in the ethical: it is consistently presented as bursting through the categories of judgement and understanding which nonetheless remain to grapple with the dilemmas it imposes. Thus, in both *Le Marin de Gibraltar* and *Les Petits Chevaux de Tarquinia*, for example, the arrival of passion both cuts through the tedium of routine existence and remains caught up in this existence: the narrator of *Le Marin de Gibraltar* takes some time to extricate himself from his life with Jacqueline, his partner at the start of the story, and liberates himself through passion only into an apparently empty quest marked by its own brand of daily tedium; and while Sara's betrayal of her husband Jacques, in *Les Petits Chevaux de Tarquinia*, is presented as an excursion from their stable life, it is also debated within, and thus also bound up with this life. While Duras is yet to develop a sustained interest in one particular ethical area, her interest in the slippery edge of the ethical is already present in her early exploration of the encounter between writing and extremity. The writing which comes out of this process becomes increasingly taut, honed down in order to allow the question of textual enactment to be explored at an increasingly large-scale textual level. *Les Impudents* and *La Vie tranquille* initiate this exploration predominantly at the level of style and syntax; by *Les Petits Chevaux de Tarquinia* and *Le Square*, it also takes place across the architectural structure of the text as a whole. By 1955, then, Duras has established sufficient expertise in the exploration of the limits of the textual instantiation of excess to be able to undertake this exploration at the levels of textual structure *and* local detail, and to begin sustained concentration on one particular ethical resonance of this excess. It is this period of preparation that I will be discussing in the following chapter.

These early texts stand in a curious relation to those for which they prepare the ground, however. Predating Duras's arrival at what she will later describe as her own, distinctive style, they are easily considered as simply a prelude to the main body of her work, and have received—in comparison to the later works—relatively little critical attention.[3] Duras herself seems uncertain about their importance: while she may at times repudiate early works, she also agrees to their republication, adds new prefaces, revises text, and so on. Duras's ambivalence is perhaps understandable, since the success of works she clearly regards as forerunners to her discovery of her proper voice may both affirm and contradict a sense of her achievements. That her public figure was also much less well established as an inevitable companion to her work at this time (although the autobiographical aspects which shade these texts are, retrospectively, gradually acknowledged and increasingly apparent) might represent a further reason for this ambivalence on the part of an older Duras to whom this figure is so important in her negotiations of the world and her career. (The gradual revelations of this autobiographical dimension—always accompanied by corresponding denials—do produce, however, the characteristically Durassian haunting of these texts, at once intrusive and nebulous; and the denials are of the essence of this characteristic structure, heightening the sense of a readerly connection which is also a separation, itself already assured by the retrospective temporality of these revelations). More pertinent, for our purposes, is the apparent critical preference for works published after the 1958 watershed.[4] It may be

[3] For Duras's positioning of *Moderato cantabile* as the crucial break in her career, see *Les Parleuses*: 'Il y a toute une période où j'ai écrit des livres, jusqu'à *Moderato cantabile*, que je ne reconnais pas' (*P*, 13).

[4] Of the articles in the bibliography to this study, for example (a fairly representative sample), only two are devoted specifically to pre-1958 texts. Duras's gradual disclosure of autobiographical dimensions in her early work may be traced, for example, in two interviews from 1963: 'L'auteur d'"Hiroshima mon amour" vous parle', *Réalités*, mars 1963, 90–5; and Pierre

that critical attention has largely focused on the post-*Moderato cantabile* era of Duras's work because her earlier texts are felt to be too derivative (particularly of Mauriac and Hemingway—although this view can obscure the extent to which Hemingway, for example, is less copied than explicitly pastiched in *Le Marin de Gibraltar*), or to demonstrate insufficiently either Duras's magnetic mature style or her contagious fascination with excessive experience.[5] And it is clearly the case, as I have just argued, that these texts do largely prepare the ground for their successors. This is far from exhausting their interest, however; these texts are just as fascinated with the irruptive beyond as any of those they precede; and, despite repeated accusations of stylistic shortcomings, they are certainly not lacking in a rich, detailed literary quality. If these early works do represent a prelude to Duras's writing as a whole, then they do so not as a mere apprenticeship, but as an overture, summarizing much of what is to be developed at greater length. In particular, they are of considerable significance for a criticism interested in the roles of excess and transgression in Duras's work—although they have been strikingly neglected by such a criticism. To the bulk of Duras criticism, for which the notions of transgression and excess provide a general framework and sensibility, these early texts will be of interest to the extent that these preoccupations are already, as I will demonstrate, both central and placed in a complex relation to the business of writing. Beyond a generalized sympathy for such notions, however, there is a more extreme approach, for which this complexity has unsettling implications. This approach, as I have argued, posits an equivalence between the literary text and its excessive concerns,

---

Hahn, 'Les Hommes de 1963 ne sont pas assez féminins', *Paris-Théâtre*, 198 (14 septembre 1963), 32–7.

[5] A view of Duras as derivative pervades responses to these early works. Alfred Cismaru, in *Marguerite Duras* (New York: Twayne, 1971), for example, is one of many to suggest that *Les Impudents* was influenced by Mauriac (20). Armand Hoog, in 'The Itinerary of Marguerite Duras' (*Yale French Studies*, 24 (Summer 1959), 68–73), states that 'Marguerite Duras, in her first manner, drew inspiration from the American novel' (68)—a view which is confirmed by Duras in an interview four years later, in which she acknowledges that 'le roman américain a exercé sur moi une grande influence, qui se retrouve dans la première partie de mon œuvre. Par la suite, j'ai pris une autre direction' (Hahn, 'Les Hommes de 1963 ne sont pas assez féminins', 35). The view that *Le Marin de Gibraltar* may be read as parody rather than mere imitation is also put forward by Mechthild Cranston (following Jean Pierrot), who describes its subversive weave of voices as 'carnivalesque'. (See Cranston, *Beyond the Book—Marguerite Duras: Infans* (Potomac: Scripta Humanistica, 1996), 21; and Pierrot, *Marguerite Duras* (Paris: Librairie José Corti, 1986)).

claiming that texts can *be* excessive or transgressive, without acknowledging the paradox inherent in this conversion of irrecuperable negativity into positive textual achievement. Duras's texts are thus claimed to instantiate the loss, passion, madness, incomprehension (and so on) they address, and are valorized on the basis of this successful enactment. The relative lack of interest in Duras's early works from this mode of criticism might well be explained by the fact that these texts already suggest its problems. For while they certainly explore the possibility of the textual enactment of excess, they also already demonstrate the impossibility of such enactment, maintaining themselves on the edge between the world and its loss. And what is more they do so, as I will try to show, at the most detailed and delicate levels of their literary texture, which ought to give at least pause for thought to the apparent critical tendency to overlook this period of Duras's work in favour of what is generally held to be her more accomplished output. A close reading of these texts will reveal that they are full of significance for Duras's work as a whole, as they set up compellingly the fascination with the ethical edge of the beyond and its encounter with writing which will characterize her entire career. They thus establish, moreover, the attenuated relationship between writing and the ethical—in which writing touches absorbingly on the concerns of the ethical without ever quite resolving the question of the nature of this relationship— which I will be following throughout Duras's career, and which represents one of Duras's most subtle and significant contributions to her various literary and philosophical contexts. The major claims which I believe it is both appropriate and necessary to make on behalf of the importance of Duras's work can hardly be made without an understanding of the ways in which many of the principal aspects of this work are announced in the texts of this early period.

This chapter will, accordingly, provide a series of close readings, in order to bring out the structure—that of impossible enactment— which Part I of this study will then trace in Duras's work until 1971. It will be my aim here to present the ways in which the texts of Duras's early career inflect the incursions of excess, to suggest some of the ethical resonances of these inflections, and—especially—to explore the complexity of the writing strategies they employ when confronting this excess. These early works sketch the extraordinary interventions of the beyond from love affairs to existential epiphanies, and hint at its overwhelming significance in part by posing the question of whether textual patterns may—perhaps—just be able to catch its irruption. The overwhelming arrival of the beyond is presented in these texts in such guises as the catastrophe of the flood of *Un Barrage contre le Pacifique*; the endless, empty quest of passion of *Le Marin de Gibraltar*; or the voracity of the natural world, set against the deathly sterility of isolation, of 'Le Boa'. These and other texts will be considered below. For now, I propose to explore the relation between irruption and textual patterning with reference to two pairs of texts which effectively circumscribe this period. Shortly, I will discuss *Les Petits Chevaux de Tarquinia* and *Le Square*, which set up a debate between continuity and irruption, symbolized as enclosure and excursion, and suggest the possible enactment of this debate within their respective structures. First, however, I will consider *Les Impudents* and *La Vie tranquille*, which initiate Duras's career, and which present principally through the figure of ellipsis the possible textual enactment of the arrival of the excessive beyond, the conjunction of passion and violence which they term 'le pire'.

Elaborating the Beyond

Le pire, tantôt insignifiant, tantôt objet d'épouvante, selon qu'on l'évoquait dans la détresse ou dans un calme relatif. Il apparaissait quelquefois dans le train quotidien de l'existence sous l'aspect défini et toujours décevant d'un crime, d'un suicide, d'un vol important. Il existait hors de la maison, telle une maladie épidémique qui rôde dans la ville, mais ne vous a pas encore atteints. Et on se contentait dans la vie d'éviter le pire . . .

$$(I, 38–9)$$

Already in *Les Impudents*, the defining traits of the irruptive beyond are evident. Its incursion is into the everyday ('dans le train quotidien de l'existence'); it is irreducible either to representation or to any of its particular manifestations ('l'aspect défini et toujours décevant'); these manifestations are criminal and deathly ('d'un crime, d'un suicide, d'un vol important'); it is inimical to established social structures ('Il existait hors de la maison'); and its catastrophic significance renders its occurrence uncertain and dread ('ne vous a pas encore atteints'). In these features, we may see 'le pire' as the first, and already quintessential instance of Duras's fascination with the borders of the ethical. It is irreducible to the structures of the world, and manifests itself in events which puncture these structures; and yet its dramatic arrival is emphatically located within the world, an indeterminate but unavoidable part of every-day existence, inseparable from but irreducible to questions of judgement, justice, right and wrong. Ethical responses are thus both demanded and exceeded by this phenomenon, which makes of it the early manifestation of the particular ethical inflection Duras gives to extreme experience. Only passion is missing for this con-stellation to present perfectly the beyond as it will repeatedly be elaborated by Duras throughout her work—and, as we shall see, *Les Impudents* is not slow to complete this final link. Over the fol-lowing pages, I will trace the various aspects of this constellation in Duras's first two literary texts, exploring in particular the gestures they make towards the textual enactment of the arrival of 'le pire'.

Both *Les Impudents* and *La Vie tranquille* map the terrible irruptions of 'le pire'. As if to underscore the links between the two texts on this question, *La Vie tranquille* has Françou, its narrator, take the very atti-tude towards 'le pire' designated in *Les Impudents* as inadequate: as her uncle Jérôme lies dying, his liver burst after a jealous assault by her brother Nicolas, Françou is desperate to keep the awful truth of the situation from the visiting doctor: 'Je lui ai demandé de ne pas effrayer Jérôme qui était très impressionnable. Maintenant, il fallait éviter le pire. Jérôme ne dirait quelque chose que dans l'épouvante' (*VT*, 28). In both texts, the arrival of 'le pire' takes place at the inter-section of passion and death. In *La Vie tranquille*, Nicolas assaults Jérôme after Françou has revealed to him that his uncle is sleeping with Clémence, the mother of his child. (Françou's motives for this denunciation, tinged with at least a hint of jealousy, will remain obscure, and will come to represent a further instance of the threat of the unknowable). Worse is to come, however: eventually, Nicolas is unable to bear the aftermath of his uncle's death. Strung between Clémence (to whom he is now indifferent) and the passionate Luce Barragues, he disappears, and the horror of his fate bursts quietly into the chatter of narrative gossip:

Pendant trois jours, après le retour de Clémence, nous ne l'avons pas vu aux Bugues. Nous pensions qu'il était chez Luce, et personne ne s'est inquiété de ne pas le voir. Luce a dit ensuite à Tiène qu'elle ne l'avait pas aperçu durant ces trois jours.

Ce n'est que le matin du troisième jour que Clémence a trouvé le corps écrasé de Nicolas sur les rails du chemin de fer. Il avait les bras allongés en avant, les pieds écartés. Il ressemblait à un oiseau mort.

(*VT*, 111)

In *Les Impudents*, the crucial irruption of 'le pire' is, equally, a passionate suicide. As the central character, Maud, is wandering nostalgically in the woods around her family's run-down country home, her eye is caught by something in the river:

Alors, dans le cirque de roseaux qui bordaient les berges, entre les deux moulins de Semoic et d'Ostel, Maud aperçut, flou comme une ombre mais cependant effroyablement précis, le cadavre d'une femme.

(*I*, 95)

In its crepuscular terror, 'le pire' is the insistent concern of these two texts. And its position in relation to this everyday is equally clear: it is the intervention of the terrible force of the beyond, which shatters the flow of the surface with the eruption of the horror of the depths.

The principal textual effects of this shattering eruption have already been in evidence in the instances above: the overwhelming beyond produces in these texts a gasp, marked by two versions of ellipsis, which I will here delineate as the first examples of Duras's writing of the beyond. The first, which intervenes with some regularity in to the narrative of *Les Impudents*, is constituted by the 'points de suspension' which trail off into the beyond, allowing its horror to echo through the text. As Maud runs from the dreadful apparition of the corpse, its horrific position on the edge of identity is portentously indicated by the '. . .', which first present this identity as enigmatic, in the question, 'Qui était cette femme? . . .' (*I*, 95) The horror of the corpse is linked to its unsettling occupation of a shady zone between identity and its dissolution, marked textually by the 'points de suspension', which negotiate undecidably between the identity of the text and the silence which surrounds it. From one side of this limbo, identity seeps into nothingness: 'Qui était cette femme? . . .' The same indicator then marks the disquieting identity of the corpse from the other side, however, as the dead woman's identity creeps back into the corpse by means of the allusivity created by the '. . .': 'Avant le coude que faisait la rivière à cet endroit, à la dernière lueur du jour Maud distingua les deux tresses noires qui traînaient le long de son corps . . .' (96) Here, the '. . .' provides the space in which the clue—'les deux tresses noires'—resonates, and sends the reader back to the point in the narrative at which the woman makes her first appearance: 'La jeune fille était en train de couper des joncs avec une petite serpe brillante. Deux longues tresses noires pendaient le long de sa tête jusque dans les herbes' (49–50). This identification of the girl, on the basis of a double repetition ('tresses noires', 'le long de'), as the lover of Maud's neighbour, Jean Pecresse, is then bluntly confirmed by a passing servant: 'Paraît que la poule à Pecresse s'est supprimée' (97). Facilitating the tracing and resolution of this enigma across the text, the 'points de suspension' also enact the unsettling instability of identity embodied in the corpse, and, as an uncertain opening from the text onto its beyond, figure its irruptive horror.

The second kind of ellipsis which marks the irruption of horror into these texts is constituted by the concrete intervention within the body of the text of its silent beyond. This incursion appears in *La Vie tranquille*, for example, as an ominous indication of the imminent revelation of Nicolas's suicide, and provides the desert across which the disaster retrospectively echoes. The full passage is as quoted above; here are just the edges of the silence with which the text marks its horror:

Luce a dit ensuite à Tiène qu'elle ne l'avait pas aperçu durant ces trois jours.

Ce n'est que le matin du troisième jour que Clémence a trouvé le corps écrasé de Nicolas sur les rails du chemin de fer.

(*VT*, 111)

The silence into which Nicolas's death crashes offers over the time of its reading a double enactment of the intervention of his suicide into the lives of those around him. As it is initially traversed, the silence marks the ignorance of these characters of his horrible end. Then, as this end becomes apparent, the textual blank figures retrospectively the horror of its discovery. In turn, then, symbolically, and as it were out of time, the absence comes to stand for that which is missing from both of these stages: namely the unnameable death itself, resistant to representation, marked at its edges by worry and bodily débris, sketched in negatively in the burst of its irrecuperable negativity.

Les Impudents and *La Vie tranquille*, then, use ellipsis to sketch the disastrous arrival of 'le pire', the conjunction of passion and violence with which they are concerned thematically. In *Les Petits*

Chevaux de Tarquinia, the awful bodily dismemberment first presented in Duras by Nicolas's death again plays a symbolic role as the shattered incarnation of the beyond. In this text, the motif of the death of the young *démineur*, blown up by one of the mines he was attempting to clear, figures the irruption manifest in the main story-line as the incursion of singular passion into the stability of estab-lished relationships. From the disaster of 'le pire', then, Duras has by now moved to consider passion *per se* as excessive enough to merit consideration in opposition to the continuity of the everyday. *Les Petits Chevaux de Tarquinia*, accordingly, is concerned with the relation between fidelity and infidelity, characterized respectively as containment and excursion; it is present in the words of the charac-ters, the symbolism of their setting, and the structures of the text. Written a decade after *Les Impudents*, *Les Petits Chevaux de Tarquinia* thus shows Duras, the success of *Un Barrage contre le Pacifique* as it were under her belt, able to explore the contrast between everyday con-tinuity and the irruptions of the beyond in a range of textual tech-niques.[6] The coding of passion as excursion also shows that it, too, is located at the edge of the ethical: while it bursts overwhelmingly into the lives of those it affects, it is nonetheless debated and assessed within these lives. (This location of passion as exceeding but bound into the debates and tedium of the world has already been apparent in *La Vie tranquille*, of course; in the run-up to *Les Petits Chevaux de Tarquinia*, it also features in *Un Barrage contre le Pacifique*, and—espe-cially—in *Le Marin de Gibraltar*).

The characters, on holiday in an Italian coastal village, discuss the rights and wrongs of infidelity in metaphors which lend their holiday setting a self-referential resonance. When Sara returns to her husband at the end of the text, after a fleeting dalliance with the enigmatic stranger who has attached himself to their group, they summarize her affair thus:

---

[6] This development has led some critics to present *Les Petits Chevaux de Tarquinia* as the turning-point in the evolution of Duras's mature style. See, amongst others, Yvonne Guers-Villate, *Continuité / discontinuité de l'œuvre durassienne* (Brussels: Éditions de l'Université de Brux-elles, 1985); David Coward, 'Marguerite Duras', in Michael Tilby (ed.), *Beyond the Nouveau Roman* (Oxford: Berg, 1990), 39–63, who remarks on 'a new sparseness of form' (42); and Jean Pierrot, who also sees the text as presenting in Duras's development 'une nouvelle forme romanesque, à la fois légère et dense, condensée par la rigueur quasi géométrique de l'intrigue' (Pierrot, 75). Displaying her constantly shifting relationship to her earlier work, Duras in 1967 repudiates *Les Petits Chevaux de Tarquinia*, as merely 'un livre plein de charme et de facilité' (Hubert Nyssen, 'Un Silence peuplé de phrases', in *Les Voies de l'écriture* (Paris: Mercure de France, 1969), 125–41 (132)).

—Ce n'était pas si grave, dit-elle. Des vacances que je voulais prendre de toi.
—Je sais. Tu es libre de les prendre.

(*PC*, 216)

Their friend Ludi, on the other hand, denies that love permits of such excursions:

—Il n'y a pas de vacances à l'amour, dit-il, ça n'existe pas. L'amour, il faut le vivre complètement avec son ennui et tout, il n'y a pas de vacances possibles à ça.

(*PC*, 219)

In contrast to the love between Sara and her husband Jacques, or that between Ludi and his wife Gina, the passion that produces itself between Sara and her lover is characterized as brutal, unexpected, mutually irruptive: the man is presented as unique, a chancy singularity in relation to the group of friends ('Il n'y avait que l'homme qui était venu ici par hasard, et non pas pour Ludi' (9)); and Sara knows that she represents for him a dramatic revelation: 'Il y avait deux jours, le matin, à la même heure, alors qu'elle arrivait de la villa, il s'était aperçu qu'elle existait, brutalement. Elle l'avait compris à son regard' (20). As the consequences of this brutal revelation begin to unwind, their passion is symbolized quite explicitly as an excursion from the enclosure of the group of friends: with the others exhibiting their exemplary sociability by forming teams to play boules, the two imminent lovers make their escape to the dance which is taking place near the coast, a move described in the phrase, 'Ils sortirent de l'enclos' (100). This excursion begins the evening which culminates in the consummation of the couple's passion; at the end of the text, contemplating the unwinding of the affair, Sara repeats the move, heading again away from the boules players and towards the mouth of the river (214). Similarly, the couple's first encounter after their initial tryst takes place on a rock away from the coast where the group spend most of their time, emphasizing still further the positioning of passion as an excursion (133–5).

Beyond these symbolizations of the excessive position of passion, its arrival is also enacted in the fabric of the text, in the empty figure of ellipsis which, as we have seen above, Duras has been using since her earliest writing to suggest the incursion of the beyond. At the culmination of the couple's evening together, romantic music carried on the breeze tropes itself negatively into silence, and the text opens within itself the space of the passionate beyond:

De l'autre côté du fleuve, on joua *Blue Moon*, et de ce côté-ci où ils étaient, *Mademoiselle de Paris*. Mais . . . ce fut surtout *Blue Moon* qui arriva jusqu'à eux et qu'ils n'entendirent pas.

L'homme était reparti depuis une heure lorsque Jacques revint de la partie de boules.

(112)

Against this elliptical irruption, the text also enacts in its overall structure the containment into which it bursts; and it is in this architectural exploration of enactment that we may see the extent of Duras's development in this area over the ten years from *Les Impudents* to *Les Petits Chevaux de Tarquinia*. No longer principally dependent upon ellipsis, she combines this figure with a symbolic geography and overall textual organization, to produce a work almost organically dedicated to the dramatization of its concerns. The four chapters both open and close with repeated phrases which establish a formulaic enclosure throughout and around the narrative, thereby performing one side of its thematic and symbolic debate. The text already opens with an implied continuity:

Sara se leva tard. Il était un peu plus de dix heures. La chaleur était là, égale à elle-même.

(7)

This continuity is then repeated at the opening of chapter III: 'Le lendemain, la chaleur était toujours là, égale à elle-même' (115). The verbatim repetition of a statement of continuity ('égale à elle-même') itself enacts a continuity of its own, elevating this continuity to the power of two. Similarly, the ending of chapter I—'Elle s'endormit dans cet espoir' (52)—is repeated verbatim at the end of chapter III (168), and with an added air of finality at the close of the narrative—'et elle s'endormit très tard, dans cet espoir' (221); and the opening of chapter II—'Mais lorsqu'elle s'éveilla, le temps, encore une fois, s'était levé' (53)—is repeated at the opening of chapter IV—'Mais lorsqu'elle se réveilla, le temps, encore une fois, s'était levé' (169)—, the repetition itself marked by the shift from 'éveilla' to 'réveilla'. This network of repeated formulae encloses the narrative in a web of continuity—and so enacts the enclosure

with which it is thematically pre-occupied. The text, between irruptive, passionate ellipsis and formulaic containment, plays out in its
own structure the symbolism of the debate about infidelity which so
concerns its characters.

The opposition between continuity and the irruptive moment
presented in *Les Petits Chevaux de Tarquinia* in relation to passion is re-
elaborated two years later in *Le Square*, here with a significance
which leans more towards the existential. The debate is pared down
to a series of exchanges between a maid and a travelling salesman in
a small public park (another symbolic enclosure); both struggling to
make ends meet, they discuss the possibility of the arrival of an
epiphanic moment of delivery from their status of a lonely, impoverished residue, the weak, vulnerable, quasi-Levinasian other for
whom Duras's concern is perpetually evident, 'les derniers des
derniers' (*S*, 65/85).[7] The debate between them centres on the
possibility of producing a decisive change in their situations by an
effort of will. The woman is determined that her situation will not
last, and that, by marrying, she will efface all trace of this sad stage
in her life. The man, more worn down by the strain of his desperate
work, is too exhausted to be able to envisage the crucial moment as
the result of an act of will, and sees it instead as irruptive: 'Il faudrait
que le changement arrive vers moi, je n'ai pas le loisir d'aller vers
lui' (*S*, 23). The deep, weary sadness of this position—sharpened by
the man's heart-rending optimism ('Je me rase en chantant, tous les
matins, que voulez-vous de plus?' (123))—becomes apparent with
the revelation that his epiphanic moment has *already* taken place. In
another public garden, this time in a small Mediterranean town, at
sunset, as the surroundings were flooded with a honeyed light, he
was filled with an inexplicable contentment:

Eh bien, j'ai été tout à coup aussi à l'aise dans ce jardin que s'il avait été fait pour
moi autant que pour les autres. Comme si, je ne saurais vous dire mieux, j'avais
grandi brusquement et que je devenais enfin à la hauteur des événements de ma
propre vie.

(54)

---

[7] The figure of the travelling salesman reappears in *Nathalie Granger* (1973), allowing Duras
to gloss his importance in her work as follows: 'Il y a un voyageur de commerce dans *Le Square*,
dans *Un Barrage contre le Pacifique*, et peut-être dans *Le Marin de Gibraltar*. La situation du
voyageur de commerce—je parle de ceux qui sont au plus bas de l'échelle, qui font du porte-
à-porte—m'apparaît toujours comme étant la plus terrible de toutes' (*NG*, 51–2).

The maid questions his story insistently, both emphasizing the untoward status of the crucial epiphany and revealing the worry that underlies her faith in her own will. What if the decisive moment were after all irruptive, not to be had by dint of desire?

> Monsieur, je voulais vous demander ceci: lorsqu'on veut une chose tout le temps, à chaque heure du jour et de la nuit, doit-on forcément l'obtenir?
>
> (83)

Her desperate rejection of the possible elusiveness of the vital moment only indicates her own worry, namely that she will fail to open the door onto her own future:

> Parfois, je crois que je ne l'ouvrirai jamais, qu'une fois que je serai prête à le faire, je reculerai.
>
> (130–1)

Against the grinding continuity of their everyday lives, the moment that might effect a change is fleeting, uncertain, possibly already gone, or even never to come—and when come, possibly unnoticed, assimilated to the banality of its everyday surroundings:

> Je crois que cela arrive soit tout d'un coup, soit si lentement que c'est à peine si l'on peut s'en apercevoir. Et quand ces choses sont là, sont arrivées, elles n'étonnent plus, on croit les avoir toujours eues. Un jour, vous vous réveillerez et ce sera fait.
>
> (111)

As with *Les Petits Chevaux de Tarquinia*, so with *Le Square*: the text's concern with the tension between continuity and irruption is dramatized in its structure. And the extreme sparseness of *Le Square* both allows its concern for its characters to resonate, and presents still more starkly the elaboration in textual structure of a thematic argument. Duras here develops to a fine art the orchestration across a whole text of the problematic of enactment. Accordingly, the openings of the text's three sections display the technique of formulaic repetition as the enactment of continuity already identified in the earlier text: the opening of the first section ('Tranquillement, l'enfant arriva du fond du square et se planta devant la jeune fille' (9)) is repeated verbatim at the opening of the final section (137), and is inflected in the opening of the central section only by the adverb 'de nouveau', itself marking the repetition both of the scene and of the phrase announcing it (77). There is here a triple repetition: of the action of the child, of its formulaic presentation (repetition to the second power), and of the technique of the formulaic repetition of repetition (repeated from *Les Petits Chevaux de Tarquinia*, repetition to the third power). The final repetition of this scene adds a quiet twist, indicating its finality by a minor-key shift: whereas the child's two previous appearances have served as a pretext for a comment from the man, in the final instance he remains silent ('L'homme, cette fois, ne fit aucune remarque' (137)), thereby both marking the text's move into the poignant uncertainty on the edge of silence with which it will close, and suggesting the enactment not so much of simple continuity, but rather of the tension between continuity and its inexplicable, silent beyond.

Thus, from the earliest to the latest texts of this period, we may trace a development: exploring the possible textual enactment of the incursion of the beyond, Duras begins by using principally the figure of ellipsis, which restricts such enactments to the local status appropriate to the phenomenon of irruption. By 1955, however, her interest is in the opposition between irruption and continuity, and this is dramatized locally, in the continuing use of ellipsis, at the intermediate level of the symbol, and at the grander level of the architecture of the entire text.

Uncertainties of Enactment

And yet, and yet. All this is far from adequate—and its failing is, precisely, adequation. Obscurity, opacity, silence, irruption, the *beyond*—how can these be *enacted*? How can we claim an equivalence, a coincidence, between something (a text, a figure) and nothing (the beyond)? That this claim is excessive loops back into enactment at a meta-level, and this spiral will wind upwards infinitely; but for as long as it is a dyadic spiral of re-confirmation, in which text and beyond find in each other their perfect image, this excess will find itself nailed to the stable floor of resemblance. The excessive residue that will always resist recuperation—which is to say, *enactment, performance, dramatization*, all of those reassuringly instrumental metaphors—irrupts (precisely) into the narcissism of this mirrored staging to declare its screaming misrecognition: nothing is not something, and—crucially—this 'not' is nothing too. There is no resolution here; and least of all the resolution of non-resolution as *excessively* significant.

While these texts do, then, present with rigour and some elegance the possibility of the textual enactment of the encounter with
the beyond, they also—insistently—demonstrate the impossibility
of such enactment. That they (and the later texts they here anticipate) may be read as instantiations of the negativity they confront
results not from critical perversity (since they clearly do, as shown
above, invite such reading), but from the failure to perceive that
such interpretation is suggested by the texts to have its impossibility
revealed in the work of their details. Read closely, these texts both
acknowledge the attraction of enactment and suggest that, when it
comes to the beyond, things are rather more tricky.

Here is Françou, peering into the muddy depths of her motivation for denouncing Jérôme and Clémence:

Moi aussi je venais de découvrir que je n'avais été dégoûtée de Jérôme et de
Clémence que parce que moi j'étais seule pendant qu'ils étaient ensemble. Mais je
me disais que j'y penserai [*sic*] plus tard.

(*VT*, 84–5)

The narrated 'je', while claiming to have located her motivation in
her lonely jealousy, refuses to draw any conclusions from this
discovery until later; the narrating 'je', however, who is Françou
thinking about things 'plus tard', makes no such conclusions apparent, thereby effacing her presence in favour of the reflections of her
earlier self. Each instance of the narrator's self defers to the other,
and the attempt to sound the depths of motivation is lost in the gulf
between the two. Which would enact in its obscurity the irretriev-
able obscurity of passionate motivation—were this not precisely a
retrieval, a recuperation of obscurity in the stable light of enactment. If the gulf is to enact the obscurity of Françou's motivation,
then it must remain obscure—which denies it the possibility of
being read usefully as enactment. It is, rather, a gulf of implosion,
towards which we are dragged through the spiral of paradox. The
gulf cannot enact obscurity—and so it remains obscure—and so it
enacts obscurity—and so it becomes a paradox—and so it again
enacts obscurity—and so its paradox is resolved—and so it is no
longer obscure—and so it cannot enact obscurity—and so it
remains obscure—. . . (Here is the beyond.)

'Mais je ne suis sûre de rien au fond' (*VT*, 157). Deep down, and
slipping through the silence, is nothing. Which, again, is not something—and so not nothing. The encounters in these texts between

writing and the terrible depths of the beyond do not lead the texts to instantiate radical negativity; the nothingness of the 'rien' whose edge cuts the fabric of these texts gives not nothing (the text as excessive—recuperated as irrecuperable, paradox found), but the wobbling 'riens' of an altogether humbler terror: that of uncertainty.

If we review the techniques sketched above as the textual enactment of the encounter with the beyond, then, it becomes apparent that this interpretation in fact represents the hasty stabilization of their oscillations. The 'points de suspension' read above as the enactment of the arrival of 'le pire', for example, may now be seen to shuttle uneasily between the here of textuality and the beyond of negativity, walking the line between expression and silence—and so failing to enact anything (including nothing) with any stability. Those scattered throughout *Les Impudents* establish it as a text with one eye constantly on the echoing beyond with which it is fascinated, and trace an uncertain line. Between Maud and her gambler brother Jacques, whose wife has just been killed in a car accident, they may symbolize the dreadful coincidence of disaster and a financial embarrassment—money and desire forming the intersection at which the plot of the novel unfolds:

—Je t'ai appelée, je n'ai plus le sou . . . J'ai emprunté pour la faire mieux soigner. Et à maman, tu comprends, je ne peux pas lui demander ça . . .

(*I*, 25–6)

Offering the thoughts of the mother herself, the '. . .' gestures towards an unspecified fear, a vague maternal existential terror:

Oui, elle aurait dû se détacher de Jacques au plus vite. Parfois, cette pensée la traversait comme un éclair, et elle en était effrayée . . . Il fallait se méfier des enfants qui vous pillent corps et biens . . . La fin de cette servitude, maintenant, il semblait qu'elle ne pût même pas l'envisager . . .

(31)

'. . .': is there anything meaningful here? The indeterminacy which necessarily affects the referent of the 'points de suspension' (and without which their allusivity evaporates) *is* terrifying, *is* 'le pire'—or is it? As the local villagers, the 'Pardaliens', discuss with relish the likelihood of Jean Pecresse marrying into the position of master of Uderan, Maud's family's property, a very particular spectre may be invoked:

Bientôt le Pardal tout entier fit le rapprochement inévitable: la fille Grant, inoccupée du matin au soir, cherchait certainement un mari. Et après tout il fallait que ce fût un bon Pardalien qui remît en état cette terre inculte, d'autant plus que, des deux fils Grant-Taneran, l'un était trop jeune, l'autre incapable . . .

(60–1)

As the subterranean work of metonymy and metaphor ('le rap-prochement') links the unmarried Maud to the dilapidated property ('cette terre inculte'), the monstrous nature of Jacques's putative inability looms at the edge of the text: not just a gambler, not just irresponsible, he is also Maud's brother . . . The hint of incest—perhaps (since Lévi-Strauss, say) the quintessential catastrophe hov-ering at the limit of the social—makes here its first silent appearance in Duras's work, precisely by also failing to appear, remaining a shadowy implication. The '. . .' indicates the beyond—the nature of which decrees that it might also not be being indicated, that the allusion might be to something altogether less dreadful than incest (simply to Jacques's gambling, for instance). There is no way of knowing, and this non-knowledge cannot *quite* be symbolized: the '. . .' is necessarily traversed in both directions, and the text is caught between here and there, on the edge of the beyond.

Equally, the alternative ellipsis practised in these texts—silence, the blank—suggests the instability of the beyond, and so produces an uncertain something, between something and nothing. At two key moments in *Les Impudents*, the text collapses into silence as Maud loses herself: first, as she loses her virginity; secondly, as she faints to the sound of the anguished cries of her mother, searching for her the morning after:

Elle eut juste le temps de s'entendre elle-même qui se suppliait intérieurement d'être faible, et très vite elle céda à cette voix, parvint à se détacher de sa volonté, comme dans le vent la feuille qui s'arrache à l'arbre et s'emporte, accomplissant enfin son désir de mourir.

(*I*, 136)

Maud tomba. Dans son évanouissement, elle entendait encore les deux chiens, mais de très loin, comme si elle se fût enfoncée lentement dans la mort.

(146)

Both of these passages announce section breaks, irruptive moments of white page. (Maud's defloration being marked, in addition, by an asterisk.) In both cases, silence enacts the loss of self described—and yet the figurative lines which open onto this silence suggest the trouble of this enactment. Maud's abandon to her inner voice finds a delicate, silent image in the falling leaf, which swirls through a moment of confusion (is 'son désir' that of the leaf, or Maud's? The two are uncertainly joined in the space of the simile), before settling on the name of negativity which slips into the silence it invokes: 'mourir'. And in her faint, Maud is already half in death, suspended on the uncertain thread of the 'comme si'; and again, it is the name of nothingness which echoes across the void from which it has stolen: 'comme si elle se fût enfoncée lentement dans la mort.' Maud faints, gives in to passion—does not die (quite); and the text too hovers on the edge of the silent beyond, almost enacting the paradox of this virtual loss in the faint names of death. 'Mourir' and 'mort' carry the text almost into the beyond, yet inevitably remain between meaning and its absence, keeping the boundaries of the text perforated—and so blocking any safe enactment of their negativity, snagging instantiation on the silenced hook of its unacknowledged 'as if . . .'

For how to enact silence? Like the wind (its most common symbol in these texts), silence is not: we have only its side-effects, its edges. Picking up the falling leaf of *Les Impudents*, and anticipating the magnolias of *Moderato cantabile*, *La Vie tranquille* offers a more or less virtual diptych:

A un moment donné, une fleur est tombée sur le rebord du parapet sur lequel je m'accoudais. Elle sentait la fleur tombée, une odeur, presque une saveur, très douce et déjà un peu pourrie.

(*VT*, 18)

On aurait pu entendre entre des pans de silence total les fleurs des magnolias se détacher de l'arbre et tomber dans le noir.

(70)

The dense negativity of these passages (decay, silence, darkness) cries out (like the dying Jérôme, whose cries form the background of the first passage) for interpretation. Yet the passages refuse to be unveiled, and keep their significance silent. The first flower to fall smells, tautologically, of a fallen flower; the falling flowers of the second passage are restricted to that which might have been heard. The second passage thus offers a triple silence: amid the total silence, there might (paradoxically) be heard that which is (paradoxically) silent (to the unaided human ear, at least); and this image, refusing to surrender a stable interpretation, remains semantically silent. But this triple silence itself remains silent, necessarily resisting

elevation to the noisy significance of enactment. The textual invocation of silence remains an edgy paradox, at the limit of the printed
page, a falling leaf never quite realizing its desire to die.[8]

Thus, these texts present the impossibility of coinciding with the
silence they evoke. So when they avert their gaze in the face of their
characters' passion, do we know where to look? Repeatedly (and
this is a technique which will recur throughout Duras's work, especially in *L'Amant* and *L'Amant de la Chine du nord*), the crucial
moments of passion between characters are marked textually by an
ellipsis. We have already seen this in the case of *Les Petits Chevaux de
Tarquinia*; it is also to be found in *Les Impudents* (as Maud loses her
virginity, as discussed above) and, notably, in *Le Marin de Gibraltar*,
which marks such moments by a combination of ellipsis and
euphemistic suggestion:

> Je n'avais pas eu de femme avant elle. Jacqueline devint cette nuit-là un souvenir
> très ancien qui jamais plus ne me fit souffrir.
>
> Nous sortîmes de la cabine vers midi. Nous avions peu dormi et nous nous étions
> fatigués.
>
> (*MG*, 153–4)
>
> On retourna à bord pour déjeuner. Puis, une nouvelle fois, on alla dans sa cabine.
> On y resta longtemps.
>
> (156)

Passion—the irruptive beyond—is here enacted in the intervention
of ellipsis and suggestion; this mode of enactment immediately calls
itself into question, however, as the gossip-column question of
whether or not the characters have actually *done it* parades its dicta-
tion to the reader of an unverifiable assumption. And so passion
remains beyond symbolization—and so it is symbolized—and so
we encounter, once again, the uncertain vortex of paradox as it
blurs the edges of efficient instantiation. This uncertainty in turn
allows *Les Petits Chevaux de Tarquinia* to toy with the scandal-hungry

---

[8] Compare Bataille's fascination at this time with the slipperiness of the word 'silence'
itself: 'Je ne donnerai qu'un exemple de *mot* glissant. Je dis *mot*: ce peut être aussi bien la
phrase où l'on insère le mot, mais je me borne au mot *silence*. Du mot il est déjà, je l'ai dit,
l'abolition du bruit qu'est le mot; entre tous les mots c'est le plus pervers, ou le plus poétique:
il est lui-même gage de sa mort.' Again, 'mort' bleeds into the (dare one say) silence which
surrounds it; and, making the connection between silence and breath/wind, Bataille will also
slip in the paradoxical uncertainty of the '. . .': 'Le silence est un mot qui n'est pas un mot et
le souffle un objet qui n'est pas un objet . . .' (Georges Bataille, *L'Expérience intérieure* (Paris:
Gallimard, 1943; texte revu et corrigé, 1954; coll. 'Tel', 1994), 28–9, original emphases).

reader, on the hunt for *confirmation* of the irruption: leaving the consummation of Sara's infidelity a silent musical enigma, it gradually teases it out into the light, first dragging out its ambiguity—'J'aime bien cette idée, dit Sara, d'avoir couché avec toi' (*PC*, 134)—before finally admitting the truth in a desire for repetition: 'Il faut que je couche encore avec toi, dit-il' (135). So now you know: they did it. And in the gap between this platitude and the lyrical ellipsis during which they were doing it (and failing to hear *Blue Moon*), there is all the uncertain space between the beyond and its symbolization— and again the reader who wants to *know* the beyond is left in mid-air.

As for silences, so for repetition: its enactment will prove, in these texts, subtly unstable. In the repeated formulae that open and close the sections of *Les Petits Chevaux de Tarquinia*, repetition and difference are repeatedly intertwined, shifting instantiation into uncertainty. The third sentence of the first chapter—'La chaleur était là, égale à elle-même' (*PC*, 7)—is *almost* repeated as the opening sentence of chapter III: 'Le lendemain, la chaleur était toujours là, égale à elle-même' (115), its substantive pre-occupation with repetition almost enacted. The ending of chapter I *is* repeated as the ending of chapter III—'Elle s'endormit dans cet espoir' (52/168)—before the ending of the text as a whole skews this repetition into frustration: 'Elle espérait que cette nuit-là, la pluie arriverait, et elle s'endormit très tard, dans cet espoir' (221). And between chapters II and IV, there is, again, a repetition that *almost* realizes itself: 'Mais lorsqu'elle s'éveilla, le temps, encore une fois, s'était levé'; 'Mais lorsqu'elle se réveilla, le temps, encore une fois, s'était levé' (53/169). The opposition between continuity and irruption sketched out in the text as a whole and picked up in miniature in these key, formulaic moments (the edges of silence, again) cannot *quite* be enacted, since this would tip it in the direction of continuity, negating the negativity it would instantiate. Instead, the text plays a game of same/difference which *might* enact the opposition between continuity and irruption, but which, leaning towards the pole of continuity and repetition without ever quite reaching it, keeps the text's architecture balanced precariously on the edge of uncertain instantiation.

A similar instability is at work between the formulaic, rhythmic patternings which open the sections of *Le Square*. Repetition between the first and final sections suggests the enactment of the thematic of continuity—'Tranquillement, l'enfant arriva du fond du square et se planta devant la jeune fille' (*S*, 9/137)—, but is prevented from quite accomplishing itself by the introduction in the opening of the central section of an element of difference—which, ironically, proclaims repetition: 'Tranquillement, l'enfant arriva du fond du square et se planta de nouveau devant la jeune fille' (77). There is a subtle, small-scale oscillation at work here between the enactment of repetition and the enactment of the tension between repetition and the unique, which itself both suggests the enactment of this tension and—as it is the formula of repetition ('de nouveau') which makes the difference—indicates the twisting paradox of such an enactment, whose stability would immediately wrench it into the camp of repetition.

In its evolution over time, moreover, its repetition of the event of its own publication, the text appears to set itself up as the very question of the possibility of the enactment of the uncertainties which it addresses. For, between its two versions, the text is itself uncertain as to where exactly it begins and ends. The opening of the later, 1990 version of the text begins, strictly speaking, with Duras's 1989 preface, which closes with a section of dialogue (beginning 'Parlez-moi encore des cafés . . .') repeated (and expanded) further on in the text (45–6)— if one accepts the preface's position as *before* the text. Chronologically, however, the preface comes *after* the text, having been composed over thirty years later. The first section of *Le Square* already repeats what it precedes: where does the text begin? The ending of the text is equally unstable. By the time of the 1990 version, the text's original ending ('Elle ne se retourna pas. Et l'homme le prit comme un encouragement à aller à ce bal') has been altered, and the final phrase omitted.[9] As the characters part uncertainly, the original text was already suggesting this uncertainty in its refusal to indicate a future resolution; the later version doubles this uncertainty, by introducing an instability over time into the text's already delicate ending. Uncertain uncertainty, then: the enactment of uncertainty? This would, however, reintroduce us to the certainty of enactment—and again we find ourselves in the spirals of uncertainty between enactment and its failure, in the field of (inevitably) uncertain enactment.

This confusing pattern facilitates the compassion of *Le Square*, walking alongside its concern without ever quite managing to achieve a coincidence that would obliterate its generous uncertainty (in its attention to the insecurities of the characters) with the

[9] On this point, see Hill, *Marguerite Duras: Apocalyptic Desires*, 165, n. 5.

confidence of a stable enactment. The spirals of the paradox of the instantiation of irruption/continuity may be resolved as meta-instantiation only by forgetting the work of the texts, which resist this collapse into stability, keeping the beyond alive precisely by refusing to come down on its side of the textual fence. A reading of the actual operation of enactment in these texts plainly suggests that the textual instantiation of the encounter with the beyond is realized only inasmuch as it remains virtual, halting, uncertain.

Hesitant Passions

So, Duras's texts of this period demonstrate that the incursion of the beyond into the continuity of the everyday cannot quite be captured in textual enactment, whether in symbols (the silent magnolias of *La Vie tranquille*, for example, or the crossing of a river in *Les Petits Chevaux de Tarquinia*), syntax, or structure. The obvious avatars of this beyond, which open the heart of the everyday onto a trembling emptiness, would, of course, be sex and death. We have already traced the dramatic presence of these in Duras's early writing (especially their conjunction in her notion of 'le pire'); we have not yet, however, examined in detail their relation to the mundanities of the everyday world. In this section, accordingly, I propose to discuss this relation as it is addressed by Duras's manipulation of narrative voice and her idiosyncratic use of symbols, which we have as yet touched upon without exploring in detail. Shortly, I will consider a key text from the collection *Des Journées entières dans les arbres*, 'Le Boa'; first, I will examine the work of the narrative voice of *Un Barrage contre le Pacifique* to maintain the irruption of passion into the tawdry financial schemings of the everyday as a matter of urgent uncertainty. Until now, this chapter has split the suggestion of enactment from its complication; henceforth, I will present both suggestion and complication together, to demonstrate the mix of drama and intricacy which characterizes Duras's texts even from this early period.

So many of these early texts (and so many of their descendants) are concerned with the contradictory intersections of desire and (financial) power—*Les Impudents*, say, or 'Des Journées entières dans les arbres', or *Le Marin de Gibraltar*. Or (for now), *Un Barrage contre le Pacifique*. And at these intersections, the excessive force of passion rubs against the windings of the contingent—which can also (as a matter of life or death) slip over into the passionate. This shifting crossroads is where Suzanne, desperately poor daughter of the mother of the disastrous dams, meets M. Jo, son of a wealthy Chinese, and encounters the passion and dialectical dilemmas of self-assertion and loss of self which, in Duras, accompany the young woman's entry as a sexual being into the world. And repeatedly, the narratives of their meetings slip, as, in an uncertain accompaniment, interior monologue and free indirect discourse render unclear the boundaries of narrative self-possession. Frequently, Suzanne's first person bursts into the narrative, a momentary flash out of the tension of the encounter, anticipating the constant oscillation between 'je' and 'elle' which structures the narrative of *L'Amant*:

—Je ne cache pas, dit M. Jo d'une voix très basse, que j'éprouve pour votre sœur un sentiment profond.
Il parlait tous les jours à Suzanne des sentiments qu'il éprouvait pour elle. Moi si je l'épouse, ce sera sans avoir aucun sentiment pour lui. Moi je me passe de sentiments. Elle se sentait du côté de Joseph plus fortement que jamais.

$(B, 95)^{10}$

It is, indeed, the figure of Joseph, Suzanne's brother, who frequently accompanies these incursions of Suzanne's 'je', establishing a contrast between the wealthy Chinese pretender and the poor white family. As M. Jo pleads his whining negotiations for Suzanne's favours, Joseph is twice cited as a relieving alternative: 'S'il foutait le camp, j'irais me baigner avec Joseph' (132); 'S'il foutait le camp, j'irais rejoindre Joseph' (152). More dramatically, and as Suzanne is about to receive from M. Jo a diamond ring which holds the possibility of her family's financial salvation, Suzanne slips into the narrative without her marking 'je', in a moment of free indirect discourse:

—Ça vient de ma mère, dit M. Jo, avec sentiment, elle les aimait à la folie. Que ça vienne d'où que ça veuille. Ses doigts à elle étaient vides de bagues.

(126)

As desire and power chiastically intersect (M. Jo: financial power, desperate desire; Suzanne: impoverished, manipulating M. Jo's

---

[10] The extent to which the twists of sex and money in this text should be considered autobiographical is discussed in Laure Adler, *Marguerite Duras* (Paris: Gallimard, 1998), 85 ff, with reference to an undated 'journal', contained in Duras's archive material at L'Institut de la Mémoire de l'édition contemporaine (whose handwriting experts have, according to Adler, situated it as having been written during the war), and which contains sketches for fragments not only of *Un Barrage contre le Pacifique*, but also of *L'Amant*.

passion), and the narrative encounters this shifting intersection, the text becomes momentarily uncertain about its voice. In the bravura scene of this unstable encounter, as Suzanne briefly reveals herself naked in the 'cabine de bains' to the overwhelmed M. Jo, the tawdry contingent and unqualified passion are indistinguishable, and the narrative winds around this knot. As M. Jo begs outside, promising a brand new His Master's Voice phonograph if he can just have a look, the text—or is it Suzanne?—debates the inevitability of her worldly consumption and circulation:

Quand même c'était là l'envie d'un homme. Elle, elle était là aussi, bonne à être vue, il n'y avait que la porte à ouvrir. Et aucun homme au monde n'avait encore vu celle qui se tenait là derrière cette porte. Ce n'était pas fait pour être caché mais au contraire pour être vu et faire son chemin de par le monde, le monde auquel appartenait quand même celui-là, ce M. Jo.

(73)

Who is speaking here—and how far is this position sanctioned by the text? 'Ce n'était pas fait pour être caché mais au contraire pour être vu': who endorses this inevitability? As Suzanne finally resigns herself to this apparent fate, and is about to open the door, M. Jo's shabby reminder of the material determinants of the situation brings a more *désabusé* gloss:

—Demain vous aurez votre phonographe, dit M. Jo. Dès demain. Un magnifique Voix De Son Maître. Ma petite Suzanne chérie, ouvrez une seconde et vous aurez votre phono.
C'est ainsi qu'au moment où elle allait ouvrir et se donner à voir au monde, le monde la prostitua. La main sur le loquet de la porte elle arrêta son geste.
—Vous êtes une ordure, dit-elle faiblement. Joseph a raison, une ordure.

(73)

On the threshold of the marketplace, Suzanne hesitates—and appears in the narrative, fleetingly, with an imagined rebellion, which however remains a mere fiction, as her first person slips into the uncertainty of free indirect discourse:

Je vais lui cracher à la figure. Elle ouvrit et le crachat lui resta dans la bouche. Ce n'était pas la peine. C'était la déveine, ce M. Jo, la déveine, comme les barrages, le cheval qui crevait, ce n'était personne, seulement la déveine.

(73–4)

With the paradox of an uncertain fatalism (is it Suzanne who decides that this ritual humiliation is just her luck, or is it the text?), the narrative emerges blinking into the tacky passion of the world; and allows Suzanne a glorious pay-off, a moment of extraordinarily complex defiance, caught impossibly between angry rebellion and naked humiliation: 'Voilà, dit-elle, et je vous emmerde avec mon corps nu' (74).

Not yet, though, not yet: for as she spits figuratively in M. Jo's face, Suzanne's voice is still uncertain—she is still not quite speaking for herself: 'Joseph disait: "Et je l'emmerde avec ma B.12", et chaque fois qu'il passait près de la Léon Bollée il lui foutait des coups de pied dans les pneus' (74). The interweaving in this scene of competing voices and interests makes it an extraordinary blend of coercion, abjection, self-assertion, integrity, manipulation, and misery; in all of these aspects, it hooks its rather claustrophobic desire insistently into the ethical, existential, and financial dilemmas of the world. Its constant raising of the question of who is narrating Suzanne's sexual coming-out means that the particular investment of the narrative in the positions it sketches out around the complex intersection of family, desire, and power remains indeterminate; the encounter between the text and the worldly edges of passion is, therefore, kept insistently uncertain.

With 'Le Boa', published first in Les Temps modernes in 1947, and then collected in Des Journées entières dans les arbres (1954), the insertion of a young woman's developing desire into the worldly socialization of passion is dramatically addressed in similar narrative subtleties and a striking use of symbols.[11] The narrator, a boarder in a *pension* run by a Mlle Barbet, experiences every Sunday a dual spectacle: first, taken to the Botanical Gardens, she watches a boa devour a chicken; then, back in the *pension*, she is presented with the sight of Mlle Barbet's withering body. The action of the boa is presented as an excessive crime, 'Ce crime impeccable', 'Ce crime sans tache' (*DJ*, 101); the boa is, moreover, itself presented as unique, 'Forme à elle seule confondante . . . nue comme l'eau et comme rien dans la multitude des espèces n'est nu' (*DJ*, 101–2). Lithe, powerful, irruptive, the boa forms the first half of an odd couple, complemented by

---

[11] An important reading of 'Le Boa' is provided by Susan D. Cohen, who argues convincingly that it contains 'elements that make this early text central to an understanding of what most deeply informs [Duras's] fictional world' (Cohen, 'The Beast and the Jungle: Longing, Learning, Love, and Luck in Marguerite Duras's "Le Boa"', in Rodgers and Udris (eds.), *Marguerite Duras: Lectures plurielles*, 35–55 (35)).

the spectacle of Mlle Barbet disrobing. The opposition is established by the narrator in advance of her presentation of this sight:
'La Barbet était, de par son âge et sa virginité très avancée, indif-
férente au boa' (102). Mlle Barbet's exhibitionism is itself irruptive
in its way; but negatively, as the implosion of a dreadful sterility:

A moitié nue. Elle ne s'était jamais montrée ainsi à personne dans sa vie, qu'à moi.
C'était trop tard. A soixante-quinze ans passés elle ne se montrerait plus jamais à
personne d'autre qu'à moi.

(103)

The narrator leaves no room for doubt: Mlle Barbet is the decaying,
stagnant embodiment of death, in contrast to the sacred, criminal
vitality of the boa: 'Je comprenais dès la première fois. Toute la maison sentait la mort. La virginité séculaire de Mlle Barbet.' (104) The
opposition is concisely formulated:

Pendant deux ans, une fois par semaine, il me fut donné d'être la spectatrice
d'abord d'une dévoration violente, aux stades et aux contours éblouissants de pré-
cision, ensuite d'une autre dévoration, celle-là lente, informe, noire.

(108)

The narrator insists that it is, precisely, the binary nature of this
opposition that lends its two terms significance:

Le boa dévorait et digérait le poulet, le regret dévorait et digérait de même la Barbet, et ces deux dévorations qui se succédaient régulièrement prenaient chacune à
mes yeux une signification nouvelle, en raison même de leur succession constante.

(108–9)

The potential Manicheism of this schema is remarked upon by the
narrator: it might have led, she comments,

jusqu'à la redécouverte d'un Dieu créateur et d'un partage absolu du monde entre
les forces mauvaises et les bonnes puissances, toutes deux éternelles, et au conflit
desquelles toute chose devait son origine; ou, à l'inverse, jusqu'à la révolte contre
le discrédit dans lequel on tient le crime et contre le crédit que l'on confère à
l'innocence.

(102)

The binary spectacle produces binary consequences: here, one
binary ('les forces mauvaises et les bonnes puissances') is opposed
in a binary schema to another (crime/innocence); elsewhere, the

vision of the world produced by this dualism is presented in a passage of extraordinary couplings:

Je me l'imaginais, ce monde, s'étendre libre et dur, je me le préfigurais comme une sorte de très grand jardin botanique où, dans la fraîcheur des *jets d'eau* et des *bassins*, à *l'ombre dense* des tamariniers *alternant* avec des flaques *d'intense lumière*, s'accomplissaient d'innombrables échanges charnels sous la forme de *dévorations*, de *digestions*, *d'accouplements* à la fois *orgiaques* et *tranquilles*, de cette tranquillité des *choses de dessous le soleil* et de *dedans la lumière, sereines* et *chancelantes* d'une ivresse de simplicité.

(110, my emphases)

The worldly couplings with which the narrator is fascinated in fact represent the coincidence of her valorization of crime and her nascent sexuality. Her developing sexual body becomes the representative within the deathly *pension* of the irruptive beyond of the boa: 'En dehors de la maison, il y avait le boa, ici, il y avait mes seins' (107). This coincidence leads the narrator to embrace the notion of prostitution, as the intersection of the criminal and the sexual, in terms which declare its allegiance to the world of natural violence inhabited by the boa:

De même que les assassins, les prostituées (que j'imaginais à travers la jungle des grandes capitales, chassant leurs proies qu'elles consommaient avec l'impériosité et l'impudeur des tempéraments de fatalité) m'inspiraient une égale admiration et je souffrais pour elles aussi à cause de la méconnaissance dans laquelle on les tenait.

(112)

The great service performed by prostitution, for the narrator, is that it allows women to be cleansed of their deathly virginity, to avoid the sterile fate of Mlle Barbet by turning their bodies into something *useful* in an economy of exchange and consumption, just as Suzanne (or the narrative voice) suspects in *Un Barrage contre le Pacifique*:

C'était un rongement de la solitude qu'on évitait sans doute en se faisant découvrir le corps. Ce qui avait servi, servi à n'importe quoi, à être vu par exemple, était protégé. Du moment qu'un sein avait servi à un homme . . . du moment que ce sein avait pu féconder un désir d'homme, il était à l'abri d'une déchéance pareille.

(114)

The natural law of devoration, 'la loi pourtant impérieuse' (114), may be borne only by being accepted, surrendered to; resistance is useless, since devoration will take place anyway, only displaced into its deathly internalization. This is the powerful binary economy with which the text comes to its conclusion, in which oppositions between vitality and decay are threaded through a world of essential sexual difference painted in the lurid colours of natural history, according to an inevitable law:

Il existait d'un côté le monde de Mlle Barbet, de l'autre, le monde de l'impérieux, le monde fatal, celui de l'espèce considérée comme fatalité . . . à la cruauté duquel, pour y accéder, on devait se faire, comme on devait se faire au spectacle des boas dévorateurs.

(115)

Here we have, then, an early example of the Romantic ethic— valorizing criminal passion precisely inasmuch as its criminality carries it beyond the mundane—which plays such a major role throughout Duras's work, as well as the clear dramatization of the dependence of this ethic on a strictly binary law. In the details of the textual elaboration of this law, however, its imperious necessity finds itself subtly contested. For the Manicheism upon which it relies— and hence the entire binary scheme of the text, inscribed, as seen above, in its symbolism, and even at the level of its style—is in fact given as a hypothesis, a conclusion which *might have been* reached, introduced with the following qualification:

C'était un spectacle qui me rendait songeuse, qui *aurait pu me faire remonter*, si j'avais été douée d'un esprit plus vif et plus nourri . . . jusqu'à la redécouverte d'un Dieu créateur et d'un partage absolu du monde entre les forces mauvaises et les bonnes puissances . . .

(102, my emphasis)

The temporality of the narrative introduces an unresolvable ambiguity: this spectacle *might have led* to the position described, which description *might* therefore be the belated realization of this potential—or, then again, might be simply its description. Similarly, the hymn to prostitution which runs through the later pages of the text is qualified, fleetingly, by a crucial parenthesis: '(je n'appris que bien plus tard le côté commercial de la prostitution)' (112). Slipped into the praise of the brothel as a temple of defloration, this interjection imports the seedy world into the devouring, metaphorical 'jungle des grandes capitales' (112), but again with uncertain consequences. Does the later realization of the material conditions attendant upon the younger self's fantasy of a 'pure' prostitution disqualify this fantasy entirely? The relative force of the text's insistent naturalizing imagery and this bracketed afterthought might indicate that, rhetorically at least, the text still sides with the violent binarism it so passionately elaborates. As the brothel is fantasized, it is initially framed: 'Je me le représentais comme une sorte de temple de la défloration' (112); but this frame gradually slips, through 'le bordel *devait être* silencieux' (112, my emphasis) and 'Je me *figurais* que les filles se mettaient un masque' (113, my emphasis), until it is all but invisible against the light of the brothel's glorious mission: 'l'on y allait se faire laver, se faire nettoyer de sa virginité, s'enlever sa solitude du corps' (113). The frame never quite disappears, however, and this indicates the quiet complication of the text. As the possibility of an ironic detachment is opened between the narrator's younger fantasy and her older awareness, there is equally offered the possibility of an ironic enactment, the suggestion that the binary patternings identified throughout the text represent the inscription of a Manicheism which the text will not quite embrace. But which it will not quite reject, either: for this ironic possibility remains (like the Manicheism it may qualify) undecidable. It is not that Duras is not fascinated by the criminal passion the narrator identifies with the boa; nor that she does not valorize this passion against the sterility of isolation. It is, rather, that the subtle details of her writing argue that, precisely inasmuch as it is excessive, such criminality can be thought to coincide with nothing, including writing. The textual fabric so drawn to capturing this excess in its symbolism and its style also marks the inevitable incoherence of this desire in the intricacies of its composition. Against the binary tide of the text's rhetoric, there is set afloat the hint of uncertainty, which will never quite realize itself, but which nevertheless prevents the text from becoming simply the grand enactment of passionate oppositions it might appear. Life/death, vitality/sterility, prostitution/virginity—yes, says the text, but . . .[12]

[12] We may see here an anticipation of *L'Homme assis dans le couloir*, which similarly presents an unstable frame hedging about a violent vision of sexuality. In the later text, however, the opposite side of the coin is displayed: whereas 'Le Boa' presents voracious, naturalized oppositions and (just about) qualifies them by a frame which, while unstable, never quite disappears, *L'Homme assis dans le couloir* presents eroticized violence through a frame whose instabilities make it uncertain whether or not it can, finally, be said to perform such qualification. This will be discussed in detail in Chapter 5, below. It is on the question of the frame in 'Le Boa' that I would disagree with Susan D. Cohen's reading: while Cohen also identifies the fleeting parenthesis ('Je n'appris que bien plus tard . . .') as the text's key moment, she sees it as clearly revising the young girl's naïve celebration of prostitution. I would suggest that the weight of the text's rhetoric (and the slippages of its framing material, as I have just described)

The possible belief that 'Le Boa' *might be* enacting in its textual patterning the polarities it addresses is, then, largely produced by the force of the text's rhetoric, which threatens extravagantly to overwhelm the detail by which, in an awkward ballet, it is also (but not definitively) qualified. This rhetoric relies principally on the symbolism which pits the law of the jungle against an old maid; were this reading not disrupted (to an extent) by the qualifying moments just discussed, we could see the irruptive beyond symbolized quasi-biblically on one side of this opposition by the voracious, criminal serpent. There is here, then, the use of a latent archetype almost to symbolize that which exceeds the musty everyday. This technique, however, is marked by the ambiguity we have observed throughout this chapter in relation to such symbolization. Were the beyond to be here, it might be symbolized; were it symbolized, signs might not quite be here.

For what, exactly, might symbolize the beyond? Already in these texts, Duras suggests her favourite answer: the sea. The endless sea of *Le Marin de Gibraltar*, the cruel sea of *Un Barrage contre le Pacifique*, the sea of *La Vie tranquille* in which the smiling stranger drowns. In *Les Petits Chevaux de Tarquinia*, the operation of this unsettling symbol is made clear: this vast figure of the beyond is, oddly, both here and there. Afraid to venture out of her depth, Sara at one point swims through a sea which acts as a symbol of the dangerous beyond of passion, with the encouragement of her future lover:

Elle s'arrêta brusquement, se rendit compte brusquement qu'elle allait vers la haute mer.
—Je ne peux pas plus, dit-elle.
—Vous avez peur. Ce n'est pas que vous ne savez pas nager.

(PC, 29)

Paradoxically, here is (to say the least) a stable symbol of excess, of the irruptive beyond—whose stability inevitably crumbles, however, as the sea is later enlisted to symbolize also the safety of continuity, the dullness of fidelity: 'Mais où aller sur la mer? L'ennui, c'est qu'on n'en sort pas' (174). Disrupting symbolic certainty, the sea remains beyond—precisely by failing to remain beyond, by seeping strangely between the overwhelming and the humdrum, and

in fact position this brief phrase as a *possible*, rather than a realized qualification; and that the text thus represents less the resolution or the celebration than the *question* of the oppositions it articulates.

thereby excessive only on condition that this movement be in turn
allowed to mean nothing. Which means: allowed not to symbolize
nothingness (as if this were possible), allowed to confuse the attempt
to sublimate its uncertainty, allowed to ebb and flow affectively here
and there. To keep moving. Still.[13]

Right at the end, asked which of her works she would single out
as her 'livre préféré absolument', Duras chooses *Un Barrage contre le
Pacifique*, prized for its evocation of her childhood (*CT*, 10). Some
years before, she had implicitly marked the distance between her
later work and such early productions, in her mockery of Roland
Barthes's 'polite' advice '*de "revenir" au genre de mes premiers romans
"si simples et si charmants"* comme Le Barrage contre le Pacifique, Les
Petits Chevaux de Tarquinia, Le marin de Gibraltar' (*YAS*, 21; original emphasis and capitalization). This mockery comprises two
main elements: Duras is ridiculing Barthes's patronizing (albeit
camp) attitude to her as a woman writer both by insisting (with some
justification, as we have seen) that her early works are not 'simples'
and 'charmants', and by laughing at the notion of a nostalgic return
to an earlier phase of her evolution. She thus manages both to bring
her early writings with her into the present (by dismissing the notion
that they might be any less accomplished and demanding than her
current work), and to mark the work of this present moment as what
is truly important. How are we to situate these early texts in relation
to Duras's *œuvre* as a whole? Their position is, plainly, ambiguous.

This ambiguity might, however, lead us into their significance for
the works they precede: for it is in their already subtle and rigorous
work on the uncertain edge of ethical extremity that these early
examples of Duras's writing both anticipate and prepare for the
later work. Throughout this chapter, I have attempted to show that,
from its very beginnings, Duras's writing rejects the notion that it
might simply coincide with, enact, or instantiate the excessive
beyond with which it is so insistently concerned. Rather, as it both
gestures towards and rules out such a relationship, this early writing
already suggests the notion of an uncertain accompaniment to
extremity, which Duras will develop through the rest of her career.
Laying the foundations for this development, these early texts both
raise and vex the question of the textual instantiation of the

---

[13] For a detailed reading of Duras's sea imagery, see Mireille Rosello, 'L'Amertume: l'eau
chez Marguerite Duras', *Romanic Review*, 78/4 (November 1987), 515–24.

encounter with the beyond in their style, their syntax, their use of symbols, and (as Duras's writing becomes both more sparse and more ambitious) their overall structure. The details of their work in all of these areas suggest that the exorbitance and extraordinary passion of Duras's writing should not simply be ascribed to an instantiation of the excessive beyond which it so often addresses, and this because such an equation offers a triple underestimate. First, of the beyond itself, which is reduced to something which could *be*, presenting a possible equivalence with a textual *something*. Secondly, of the edgy intricacies of Duras's writing, neglected in the rush to locate it in (a misprision of) the beyond. And thirdly, then, of the particular, paradoxical elaboration of the beyond wound through these intricacies, in which it is *almost* caught. To read Duras's writing as excessive *per se* is to reduce both this writing and the truths about excess which it *almost* reveals. Close reading of the incursions of the beyond into Duras's early texts indicates that this realm may be excessive precisely in its refusal to remain *simply* beyond, in its unstable occupation of a hesitant limit, the line *between* here and the beyond.

In this period of Duras's work, then, this line is already elaborated as the awkward limit of the beyond, on which the texts which both address and refuse the notion of the textual enactment of excess do their work. That it is also, as I have suggested, the edge of the ethical is perhaps less apparent at this point. While the extreme experiences presented in these texts do occupy the uneasy position at the limit of the ethical which Duras will explore throughout her career, they do not offer the continuity of concern which will mark her later, more sustained explorations of specific ethical areas. Only with *Moderato cantabile* will Duras begin to address a coherent area of ethical concern over a prolonged period; to this limited extent, we might see these texts as a preparation for the later writing. It is only the confidence to draw out the encounter with a particular ethical question over several years and an extra textual dimension that arrives in 1958, however. The characteristic structure of this encounter—in which writing refuses simply to enact the extremity of the ethical material it confronts, and, in the twists of this impossible enactment, situates itself as an uncertain accompaniment to this extremity—is emphatically already present in these early works.

The ethical is not absent from these texts, however, as the multiple examples discussed in this chapter testify. And it is already present in a manner which suggests both the claims made for its status and the necessity of a reading practice which will respond to this status. It is vital for Duras that the ethical be recognized as both essential and irresolvable, the realm of dilemmas which are both lived, and lived as beyond our mastery. That this recognition is necessary to respect the demands of the ethical is clear from Duras's writing, which winds these demands into the everyday even as it maintains them as excessive, bound into a textual weave which refuses quite to envelop them. To respect in turn this writing, we need to read Duras with an eye to this combination of excess and detail—presented paradigmatically in this extract from *Le Square*, a moment of great and significant delicacy:

—Oui, vous avez dit que vous aviez été malheureux autant qu'il est possible de l'être. Et vous le croyez encore?
—Oui.'
Ce fut la jeune fille qui se tut.
'Ne pleurez pas, Mademoiselle, je vous en prie, dit l'homme en souriant.

(*S*, 129)

Across the ellipsis, as it is read, the young woman's tears suddenly emerge, tenderly suggested in a moment which both (retrospectively) indicates their arrival and (gently) refuses to efface their pain by an assertive, positive representation. As the man's compassion attempts to dry them, the tears offer silently the uncertainties of a pain which is almost too much: both excessive and commonplace, in the hesitant gap between here and the beyond. The woman's pain is snagged beyond, caught on the edge of symbolization as that which is already, softly, lost.[14]

The excessive moment of weeping is caught up in the text, without for all that being quite dramatized in its intricate machinery; its ethical demand, to which the man's smile responds, demands also that it not be reduced by a reading looking only for equivalence. The tears are between invisibility and textual representation; as the woman weeps during a line in which her weeping is not described, their track both is and is not the line describing the silence in which they fall. And to read this line as the textual incarnation of their silent irruption dries them immediately, effacing their upsetting,

---

[14] The pathos of the conversations between the characters of *Le Square* is also addressed in Blanchot's piece on the text. See Maurice Blanchot, 'La Douleur du dialogue', in *Le Livre à venir* (Paris: Gallimard, 1959; coll. 'Idées', 1986), 207–18.

ambiguous presence with the recuperating stability of instantiation. The wetness on the young woman's cheek is (almost) the uncertain line on which writing and the ethical meet, requesting a reading which notes both the awkward position of writing on the edge of beyond, and the troubling work along this edge of the unsettling urgency of the ethical. Binding the reader, moreover, into this troubling work in the dual pathos of the scene described and the delicacy of its textual elaboration; a bond, however, which is also dissolved by this teary, pathetic fragility. As Duras's writing moves more confidently into its sustained encounters with specific ethical areas, this line (the uncertain meeting of writing and the ethical) will continue to mark its explorations (and, incidentally, its role in this awkward readerly implication will come properly to the fore); and it will be this soft, overwhelming line which I will aim to trace.

Throughout this period of Duras's work, we have seen her frequent concern with the irruptive moment, the moment of violence, passion, disaster, joy, sadness, and the textual uncertainty around the difficult, worldly edges of this moment. We have also seen her increasing interest in addressing the possible textual enactment of the arrival of this moment at the level of overall textual structure. In 1958, with *Moderato cantabile*, Duras initiates a period of her work in which the ethical questions raised by the temporality of the arrival of excess—primarily questions of the possibility of retrospective judgement—are repeatedly explored in both narrative structure and local detail. The work done in these early texts on the impossible enactment of ethical extremity, then, enables Duras to move on with *Moderato cantabile* to debate across whole texts the consequences of the irruptive moment; this irruption, whose edges are the demands of ethical and judicial judgement, will fascinate her writing for the next decade, in the guise of the criminal/erotic event.

THE TEMPORALITY OF THE EVENT

S'il y a sens, il se dégage après.
Les Parleuses

In the opening section of *Hiroshima mon amour*, the French actress and her Japanese lover debate the status of the traumatic event for which the name 'Hiroshima' forms a kind of desperate shorthand. Is it possible to know such an event? Or to remember it? Can it be reconstructed, for those to whom it has always represented an alien experience? Or does it represent a radically alien experience, even to those to whom it has happened? Is it, by virtue of its status as trauma, beyond such categories as knowledge, memory, and reconstruction? In this debate, the museum in Hiroshima becomes the very figure of reconstruction, embodying the simultaneous impossibility and necessity of living with the traumatic event. The museum preserves the terrible evidence of the event, for contemplation by tourists, for example, and other visitors, such as the French actress:

J'ai regardé moi-même pensivement, le fer . . . Des peaux humaines flottantes, survivantes, encore dans la fraîcheur de leurs souffrances . . . Des chevelures anonymes que les femmes de Hiroshima retrouvaient tout entières tombées le matin, au réveil.

(*HMA*, 24)

In front of the remnants of the event, the actress is face to face with the dilemmas of memory after trauma. She responds by insisting on the validity of retrospective knowledge ('l'Histoire') guaranteed by brute visual evidence, this faith marked by her mantra, 'J'ai vu . . .':

J'ai vu les actualités . . . Des chiens ont été photographiés.
Pour toujours.
Je les ai vus.
J'ai *vu* les actualités.
Je les *ai vues*.

(*HMA*, 27, original emphasis)

The actress is opposed by her Japanese lover: supposedly closer to the trauma, he insists on its radical unavailability to knowledge, refusing both her visual certainty—'Tu n'as *rien* vu à Hiroshima. Rien' (22, original emphasis)—and her emotional response: 'Sur *quoi* aurais-tu pleuré?' (26, original emphasis). Against this, however, the actress argues in turn that some attempt, however inadequate, to remember the event is inevitable: 'Pourquoi nier l'évidente nécessité de la mémoire?' (33). The reliance on insufficient, fragmentary evidence is all that can be hoped for after the event: reconstructions, carried out as responsibly as possible ('Les reconstitutions ont été faites le plus sérieusement possible' (25)), bear the burden of testimony in their very inadequacy:

Les gens se promènent, pensifs, à travers les photographies, les reconstitutions, faute d'autre chose, à travers les photographies, les photographies, les reconstitutions, faute d'autre chose, les explications, faute d'autre chose.

(24)

The museum thus figures the dilemma imposed by the traumatic event, which cannot simply be remembered or known (since its status as trauma challenges such categories), and yet whose memory must be preserved, reconstructed precisely in its impossibility.[1]

This dilemma is far from solely intellectual, to be resolved by discussion: it is, as the film makes clear, to be *lived*. The debate itself takes place as part of the affair between the two characters, which represents the repetition of the other of the film's twin traumas, namely the passion of the actress when young for a German soldier. Thus the encounter (the lived experience of the characters) is also governed by the logic of the event: 'Tu me plais. Quel événement. Tu me plais' (35). The passionate singularity of the encounter resembles the event by also exceeding the grasp of knowledge and understanding, but, in addition, it repeats a previous encounter, doubling itself precisely in its paradoxical singularity. (This repetition also produces a chiastic reversal in the positions of the protagonists on the status of the event: in repeating her past trauma, the

---

[1] Writing in *France-Observateur* in 1958, Duras presents the making of the film as itself the reconstruction of a phoenix of memory after the event which, while refusing to address the catastrophe directly (here, in part for reasons of cultural humility), would let its ungraspable meaning resound: Resnais explained, she writes, 'que le dessein majeur du film était d'en finir avec la description de l'horreur par l'horreur, car cela avait été fait, accompli jusqu'au bout, par les Japonais eux-mêmes, mais qu'il fallait faire renaître l'horreur de ses cendres en en conservant le sens implacable et éternel' (Marguerite Duras, 'Travailler pour le cinéma', *France-Observateur*, 31 juillet 1958, 20).

actress comes to refuse her earlier insistence on the possibility of knowledge—'On croit savoir. Et puis, non. Jamais' (109)—, while her lover embraces *her* trauma as knowable, 'dans une joie violente': 'Il n'y a que moi qui sache. Moi seulement' (103).) Split within itself by its status as repetition, the encounter cannot be known; it will inevitably, however, give rise to reconstructions and attempts to comprehend it ('Il n'y a que moi qui sache'); it represents, to this extent, a further event, and demonstrates that the event imposes itself as lived experience, even as it removes itself as passion and repetition from the categories of an experience which could quite be known or possessed. And as lived experience, the event-encounter deals in the highest stakes: it is, quite explicitly, a matter of life and death, be this the incomprehensible mass destruction of Hiroshima, or the symbolic death and real disgrace of the young actress in Nevers (and the real death of her German lover). While it represents an experience which is not simply available to knowledge, the event nonetheless imposes consequences which, as they are lived, raise inevitably the question of judgement. Her head shaved as the mark of her criminal passion, the young actress embodies the terrible logic of the event: the trauma or passion that renders the event inaccessible also brings with it the compulsion to produce judgement despite and in necessary denial of this inaccessibility. The drives to reconstruct and to judge are produced by precisely those events which render reconstruction and judgement uncertain. Imposing reconstruction, the event both ruins and calls forth judgement. Neither term of this impossible couple cancels the other—the trauma of the event leaves judgement caught between its inadequacy and its urgency.[2]

[2] For a detailed discussion of Duras's sustained exacerbation of the traumatic event into the realm of historical trauma, see Chapter 4, below. *Hiroshima mon amour* represents an initial example of this concern; it will, however, have to wait until 1979 for concerted elaboration. We should also note, at this point, the resemblance between the Durassian event and Lyotard's account of the same phenomenon. See, for example, Jean-François Lyotard, *Le Différend* (Paris: Minuit, 1984), 120: 'En somme, il y a des événements: quelque chose arrive qui n'est pas tautologique avec ce qui est arrivé.' Bill Readings, in his *Introducing Lyotard* (London: Routledge, 1991), emphasizes the link between the event and judgement: 'The event is the fact or case that something happens, after which nothing will ever be the same again. The event disrupts any pre-existing referential frame within which it might be represented or understood. The eventhood of the event is the radical *singularity* of happening, the "it happens" as distinct from the sense of "what is happening". It leaves us without criteria and requires *indeterminate judgement*' (xxxi, original emphasis). That Lyotard's description of the event is given in the context of a meditation which includes consideration of the Holocaust also suggests that Duras's concern for historical trauma is part of a general cultural move-

The disaster at Hiroshima provides a powerful example of the phenomenon which comes to fascinate Duras from 1958, and which will represent the focus of her work from *Moderato cantabile* to *L'Amante anglaise*: the event, or irruptive moment. The skill with which, by 1955, Duras can address the dramatic incursions of ethical extremity into the everyday in a range of textual features, from syntax to overall textual structure, allows her now to capitalize on the achievements of her earlier work, by singling out one aspect of these incursions for detailed attention. This aspect, explored repeatedly in the period of her work inaugurated by *Moderato cantabile*, is the significance for narrative and judgement of the temporality of the event. The excessive moment which is already of striking importance in Duras's early work (as the drownings of both *Les Impudents* and *La Vie tranquille*, for example, the death of the *démineur* of *Les Petits Chevaux de Tarquinia*, or the existential epiphany of *Le Square*) now has the formal and ethical consequences of its temporality—which I shall outline shortly—investigated in detail.

For Duras, the event is primarily criminal and/or erotic; as in her early work, it is the dramatic arrival in the everyday of the overwhelming beyond, which she had initially called 'le pire'. Demonstrating the fascinating extremity which characterizes the Durassian ethical, it is the *crimes passionnels* and erotic encounters of *Moderato cantabile* and *Dix heures et demie du soir en été*; the *ravissement* of Lol V. Stein; the explosion of inexplicable violence in *Le Vice-Consul* and *L'Amante anglaise*. In each case—and it is this new unity of concern that marks this period of Duras's work—the event in question imposes a work of reconstruction, ranging from the compulsive symbolic re-enactment of the event (in *Moderato cantabile*) to its judicial/forensic reconstruction (in *L'Amante anglaise*). In the aftermath of the exorbitant moment, the reconstructions and repetitions to which it gives rise are entwined with the everyday existence and intimate passions of those caught up in its tremors. Involvement in the reconstruction of the event is not an option for these characters: they are already—and vitally—entangled in its windings. At stake in the reconstruction of the event as Duras presents it are at

ment towards interest in these areas; this point will be discussed in Chapter 4, below. The connection between Duras and Lyotard is also made by Bernard Alazet, in his 'La Tentation du sublime', in Vircondelet (ed.), *Duras, Dieu et l'écrit*, 85–101. The connection between the event and a problematic of judgement is also evident in much of Duras's journalism of this period, demonstrating well the imbrication of her writerly and ethical concerns; sadly, I do not have room to consider this here.

least questions of identity and desire, most often life and death. Accordingly, characters struggle with each other and with themselves to produce and to live out stories which, for all their inevitable inadequacy, imply their most vital passions. Anne and Chauvin come to repeat symbolically the story of the event *via* a reconstruction that is both collaborative and a tense ballet of passion and shifting power; the agencies of colonial Calcutta, from society gossip to ambassadorial files, scrabble to gain some purchase on the incomprehensible action of the Vice-Consul; Lol's story oscillates maddeningly between voice and silence in the interstices of Jacques Hold's telling.

Duras herself positions 1958 as the date of a decisive break in her writing, locating the gap between *Le Square* and *Moderato cantabile* as the site of an excessive, passionate encounter, after which nothing was the same:

> Une expérience érotique très, très, très violente et—comment dire ça?—j'ai traversé une crise qui était . . . suicidaire, c'est-à-dire . . . que ce que je raconte dans *Moderato cantabile*, cette femme qui veut être tuée, je l'ai vécu . . . et à partir de là les livres ont changé . . .
>
> (*P*, 58–9)

We saw above how Duras's writing career began in crisis, with suicide threats and high anxiety; in her own account of this career, it is with *Moderato cantabile* that writing itself is first touched by this crisis: 'C'est à partir de là que j'ai hésité à faire des livres. A partir de là que mon écriture est devenue dangereuse. Qu'elle a quitté le stade de travail pour arriver à un état de crise.'[3] In terms of the biographical story as she tells it, then, Duras's writing proper comes into being *after the event*, and begins with *Moderato cantabile*. Subsequently, moreover, it appears to have become possible to detail the nature of this event, to tie the 'expérience érotique' down: namely, to Duras's liaison with Gérard Jarlot (the 'G. J.' to whom *Moderato* is dedicated), seemingly drunken, violent, revelatory, a liberation which allows her to become herself, to write in her own voice at last.[4]

---

[3] Jack Gousseland, 'Le Feu d'artifice de Marguerite Duras', *Le Point*, 14 février 1977, 83–5 (84).

[4] Duras also tells the tale of this passionate encounter at the root of *Moderato cantabile* to Hubert Nyssen (see Nyssen, *Les Voies de l'écriture*, 129–30), to Bettina L. Knapp (see interview with Duras by Knapp in *The French Review*, 44/4 (March 1971), 653–9), and, most comprehensively, in the piece 'Le Dernier Client de la nuit', in *La Vie matérielle* (*VM*, 17–19). For its detailed exposition, see also Adler, *Marguerite Duras*, 318–21. Interviewed in 1963, however, Duras denied that *Moderato cantabile* possessed an autobiographical dimension: see 'L'Auteur d' "Hiroshima mon amour" vous parle', esp. 92.

Such an account offers a biographical explanation which simultaneously undoes itself, however, since it takes the form of a reconstruction inevitably powerless to grasp the passion in which it would ground itself. Duras remains, as ever, on the edge of her texts, this biographical link unravelling even as it is established, a connection that is also a separation, in the familiar structure of Durassian articulation. Reconstructing the originary moment of this chapter (already a gap, between 1955 and 1958), we find a passionate encounter which, as such, is not available for adequate reconstruction—and whose unavailability is rehearsed repeatedly throughout the next ten years of Duras's work.

The ethical significance of the event is directly related to this unavailability: straining the limits of comprehension, the event poses a substantial challenge to notions of judgement and responsibility. It is in the nature of the Durassian event that it has always already taken place, or is always still to come. It can be understood only retrospectively—and this calls into question the understanding that might be thought to take place after the event, as the reconstruction imposed is dramatically incommensurate with the trauma it would reconstruct. This view of the event is a constant throughout Duras's career; she expresses it for example in an interview from 1984: 'Tandis qu'on est à vivre un événement, on l'ignore. C'est par la mémoire, ensuite, qu'on *croit* savoir ce qu'il y a eu.'[5]

The consequences of this temporality for judgement are clear: an event so overwhelming as to suspend understanding as it takes place will provoke an evaluative response (of compassion, condemnation, resignation, celebration, and so on) whose purchase it simultaneously avoids. Duras's texts of this period repeatedly present the inevitable attempt to grasp the event in retrospective reconstruction—as well as the inevitable failure of this attempt. The event thus allows Duras to further her fascination with ethical extremity, as its temporality places it right on the edge of the ethical, where judgement and understanding are punctured, but—and this is crucial— still not suspended. Both the need and the attempt to judge after the event remain in this period of Duras's writing, painfully juxtaposed with their failures, as the ethical is carried just beyond its elastic limit, stretched but still (somehow) in place.

[5] Hervé Le Masson, 'L'Inconnue de la rue Catinat', *Le Nouvel Observateur*, 28 septembre– 4 octobre 1984, 92–4 (92), original emphasis.

If judgement remains open after the event, it is open not as a happy tolerance, but rather as a tear. Judgement gapes *and must speak*, and this is its pain. Duras couples reconstruction to the event as an inevitability; she also indicates the awkward insistence of the question of narrative responsibility in this coupling. The traumatic event is both fascinating and compelling, but it is also devastating, and subject to its devastation are, *inter alia*, the stories to which it gives rise. Which, inevitably, questions the status of the texts in which this logic is elaborated. The structures of reconstruction and repetition in question are extensively performed in the narratives of these texts; as the texts are read, the dramas of reconstruction are played out in the time of the reader's experience. The developing confidence which in *Les Petits Chevaux de Tarquinia* and *Le Square* had allowed Duras to explore the encounter with extremity at the level of textual architecture, now facilitates the continuation of this exploration at the new, dynamic level of the time of the reader's experience. To remain with this experience as an adequate recuperation of the dilemmas of reconstruction would, however, produce by formal *fiat* a stable frame undisturbed by their shock—and would thus annihilate what it thought to recuperate. As seen in Chapter 1, above, Duras's early writing argues that the irruption may not be recuperated, and this includes recuperation by formal enactment, which is both suggested and frustrated by the patterns of writing generated by the encounter with ethical extremity. Tracing the elaboration of the temporality of the event and its narratives of reconstruction through the texts of this later period, we will see that the presence of such narratives in these texts takes the form less of enactment than of an uncertainty, a painful performance that cannot quite realize itself. And which thus—inevitable but inadequate—performs the dilemma of judgement after the event—and so becomes an enactment—and so paradoxical: the familiar Durassian spiral here twists through the narratives of the event, and offers in relation to the ethics of judgement her signature drama of impossible enactment, the uncertain accompaniment of ethical extremity, extended during this period to include the time of the reader's experience.

Throughout these texts, then, the reader is kept on the edge of the ethical precisely inasmuch as the reading experience refuses quite to enact this structure. In order to map Duras's elaboration of this impossible enactment in relation to the temporality of the event, I will begin by elaborating the logic of reconstruction as it is presented in the texts of this period. I will then discuss the relation between reconstruction and repetition, and consider some of the implications of Duras's understanding of this latter; finally, having addressed the inevitably conflictual nature of reconstruction, I will explore the consequences of these questions for an ethics of judgement, and discuss their uncertain enactment in the writing and reading of the texts.

Reconstructing the Event

In Duras's writing, the event never takes place. Throughout her earlier texts, its exorbitance is most often evident in its already having happened: *La Vie tranquille* opens just after the fatal fight between Jérôme and Nicolas, for example, the *démineur* of *Les Petits Chevaux de Tarquinia* has already been blown up, the existential epiphany of *Le Square* has been and gone. This anteriority continues to characterize the event in this subsequent period of sustained elaboration, as in *Dix heures et demie du soir en été*, *Le Ravissement de Lol V. Stein*, *Le Vice-Consul* and *L'Amante anglaise*, in which the crucial event has already taken place before the narrative begins. Two departures from this pattern are developed during this period, however: the event may take place off-stage, on the margins of the narrative, as in *Moderato cantabile*; or it may never quite take place, suspending the narrative in the frustrations of an apparently interminable period of waiting, as in *L'Après-midi de M. Andesmas*.[6] With the exception of this last text, concerned with the event's sleepy deferral, the absence of the event from the narratives it dominates imposes the burden of reconstruction, generally in at least one of two forms: as the reconstruction of the event as origin of its consequences; or as the reconstruction of the origins of the event. In both cases, the drive imposed in the wake of the event is that of an epistemophilia whose passion simultaneously complicates and motivates the urge to comprehensive

---

[6] As it deals with repetition in terms of deferral rather than reconstruction—and as the range of texts covered in this chapter is already substantial—I will unfortunately be unable here to consider *L'Après-midi de M. Andesmas*. As a screenplay, *Hiroshima mon amour* will serve primarily as illustrative contextualizing material; I will not be discussing it in detail. An outstanding discussion of *Hiroshima mon amour* in terms of these questions of repetition and re-enactment may be found in Emma Wilson, '"Mon histoire de Lol V. Stein": Duras, Reading, and Amnesia'.

detection. Intricately caught in the implications of the event, there yet remains the drive to know, to understand.

The combination of these types of reconstruction is perhaps most clear, and most necessarily convinced (at least pragmatically) of its adequacy in the judicial reconstruction of a crime and its motives; such reconstruction is explored in this period of Duras's writing primarily in *L'Amante anglaise*. This 1967 text is itself a re-working of *Les Viaducs de la Seine-et-Oise*, a play from 1960 based on a 'fait divers' about a small-town murder whose motives had never been established—despite the apparent willingness of the criminal to assist in shedding light on her act. The origin of Duras's fascination with this story is, then, an absence, a motivational blank which simply refuses to be filled, as she suggests in an interview in 1963: 'Ce qui a retenu mon attention, c'est la bonne volonté de la femme: elle voulait sincèrement aider la justice, mais elle n'a pu expliquer son geste.'[7] This fascination is then announced in the 'Texte d'informations', read to the public before performances of *Les Viaducs de la Seine-et-Oise*: 'Les efforts conjugués de la justice et de ses auteurs ne vinrent pas à bout des raisons de ce crime. Il resta donc inexpliqué' (*VSO*, 10).[8]

The reconstructions which follow this originary lacuna attempt to fill it with retrospective significance; their tribulations are traced through *L'Amante anglaise* in a series of interviews by an unnamed interrogator with, respectively, a bar-owner (Robert Lamy), the husband of the murderer (Pierre Lannes), and the murderer herself (Claire Lannes). Eventually, the originary absence will remain, as Claire Lannes both refuses to reveal the location of the final piece of evidence (her victim's head), and is herself ultimately unable to illuminate her motives, for all that possible connections are made (her unhappy romantic history, her unconventional intelligence, her discomfort with the role of homemaker . . .). The origin is lost, but edged about with attempted explanation.

The first move in this attempt to explain the criminal event consists in the establishment of guilt. Thus, in the opening part of *L'Amante anglaise*, an indented section of text presents a tape-recording of the crucial scene in the police reconstruction of the

[7] Hahn, 'Les Hommes de 1963', 32.

[8] Duras cites a similar, fascinating silence on the part of Rodrigo Paestra, the murderer of *Dix heures et demie du soir en été*: 'Il sera mort d'amour, dans le refus ou l'impossibilité de toute explication, dans le mépris de toute explication' (Marguerite Duras, 'Melina la superbe', *Arts-Loisirs*, 1–7 février 1967, 20–3 (23)).

event itself (the murder of an initially unidentified woman), as two undercover officers piece together the narrative of the crime, eventually provoking Claire Lannes into what amounts to a confession: 'Ce n'est pas dans la forêt qu'elle a été tuée, Marie-Thérèse Bousquet, c'est dans une cave à quatre heures du matin' (*AA*, 47). The forensic approach to the unavailability of the event to knowledge is to establish information retrospectively, to work backwards from the disparate evidence to the positing of a unitary event (preferably supported by a confession). This method is figured in *L'Amante anglaise* by the reconstruction of the victim's body, which has been cut into pieces and thrown into a succession of goods trains. The tracing of the routes of these trains ('le recoupement ferroviaire') reveals that they all passed under one bridge, which thus identifies Liorne as the scene of the crime. The forensic move from disparity to unification is thus figured both physically and geographically, while being reproduced in reverse in the grisly irony of the role of the key term 'recoupement' in the case of a dismembered body.

The next move in this narrative of detection is from the search for the event-as-origin to the search for the origins of the event, in the form of motives. The bulk of *L'Amante anglaise* thus consists of the staging of various attempts to find the story of the criminal event, by reconstructing the past of the murderer, Claire Lannes. These reconstructions take the classic form of interviews, although here the interviews are carried out not by police officers, but by an unnamed character, supposedly engaged in producing a book on the crime. The text also includes a debate on the rights and wrongs of such explanatory reconstructions, primarily between the main police officer and the bar-owner, Robert Lamy. Lamy, partly motivated by fear for his friends the Lannes, whose implication in the events is fast becoming apparent, attempts to stop the developing narrative by rejecting all attempts at explanation:

Moi, j'estime, pas d'explication, précisément. Ne pas commencer avec l'explication, sans ça où va-t-on? Ne pas l'aborder du tout. Se contenter de la preuve. Un point c'est tout.

(*AA*, 33–4)

Unsurprisingly, the police reject Lamy's position, in the name of the public interest:

Comprendre, monsieur Lamy c'est un bonheur, un si grand et réel bonheur et

auquel on aspire si naturellement qu'il est un devoir de n'en priver personne, ni le
public, ni même les juges, ni même parfois les criminels.

(34)

This position represents, in Durassian terms, a domestication of the
inevitable drive to the reconstruction of the event: Robert Lamy is
perhaps wrong to imagine that the production of narratives can be
avoided after the event, but the police officer's pompous civic
rhetoric indicates an ironization of his comfortable justification of
this production in terms of a 'natural' aspiration towards understanding. For understanding is precisely what is obstructed by the
event: it remains unrealized, precisely as an aspiration, an unavoidable compulsion to produce compensatory stories. The attempt to
calm this compulsion with the name of 'nature' can only lead to the
effacement of the terror that echoes from the naked event—a terror
which, for Duras, is only exacerbated by the inability of reconstruction to do anything other than sketch the tattered edges of the event
which has punctured understanding.

As the trauma of the event wrecks its recuperation within the field of
knowledge, the forensic search for the origins of the event involves
less the establishment of a stable, truthful story than the production
of partial, particular narratives which are as inadequate as they are
inevitable. And this position applies just as much to official narratives as it does to private ones. Thus the Ambassador in *Le Vice-
Consul*, seeking explanations of the extraordinary violence of the
Vice-Consul, searches his childhood for clues; challenged (in a
letter) by the Vice-Consul's aunt to content himself with what he
can know of the event itself ('Pourquoi remonter à l'enfance pour
expliquer sa conduite à Lahore? Ne faudrait-il pas chercher aussi à
Lahore?'), he declares, with weary irony, 'Je préfère qu'on en reste
aux conjectures habituelles' (*VC*, 42). Despite the clear criticism of
'official' reconstructions in such passages, however, the 'truth' of the
logic of reconstruction does not necessarily lie with those who
oppose them: neither the Vice-Consul's aunt nor Robert Lamy can
be taken at face value. Both appeals to refuse the production of
explanatory narratives feature more than a suggestion of special
pleading (Lamy for his friends, the aunt for her nephew), and both
miss the most disconcerting feature of the phenomenon of reconstruction: despite its inadequacy, it will happen anyway. While
Duras emphasizes the unavailability of the event to retrospective

understanding, then, she does not conclude from this that reconstruction may simply be abandoned: rather, she also emphasizes the compulsive, inevitable character of such reconstruction. There is no separating the irruptive moment from the desperate retrospective stories it produces. To stress this, Duras shows the drive to reconstruct narratives for the event to be shared not only by those with official functions to fulfil and those immediately concerned by the event, but by chance witnesses, with no a priori involvement in the narratives they find themselves producing. Thus, the French actress is, initially, desperate to comprehend the enormity of Hiroshima; and Anne Desbaresdes and Chauvin, in *Moderato cantabile*, reconstruct between them the story which led up to the *crime passionnel* by which they are fascinated. Although motivation is unknowable, precisely because of the trauma of the event ('Lui le savait. Il est maintenant devenu fou, enfermé depuis hier soir. Elle, est morte'), the desire to produce its narrative remains, driven by the force of the unknown to search the very origin: 'Je voudrais que vous me disiez le commencement même, comment ils ont commencé à se parler. C'est dans un café, disiez-vous . . .' (*MC*, 36/58).

The partial, conjectural status of the reconstructions produced in response to the event—and even an awareness on the part of those involved in their production of this status—in no way lessens the strength of the drive to produce such reconstructions. Anne and Chauvin stress continually their ignorance, undermining the epistemological status of their reconstruction without mitigating its urgency:

Vous savez, je sais très peu de choses. Mais je crois qu'il ne pouvait pas arriver à avoir une préférence, il ne devait pas en sortir, de la vouloir autant vivante que morte. Il a dû réussir très tard seulement à se la préférer morte. Je ne sais rien.

(*MC*, 116)

'Il n'y a pas d'explication, je crois, à ce genre de découverte-là' (57): such knowledge of the unavailability of what is reconstructed motivates rather than cancels its reconstruction. As Maria puts it, in *Dix heures et demie du soir en été*, 'Ce sont ces parties perdues là [*sic*] qui vous portent à épiloguer sans fin' (*DH*, 131). And the compulsion to reconstruct the event is sufficiently powerful to produce both attempts at self-justification—'Ce cri était si fort que vraiment il est bien naturel que l'on cherche à savoir'—and a surrender to the inevitability of the reconstruction: 'J'aurais pu difficilement éviter de le faire, voyez-vous' (*MC*, 35).

Such, then, are the primary features of the phenomenon of reconstruction as it is elaborated in Duras's work of this period: at issue in any reconstruction are either the event or the origins of the event; particular reconstructions will be inadequate, partial, and hypothetical; but the compulsion to reconstruct will be unaffected by awareness of this. Indeed, as a compulsion, reconstruction imposes itself as inevitable. And the mode of reconstruction in which its inevitability is perhaps at its most evident is that mode which might perhaps be most readily associated with compulsion: repetition.

Repetition (i): Past

It would be tempting to appeal to psychoanalytic categories at this point: by claiming, for example, that characters such as Anne Desbaresdes and Chauvin are subject to the compulsion to repeat. A psychoanalytic definition of this compulsion makes its differences from Durassian repetition apparent, however:

> Le sujet se place activement dans des situations pénibles, répétant ainsi des expériences anciennes sans se souvenir du prototype et avec au contraire l'impression très vive qu'il s'agit de quelque chose qui est pleinement motivé dans l'actuel.[9]

There is a strong sense that Anne and Chauvin, for example, are devastatingly aware that they are repeating a previous experience; moreover, it is not their experience that is being repeated, but that of the couple whose *crime passionnel* constitutes the event which is being reconstructed. For Duras, however, the event cannot properly be identified as anybody's experience: those who undergo it can no more 'own' it as 'their' experience than bystanders such as Anne and Chauvin. (The woman is killed, the man driven mad: there is no one left to whom the experience of the event might belong). It is possible, then, that the event will be repeated not by its original subjects, but by others, whose repetition will take the form of an enactment of the narrative of the pre-history of the event, as in *Moderato cantabile*.

---

[9] Jean Laplanche and Jean-Baptiste Pontalis, *Vocabulaire de la psychanalyse* (Paris: PUF, 1967), 86.

In order to reconstruct the event (the man's murder of the woman), Anne and Chauvin *become* the couple, repeating the narrative of their encounter as they construct it. This process begins with Anne's initial moment of empathy with the woman, as she begins the *via dolorosa* of repetition, of reconstruction as passion:

—Je n'ai rien dit, répéta l'homme. Mais je crois qu'il l'a visée au cœur comme elle le lui demandait.
Anne Desbaresdes gémit. Une plainte presque licencieuse, douce, sortit de cette femme.

$(MC, 44)$[10]

In her anonymity ('cette femme'), Anne is aligned with the murdered woman, this alignment intensified by her erotic empathy. Later, she explicitly identifies herself with the woman, the reference to childbirth emphasizing this identification as gendered:

Une fois, il me semble bien, oui, une fois j'ai dû crier un peu de cette façon, peut-être, oui, quand j'ai eu cet enfant.

(54)

Chauvin then strengthens this link, by recalling it as he (re)constructs the beginnings of the couple's story (the ambiguity as to which couple is here in question demonstrating the collapse of reconstruction into repetition):

Ils s'étaient connus par hasard dans un café, peut-être même dans ce café-ci qu'ils fréquentaient tous les deux. Et ils ont commencé à se parler de choses et d'autres. Mais je ne sais rien. Ça vous a fait très mal, cet enfant?

(54)

The explicit interweaving of the narrative of the origins of the event and the interaction between Anne and Chauvin thus produces their reconstruction as an enactment of the narrative in question, again largely on the basis of an identification between Anne and the woman of their story:

Il lui tend un verre de vin tout en riant.
—Cette femme était devenue une ivrogne. On la trouvait le soir dans les bars de l'autre côté de l'arsenal, ivre morte. On la blâmait beaucoup.

(75)

---

[10] The textual details of this intertwining are presented in tabular form in Najet Limam-Tnani, *Roman et cinéma chez Marguerite Duras: Une Poétique de la spécularité*, 36.

Within this enactment, however, the truth-value of the story constructed—and so the enactment itself—is always suspect. The repetition is highly self-conscious, and appears at times to lapse into role-play ('Anne Desbaresdes feignit un étonnement exagéré' (75)); the characters' passionate investment in their reconstruction plainly complicates any notion of epistemological validity; moreover, details of the story are openly contested between the two. Anne challenges Chauvin ('Ce que vous m'avez dit sur cette femme est faux, qu'on la trouvait ivre-morte dans les bars du quartier de l'arsenal' (78)), and Chauvin returns the compliment, casting doubt (with an innuendo) on the very identification which initiated their reconstruction-repetition of the event: 'Jamais vous n'avez crié. Jamais' (83). What is at issue, then, is not a faithful reconstruction of a known story (impossible, given the status of the event), but rather an on-going repetition, driven not by an attention to literal detail, but by the fascinated, passionate inevitability of reconstruction. The truth-value of the enactment lies not in its fidelity (which cannot be ascertained), but in its qualitative repetition of the transgressive force of the event. Anne and Chauvin thus move to an increasingly explicit acting-out of the story they reconstruct, its violent implications drawing ever nearer:

—Puis le temps est venu où il crut qu'il ne pourrait plus la toucher autrement que pour . . . Anne Desbaresdes releva ses mains vers son cou nu dans l'encolure de sa robe d'été.
—Que là, n'est-ce pas?
—Là, oui.

(121)

By the time of the final scene of the story, after Anne's social disgrace (the symbolic 'death' produced by her scandalous liaison), she has completed her occupation of the position of the woman in the couple, and is discussed in the third person, as the 'elle' of their reconstruction:

—Elle ne parlera plus jamais, dit-elle.
—Mais si. Un jour, un beau matin, tout à coup, elle rencontrera quelqu'un qu'elle reconnaîtra, elle ne pourra pas faire autrement que de dire bonjour. Ou bien elle entendra chanter un enfant, il fera beau, elle dira il fait beau. Ça recommencera.
—Non.

(151)

Chauvin here attempts to provide an extension to the reconstructed narrative, to resurrect the dead woman, to recuperate his loss;

Anne, as the (symbolically) dead woman, refuses this offered resurrection, and embraces her death, producing as the climax of their enactment a *Liebestod* confirmed by their first kiss:

Elle s'avança vers lui d'assez près pour que leurs lèvres puissent s'atteindre. Leurs lèvres restèrent l'une sur l'autre, posées, afin que ce fût fait et suivant le même rite mortuaire que leurs mains, un instant avant, froides et tremblantes. Ce fut fait.

(152–3)

This deathly kiss completes Anne's social disgrace, and so perfects the repetition:

—Je voudrais que vous soyez morte, dit Chauvin.
—C'est fait, dit Anne Desbaresdes.

(155)

The original event is finally attained, at the end of the narrative of its repetition. It is, therefore, firmly non-originary, radically unavailable before the reconstructions which attempt to address its consequences, and taking place in its repetition. Anne's 'C'est fait' refers as much to the original event as to its repetition; having been repeated, reconstructed, the event may now be said to have taken place—although this logic, condemning the event to an uncertain happening in repetition, means that this 'happening' remains inevitably divided from itself. The Durassian event has thus both always already and never quite taken place, hovering at the edges of occurrence.

Reconstruction of the event may thus impose itself as repetition, in the mode of the enactment of the event. When such reconstruction is undertaken by those most intimately affected by the original event, however, this re-enactment provides an example of repetition that dramatically confirms the radical unavailability of the event, which remains beyond even those to whom it has (almost) occurred. This is the case, famously, with Lol V. Stein.

Le Ravissement de Lol V. Stein has generally been read at the intersection of the various discourses it puts into play: narrative structure, gender, psychoanalysis, and so on. Picking up on this interpretative context, I will here try to show how it is itself shaped by Duras's overriding concern at this time for the temporality of reconstruction. No interpretative discourse that seeks to make sense of this text in terms of its own categories is likely to make more than limited headway, however; one reason for its status as a favoured object of interpretation must doubtless be the seductive double gesture of invitation and escape offered by the text to such discourse. Taking 'reconstruction' as a master-trope to organize a reading of *Le Ravissement de Lol V. Stein*, then, I will be attempting to demonstrate how this move is invited by the text, only simultaneously to be frustrated; I will, accordingly, ultimately be addressing the question of whether this frustration itself (the reader welcomed inasmuch as s/he is also excluded) may be read as meaningful.

First, though (as in any good reconstruction), the facts as we know them. Lol's reconstruction of her 'ravissement' entails two types of repetition: both the return to the scene of the traumatic event, the ballroom at T. Beach where she was abandoned by her fiancé for Anne-Marie Stretter; and the attempt to fix the moment of the event—and, more particularly, her absent, vacant role in the event—by repeating it and its fantasized consequences in the triangular orchestration of voyeuristic scenarios. Lol's project, after the original traumatic moment, is explicitly given as one of reconstruction: 'Lol progresse chaque jour dans la reconstitution de cet instant' (*RLVS*, 46).[11] Jacques Hold (more or less the book's narrator—and the consequences of this 'more or less' will be considered below) and Tatiana Karl, a school friend of Lol's, hypothesize that Lol's concern, during these repetitions, is to order in her memory the chaos produced by the traumatic event. In this account, Lol is attempting to reconstruct the lost, fateful moment:

Dans les multiples aspects du bal de T. Beach, c'est la fin qui retient Lol. C'est l'instant précis de sa fin, quand l'aurore arrive avec une brutalité inouïe et la sépare du couple que formaient Michael Richardson et Anne-Marie Stretter, pour toujours, toujours.

(46)

---

[11] The definition of 'ravissement' provided by Roland Barthes makes clear its imposition of the logic of reconstruction: 'La scène initiale au cours de laquelle j'ai été ravi, je ne fais que la reconstituer: c'est un *après-coup* . . . toute la scène reconstruite opère comme le montage somptueux d'une ignorance' (Barthes, *Fragments d'un discours amoureux* (Paris: Seuil, coll. 'Tel Quel', 1977), 228–9). (These phrases are also cited in Michael Sheringham, 'Knowledge and Repetition in *Le Ravissement de Lol V. Stein*', *Romance Studies*, 2 (Summer 1983), 124–40). The absence of Duras from the references provided by Barthes in his account of 'ravissement' is striking, given both the similarity of his account to that found in Duras's novel (thirteen years old by the time of the *Fragments*, and hardly obscure) and the intertextual routes connecting the two (Lacan, for example, whose piece on Lol will be discussed below, is cited throughout by Barthes). Later evidence of friction between Duras and Barthes (see, for example, *Yann Andréa Steiner*, 21, as quoted in Chapter 1, above) renders her absence, while eloquent, perhaps not all that surprising.

Moreover, this reconstruction has imposed itself because of the pure, empty temporality of the moment, its traumatic unavailability to comprehension: 'Il ne reste de cette minute que son temps pur, d'une blancheur d'os' (47). Lol is thus suffering from the eventhood of the event, from its radical unavailability and its consequent imposition of the temporality of reconstruction: 'J'ai le temps, que c'est long' (29).

Lol's mode of reconstruction is, then, repetition: she attempts to repeat a triangular structure from which she would no longer have been expelled before its *dénouement*: 'Une place est à prendre, qu'elle n'a pas réussi à avoir à T. Beach, il y a dix ans' (60). This position (brought out especially in Lacan's reading of the text, which will be discussed shortly) is the third term in a triangular structure, that of a voyeur before the scene of the unveiling of the other woman—a scene apparently fantasized by Lol as the consequence of the traumatic event. (See *RLVS*, 49). Lol's driving desire is to see this scene (her response to Jacques Hold's 'Que désiriez-vous?' is 'Les voir' (105)); its status as fantasy is apparent for example in the tense of its narration:

Il l'aurait dévêtue de sa robe noire avec lenteur et le temps qu'il l'eût fait une grande étape du voyage aurait été franchie.

(49)

Lol's repetition of this triangular, voyeuristic structure positions Tatiana Karl as Anne-Marie Stretter and Jacques Hold as Michael Richardson in the scene of the consummation of her expulsion from the couple. Her desire is not simply to repeat the event, but rather to repeat the fantasized consequences of the event, to insert herself into a triangle from which she was prematurely expelled. The culmination of this repetition is thus Lol's abolition, her timely, rather than untimely, expulsion: 'Cet instant d'oubli absolu de Lol, cet instant, cet éclair dilué, dans le temps uniforme de son guet, sans qu'elle ait le moindre espoir de le percevoir, Lol désirait qu'il fût vécu. Il le fut' (123). Lol's desire is, then, a matter of time, the repetition of a moment within a narrative according to a certain tempo. Again, the originary moment takes place only in its repetition: the moment Lol is repeating is not the event, but rather an instant in her fantasy narrative of its consequences, the disrobing of Anne-Marie Stretter by Michael Richardson. To this extent, Lacan is right in his haughty dismissal: 'On pensera à suivre quelque cliché, qu'elle répète l'événement. Mais qu'on y regarde de plus près.'[12] Lacan claims that Lol is not repeating an event but re-forming a knot: it is a question not of an experience but of a structure, dictating positions. Lol *is* repeating the event, however, inasmuch as the Durassian event is brought into meaningful existence only in its repetition. The repetition creates the event it repeats: Lacan is right inasmuch as there is no actual, knowable moment that can be adequately repeated as part of a process of 'working-through', wrong inasmuch as it is precisely this absence that defines the Durassian event. Inevitably drawn into the distorting glare of reconstruction, the event begins to crumble, to crack: split within itself (as the moment of betrayal *and* the fantasized encounter which follows) *and* generated by its repetition, it withers into a worrying uncertainty. Snagged in and as paradox, the Durassian event is, awkwardly, just what it is for Lol, which is to say—nothing; and everything, a defining trauma.[13]

Lacan's rejection of the possibility of the repetition of an event is no doubt motivated by the desire to exclude a simplistic notion of repetition as therapeutically beneficial, a notion he attributes to a type of therapy dismissed as 'goujaterie' (Lacan, 'Hommage . . .', 94). And indeed, Lol's repetition can in no way be counted as a process of healing: rather than an assimilation of the past by working-through, it both invites and mocks interpretations based on such wholesome clichés, representing instead the annihilation of the past by its doubling:

Cet endroit du monde où on croit qu'elle a vécu sa douleur passée, cette prétendue douleur, s'efface peu à peu de sa mémoire dans sa matérialité . . . En quelque point

---

[12] Jacques Lacan, 'Hommage fait à Marguerite Duras, du ravissement de Lol V. Stein', in François Barat and Joël Farges (eds.), *Marguerite Duras* (Paris: Albatros, coll. 'ça/cinéma', 1975), 93–9 (94). Emma Wilson argues that Lol seduces Jacques Hold (which may or may not be the case, as will be seen) in order to adopt the position of Anne-Marie Stretter (with, respectively, Jacques Hold as Michael Richardson and Tatiana Karl as Lol). (See Wilson, 176.) While this is one possible identification suggested by the text, I would suggest that it functions primarily to blur the edges of the triangular repetition of the consequences of the lost, originary event (in which Lol repeats her own position, with Hold as Richardson and Tatiana as Anne-Marie Stretter, with Lol as excluded third term), which provides the principal object of Lol's attempts at reconstruction. The text, in fact, both sets up this principal, triangular object and overlays it with opaque layers of possible binary imaginary identifications, in order to stage and wreck the business of reconstruction. On this, see also Hill, *Marguerite Duras: Apocalyptic Desires*, 77.

[13] See on this point Sheringham: 'Duras places at the heart of the text an experience—Lol's "ravissement"—which, like desire itself, can be endlessly repeated but never known, because it never did and never can belong to the order of knowledge' (Sheringham, 'Knowledge and Repetition', 137).

qu'elle s'y trouve Lol y est comme une première fois. De la distance invariable du souvenir elle ne dispose plus: elle est là.

(*RLVS*, 42–3)

Amateurs of the gossip of armchair psychology might read Lol's progress from ontological fragmentation, as recalled by Tatiana Karl and figured typographically—'il manquait déjà quelque chose à Lol pour être—elle dit: là' (12)—to existential presence, free from typographical interruption ('elle est là') as a narrative of healing. This passage, however, both ironizes this position ('on croit') and demonstrates that Durassian trauma can never be owned, never assimilated: hardly having taken place (*'on croit qu'elle a vécu* sa douleur passée'), it can only be doubled and repeated. So, when Lol re-enters the scene of the trauma, by returning to the ballroom at T. Beach, she does not re-live her memories: rather, she buries them:

Le bal sera au bout du voyage, il tombera comme château de cartes comme en ce moment le voyage lui-même. Elle revoit sa mémoire-ci [*sic*] pour la dernière fois de sa vie, elle l'enterre.

(175)

Moreover, the traumatic past is being annihilated by its present repetition, which takes (its) place in its wreckage:

Dans l'avenir ce sera de cette vision aujourd'hui, de cette compagnie-ci à ses côtés qu'elle se souviendra. Il en sera comme pour S. Tahla maintenant, ruinée sous ses pas du présent.

(175)

And when Lol finally enters the ballroom, the very site of her trauma, and, lifting a curtain, might be thought to be lifting the veil on her repressed memories, she finds—nothing:

Lol passe la tête à chaque issue et rit, comme enchantée par ce jeu de revoir . . . Elle rit parce qu'elle cherche quelque chose qu'elle croyait trouver ici, qu'elle devrait donc trouver, et qu'elle ne trouve pas. Elle vient, revient, soulève un rideau, passe le nez, dit que ce n'est pas ça, qu'il n'y a pas à dire, ce n'est pas ça.

(179)

Lol's repetitions are thus in no way therapeutic. Neither, however, are they simply pathological: paradoxically, since they are imposed as inevitable by the temporality of the traumatic event, they cannot be so easily determined. Reading *Le Ravissement de Lol V. Stein*

78 THE TEMPORALITY OF THE EVENT

alongside Duras's other texts of the period, we would have to resist the pathologization of Lol, since her particular crisis—the temporality of the event—is shared by so many of her Durassian contemporaries. We should also, however, resist the temptation simply to avoid the judgement of Lol as pathological, since her difference from other Durassian figures does undoubtedly lie in her greater proximity to detailed descriptions of neurosis. A psychoanalytic reading of the text is thus, of course, strongly invited (if not positively imposed by Lacan's contribution); and it would be to underestimate the extraordinary achievement that is *Le Ravissement de Lol V. Stein* to minimize its fascinating ability to offer apparently ideal material for a critical model on the look-out for literary confirmation of its psychoanalytic tenets. A reading might be available (at the juncture of psychoanalysis and feminism, say) according to which Lol, as a result of the laborious working-through of her trauma in its repetition, takes increasing control of the narratives which have flowed from this trauma, thus achieving some sort of cure. Even a committed psychoanalytic reading would have to baulk at this suggestion, however, since it so plainly fails to attend to the haunting emptiness and repetition on which, for example, the text ends. The closest one can come to grasping the text in these terms, it would seem, is to acknowledge that it sets up this reading—precisely also to baffle it. And this bewilderment takes place not only within the structure of the diegesis, as just described, but also—and crucially—within a dimension of the text with which a character-orientated psychoanalytic reading will always have problems: the terrible difficulties imposed by the ways in which this tale is told.[14]

---

[14] Carol Hofmann, in her *Forgetting and Marguerite Duras*, provides a good example of a psychoanalytic reading of the text as outlined here which seems progressively to discover its own insufficiencies: having initially presented Lol as gaining increasing conscious control over her stories of repetition, Hofmann eventually exposes this momentum as deceptive, concluding that Lol 'embraces forgetting [a questionably active formulation], which is a constant remembering as well as the dissolution of memory into an endless series of repetitions and displacements' (Hofmann, 113). Radicalizing this realization, Emma Wilson describes Lol as adopting—instead of a supposedly therapeutic 'access to memory' *via* 'restorative narrative'—'a more dangerous strategy of erasure through re-enactment' (Wilson, 175). Wilson's important reading of *Le Ravissement de Lol V. Stein* demonstrates how Duras challenges normative, clinical discourse, by offering the reader 'the illusion that the text will enact the discovery of curative analysis', only for this reader to discover that 'this is in no sense achieved' (Wilson, 176). Wilson thus contests Kristeva's argument in *Soleil noir*, celebrating the very disintegration which Kristeva had seen as dangerous. For Wilson, the text enacts the insufficiencies of a clinical discourse based on normative models of identification, spreading instead the (valorized) contagion of irrecuperable loss. I will argue, however (and it is here

Lol's incessant ambiguity is the direct result of the almost impossible instability of the narrative of *Le Ravissement de Lol V. Stein*. Any access one might have to Lol's repetitions is itself gained via the narrative reconstructions of the text, primarily—or exclusively—those of Jacques Hold. Everything we can say about Lol may be based solely on the house of cards that is Jacques Hold's imagination. The fantasized consequences of the event may be his fantasy of Lol's fantasy. Or he may be telling the truth, lying when he says he is lying: 'Voici, tout au long, mêlés, à la fois, ce faux semblant que raconte Tatiana Karl et ce que j'invente sur la nuit du Casino de T. Beach' (14). If Jacques Hold says he is lying, why should we believe him? This spiral may mean that he is in fact telling the truth, presenting Lol to us as she is. Or the truth may be somewhere between these two poles. Not only do we not know Lol—we do not even know for sure that we do not know her. We are presented here with the dilemmas of reconstruction, which has always already lost its object—and which can never know, therefore, the extent to which it has accurately recuperated this object in its retrospective stories. The text thus suggests the enactment of the reconstruction it describes, as when the identity of Jacques Hold as narrator is belatedly revealed, after seven sections of text in which he has (we retrospectively surmise) been oscillating between 'je' and 'il'; the moment in question thus produces a dizzying coincidence between narration and diegesis, in Hold's remark, 'la distance est couverte, moi' (74). The instability of reconstruction means, however, that the notion of safe textual enactment is severely questioned even as it is suggested. It is, precisely, the question of the certainty and efficacy of enactment after the event that is at stake in this narrative—and so the narrative jolts against moments which, while they may be recuperated as the enactment of the uncertainties of reconstruction, also resonate more simply as moments of utter opacity. We might reconstruct them (as the enactment of reconstruction), and so make them meaningful—but on condition that they immediately lose the meaning (that of the lost object of reconstruction) so gained. Reconstructing/fantasizing Lol's imagining of the aftermath of the ball,

---

that I will disagree with Wilson's interpretation), that any reading of the text based on a model of enactment will be bound to cure this celebrated contagion, by reinstalling the reliance on identification it had sought to dismantle; and that the notion of enactment, therefore, offers a key to these texts only to the precise extent that it is questioned by them.

the narrative is interrupted by a voice which quite simply cannot identified:

Lol retient ce souffle: à mesure que le corps de la femme apparaît à cet homme, le sien s'efface, s'efface, volupté, du monde.
—Toi. Toi seule.
Cet arrachement très ralenti de la robe de Anne-Marie Stretter [*sic*], cet anéantissement de velours de sa propre personne, Lol n'a jamais réussi à le mener à son terme.

(50)

Incompletion may be brought to some kind of conclusion by a framing supplement, as Jacques Hold demonstrates:

—Pourquoi ne rien dire? Pourquoi? Pourquoi y aller?
—Je croyais que
Elle ne termine pas. J'insiste doucement.
—Essayez de me dire. Que . . .
—Vous auriez deviné.

(153)

The echoes of Anne and Chauvin are unmistakable. This method will not always work, however:

—C'est la première fois que vous vous trompez.
—Ça vous plaît?
—Oui. Surtout de cette façon. Vous êtes si près de
Elle raconte ce bonheur d'aimer, matériellement.

(169)

The gulf at the too-rapid end of Lol's words cannot be filled; its jolt cannot be redeemed. Confusion—as confusion—is not available for symbolic recuperation; as will be discussed below, the fascination of *Le Ravissement de Lol V. Stein* is in part the result of the fact that, whatever the stakes, its uncertainties will not be resolved. Its haunting, disembodied voices (anticipating the 'voix brûlées' of *India Song* and *La Femme du Gange*)—'Toi. Toi seule'—, its awkward collapses— 'Vous êtes si près de'—just remain. The uncertainties of Jacques Hold's narration offer a strong suggestion that, for Duras, repetition/enactment is no more a therapeutic option textually than it is psychologically, as the attempt to make these jagged moments meaningful—for example as the textual enactment of the painful reconstruction of the irruptive event—produces only paradoxical meaning, bound to puncture itself on the absence/instability it seeks to repeat, but can only—as enactment—lose.

Repetition (ii): Present

Just as the past event is never available other than in its reconstructions and repetitions, so the present event is divided from itself by its status as repetition. It is, as it were, never present. The primary example of this in Duras's writing of this period is the erotic encounter, as elaborated for example in *Dix heures et demie du soir en été*. In this text, the encounter (between Pierre, the husband of the main character Maria, and Claire, a friend of theirs with whom they are holidaying) is one of two events that combine to form the moment of the title (the other being Maria's sighting of the hunted murderer Rodrigo Paestra). As this structure suggests, however, neither of these events may simply be said to take place: in their simultaneity, they vie for possession of the moment. Moreover (and more significantly), the encounter between Pierre and Claire is presented as the repetition of the origin and subsequent history of the relationship between Maria and Pierre. Claire is thus, in relation to Pierre and Maria, 'ce fruit si beau de la lente dégradation de leur amour' (*DH*, 67); and Maria haunts the beginnings of her husband's affair, another non-originary origin:

S'ils ne se regardent plus comme la veille, s'ils évitent de le faire c'est qu'ils se sont avoué leur amour, tout bas, quand le ciel fut rose au-dessus du blé et que le souvenir de Maria leur est revenu avec cette aurore, poignant, abominable en raison même de la force de leur nouvel amour.

(102)

The event of the encounter between Pierre and Claire is thus divided from itself, split by its function as repetition of the encounter between Pierre and Maria.[15]

The temporality of the affair also conforms to the temporality of the Durassian event: its origin is produced retrospectively by Maria,

---

[15] In 1967, Duras glosses Maria's acceptance of this inevitable repetition: 'Le temps défait tout amour et celui que vit Maria avec Pierre aussi. Maria accepte avec un calme désespoir l'inévitable échec, l'âge, la fin, toutes les fins' (Duras, 'Melina la superbe', 22–3).

in a flashback ('Ils n'ont pas vu Maria. C'est alors qu'elle a découvert leurs mains se tenant l'une l'autre avec décence, le long de leurs corps rapprochés' (19)), and its consummation is continually delayed. Just as the event cannot quite be said to have taken place, precisely because it has already taken place, and is available only in its repetition, so the encounter, as repetition, will never quite take place. The initial erotic encounter between Pierre and Claire, on the balcony of the hotel where they are spending the night sheltering from the storm, is observed by Maria at the very moment that she also spots Rodrigo Paestra; its moment split, the encounter is thus already prevented from fully taking place. Matters are complicated further, however, by the mode of the encounter's narration. Caught within a voyeuristic triangle, the encounter is narrated (from Maria's point of view) as an indeterminate mixture of observation and fantasy:

Ça doit être la première fois qu'ils s'embrassent . . . Tandis qu'il l'embrasse, les mains de Pierre sont sur les seins de Claire. Sans doute se parlent-ils. Mais très bas. Ils doivent se dire les premiers mots de l'amour. Ils leur montent aux lèvres, entre deux baisers, irrépressibles, jaillissants.

(42)

Does the encounter take place? The movement from observation ('Tandis qu'il l'embrasse . . .') to fantasy ('Ils doivent se dire les premiers mots de l'amour'), to fantasy presented as (impossible) observation ('Ils leur montent aux lèvres . . .') so complicates the status of the action 'observed' that little certainty remains. The subsequent progression from this initial (and highly problematic) encounter to its consummation is, moreover, tortuous, and again structured by Maria's hypotheses-cum-fantasies:

Est-ce fait maintenant? Dans un autre couloir noir, étouffant, il n'y a peut-être personne—qui les connaît tous?—celui qui se trouverait dans le prolongement de leur balcon, par exemple, au-dessus exactement de celui-ci, dans ce couloir miraculeusement oublié, le long du mur, par terre, est-ce fait?

(45)

Maria's answer to her own questions, minutes later, is that, of course, the consummation of the encounter has not taken place: 'L'amour ne s'est pas fait ce soir dans cet hôtel' (45). And even if this consummation were to take place, it would represent not simply an encounter, but the repetition of a structure, the redistribution of positions:

Les mains de Pierre sont ballantes le long de ses jambes. Huit ans qu'elles lui caressent le corps. C'est Claire qui entre maintenant dans le malheur qui coule, de source, de ces mains-là.

(47)

Thus, when the encounter will happen, for Maria, 'la conjugaison de leur amour s'inversera' (138). This status as the repetition of a structure means, however, that when the encounter does finally take place (is consummated), its temporality is still the subject of debate. Claire wants to seal it off, to preserve it as the locatable origin of a narrative (that of her relationship with Pierre): 'Tu n'aimes plus Maria, crie-t-elle. Rappelle-toi, tu n'aimes plus Maria' (142). But Pierre is perhaps more attuned to the implication of the present moment in the past: 'Je t'aime. J'ai aimé Maria. Et toi' (141). So: the consummation of the encounter (which is already in a sense the delayed happening of the encounter) does not simply take place. It represents, rather, what *Moderato cantabile* calls 'la consommation d'un événement inconnu' (*MC*, 22). Moreover, it is repeated, at the end of the novel, in a final encounter between Maria and Pierre, in a hotel in Madrid, itself presented as the repetition of a similar encounter in Verona, which is now situated as the origin of *their* relationship (149). The repetition (Pierre and Claire) is repeated in an encounter (Pierre and Maria) of which it is the repetition, and which is itself the repetition of its own origin. This complicated temporality is shared by all of the principal erotic/romantic encounters presented by Duras in this period: Anne and Chauvin repeat the story of the origins of the *crime passionnel*; the French actress and her Japanese lover repeat her encounter with the German soldier, and name themselves after the respective traumas they are somehow supposedly repeating, 'Nevers' and 'Hiroshima'; Jacques Hold and Lol repeat Lol's fantasy of the consequences of her traumatic moment. So thoroughly governed by the logic of repetition, the passionate encounter—lived experience of incomparable force, in Duras— would appear never, in the strong sense of the term, to take place.

The vexed status of the present event as repetition of its lost origin also affects the future event, imposing it as something one could only call 'fate'. Inasmuch as it will be repeated, the past event dictates its future double. Thus, for example, Maria's certainty of the inevitability of the encounter between Pierre and Claire:

Maria referme de nouveau les yeux. Ça va être fait. Dans une demi-heure. Dans une heure. Et puis la conjugaison de leur amour s'inversera.

(*DH*, 138)

Again, however, the event defies certainty: it will take place, but it has also always already been taking place, as it has already been determined by the past event, of which it will be the repetition:

Elle voudrait voir se faire les choses entre eux afin d'être éclairée à son tour d'une même lumière qu'eux et entrer dans cette communauté qu'elle leur lègue, en somme depuis le jour où, elle, elle l'inventa, à Vérone, une certaine nuit.

(138)

While none of the three events—the past event and its repetitions as the present moment and the future event—can be said fully to take place, the logic of repetition nevertheless powerfully imposes inevitability as the mode of anticipation of the future event, inserting the characters into a fated narrative which has already exceeded their control. Once Anne and Chauvin are compelled to re-enact the story of the *crime passionnel*, the end—the death of the woman— is inevitable, albeit transposed from the literal to the symbolic. This sense of inevitability turns the future into an abyss, both known (in its inevitability) and unknowable (in its eventhood), as in Maria's anticipation of the encounter between Pierre and Claire:

Dans les deux jours qui viennent Pierre et Claire se rejoindront . . . Ce qui s'ensuivra est encore inconnu, imprévisible, un gouffre de durée.

(60)

This abyss, the gap between anticipation and its fulfilment, imposes a difficult mixture of tension and inevitability, the uncomfortable experience of the 'durée'.

The inevitability which, for Duras, marks the reconstruction/ repetition of the lost event also provides an initial approach to the ethical implications of its temporality. With Duras's characters caught up in apparently inevitable stories at the level of their most intimate passions, responsibility for their apparently inevitable actions becomes vexed. The will of the characters may still be operative ('Je *voudrais* que vous soyez morte'), but it is *already* positioned, the product of a repetition at the end of a process of reconstruction.

The often terrible outcomes of these reconstructions—madness, passion, death—provoke reference to an ethical framework which is simultaneously haunted by the suggestion of inadequacy. The emergence of the temporality of the event as a principal feature of Duras's work at this time may thus in part be explained by the drama with which it situates extreme experience at the edge of the ethical, precisely that location which constitutes Duras's insistent fascination. In the case of the repetition of the lost event, the quint-essential structure of the Durassian ethical—ruptured, but not for all that removed—is particularly clear. The forms taken by inevitable repetition (say, a symbolic death, or a possible rape) invoke a notion of responsibility which is simultaneously cut through by the apparent logic of repetition (this death, this possible rape take place at the very limit of notions such as consent—which are not, therefore, simply dissolved). There emerges the horror of an impossible responsibility, which would be positioned at the edge of the ethical, at its elastic limit, stretched beyond itself without thereby being suspended. The residual agency and responsibility operative here are those of tragic inevitability, in which divinity has been replaced by the aching emptiness of the event. Vitiated by the inevitability it imposes, their question nevertheless remains, ratcheting up the horror of the event's bloody puncture by sullying its excessive purity with the haunting edge of the ethical.

Reconstruction, Gender, Power

As is suggested by these examples, the forceful but uncertain oper-ation of power within the reconstruction of the event is also apparent in what might be termed the sexual politics of reconstruction. In *Moderato cantabile*, *Le Ravissement de Lol V. Stein* and *L'Amante anglaise*, it is a woman who is the primary object of the reconstructed narrative, the reconstruction being orchestrated in the first instance by a man.[16] In *Moderato cantabile*, for example, the reconstruction is shaped by Chauvin, with Anne as its object; it is also the

---

[16] Marilyn R. Schuster locates the origin of this pattern in *Le Marin de Gibraltar*, and describes its workings as comprising: 'A man seeking to tell a woman's story, to prod her to tell her own story; a woman, compliant or withholding, who uses the male interlocutor to claim the story she dreads and desires' (Schuster, 'Reading and Writing as a Woman: The Retold Tales of Marguerite Duras', *The French Review*, 53/1 (October 1984), 48–57 (48)).

reconstruction of Anne's life, produced out of Chauvin's mostly voyeuristic knowledge. Chauvin drives the reconstruction, with his incessant refrain 'Parlez-moi' (*MC*, 55 *et passim*), and decides when the conversation will switch from explicit reconstruction of the story of the couple to discussion of Anne's life. Anne is thus an enigma within a narrative orchestrated by a man, who, moreover, insists against her will that she participate in this narrative:

—Maintenant, parlez-moi.
—Ah, laissez-moi, supplia Anne Desbaresdes.
—Nous avons sans doute si peu de temps que je ne peux pas.

(111)

Chauvin proceeds to insult Anne (113), and appears to control the consequences of their reconstruction in her life:

—Vous allez arriver plus tard que d'habitude dans cette maison, vous y arriverez plus tard, peut-être trop tard, c'est inévitable. Faites-vous à cette idée.

(114)

The implicit violence of this apparent control repeats symbolically the final, bloody encounter of the couple whose story Anne and Chauvin are re-enacting. This repetition, however, begins to suggest that the entwinings of power and knowledge within this re-enactment are not so simple as those sketched above. For this version of the story (male subject, female object) will not quite fit. The reconstruction is not simply driven by Chauvin: it is also propelled by Anne's desire to know, and is initiated as a question-and-answer session, Chauvin's limited knowledge being probed by Anne's questions (see *MC*, 35ff.). Anne also contests Chauvin's statements ('C'est aussi faux que ce que vous m'avez dit sur cette femme ivre-morte tous les soirs' (79)), and has had knowledge of his identity of which he was unaware (77). But the power at work within the reconstruction is not simply more evenly distributed than might have been thought: it is complicated precisely as power by the status of the reconstruction as desirous repetition. The inevitability of the consequence of their reconstruction (Anne's 'death') means that Chauvin cannot *simply* be held responsible for these consequences.[17] His responsibility is not just complicated because Anne

---

[17] In 1960, Duras appears to want to excuse Chauvin entirely: 'Qui n'aurait pas agi comme lui? Anne Desbaresdes attend la mort, elle l'attend de lui, il le sait . . .' (Interview with Duras by Madeleine Chapsal, in Chapsal, *Quinze écrivains* (Paris: René Juillard, 1963), 57–64 (61)).

has consented to this reconstruction (although she certainly appears to have done so), but because questions of consent or coercion are radically preceded by the logic of repetition, which has inserted the pair into the reconstruction of a particular narrative before faculties such as consent can be said to be operative. Moreover, they are caught up in this narrative by their passion, and cannot, therefore, be considered to be in control of the knowledge they manipulate. Chauvin's frequent avowals of ignorance (e.g. 'Vous savez, je sais très peu de choses . . . Je ne sais rien' (116)) need not be read as rhetorical disavowals of discursive authority: they may be taken at face value. For, governed by the desire according to which he participates in the narrative he reconstructs, Chauvin is quite clearly not in possession of the knowledge with which he operates. Moreover, the object of their repetition is, precisely, the point at which desire becomes overwhelming. Anne's mime of this point, of her death, is thus devastating for Chauvin: 'Je voudrais que vous partiez, murmura Chauvin . . . Chauvin resta assis, accablé, il ne la connut plus' (121). And yet: while Chauvin is devastated by Anne's symbolic repetition of the woman's *Liebestod*, it is Anne who is disgraced; while the man in the original couple is driven mad by his crime, it is the woman who dies. These structures may be subtended by desire, but their object—women—appears to remain the same, according to a depressingly familiar distribution of roles. If the structures of reconstruction and repetition are inevitable, are their gender politics fixed? If their power structures are complicated by desire, does there remain a residue of domination, which might be evaluated? If the repetition of the passionate event stretches responsibility beyond its elastic limit, what would this distended, residual responsibility look like? Chauvin is not simply responsible for the repetition in which he is engaged. But nor is he simply excused on the basis of this repetition, since the scandal in which it culminates continues to refer inevitably to notions of responsibility and judgement. As Anne is lost in the sunset, the narrative ends in the banality of the café, punningly hints at the force of Anne's disgrace as a moment of rebellious strength, and so keeps the scandal on the edge of the world, touched by the residues of categories which mark it but gain no purchase: 'Après son départ, la patronne augmenta le volume de la radio. Quelques hommes se plaignirent qu'elle fût trop forte à leur gré' (*MC*, 155).

A similar structure of residual responsibility and domination is at work in what is perhaps Duras's masterpiece of narrative reconstruction, *Le Ravissement de Lol V. Stein*. Jacques Hold, narrator-cum-protagonist, reconstructs the story of a female enigma, Lol; and his narrative may even (to an extent) be read as the pathologization of the woman-as-enigma, as the oppressive reconstruction of her story as a narrative of insanity. Once again, a woman is the object of male epistemophilia. But, once again, the dominant principle in the narratorial epistemophilia is desire: 'Je connais Lol V. Stein de la seule façon que je puisse, d'amour' (*RLVS*, 46). Jacques Hold is in the narrative he is reconstructing, and structures it according to his fantasies, thus undercutting its epistemological status. The principal refrains with which his narrative is punctuated are 'J'invente' and 'Je vois', the admission of fantasy in the former turning the apparent voyeuristic domination of the latter into the vagueness of pseudo-prophecy.[18] Moreover, Jacques Hold is within the repetitions which constitute the narrative he is reconstructing, is positioned by them, and indeed overwhelmed by them. Lol's fantasized vision of Tatiana Karl 'nue sous ses cheveux noirs' as she makes love to Jacques Hold (itself a repetition of Lol's fantasized image of Anne-Marie Stretter, disrobed by Michael Richardson, naked beneath her black dress—and all of this, quite possibly, Jacques Hold's fantasy) is as devastating to Jacques Hold as was Anne's mime of her own death to Chauvin:

> Il est vrai que Tatiana était ainsi que Lol vient de la décrire, nue sous ses cheveux noirs . . . L'intensité de la phrase augmente tout à coup, l'air a claqué autour d'elle, la phrase éclate, elle crève le sens. Je l'entends avec une force assourdissante et je ne la comprends pas, je ne comprends même plus qu'elle ne veut rien dire.

(116)

The 'force assourdissante' in question is Jacques Hold's desire, and his double passivity before both its intensity and the repetition in which he is now involved. The blind spot of Jacques Hold's narrative is his own position within it; he is no more insulated from the disabling effects of the event (in its repetition) than anyone else. On becoming aware of Lol's voyeuristic presence in the rye field

---

[18] See *Le Ravissement de Lol V. Stein*, *passim*, and especially 56, where the juxtaposition 'J'invente, je vois' produces an implicit epistemological equivalence. As Wilson puts it, 'Jacques's desire for Lol is the pre-condition for his assumption of subject position within the text, yet also the very factor which will undermine the stability of this position and the security of the reader's faith in the veracity of his narrative' (Wilson, 167).

outside the hotel room where he is about to make love to Tatiana
Karl, he appears to experience a moment of crisis:

J'ai étouffé un cri, j'ai souhaité l'aide de Dieu, je suis sorti en courant, je suis revenu
sur mes pas, j'ai tourné en rond dans la chambre, trop seul à aimer ou à ne plus
aimer, souffrant, souffrant de l'insuffisance déplorable de mon être à connaître cet
événement.

(120)

This realization of his inclusion in a repetition bursts through
Jacques Hold's knowledge with the irruptive force of the event, and
so places in question the supposed mastery of his position. And yet:
despite her adoption of a voyeuristic position, Lol remains the
object of Jacques Hold's reconstruction, however much thus is vitiated by the operation of his desire. The roles of narrator and object
are complicated, but, ultimately, not quite displaced. How, then,
might this complication and its apparent residual oppression be
assessed in terms of its apparently gendered power relations?

A first move in the attempt to produce such an assessment would
perhaps be to note the extent to which scenes such as the above crisis are staged within the narrative of Jacques Hold's desire. His sight
of Lol is uncertain (introduced by 'j'ai cru voir' (120)), and his supposed reaction may have been largely invented: 'Je mens. Je n'ai pas
bougé de la fenêtre, confirmé jusqu'aux larmes' (121). (But can Hold
be believed when he says he was lying?). No decision can be made:
the moment of narratorial crisis remains, but the status of its details
is impossible to ascertain. One might, then, assess the status of the
narrator. Much like Chauvin, he is happy to avow his ignorance:
'En ce moment, moi seul de tous ces faussaires, je sais: je ne sais rien'
(81), and apparently accepts the blind spot of his knowledge:

alors je serai devant une certitude.
Laquelle? Elle concernerait Lol mais j'ignore comment, le sens qu'elle aurait, quel
espace physique ou mental de Lol s'éclairerait sous l'effet de mon désir comblé de
Tatiana, je ne cherche pas à le savoir.

(91)

But, like Chauvin, Jacques Hold remains the dominant force in the
narrative. If his dominance is residual, however, how is it to be
evaluated?

One type of feminist reading of *Le Ravissement de Lol V. Stein* has
Jacques Hold as omnipresent narrator: the text represents exclusively

his narrative reconstruction of the story of a female object. This reconstruction is bound to fail, however: Jacques Hold's epistemophilia cannot comprehend Lol's otherness. Thus, *Le Ravissement de Lol V. Stein* constitutes a dramatized critique of a certain type of narrative-as-possession coded as masculine, in which the gaps and interstices of Jacques Hold's narrative allow the undoing from within of its supposed hegemony by the buried, implied voice of its other, Lol.[19] Lol would be raised from the tomb of Jacques Hold's narrative, and resurrected in her own reconstructed story. This approach necessarily seeks to convert absence into presence, silence into voice. As Alice Jardine points out, 'For the feminist reader, it is a question of this Lol who is prevented from being *there*.'[20] Such a gendered archæological reading is plainly invited by the text. We may see here, however, an example of Duras's ability to align herself with a particular approach while simultaneously avoiding its grasp. It is hard to avoid the suspicion that this type of feminist reading is invited by the text in part in order to be qualified, for it remains simply unable to address the uncertain aspects of the text which are neither silence nor voice, but hover between the two.[21] 'Toi. Toi seule.' Is Lol *there* or not? If she resides in the interstices, then it can be by no means clear that she does so solely as an oppressed absence waiting to be realized. When Jacques Hold locates Lol in a painful limbo beneath or beyond subjecthood, is he effacing her as a subject?

La prostration de Lol, dit-on, fut alors marquée par des signes de souffrance. Mais qu'est-ce à dire qu'une souffrance sans sujet?

(23)

Or is he reporting the truth—that Lol's suffering *has* exiled her from whatever we might understand as subjecthood? The details of this shifting narrative insist that Lol is, troublingly, both there and not

[19] Such a reading is provided for example by Martha Noel Evans, in her *Masks of Tradition* (London: Cornell University Press, 1987). Susan D. Cohen argues explicitly that Jacques Hold maintains Lol in this buried state: 'Moved by a desire for endless knowledge-possession rather than by love, Hold had no thought of helping Lol out of neurosis' (Cohen, *Women and Discourse*, 37). Wilson, who also acknowledges the extent to which this type of archæological reading is invited by the text, suggests nonetheless that it limits the workings of the text, by reducing these to a binary stand-off between Lol and Jacques Hold, and thereby excluding the role played by Tatiana Karl. (See Wilson, 169).

[20] Alice A. Jardine, *Gynesis: Configurations of Woman and Modernity* (London: Cornell University Press, 1985), 175.

[21] On this point, see Hill, *Marguerite Duras: Apocalyptic Desires*, 71–3.

there, suffering in the wings, this suffering both reported and repeated in Jacques Hold's attempts at narrative appropriation. Lol is not there, yet there she remains—and it is this residual presence, caught on the edge of a story which may or may not be hers, which gives her her extraordinary aura, and which resists, in its textual uncertainty, conscription into a dichotomy of enforced absence and recuperated presence.[22]

And yet: again, as categories of judgement are rendered uncertain after the event, Duras presents a case which would seem to demand that judgement remain firm. Should the sexual encounter between Lol and Jacques Hold after the return to the ballroom at T. Beach be read as rape? Lol (who has apparently initiated the situation, asking Jacques Hold to find a hotel room (185)—or is this just his supposedly justificatory invention?) certainly protests (although this protest is strangely, unsettlingly flattened by the absence of punctuation): 'Oh que vous me faites mal' (188). Jacques Hold continues his caresses, until Lol no longer complains, and her anxiety shifts to questions about their identity: 'Qui c'est?' (188). Two disturbing elements of this scene are prominent. First, Jacques Hold's response to Lol's question ('Tatiana Karl, par exemple' (188)), indicates—not least via its oddly generalizing tag—that this encounter is a further repetition, another modulation of (Jacques Hold's fantasy of) Lol's fantasy of the consequences of the event. The status of the encounter is, therefore, unclear. Secondly, it is *precisely* from this lack of clarity that the scene gains its unsettling force. Jacques Hold is not simply responsible for an assault on Lol, first because it is not certain that he is assaulting her, and secondly because, even before his undoubted attempts to master Lol's story,

[22] The need to recuperate Lol from the interstices of Jacques Hold's story may, then, lead to a reading motivated more by a readerly agenda than by the details of the text, as when Laurie Edson writes that 'When I say that this is not the story of a subject, I do not mean to imply that Lol is not a subject in her own right. I mean that Jacques, in his desire to know her, to figure her out, effaces her status as a subject by objectifying her, and is thus incapable of recognizing her as a subject' (Edson, 'Knowing Lol: Duras, Epistemology and Gendered Mediation', in *Sub-Stance*, 21/2 (1992), 17–31 (19)). How exactly might one go about 'recognizing [Lol] as a subject', however? It is simply not clear that the text is ironizing Hold's obsession in order to dramatize the violence of his appropriation: the text is, rather, suggesting that it might be doing this (and that, consequently, it might consider Lol to be 'a subject in her own right')—but that it might also be presenting the inadequacies of such appropriation in front of a figure who is evasive precisely because she is *not* a subject in her own right. This tension can be decided—but only by readerly fiat, not on the basis of the operation of the text.

he is already caught up in a repetition which exceeds his control. And yet these arguments may be insufficient: he may still be raping Lol. There is no way of knowing. And this is the pain of the text: again, judgement is simultaneously invoked and cut through by the overwhelming repetition of the lost event.[23] Jacques Hold remains as the focus for the strong anxieties provoked by the text, but the responsibility with which he is confronted is itself, inevitably, re-sidual—hence agonizing, impossible, and unavoidable. Thus, while it is impossible simply to denounce Chauvin and Jacques Hold as phallocratic appropriators, so is it impossible to ignore the gender-ing—not absolute, but marked—of the power relations which obtain within their reconstructions. Judgement becomes, in these cases, a residual presence in narratives of residual domination. We may feel that this is not good enough, that the more or less violent appropriations by men of the stories and identities of women boxed into the role of victim deserve less ambiguous criticism—but such mutual implication, impossible responsibility, and residual judge-ment are all Duras leaves us with after the event.

Readerly Reconstruction

Nor is the reader of Duras's work of this period immune to the inevitability of the dilemmas of reconstruction: its structures are sketched within the narratives of the texts themselves, thereby sug-gesting in the temporality of the reader's experience the enactment of the questions raised by the event. By 1958, however, Duras's reader is well aware that the enactment of the encounter with eth-ical extremity, while suggested by her texts, is also presented as ultimately impossible. I will now trace in detail the presence of this

---

[23] Duras's own unsettling gloss on this scene claims—ambiguously—that it represents Lol's first experience of a typically female happiness; that she has finally broken free of living by proxy; and that this freedom cannot be claimed as a liberation, since the force of this direct experience completes the disintegration of her mind, removing the self who might have had the experience. All of this serves primarily to exacerbate the scene's complexity: 'Lol va dans une chambre d'hôtel avec l'homme qu'elle aime et connaît la même expérience du bonheur que les autres femmes en général. Je veux dire par là que, pour la première fois, elle ne vit pas à travers quelqu'un d'autre. Elle vit directement. Le choc de cette expérience est si violent qu'elle perd complètement la tête.' (Interview with Duras by Knapp, 656.) For a reading of the encounter as rape, which would have considerable (if ambiguous) significance for our understanding of Duras's notion of female happiness, see Evans, 139.

impossible enactment—which we have encountered briefly above in *Le Ravissement de Lol V. Stein*—in this period of Duras's writing, where its arena becomes that of readerly experience. Beginning with the gestures made throughout these texts toward the dramatization of reconstruction in the reader's experience, I will gradually bring out the ways in which this dramatization is marked by the *loser wins* of Durassian impossible enactment. Reconstruction has always already lost its object; to dramatize this experience successfully is, therefore, to lose it precisely by grasping it—which means, as these texts demonstrate, that the enactment of reconstruction can avoid betraying its object only by failing quite to enact it, disturbing this dramatization with odd, ungraspable details. (At stake here is also Duras's relation to a literary fashion for self-referentiality: clearly happy to indulge in this kind of play, as we have seen, Duras nonetheless characteristically insists on rupturing its possible self-sufficiency on the irrecuperable spikes and collapses of ethical extremity).

First, then, the suggestion of enactment. At an initial, obvious level, the event has always already taken place before the narrative begins, or it takes place off-stage, as in *Moderato cantabile*, or it is the repetition of an already-lost origin. Neither Anne Desbaresdes nor the reader witnesses the *crime passionnel* of *Moderato cantabile*; it is signalled only by its side-effect, the woman's scream. In *Dix heures et demie du soir en été*, Rodrigo Paestra has already murdered his young wife and her lover; and the encounter between Claire and Pierre is the repetition of those between Pierre and Maria. Lol's abandonment by Michael Richardson took place years before the telling of her story. The Vice-Consul has already fired his inexplicable shots into the gardens of Lahore. Claire Lannes has already murdered Marie-Thérèse. This structure, which imposes the retrospective reconstruction of meaning as characteristic of the reader's experience of the text, is also operative at the most local level, as in this passage from *Moderato cantabile*:

—Pauvre femme, dit quelqu'un.
—Pourquoi? demanda Anne Desbaresdes.
—On ne sait pas.

(*MC*, 23-4)

Anne's question here changes status (from a response to the first remark to an enquiry about the motivation of the murder) *après-coup*, with the addition of the third comment. These lines thus provide a tiny example of the retrospective reconstruction of meaning—in a passage in which the action consists of an attempt to discover retrospectively the meaning of the event. The structure in question is thus enacted in the temporality of its reading. Throughout *Moderato cantabile*, information is constantly revealed belatedly (such as Anne's identity, or the details of her life), thus implicating the reader immediately in the structures of reconstruction that are at work in the narrative. Undergoing within the experience of reading the temporality which determines the actions of the characters, the reader enacts the re-enactment of the event, and becomes the participating site of its inevitable end, given a taste of impossible, residual responsibility, impelled by the structures of the text to rush in horror towards (for example) Anne's symbolic death.

The reader's role in the reconstruction of meaning within the text is treated explicitly in *L'Amante anglaise*:

—La différence entre ce que je sais et ce que je dirai, qu'en faites-vous?
—Elle représente la part du livre à faire par le lecteur. Elle existe toujours.

(*AA*, 9–10)

Such moments of self-referentiality double the reader's experience: as well as an experience of the text akin to that of the reader of the thriller, who also has to make decisions about guilt, motivation, and so on, there is added a meta-experience of the question of narrative reconstruction in relation to responsibility. For the text's self-referentiality means that the reader's attention is focussed both on the substantive questions of guilt staged within the text and, crucially, on the fact that the text is demanding such decisions within a particular temporal logic. If one's interest in *L'Amante anglaise* is limited to establishing Claire Lannes's motives, then the text is limited to the status of a thriller and a meditation on the factors at work in the production of female murderers. It is of course to an extent both of these, but it is also, primarily, an investigation, in the rhythms of the reader's experience, of the relationship between the reconstruction of the event (with all that this implies for the impossibility of adequate knowledge of this event) and its judgement. It is a question less of whether Claire Lannes is bad, mad, evil, and so on, than of the framework according to which such judgements are (or are not) possible. As Claire Lannes takes increasing, pleading control of her interrogation towards the end of the text, this self-conscious framework raises questions about the ownership of narrative and the possibility of truth ('Ce que dit une folle ça ne compte pas' (*AA*, 192)) in which the reader has already been implicated. Claire keeps the origin of her reconstructions (Marie-Thérèse's head) hidden, desperately playing with its possible revelation as a way of attempting to force the narrative to continue, and (in one interpretation) symbolically keeping open the interpretative gap into which the reader has been invited.[24] And yet the symbolic interpretation of this gap—as either a rebellion by Claire against her interrogator, or the space of a readerly participation in the narrative—immediately closes it, producing an interpretation which, while thinking to enact the structure of reconstruction (a gap is retrospectively filled with meaning), misses the point of Durassian reconstruction: rather than being filled, the gap remains to resonate through the narratives which grasp after its puncture. For Claire's maintenance of the absence of the head (the event-as-origin) represents a displacement of her *inability* to reconstruct the motives of her crime, the origins of the event. The origin will always be lost; a refusal to reveal constitutes only a small synecdochic protest against the *inevitable* gap at the head of the narrative which has already defeated any conscious strategy on the part of the protagonists, and into which the reader is invited, therefore, on the condition that it remain open, unavailable, disruptive—meaningless.

The reader, then, is not quite the heroic protagonist s/he might have thought on the basis of the self-conscious configuration of

[24] On this point, see Schuster, 'Reading and Writing as a Woman', 53–4. A similar absence is opened up by the text's evolution over time. According to Liliane Papin, Duras stopped all publication and performance rights for *Les Viaducs de la Seine-et-Oise* in 1967—the year of *L'Amante anglaise*. The intertextual origin finds itself effaced, as Duras produces a legal metaphor of Claire Lannes's concealment of Marie-Thérèse's head. (See Papin, *L'Autre Scène: Le Théâtre de Marguerite Duras* (Saratoga: Anma Libri, 1988), 24). The original edition of *L'Amante anglaise* makes no reference to *Les Viaducs de la Seine-et-Oise*: the hypotextual origin is effaced in its hypertextual repetition. The subsequent edition of the text in the collection 'L'Imaginaire', on the other hand, *does* present the later text as a repetition of the play, as its back-cover blurb reveals that 'Le même fait divers a inspiré *L'Amante anglaise* et *Les Viaducs de la Seine-et-Oise*', reconstructing the origin of the prose piece retrospectively. (See *AA*, back cover). With *Le Théâtre de l'Amante anglaise* (1991), however, the version of this 'fait divers' given in *Les Viaducs de la Seine-et-Oise*—the apparent origin, until now—is revealed as a distortion: the crime, perpetrated by one Amélie Rabilloux, took place in Savigny-sur-Orge in 1949 not 1954, and the husband ('Pierre Lannes' of *L'Amante anglaise*) was neither a participant in nor a bystander to the crime—but rather its victim. (See Marguerite Duras, *Le Théâtre de l'Amante anglaise* (Paris: Gallimard, coll. 'L'Imaginaire', 1991), 9–11). As the origin is reconstructed, another origin (the original play) is effaced, maintaining a gap (even as it is filled) at the head of this intertextual story.

these texts, so tempting to read as an invitation . . . Rather, we are detained on the border, invited into the text to the precise extent that our place there is also frustrated. Duras's classic relation to her reader emerges once more: whether it be by our affective relation to her unavoidable persona, or by our equally emotional engagement with overwhelmingly poignant moments of pathos, or (as here) by our enthusiastic attempts to occupy a position which remains radically open, thereby ruling out this occupation even as it is suggested, we find ourselves pathetically bound to Duras and to her texts by a bond which is also a gap, the failure of connection which is precisely where this articulated link is constituted.

Reconstructing Durassian reconstruction, it becomes apparent that this process will get us nowhere; other than wound round the spirals it imposes, which is to say caught on the edge of the ethical—which is to say, then, that this will also get us to a location whose importance could hardly be overstated. Consider, for example, the self-referentiality of *Le Vice-Consul*. The text opens, and we are already *en abyme*: 'Elle marche, écrit Peter Morgan' (*VC*, 9). This *mise en abyme* is, moreover, primarily a matter of reconstruction. As Peter Morgan breaks off from writing and moves out into Calcutta, he sees: 'elle', the 'mendiante', whose history he has just been writing:

Elle est là, devant la résidence de l'ex-vice-consul de France à Lahore. A l'ombre d'un buisson creux, sur le sable, dans son sac encore trempé, sa tête chauve à l'ombre du buisson, elle dort.

(29)

Peter Morgan thus appears as a variant of Jacques Hold, weaving a retrospective narrative from threads of information, raising by his virtual expropriation the question of the ownership of reconstructed narrative—here with a colonial inflection:

Peter Morgan sait qu'elle a chassé et nagé une partie de la nuit dans le Gange, qu'elle a abordé les promeneurs et qu'elle a chanté, c'est ainsi qu'elle passe ses nuits. Peter Morgan l'a suivie dans Calcutta. C'est ce qu'il sait.

(29)

Moreover, this narrative presents *inter alia* the attempt by the 'mendiante' to reconstruct the story of her expulsion by her mother—and so becomes the reconstruction of a reconstruction. At this level of self-referentiality, the text's 'méta-récit' (the narrative woven about the 'mendiante') stages the vagaries of reconstruction: for the story so woven is blatantly hypothetical, mythical in its geographical impossibility, and is marked as such in part by the magical coincidence which, as Peter Morgan stops writing, transports the 'elle' from the virtuality of the 'méta-récit' to the pain of Calcutta, tracing precisely the line of the Durassian ethical, between writing and its agonized beyond, refusing the self-conscious text any clear purchase on the ethical extremity it insistently addresses: 'Elle est là.' This story is, moreover, revealed as the reconstruction of a reconstruction *retrospectively*, belatedly—and so offers, in addition to a 'méta-récit', a double meta-reconstruction. Again, however, it is primarily the gaps of reconstruction that are reconstructed: for, as we reconstruct Peter Morgan's writing as reconstruction, we discover that reconstruction is a matter of fantasy and hypothesis— which conclusion is immediately self-subverting. This uncertainty of enactment is confirmed by a return to the opening of the text, which, after an initial framing line, explodes into a cacophony of unattributable voices (remember Lol) which neither the fragile frame nor retrospective confirmation can accommodate:

Elle marche, écrit Peter Morgan.
Comment ne pas revenir? Il faut se perdre. Je ne sais pas. Tu apprendras. Je voudrais une indication pour me perdre.

(9)

We may clutch at categories such as 'interior monologue'—but their purchase on the experience of this babble is slight. 'Je voudrais une indication pour me perdre': this might serve as a motto for our readerly intoxication at this point, reconstructing the reconstruction of a reconstruction, to discover both that reconstruction produces no stable knowledge or discovery, and that its production spills out elements which it cannot quite contain, tearing self-referentiality on the shards of the ethical. 'Je voudrais une indication pour me perdre' would thus be emblematic on the condition that it accept its failure to embrace that for which it stands, namely the unembraceable swirl of reconstruction which cannot *quite* be grasped by a model of textual enactment. The sublime blazon of this 'mise en abyme' might be the 'mot-trou' of *Le Ravissement de Lol V. Stein* ('On n'aurait pas pu le dire mais on aurait pu le faire résonner'), featuring at its centre the abyss ('creusé en son centre d'un trou')—which it could therefore not represent ('de ce trou où tous les autres mots auraient été enterrés'), but whose edges it could map: as the uncertainties of the enactment of reconstruction (*RLVS*, 48).[25]

In this chapter, we have seen that, in this period of Duras's work, the irruption of the excessive into the everyday is grasped at its edges, in cases which both invoke and challenge the categories of the ethical operative this side of the beyond. The event is such that it demands reconstruction; be it as criminal or pathological or passionate, the incursion of excess invites its own retrospective narrativization—while slipping immediately *just* beyond the *complete* purchase of such narrative. The beyond is grasped after. The suggestion of the good enactment of this structure in this period of Duras's work again produces the twisting paradoxes of stable instability traced in Chapter 1, now orchestrated primarily within the time of the reading of the texts. As the reader's experience suggests the possible enactment of the reconstruction with which Duras is predominantly concerned at this time, these texts scatter unresolved details through their readerly reconstructions to insist on the uncertainties of their enactments. *L'Amante anglaise* claims that 'la part du livre à faire par le lecteur' always exists. And that it exists as—a gap, a difference: 'La différence entre ce que je sais et ce que je dirai, qu'en faites-vous?' (*AA*, 9–10). If the texts of this period enact safely the temporality of reconstruction, then this emptiness represents a utopia, the safe openness of a liberal interpretative plurality. No gap remains, as the gap is filled with meaning—as the sign of an active readerly participation in the text, as the recognition of the inadequacy of any single reconstruction, as the redemptive symbol of the (feminine) otherness effaced by (masculine) self-proclaimed lucidity, as the mark of the reader's imitation of the loss dramatized within the texts. One tiny uncertainty interrupts all

---

[25] For Wilson, in the case of *Le Ravissement de Lol V. Stein*, 'Duras's narration reiterates and imitates Lol's inability to remember and her refusal to forget as the reader fails to assimilate the text, and doubt destabilizes interpretation' (Wilson, 181). Again, however, this kind of interpretation of the text or the reading experience as the good enactment of these manifold articulations of loss (dependent upon a relation of identification between text, diegesis, and readerly experience) will indeed assimilate the inassimilable—into a secure embodiment of insecurity. Wilson is right, then, to state that '[Duras's] reader engages in an activity which is distressingly mirrored in the text s/he consumes, but this mirroring offers only insecurity' (191); I would want to push the implications of this further, however, by arguing that not just the two sides of the mirror, but the mirroring itself needs to be understood as endlessly insecure.

these gestures of recuperation, however. To Robert Lamy's question about the recuperability of this gap ('qu'en faites-vous?'), the anonymous interrogator answers that it always exists, waiting to be actualized by the reader: 'Elle existe toujours' (10). Or—that it *still* exists. That it remains, after this actualization, to question its realization. This uncertainty, itself elusive, caught in the semantic interstices of 'toujours', prevents uncertainty from *quite* becoming useful, keeps its unsettling work operative within the reader's recuperative symbolization of its empty space as the site of her/his (failed) activity. Even as this readerly position is quite explicitly promoted, it is cut through by the awkwardness it is invited to gather up. Enactment is here positioned on the edge of its own contestation, along with the ethical—whose dilemmas after the event it therefore *almost* (not quite) enacts: an uncertain accompaniment.

This edge is a delicate place. The ethical remains, even as it is contested, as an uncertain, nagging question. In her early work, Duras had already taken the ethical to its very limit, interested in crisis experiences which both challenged its competence and invoked its categories; and she had addressed the encounter with this limit point by the uncertainties of its impossible enactment in her writing. During the period of her work discussed in this chapter, we have seen how this limit is again engaged, now in the exacerbated form of the elastic limit of the ethical: after the event, categories such as judgement and responsibility are not only challenged in Duras's writing, they are rendered both impossible and yet still necessary. The sustained exploration of the temporality of the event thus allows Duras to push her fascination with the irruptive beyond to the point where certain of its ethical implications are brought dramatically into focus, and to address these implications at the new level of the reader's experience, which becomes the further site for the impossible enactment of their dilemmas.

From 1969, Duras's work continues this development, twisting uncertainty across deserted landscapes and shattered figures, partly in an attempt to respond to the extraordinary political rupture of May 1968. From the temporality of the event to the writing of *les événements*, readerly uncertainty is wrenched into its impossible, negative apotheosis: incomprehension.

3

THE POLITICS OF INCOMPREHENSION

C'est à votre incompréhension que je m'adresse toujours.

L'Homme atlantique

Jusqu'en 68, j'ai toujours écrit très régulièrement. Après 68, je n'ai pas pu écrire pendant onze mois. Ça ne m'était jamais arrivé. Pas un mot. Et tout d'un coup, en six jours, j'ai fait *Détruire*. Et depuis, mes livres ont été faits comme ça, ainsi que mes films.[1]

Ten years after the radical break that was *Moderato cantabile*, here is another: *Détruire dit-elle.* '*Détruire*, le livre *Détruire*, est un livre cassé du point de vue romanesque. Je crois qu'il n'y a plus de phrases'.[2]

The excessive moment with which Duras's work of 1958 to 1967 has been concerned is characterized both by its unavailability to comprehension and by the subsequent narratives which attempt to catch it up; the tensions and drama of these narratives are evident throughout Duras's writing of this period. By the end of *L'Amante anglaise*, Duras's reader is caught at the limits of understanding, between a sense of the irrecuperability of the event and the desperation to produce explanatory reconstruction. With the arrival of *Détruire dit-elle*, this fraught position is exacerbated, a novelistic concern with narrative broken: 'il n'y a plus de phrases'. Whereas Duras's writing from *Moderato cantabile* to *L'Amante anglaise* dramatizes (impossibly) within the time of the reader's experience the impossibility of reconstructing adequately the lost event, her work of 1969 to 1971—*Détruire dit-elle, Abahn Sabana David*, and *L'Amour*—shifts this dynamic experience into a more static, brute encounter with incomprehension. The fascination with the overwhelming beyond with which Duras's writing begins, and which winds through the exploration of the criminal/erotic event, now really does seem to be on the verge of its textual realization, as Duras

---

[1] P. Bregstein, '"Parce que le silence est féminin"', *Cinématographe*, 13 (mai–juin 1975), 22–4 (23).

[2] Jacques Rivette and Jean Narboni, 'La Destruction la parole', *Cahiers du cinéma*, 217 (novembre 1969), 45–57 (45).

stretches the puncture with which she has constantly been preoccupied (from 'le pire' of *Les Impudents* to the missing head of Marie-
Thérèse Bousquet) into a widespread failure of understanding
which permeates the texts of this period.

Rather than suspending the spiral of impossible enactment
which, as we have seen, marks the encounter of Duras's texts with
this beyond, however, the arrival of this exhausting sense of incomprehension represents the winding of this spiral to an ultimate point
of tension. For these texts also suggest that the incomprehension
they produce in their reader may, in some way, be meaningful. The
paradoxes which we have met throughout Duras's tracing of the
edge of extremity thus continue to mark this new experience of readerly incomprehension: invited to interpret this experience itself as
meaningful, one cannot but betray it, comprehending incomprehension in a theoretical move which effaces the experience it
attempts to preserve. And this paradox repeats the experience of
incomprehension—and so may be meaningful—and so is paradoxical—and so on. The valorization of incomprehension, invited by
these texts in ways examined below, thus represents the paring down
of the spiral of impossible enactment to its most elemental form: the
textual instantiation of an experience of incomprehension understood as significant, meaningful meaninglessness.

We may see in these texts, then, the culmination of a development evident throughout the early part of Duras's career. This culmination is far from merely formal, the repetition of an empty
figure, however. Duras is still concerned to keep her reader (just) on
the edge of the world: as 'le pire' bursts into everyday experience,
and the event is grasped after within the lives it also tears open, so is
incomprehension littered with débris which indicate its continuing
(if perplexing) relationship with the world it almost suspends.
Where Duras has previously kept excess uncertainly hooked into
the world by tracing its incursions as the edge of the ethical, however, her work of 1969 to 1971 gives this edge a new inflection, drawn
from a realm with which Duras's literary work has as yet rarely
engaged closely, but which now intervenes dramatically: the realm
of the political. For in addition to the internal dynamic of Duras's
writing, there exists an external factor which motivates the emergence of readerly incomprehension as a significant element of
Duras's writing in 1969; and this factor is located in the political
events which immediately precede this period. Over the course of

this chapter, I propose to explore how the broken, rapid writing which Duras says emerges with *Détruire dit-elle*, and the spiralling problematic of recuperation it imposes, represent not only the culmination of Duras's interest in the question of impossible enactment, but also a possible response to the politics of the socio-cultural rupture of May 1968.

1968 comes as an event, then, in Duras's writing career as she presents it, as another moment after which nothing will be the same. Which is also how the crisis of May 1968 was experienced at the time, according to certain commentators.[3] This irruptivity so closely resembles the interest in the temporality of the event in Duras's work over the last ten years that it is compelling to read the significance of May 1968 in Duras's writing as in part the embrace of the political manifestation of a concern which has been live for her for some time. The internal and external factors which produce the politics of incomprehension as a pressing concern for Duras at this time converge, at this point: the fascination within Duras's work with the incursions of extremity finds in the external world a politics which seems to share its interest in the overwhelming moment at which the world is almost suspended. To this extent, the politics of May 1968—while also importantly of political significance—may be seen as responding to Duras's ethical preoccupations, both because they feature (as we will see) a range of demands which fragment a positive political position into a more diffuse ethical outcry, and because the interest of some of the protestors in the rupture of the everyday world by passion, imagination, refusal, play, and so on, offers Duras a politics relatively freed from the constraints of dogma and marked by the fascinating edge which is the location of her ethical interest. As well as being active in the May events, Duras is also able to address certain of their implications in her work in ways which develop directly out of her established concerns. Shortly, I will discuss some of the particular features of the May events which facilitate this coming-together of a literary *œuvre* with its general context. First, however, I shall explore what we know of the involvement of Duras and her circle in the *événements*.

Duras is directly involved in the events of May 1968. Along with Sartre, de Beauvoir, Claude Roy, Michel Leiris, and other writers,

---

[3] See Keith Reader and Khursheed Wadia, *The May 1968 Events in France* (Basingstoke: Macmillan, 1993), 8.

she gives public support to the occupation by a 'literary com-
mando', comprising Michel Butor, Nathalie Sarraute and others, of
the headquarters of the Société des Gens de Lettres, and the consequent foundation of L'Union des écrivains, 'ouverte à tous ceux qui
considèrent la littérature comme une pratique indissociable du
procès révolutionnaire actuel'.[4] Active in the campaign to boycott
the ORTF, she is also, along with Sarraute, Maurice Blanchot,
Dionys Mascolo, and others, involved in the foundation of the
Comité d'Action Étudiants-Écrivains, a communal grouping
founded on 18 May 1968, described by Patrick Combes as 'la première initiative significative dans le domaine littéraire' (Combes, 49).
Such texts as remain from the Committee's various tracts and com-
muniqués show, among other aspects, its insistence on the political
importance of the notion of refusal, its celebration of this force
among 'les jeunes', its absolute hostility to the PCF as well as to
de Gaulle, and its inevitable, fractious self-redefinition.[5]

Duras's own piece '20 mai 1968: texte politique sur la naissance
du Comité d'Action Étudiants-Écrivains', originally published in
Les Lettres nouvelles (June–July 1969) as part of a 'one year on'
retrospective on the May events, and collected in Les Yeux verts in
1980, was produced during the group's sessions, and intended as a
public statement of its origins, workings, and aims. Despite having
been rejected by the Committee—'Il a été jugé soit trop "personnel",
"littéraire", "malveillant", "faux"' (YV, 82)—it shows the work of
the CAEE to have been characterized by an experiment in collective authorship, guided by an overall principle of radical refusal.
The Committee represents what Blanchot, following Bataille,
terms a negative community, founded on rejection, identified by its
impossibility, bound together only by the negativity of its refusals.
As Duras puts it, 'Rien ne nous lie que le refus' (YV, 77). In this, the
CAEE takes up a tradition of anti-Gaullist protest in Duras's milieu
dating back to opposition to de Gaulle's prise de pouvoir in 1958. It
was at this time—principally in the journal Le 14 Juillet—that
Mascolo, Blanchot, and Duras elaborated the notion of a politics of
refusal which would found a strange, articulated form of solidarity,

[4] Union des écrivains, declaration of 21 May 1968, quoted in Patrick Combes, La Littérature et le mouvement de mai 1968 (Paris: Seghers, 1984), 268. Further details of Duras's involvement in the events of May are to be found in Adler, Marguerite Duras, 418 ff.
[5] Material produced by the CAEE is collected in Lignes, 33 (Paris: Hazan, 1998). See also
Dionys Mascolo, A la recherche d'un communisme de pensée (Paris: Fourbis, 1993), 299–363.

a community based on the irreducible fragility of those who have nothing left but their implacable refusal.[6] As Mascolo puts it in 1958: 'Que notre premier et dernier mot soit NON' (Mascolo, *A la recherche*, 149).

And this position—which evolves into opposition to the war in Algeria, and hence into the 'Manifeste des 121'—next finds dramatic political expression in the involvement of many from this context in the events of 1968. A politics of the irreducible, of the residue of radical refusal which gives onto a fundamental compassion, will become especially important to Duras's concern, in her later writing, with both immigrant identity and the figure of the residual self; these aspects will be considered in detail in Chapter 6, below. Its resonance for Duras in 1968 is perhaps easy to appreciate in terms of the concerns already apparent throughout her work. For the impoverished, devastated figures who people her texts of 1969 to 1971 clearly issue from the gradual erosion of character evident in her work of the previous fifteen years; and, like the tenderly sketched 'derniers des derniers' of *Le Square*, they also pick up, in their delicacy and impoverishment, the concern for the marginal— immigrant workers, criminals, down-and-outs—apparent in her journalism of the 1950s and 1960s. The May protestors identified themselves vociferously with a great range of marginal and oppressed figures, including prisoners, the mentally ill, immigrant workers, old people, homosexuals, prostitutes, the poor, the people of the Third World, Jews, and the uneducated, in a clamour against injustice which demonstrates vociferously their dispersal of a positive political project in favour of repeated ethical demands.[7] In 1969, Duras includes in her list of valorized marginal groups the exploited ('le dernier coolie'), the mad, and Jews (Rivette and Narboni, 51). Thinking of *Le Square*, of the Vice-Consul and the *mendiante*, we may perhaps glimpse something of the literary pre-history of Duras's embrace of the residual alignments at work within the May groupings with which she was involved. We should also, of course, note the proximity of these alignments to their philosophical

[6] See Maurice Blanchot, 'Le Refus', in *L'Amitié* (Paris: Gallimard, 1971), 130–1; Duras, 'Assassins de Budapest' (*O*, 88–91); and Mascolo, 'Refus inconditionnel', in *A la recherche d'un communisme de pensée*, 147–9. The notion of a negative community, which I have been using to describe the CAEE, is attributed by Blanchot to Bataille, as 'la communauté de ceux qui n'ont pas de communauté' (Maurice Blanchot, *La Communauté inavouable* (Paris: Minuit, 1983), 45). This text also, of course, contains Blanchot's reflections on the May events.

[7] See Ingrid Eichenberg, *Mai 68 im französischen Roman* (Marburg: Hitzeroth, 1987), 15–16.

and other cultural contexts: to anti-psychiatry, of course (and thus to Foucault), anti-colonialism, feminism, gay liberation; but also, importantly, to the Levinasian conception of the ethical as founded in the overwhelming encounter with the vulnerable other (Blanchot's recollection of May 1968 in *La Communauté inavouable* is situated within a heavily Levinasian approach), as well as to later models of community as shared dereliction, exposure, finitude (as offered, for example, by Nancy) which, in addition to their Bataillean connections, seem to owe much to the practice of negative or heterogeneous community elaborated by and around Duras, Blanchot, and Mascolo from 1958 on.

Duras's enthusiasm for the aims and activities of May, for their irreducible, passionate demand for justice, remains, even after the events are over. She refuses to assess the events according to straightforward criteria of success and failure, producing instead apparently paradoxical verdicts that challenge the positive teleologies of political programmes. In 1969, she declares, 'Mai était une chose réussie. C'est un échec infiniment plus réussi que n'importe quelle réussite au niveau de l'opération politique' (Rivette and Narboni, 51). Eight years later, to Michelle Porte, this position is expanded:

C'est l'utopie qui fait avancer les idées de gauche, même si elle échoue. 68 a échoué, ça a fait un pas en avant fantastique pour l'idée de gauche . . . Il n'y a qu'à tenter les choses, même si elles sont faites pour échouer . . .
Les esprits courts, les esprits faux, les esprits sans générosité disent: '68 n'a pas abouti, donc c'est un échec', et 68 est là encore maintenant, complètement, c'est un acquis total, c'est complètement positif, même si ça a échoué.

(C, 114–15)

The maxim offered in *Le Camion*—'Que le monde aille à sa perte, c'est la seule politique' (*C*, 25)—demonstrates Duras's continuing espousal, through the 1970s, of a politics of negativity, of destruction, which refuses projects in favour of loss, rejecting militancy and dogma in favour of a negative utopia associated with poetry and love (*C*, 113). This approach represents a politics based less on predetermined, positive programmes, than on specific, particular resistances and blockages, designed to effect provisional breaches and reveal possibilities. Criteria of success and failure are perceived as belonging to a positive, teleological narrative associated with precisely the sort of institutions opposed by the protestors; and this opposition is maintained by Duras long after the May protests are

over. In 1974, her negative utopian credo is blunt: 'Je rêve d'un programme politique entièrement négatif, comme ça' (P, 108).[8]

Radical refusal, a politics of loss and paradox, the importance of
Jewishness, a valorization of madness: these may serve as just some
of the elements of the May protests which appear in Duras's work of
this period, and which may encourage a reading of this work alongside the politics of the 'événements'. The demands of the protestors
for a liberation of the imagination, and for the dismantling of the
bourgeois state, and their violent challenge to the violent repression
of those demands by the agents of this state, are perhaps doubled in
Duras's writing by the juddering, lyrical dismantling of such notions
as identity and agency, and the production and valorization of an
experience of incomprehension. It seems possible, then, to read
these texts as responses to the political upheavals of 1968, as the literary elaboration of a radical rejection of bourgeois values. Thus,
for example, Alain Vircondelet writes in 1972: 'Cet au-delà espéré,
ces plages, cette grève internationale par laquelle les hommes
devront passer avant de recommencer, n'est-elle pas déjà symbolisée
par cette agraphie envahissante?' And Yvonne Guers-Villate also
locates these texts as the literary manifestation of Duras's engagement with the new political demands of the time: 'La "tabula rasa"
que Duras proclamait nécessaire en matière politique, elle la met en
pratique dans le domaine littéraire.'[9] How, though, do these texts
respond to the events of 1968? Does the symbolization of a political
tabula rasa in fragmented, ruined texts represent the literary staging
of issues raised during these events, a privileged literary working-
through of problems from the political arena? A more or less
straightforward recuperation of a politics of loss and refusal in literary texts will, inevitably, be subject to the paradoxes of impossible
enactment we have traced through Duras's career so far. Indeed, the
paradoxical relationship between this politics and its impossible
enactment is precisely what allows the politics of May to enter into

---

[8] The refusal of teleology by the protestors is stressed at the time by Daniel Cohn-Bendit:
'le gouvernement n'arrive pas à imaginer que 15000 à 20000 jeunes gens puissent, en une
semaine, apprendre à manifester, apprendre à se défendre, à s'organiser. Pour lui, il faut qu'il
y ait eu un cerveau, un plan. Vendredi, les étudiants ont prouvé le contraire. Il n'a pas eu de
plan. Il n'y avait pas de commandement unifié, aucun plan préétabli' (Cohn-Bendit, 'Notre
Commune du 10 mai', *Le Nouvel Observateur*, 15 mai 1968, 32–4 (33)).

[9] Alain Vircondelet, *Marguerite Duras ou le temps de détruire* (Paris: Seghers, 1972), 120; and
Yvonne Guers-Villate, *Continuité/discontinuité de l'œuvre durassienne* (Brussels: Éditions de l'Université de Bruxelles, 1985), 13.

Duras's work, since it enables her to respond to a major political moment while developing concerns which already characterize her work. (It is notable, for example, that no similarly clear literary response is produced by Duras's opposition to the French campaign in Algeria at the start of the 1960s). In order to address the nature of this response, I shall first investigate the particular features of these texts which produce an experience of readerly incomprehension, relating these features, where appropriate, to issues relevant to the politics of the period. I shall then discuss the political references present in the texts, and the implication, in the manner in which these references are made, of a valorization of incomprehension. Finally, I shall argue that it is in the twisting, impossible relation between the experience of incomprehension and the re-symbolization of this experience as politically significant that the relation between these texts and the politics of 1968—and their development of the characteristic concerns of Duras's writing—may be located.

Techniques of Incomprehension

First, then, I propose to explore the ways in which Duras's writing of this period produces in its reader an experience of incomprehension. Specifically, I will be discussing: the fragmentation of identity, agency, and action; Duras's technique of incomplete symbolism; the refusal of logic and the production of paradox; and the erosion of the fabric of the texts. Even this approach has already betrayed the experience of the text, of course, since the reader encounters the incomprehension produced by these techniques not as a series of discrete features, but rather as a concatenation of bewilderment; yet the attempted re-symbolization of this experience is also invited by the writing in which it is produced. The resulting spiral of punctured interpretation will be essential to the notion of a politics of incomprehension; it will, then, be vital that this analysis first lose its object by tracing the experience of loss it imposes.[10]

[10] In her reading of *L'Amour*, Claire Cerasi traces a similar double movement, but recuperates an initial incomprehension into the later recognition of a deeper significance: 'Frappé par l'hermétisme du texte, le lecteur doit cependant dépasser son "incohérence", et découvrir la cohérence qui sous-tend l'œuvre, cohérence interne masquée, mais essentielle' (Cerasi, *Du Rythme au sens: Une Lecture de* L'Amour *de Marguerite Duras* (Paris: Archives des Lettres Modernes, 1991), 6). I will be arguing, by contrast, that the essential coherence of

An initial degree of incomprehension is created in the reader of these texts by the dismantling of any stable sense of identity, a feature of Duras's writing which, by 1969, has been progressing intermittently for some time—notably in *Le Ravissement de Lol V. Stein*—but which here begins powerfully to resist retrospective recuperation. Characters are dispersed through the texts, their identities barely locatable, thanks to different techniques of dissolution, which leave the reader with an extreme experience of confusion. As Blanchot indicates in his article on *Détruire dit-elle*, these are obscure figures, 'des hommes, des femmes, des ombres', who find themselves 'en position de personnages' without fully occupying these positions.[11] Their names are abbreviated, truncated markers, which, in the manner of so much in these texts (as will be seen below), gesture towards a possible meaning while remaining resolutely enigmatic (Alissa, Stein); or else they hover on the edge of the mythical (Abahn, Sabana, David); or else they are not names at all, are simply role-markers—or even just a pronoun ('le voyageur', 'le fou', 'elle'). (Only the representatives of the bourgeoisie are granted full names—Bernard Alione, Élisabeth Alione—which, in the midst of these pared-down markers, become parodic indicators of bourgeois substance, independence, self-possession). They communicate fitfully, their psychology is displaced into the echoes of unspecified trauma, and their identities blur into each other with alarming frequency. Thus, for example, third-person pronouns frequently float away from their supposed referents, replacing characters with their shadows. In the opening paragraphs of *Détruire dit-elle* they arrive, miming reference to pre-textual characters, but—in the temporality of readerly experience—utterly opaque:

Du côté de la salle à manger où il se trouve, on ne peut pas voir le parc.
Elle, oui, elle voit, elle regarde. Sa table touche le rebord des baies.

(*Dd*, 9)

This initial opacity is complicated further by the doubling of the already-obscure pronoun with the arrival of a third figure:

Il relève la tête et le reconnaît. Il a toujours été là, dans cet hôtel, depuis le premier

these texts lies in their refusal quite to allow the reader to complete this recuperation, their suggestion that loss (of understanding) may be recuperated only in paradox, only by being lost.

[11] Maurice Blanchot, 'Détruire', in *L'Amitié*, 132–6 (133).

jour. Il l'a toujours vu, oui, soit dans le parc, soit dans la salle à manger . . . Son âge n'est pas ce qui apparaît, mais ses yeux.

(Dd, 15)

The ambiguity of the pronouns in this extract is, ultimately, not quite resolvable: in the phrase, 'Il l'a toujours vu', which of the subjects of the previous two sentences is subject, and which object? The suspicion that the first 'il' continues as subject is allowed only insofar as it is questioned by the possibility of its reversal. As the resulting dialogue progresses, this ambiguity becomes ever more troubling, culminating in the statement 'Il se tait' (15), in which the two identities are collapsed. The 'elle' of the opening paragraphs is subject to similar instability, producing for example the following slippage:

Anita doit avoir quatorze ans.
Le mari d'Élisabeth Alione est peut-être plus jeune qu'elle.

(32)

This moment of opacity may be quickly clarified by the anxious reader, who insists that of course Bernard Alione isn't younger than his fourteen-year-old daughter! Nothing in the text, however, and certainly nothing in the text as it is experienced over the time of its reading, allows the complete resolution of the panic produced by such momentary instability, and its trace remains to gnaw at the reader's interpretative ventures.

In *Détruire dit-elle*, then, the instability of third-person pronouns is operative between characters—indeed, it collapses characters precisely into this between, into a gulf where their identities can no longer quite be separated. In *L'Amour*, this instability spreads, to produce confusion between characters and the external objects and phenomena which surround them. Thus, 'elle', the elliptical 'name' of the woman on the beach, shifts its referents until it is no longer quite clear whether it refers to the woman, or to the light and mutable sea which flood the landscape:

La lumière change d'intensité, elle change.
Elle blanchit, elle se change, change. Il dit:
    —La lumière change.
Elle se tourne vers lui, à peine, elle parle.

(Ar, 14–15)[12]

[12] The status of the name of the woman on the beach is of course a key question in *L'Amour*, and play is made of it towards the end of the text, where it is mentioned by the caretaker of the ballroom but not recorded in the narrative—and is said to be even at this point only an

Elle la montre, c'est la mer du matin, elle bat, verte, fraîche, elle avance, elle sourit, elle dit:

—La mer.

(59)

Is the sea or the woman the subject of 'elle avance'? If the sea, is 'elle sourit' a metaphor? These questions simply cannot be answered: the woman remains irretrievably entwined with the feminine nouns which constitute the beachscape. An interpretation is tempting here: is there a suggestion that the woman—or even women, or even Woman—is/are in some sense disruptive of stable identity, by her/their mystical proximity to the rhythms of the natural world, to the ebb and flow of the tides? This is, in fact, a quintessential inter-pretative venture before *L'Amour*: nothing in the text can quite rule it out—but no further textual elements emerge to move it beyond the status of a mere suspicion. The text both invites and refuses interpretation in the same, enigmatic moment.

Rather less mystical is the conflation of the woman who con-fronts the traveller in the hotel—his wife, quite possibly, and almost certainly the mother of his children—with a hotel door:

Elle pousse dans le dos, fait avancer, pousse, pousse de toutes ses forces vers la porte du hall.
La porte.
Elle est atteinte.

(*Ar*, 100)

In this case, the ambiguity is resolved rather more easily: the pun fits comfortably into the general (if sketchy) caricature of the wife as ridiculously over-emotional, a classifiable version of the more rad-ical madness offered by either the woman on the beach or 'le fou'. And yet: nothing can quite determine that this is *not* the woman from the beach. The same 'name'—'elle'—is used, for example, and no further clues to her identity are available. So perhaps this pun—a comfortable, restricted moment of equivocity—is in fact unstable at a further level, both simple pun and the confusion of this strand of the narrative discourse (caricature) with the general,

invention (*Ar*, 131). Since the name in question may or may not be 'Lol' (as it is declared to be in 1974: see *Les Parleuses*, 199), its possible abbreviation to the initial 'Elle' provides a further instability in the operation of the pronoun. For a similar example of Duras's play between the pronoun 'Elle' and the letter L, see *L'Amant*, where the game becomes triangular, between 'Elle', 'H.L.', and 'Hélène Lagonelle' (*At*, 90).

bewildering narrative flow? Which would suggest, then, that even a literary accommodation of uncertainty (as semantic richness, poetic licence, and so on) were being teased apart, by itself being— perhaps—uncertainly merged with a generalized uncertainty which is hardly recuperable within any attempted interpretation. In this tautological, dialectical parody (the instability between instability and instability), not just the traveller's wife, not just the hotel door, not just the woman from the beach, not even just the narrative, but ultimately the reader herself is 'atteinte', both reached and maddened by the contagious narrative. Or maybe 'elle' just means the door, after all. Before the reader's very eyes, the (non-)presence of such unstable pronouns reduces 'characters' and their 'identities' to a baffling, rattling skeleton, in which apparent meaning is evacuated immediately it suggests itself, ultimately remaining always on the horizon.

Nor does the granting of names to these characters lessen the opacity of their identities. In *Abahn Sabana David*, Abahn, 'le juif', is soon doubled by a second Abahn. The two are temporarily distinguished by the former's epithet; this distinction is quickly collapsed, however:

—Il s'appelle aussi Abahn mais lui, on l'appelle le juif.

(*ASD*, 18)

—C'est toi Abahn le juif, Abahn le chien?
—C'est moi aussi. Tu m'as reconnu?

(38)

Moreover, the formulae used to introduce the two figures into the narrative are identical: 'Un homme grand et maigre, aux tempes grises' (7/18). This indistinction in turn produces moments of irreducible confusion over the characters' identity: there is no longer any stable difference between the two Abahns:

Abahn, à son tour, vient.
—David, appelle Abahn.
Abahn n'a pas crié. Sabana se retourne: elle voit qu'Abahn s'est adressé à elle, Sabana.
Le regard bleu de Sabana reste sur Abahn.

(55)

It is not only the two Abahns who wreck the stable distribution of identities, however. David, a manual labourer, member of 'le Parti de Gringo', and charged with the execution of 'le juif', bears an emblematically Jewish name, the symbolic charge of which under-mines the anti-Semitic distinction which marks Gringo's politics of hatred. Indeed, precisely this manner of classification is placed in question by the text, which—particularly around the figure(s) of the Jew(s)—piles noun upon noun until attempts to separate the terms end in confusion:

—On l'appelle aussi Abahn le juif, Abahn le chien.
—Et aussi bien le juif ? le chien?
—Oui.
—On appelle juifs les autres, ici?
—Oui.
—Et chiens?
—Les juifs—elle attend—et là d'où tu viens?
—Aussi.

(20)

This disturbance in the distribution of identity undoes the logic of fixed, determinable positions on which political persecution depends, producing instead an impossible logic:

—Les racistes sont exécutés ici.
Le bleu des yeux est très sombre.
—Je suis raciste, dit Abahn.

(38)

Abahn's implicit broken syllogism ('Racists are killed here/I am to be killed here/Therefore I am a racist'), turning upside-down causal relations in the realm of identity, shakes the ground on which 'identity' might be understood. As with the conflation of the woman of *L'Amour* and the surrounding landscape in the pronoun 'Elle', interpretation is here invited by the fragmentation of identity pro-duced around the code of 'Jewishness' in *Abahn Sabana David*: the text gestures towards claims that the figure of the Jew is productive of a disturbance in the field of stable identity, and that anti-Semitic violence is related to this disturbance. As in *L'Amour*, however, this interpretation is both made available and denied any final ground-ing, more flirtation than invitation, as the adoption of this as a stable interpretation cannot avoid an embarrassed, anti-climactic flatness in comparison with the uncertainty it would recuperate.

Writing on *Détruire dit-elle*, Blanchot describes the difficult fluidity of these perplexing characters, and indicates what he sees as the ethical significance of the fragmentation of character, of the erosion of stable identity in favour of a gentle openness: evoking briefly a Levinasian ethics, he presents these figures as 'des êtres déjà radicalement détruits', and consequently 'libérés pour la douceur, pour l'attention à autrui, l'amour non possessif, non particularisé, non limité' (Blanchot, 'Détruire', 134). In 1969, reading to Rivette and Narboni from the 'film-annonce' to *Détruire dit-elle*, Duras defines 'un fou'—one of the privileged underprivileged celebrated by the May protestors—as 'un être dont le préjugé essentiel a été détruit: les limites du moi' (Rivette and Narboni, 51).[13] Slipping between identities, these 'êtres radicalement détruits' have surpassed these limits, shattered these prejudices—and are, therefore, from a certain perspective, mad. When Alissa declares her love and desire for Élisabeth Alione—based on their mutual resemblance, the blurring of their identities—the latter's appalled reaction is, simply, 'Vous êtes folle' (*Dd*, 102); the dictatorial Gringo delivers a similar verdict on Sabana ('Gringo dit qu'elle est folle' (*ASD*, 102)); in *L'Amour*, the woman on the beach ('elle') and 'le fou' offer examples of mental alienation in which any sense of 'self' lies in tatters, so much flotsam and jetsam on this desolate beach, 'Lol' (already a vexed identity) withered (perhaps) to 'L'. The importance of madness and the writing of fragmented characters converge at the point of the revolutionary force of the dissolution of the ego: as the 'texte politique sur la naissance du Comité d'Action Étudiants-Écrivains' puts it, 'cette promotion de la dépersonne nous paraît être la seule révolutionnaire' (*YV*, 82). This is what *Détruire dit-elle* calls 'la destruction capitale' (*Dd*, 59), glossed in the 'film-annonce' as 'la destruction de l'être personnel' (Rivette and Narboni, 51); it is to be inaugurated by the hands of Alissa, the emblematic figure of the porous, fluid individual, whom Blanchot calls 'l'adolescente nocturne', alone able to announce the messianic (non-)truth of destruction (Blanchot, 'Détruire', 134). Both the loss of the self as ethical imperative, à la Blanchot—the opening of the individual to the (love of the) other via the destruction of the ego—and the political embrace of madness in the events of May perhaps find a way into these texts in the dismantling of individual characters.

---

[13] Duras gives an explicit valorization of madness in an interview with Alain Vircondelet published in 1972, linking it in anti-psychiatric fashion to the notion of refusal: 'La folie augmente partout . . . Ça veut dire qu'il y a une réaction très sensible, très intelligente. Ça veut dire que la sensibilité grandit, les gens deviennent fous pour ne pas subir. C'est en cela que je me réjouis . . .' (Vircondelet, *Duras ou le temps de détruire*, 164).

Just as characters are dispersed around these texts as so many traces, so is the concept of agency ceaselessly dismantled, acts divorced from their subjects until they become virtually arbitrary incursions, almost beyond even symbolic interpretation. Again, it is the *almost* that is significant: it is the neither/nor quality of action in these texts, its suspension between significance and insignificance, that allows it to produce their particular incomprehension. The challenge to agency and responsibility apparent in Duras's writing on the event is here pushed to the point where action seems all but divorced from figures who, eroded as characters, have barely any agency left. Both *Détruire dit-elle* and *L'Amour* are traversed by haunting, apersonal cries, which may become attributable to a possible agent, but which arrive as flat enigmas:

Septième jour. Mais dans la torpeur de la sieste une voix d'homme éclate, vive, presque brutale.
Personne ne répond. On a parlé seul.

(*Dd*, 12)

Tout à coup, une plainte.
Tout à coup, entre le bruit des moteurs et le bruit de la mer, s'insère une plainte d'enfant. Il semblerait qu'elle parte de l'endroit où elle dort.

(*Ar*, 44–5)

As is apparent from the first two of these examples, the dissolution of agency is in part a function of the slippage between already unstable pronouns and the impersonal 'on'. Whereas elsewhere in Duras's writing, 'on' is generally used as the voice of oppressive, petty moralizing, here it is no longer opposed to the more valorized sensibilities of ruined characters; rather, it suggests that these characters are no longer distinct from anonymity. Thus, when the Jew (but which one?) weeps, in *Abahn Sabana David*:

—Il pleure, dit Sabana.
On ne voit plus les yeux du juif.
—On pleure, dit Sabana. Quelqu'un pleure.

(*ASD*, 118)

Not content with blurring agency by sliding from 'Il' to 'Quelqu'un', *L'Amour* even blurs the issue of whether or not this blurring has taken place: is this next 'Quelqu'un' the traveller, or another figure, 'le fou', also called 'L'homme'?:

L'homme marche toujours, il va, il vient, devant la mer, le ciel, mais l'homme qui
regardait a bougé.
Le glissement régulier du triangle sur lui-même prend fin:
Il bouge.
Il se met à marcher.

Quelqu'un marche, près.

(*Ar*, 9)

Not only does *L'Amour* blur the distinction between 'personal'
pronouns and apersonal terms, however; it goes so far at times as to
abolish these pronouns altogether, presenting isolated verbal phrases
for which subjects may or may not be found. The blank 'Attendent,
encore' (25), while briefly unsettling, may reasonably be stabilized as
a development of 'Ils attendent', six lines above; similarly, the absent
subject of 'Ne ressent pas être vue. Ne sait pas être regardée' (10) is
identifiable as the woman on the beach both from the preceding
pronoun ('Elle', twice the subject of the preceding paragraph) and
from the feminine marking of the past participles. (Paradoxically, the
absent subject of 'Reste rivé au sable' (104) is identifiable as 'Il'
precisely from its *lack* of marking, one lack coming to supplement
another). The absence of a subject pronoun from the phrase 'Ne les
appelle pas' (68) creates a further degree of confusion, however. In
keeping with the practice of much of the text, the absent subject is
most likely 'Elle', the subject of the preceding paragraph. And yet
this bald statement also mimes an imperative. There is no reason to
conclude that the phrase *is* an interpellation of the reader—and
familiar at that—but then nor is there any reason to conclude that it
is *not* such a cry. 'Does/do not call them': who, precisely, is (not) speaking? Profoundly undecidable, agency in this text is now so fragmented that its apersonal subjects are strung out in the interpretative
chasm between the text and its reader, dragged into the textual
drama to the precise extent that s/he is also left, uncertain, in the
wings, wondering how (or whether) to respond to the pale, halluci-
natory voice which, from earlier moments of odd interruption
('Toi. Toi seule') has here become Duras's characteristic tone.

As the figures of the woman in *L'Amour* and the Jew(s) in *Abahn
Sabana David* illustrate, these texts produce their particular experience of incomprehension in part by miming invitations to interpretation, gesturing towards symbolism without allowing such

interpretations ever to be fully justified. Such incomplete symbolism is a technique we have met throughout Duras's writing so far, and which has consistently functioned to sketch the edges of the irruptive beyond, while failing (just) to bring it into the text. To recall just one example: in *L'Amante anglaise*, Marie-Thérèse Bousquet's head *might* symbolize the originary absence which motivates both characters and reader to attempt the reconstruction of Claire Lannes's story—on condition that this symbolic reading, which fills this gap with meaning, also fail. The Durassian symbol habitually operates as a desperate hole, calling up all manner of excessive meaning, but simultaneously bleeding this meaning dry in the encounter of this overdetermination with the inability of any of its elements quite to realize the virtual meanings towards which they gesture. The most consistently over-full (and therefore punctured) symbol in these texts is that of the forest, which appears in both *Détruire dit-elle* and *Abahn Sabana David* as an archaic, semi-mythic space both hinting at and frustrating symbolic interpretation.[14] In *Les Lieux de Marguerite Duras*, Duras discusses her use of the symbol of the forest in *Jaune le soleil* (the film version of *Abahn Sabana David*) and *Détruire dit-elle*, emphasizing its disturbing mystery:

> La forêt, c'est l'interdit. C'est-à-dire, je ne sais pas exactement ce que c'est que cette forêt de *Jaune le soleil*, que j'appelle la forêt du nomadisme, la forêt des juifs, je ne sais pas quel est le lien entre cette forêt-là et la forêt de *Détruire*, dont les gens ont peur, dont une certaine bourgeoisie a peur, dont les hommes ont peur et qu'ils massacrent.

(*L*, 15–16)

The potential symbolic function of the forest as representing the rejection of bourgeois values is marked in *Détruire dit-elle* by its position as the site of Élisabeth Alione's vomiting, a moment which recalls Anne Desbaresdes's final disgrace in *Moderato cantabile* (see *Dd*, 112, and *MC*, 140). In the 'film-annonce', Duras says of the forest, 'C'est aussi Freud' (Rivette and Narboni, 51); it is—'also'—the unconscious in its role as disturbance of identity. It is, therefore, particularly associated with the figure of Alissa, the incarnation of the

---

[14] Madeleine Borgomano, in her essential survey of Duras's core imagery, calls this ruined use of the symbol 'le signifiant "troué"' (Borgomano, *Duras: Une Lecture des fantasmes* (Paris: Cistre, 1985), 13). For a survey and analysis of the role of forests in Duras's work, see Borgomano, *Duras: Une Lecture des fantasmes*, 55–61.

revolutionary loss of self proclaimed by the text, who tries to per-
suade Bernard Alione to enter it with her, to the horror of Élisabeth
Alione:

—Venez dans la forêt, dit Alissa—elle ne s'adresse qu'à lui,—avec nous. Ne nous
quittons plus.
—Non, crie Élisabeth Alione.
—Pourquoi? demande Bernard Alione. Pourquoi dans la forêt?
Silence.

(*Dd*, 126)

As indicated by the mystery and terror it produces in this passage,
however, the importance of the forest lies less in what it may be said
positively to symbolize than in its unsettling status as a shifting,
uncertain symbol, both incomplete and overdetermined, never
quite being identified with any single referent, while gesturing
towards many. (In *Les Parleuses*, for example, it is associated with
childhood (*P*, 135); in *Les Lieux*, with femininity (*L*, 16).) It is productive of a vertiginous plurality of interpretative possibilities, a constant slippage of signification in which its meaning will never quite
become present: 'C'est *aussi* Freud'. Writing on *Jaune le soleil* in 1971,
Duras links its enigma explicitly to the politics elaborated from
Détruire dit-elle on: 'LE REFUS EST ICI ENCORE LA FORET . . . LA FORET EST
LA DESTRUCTION. Donc L'AMOUR'.[15] Poised on the verge of meaning
in its oscillation between opacity and overdetermination, the forest
demonstrates the dynamic of ruptured interpretation in its incomplete symbolism. The forest *may* mean (childhood, Jewishness, the
unconscious, the destruction of bourgeois values)—and (therefore)
it *may not* mean. And this failure of meaning *may* be reconverted into
significance—and so fails again quite to become meaningful.
Duras's signature spiral—in which the impossibility of converting
negativity into significance becomes itself significant, only to be
punctured itself by impossibility—means here that we do not know
what the forest means ('je ne sais pas exactement ce que c'est que
cette forêt'), and that this is also its meaning, and that this is impossible, and that this is also its meaning . . .
    A similar gesture to this technique of incomplete symbolism is
made by the texts' repeated simultaneous evocation and subversion

[15] Marguerite Duras, 'Remarques générales sur "Les Juifs" de *Jaune le soleil*' (1971), *Cahiers
du cinéma*, 400 (octobre 1987), 20–1 (20).

of extreme experience and significance, suspending the reader between terror and uncertainty. *L'Amour*, which ends in an imminent apocalyptic blaze, refers both provocatively and blankly to 'Dieu en général' and 'Dieu? . . . ce truc?' (*Ar*, 46/143), daring the reader to produce a theological frame for the narrative, both confirmed as a negative theology and parodically refused in its oxymoronic formulations. The cries that haunt the texts suggest the possibility of existential interpretation, capturing perhaps a Munchian angst sketched out in Alissa's ambiguous 'Comment vivre?', caught between the ethical and the existential (*Dd*, 107). Unmotivated extremity is everywhere, confronting the reader with a succession of strange, jarring cries of despair, from Stein—'Je tourne en proie à des pensées exténuantes' (*Dd*, 16)—to Sabana:

—C'est une souffrance, dit-elle.
—Terrible?
Elle cherche encore.
—Non, entière.

(*ASD*, 27)

to the traveller's exhausted letter (which recalls, in its odd absence of punctuation, Lol's unsettling protest, 'Oh que vous me faites mal' (*RLVS*, 188)): 'Ne venez plus ce n'est plus la peine' (*Ar*, 22). The (non-)action of the texts staggers along a narrative suspended between the intimation of inexplicable past tragedy (Élisabeth Alione's 'pillules blanches' (*Dd*, 9–10), *Abahn Sabana David*'s 'chambres à gaz' (*ASD*, 22)) and an imminent 'destruction capitale', caught between the suggestion of overwhelming, urgent meanings and the impossibility of quite understanding these shifting hints, even as the impossible emblems of the failure of understanding. And the reader, accordingly, encounters the burden of attempting to understand in a looking-glass world in which the rules of understanding are repeatedly flouted, in which notions of identity and agency have been exploded, meaning caught between incompletion and excess, and in which unmotivated extremity is liable to explode at any moment. Kristeva might be right: 'il ne faut pas donner les livres de Duras aux lecteurs et lectrices fragiles' (Kristeva, 'La Maladie de la douleur', 235).

Not books for fragile readers, perhaps; they are, however, fragile books, assemblages of fragmented text, with incomprehensibility flourishing in the many cracks in their textual walls. Their dialogue,

for example, is hardly worthy of the name, inexplicable questions
followed by non-answers:

—Qui êtes-vous?
La musique continue encore. Elle répond:
—La police a un numéro.

(Ar, 39)

At times, the 'dialogue' is as shattered as the 'characters', stumbling
towards incoherent juxtaposition:

—Vous avez peur, crie Sabana, où êtes-vous?
—Là devant toi, dit Abahn.
—Pas lui—elle le désigne—pas lui.

(ASD, 84)

—Quelque chose est arrivé, n'est-ce pas?
—Je ne sais pas.
Voici Stein. Il sort de l'hôtel.
—Que je peux comprendre?
—Oui.

(Dd, 38)

Moreover, the borderlines between this incoherent dialogue and
the narrative that surrounds it are far from clear. Unattributable dialogue may, for example, 'answer' a question posed by the narrative:

Elle est belle. C'est invisible.
Le sait-elle?
—Non. Non.
La voix se perd du côté de la porte de la forêt.

(Dd, 13)

or 'characters' may repeat sections of previous narrative: 'Aujourd'hui
le bruit des balles frappe dans les tempes, le cœur'/'—Aujourd'hui
le bruit des balles frappait dans les tempes, le cœur, vous ne trouvez
pas?' (<i>Dd</i>, 13/18). This blurring might be resolved by the retrospective understanding of the first of these instances as interior monologue; it remains, however, unmarked as such in the text, and this
interpretation must remain only a hypothesis—and so, caught in
the glare of its arbitrariness, in fact reconfirms the uncertainty it
might have dispelled. This intercalation of narrative and dialogue
produces effects which are observable only on the printed page,
dependent on the presence or absence of punctuation (such as the

transformation of 'Elle fait signe: non' into 'Elle fait signe:—Non'
(*Ar*, 25–6)), unsettling a hierarchy between dialogue and narrative
so that each may quote the other:

Il a répondu:
le mouvement de la lumière reprend, le bruit de la mer recommence, le regard
bleu de l'homme qui marche se retire.

(*Ar*, 19)

La plainte appelle. La plainte crie:
Le voyageur dit:
—J'ai du mal à rentrer à l'hôtel, j'ai du mal à m'éloigner d'elle . . .

(*Ar*, 47)

Repetition between narrative and dialogue may produce either flat
confirmation—

Elle ne sait pas.
—Je ne sais pas.

(*Ar*, 35)—

or bless the characters with an empty divine Verb, a negative *fiat*:

Il dit:
—La couleur disparaît.
La couleur disparaît.

(*Ar*, 26)

Even the titles of the texts are not immune from this disturbing it-
erative logic, in which any phrase may find itself displaced elsewhere.
Détruire dit-elle, for example, is *almost* a quotation from the narrative
which it names, in which it features as '—Détruire, dit-elle' (*Dd*, 34),
the presence/absence of punctuation placing the title in an unstable
position between itself as title, bordering the text it names, and this
text itself, with all its confusions. The title is located between title
and text, neither/both stable frame nor/and unstable quotation.
Similarly, when the titular 'Amour' appears in *L'Amour* (*Ar*, 124), it
functions as term of address, noun, and quotation of the text's title,
which is thus, again, put into play by the instabilities of the text it
would also legitimize, again slipping between the multiplication
and the resulting erosion of its roles.

The operation of typography—particularly punctuation—in
these texts is, then, a further factor in the bewilderment of the

reader. The absence of punctuation leaves phrases apparently incomplete—

Le voyageur dit:
—La lumière

(Ar, 16)

and flattens both narrative and dialogue, reducing them to a halting series of gaps and interruptions:

—Je ne vous dérange pas?
—Non non.

(Dd, 15)

—Vous avez entendu on a crié.

(Ar, 15)

Une brume arrive, très ténue, des embouchures. Elle danse devant les yeux elle tombe, la mer la déchiquette, mais d'autres rangs de brume arrivent, dansants.

(Ar, 49)

Such momentary failures of regulatory punctuation are already familiar from *Le Ravissement de Lol V. Stein*; here, they multiply into a regular tremor. Typography becomes yet more confusing when it appears to invite interpretation, as symbolically significant, using capitalization in a way Duras had already employed in her text on the CAEE:

Le juif sourit, il fait un signe.
—PLUS RIEN? demande Sabana.
—Non, dit Abahn, AUTRE CHOSE. Il ne sait pas quoi.

(ASD, 86)

The exaggerated gesture of the capitalized text is, once again, a double gesture of invitation and refusal, almost emphasizing the role of the Jew(s) as advocate(s) of radical refusal, but—by virtue of the gap between its dramatic arrival and the comparative flatness of any interpretation—leaving this emphasis incomplete. The nothingness which would be symbolized in its capitalization remains to ruin this symbolization, in a melodrama of destruction in which meaning is inflated just past bursting point, left far too full yet strangely empty, a cry which takes its emphasis just beyond the realm of comprehension.

Finally, beyond the puncturing of the weave of the text by the absence of punctuation or the excesses of typographical emphasis, the reader is exposed to the breakdown of the textual fabric into ragged, torn strands, twisted permutations which litter the texts with their verbal debris:

—Je veux les chiens du juif pour David aller dans la forêt.

(*ASD*, 66)

—Elle crie de désespoir, dit Sabana.
—Un chien? demande David
—On ne sait pas, dit le juif.
—De-désespoir-un-chien? murmure les mots, David.
—On ne sait rien, dit Abahn.

(*ASD*, 113)

A Politics of Incomprehension?

Thus, the texts of this period of Duras's writing produce the experience of anxious incomprehension in the reader by a variety of means, from the dismantling of character and action to the fragmentation of textual material. These are texts that simply refuse to give up their secrets, that remain enigmatic in the very moment of the reader's attempt to understand. And yet such attempts are in no way dismissed by the texts: as has been apparent throughout this discussion of their imposition of an experience of incomprehension on the reader, they gesture towards interpretation even as they cloak themselves in mystery, drawing the reader's curiosity out, only to frustrate it with their incomplete allusions, their elusive metaphors, their exaggerated intimations of extreme, unmotivated terror. And one set of gestures towards interpretation evokes specifically the politics of May 1968, including not just such 1968 themes as the celebration of madness and the destruction of the bourgeois individual, but also more specific political and historical references. To which the anxious reader might perhaps cling, grasping at interpretative straws? How does politics enter this field of incomprehension?

Duras presents this period of her work as in part a response to the events; in her 1969 interview with Rivette and Narboni, for example, her frequent references to May make the connection between *Détruire dit-elle* and 1968 quite explicit. And in 1974, she insists that the text was received in this light: 'C'est un livre politique, qui exprime je crois mai 68. Il a été pris d'ailleurs comme ça par la jeunesse.'[16] And with its valorization of destruction, of a politics which refuses to cohere into a positive project, and its assault on notions of identity coded as bourgeois, *Détruire dit-elle* clearly resonates with the shock of 1968. The most explicit political references to be found in these texts are, however, located in *Abahn Sabana David*, which, in the midst of its bewildering textual flow, gestures repeatedly towards major moments in twentieth-century history. Details of its setting are mythically sparse, but indicate potential political references: a small, virtually anonymous town ('Staadt'), featuring immigrant workers, Jews, a Comité d'Entreprise, a Société Immobilière, heavy industry, and a violently oppressive ruling Party. Duras gives a gloss to Staadt which is—appropriately, as will be seen—both mystical and political: 'Dans la nuit future, il y a des milliers de Staadt. Frontières fermées de la méfiance réciproque. Voix grises des haut-parleurs des Comités Centraux et des Démocraties-bidons. Nuit noire sur Staadt et sur la liberté' (Duras, 'Remarques générales sur "Les Juifs" de *Jaune le soleil*', 20). 'Le Parti de Gringo', dependent upon the support of manual labourers such as David, led by rhetoric ('Je vais parler au nom de notre grand Parti. Je ferai mon devoir') and jargon ('ouvrier indigne sans conscience de classe') is a critical nod towards the monolithic Party of Soviet communism and the PCF, demanding obedience and disparaging—not least in 1968—any 'esprit d'anarchie et d'insoumission' (*ASD*, 144). The other pole of political reference in the text is provided by the Holocaust, with repeated references to the gas chambers and to the continued persecution of Jews:

—On les tue un par un maintenant—elle s'arrête—les chambres à gaz étaient nazies?
—Oui. Il n'y en a plus. Il n'y en a plus nulle part . . .
Elle dit:
—Ce n'était pas ces juifs-là dans les chambres à gaz.
—Non. C'était d'autres.

(*ASD*, 22–3)

The codes of Soviet communism and the Holocaust are linked, moreover, in their anti-Semitism: one of the tenets of Gringo's Party

---

[16] Jean-Louis Ezine, 'Ce que parler ne veut pas dire . . .', *Les Nouvelles littéraires*, 15–21 avril 1974, 3. Of *Jaune le soleil*, Duras claims in 1971 that 'Ils [i.e. les jeunes] manifestent dans la rue. Nous faisons ce genre de films. C'est pareil' (Duras, 'Remarques générales sur "Les Juifs" de *Jaune le soleil*', 21).

is a belief in an international conspiracy: 'Gringo a dit que le juif recevait de l'argent des grandes puissances étrangères' (*ASD*, 61–2). While *Abahn Sabana David* valorizes the figure of the Jew as bringer of a revolutionary loss of identity, it does so in part by its parodic scorn for the paranoid displacement of this supposed force into the fantasy of international Jewish financial machination. Combining mourning for the six million victims of the Holocaust (the title originally planned for the book was *L'Écriture bleue*, recalling the serial numbers tattooed on the wrists of the prisoners of the camps) and parodic critique of the institutionalized violence of totalitarianism, the text positions itself as an explicitly political object. The horrors of Stalinism and anti-Semitism overlap, and *Abahn Sabana David* becomes the site of an attempt to address the trauma of its century. This site is, moreover, also recognizably that of May 1968. From Abahn's declaration that 'Nous sommes tous de la ville d'Auschstaadt' (*ASD*, 102) and Alissa's identification of herself, Stein and Max Thor as 'Des juifs allemands' (*Dd*, 111), one may reconstruct across the two texts the slogan 'Nous sommes tous des juifs allemands', producing a double political context: both in the events of May 1968, where the slogan originated, and in the remembrance of the Holocaust.[17] And in *L'Amour*, such remembrance provides one example of the apparently unmotivated evocation of trauma, exceeding in its distress this status as one example among many, in the shattered words of 'le fou': '—De partout—il s'arrête—ils étaient nombreux: des millions—il s'arrête encore—tout est dévasté' (*Ar*, 30).

Thus the texts, while imposing upon the reader an experience of incomprehension, nevertheless may be situated—and thus, to an extent, understood—as interventions into their political and historical context. And yet, as the dispersal of the 'mot d'ordre de Mai' across two separate texts indicates, the angle of intervention is here tangential. Indeed, the political references of these texts, like

[17] In the 'film-annonce' to *Détruire dit-elle*, Duras glosses the slogan thus: 'Il faut entendre: Nous sommes tous des juifs allemands, nous sommes tous des étrangers. C'est un mot d'ordre de Mai. Nous sommes tous des étrangers à votre état, à votre société, à vos combines' (Rivette and Narboni, 51). The slogan apparently originated as a protest against anti-Semitic attacks on Daniel Cohn-Bendit (see Hill, *Marguerite Duras: Apocalyptic Desires*, 133); its importance to the politics of its time may be indicated by the spectacle of Gaullist demonstrators, marching triumphantly on 30 May, the day after de Gaulle's address to the nation, chanting, 'Cohn-Bendit à Dachau!' (See Patrick Seale and Maureen McConville, *French Revolution 1968* (London and Harmondsworth: Heinemann and Penguin, 1968), 211, and Reader and Wadia, 17).

their other invitations to interpretation, abandon the reader on the edge of reference, searching, in the face of the suffering evoked, for a clarity that its oblique evocation frustrates. Such references as are introduced are invariably complicated, folding in upon themselves until the referentiality they mime both gestures beyond and points back towards their unstable textuality. Staadt, the location of *Abahn Sabana David*, is in this respect typical. Its Germanic form suggests a *Mitteleuropa*; indeed, it all but sets the action of the narrative in an archetypal 'Everytown' ('Stadt'). Its form maintains this reference as virtual, however: despite its proximity, the town's name *just* fails to name this atopian archetype—and inflates it in the direction of the structures of oppression, the machinery of the state ('Staat'). Moreover, as close to a specific place name ('Gstaadt') as it is to the archetypal 'Stadt', the town remains suspended between two potential modes of referentiality, neither historical nor allegorical. Its expansion into the name 'Auschstaadt' can only complicate matters further: with two incomplete geographical/historical references ('Auschwitz', 'Gstaadt'), and one incomplete allegorical reference ('Stadt'), the name is no longer simply suspended between the two referential poles: rather, it is now suspended between this suspension and the pole of political reference. Historical hooks keep the reader dangling over an enigmatic limbo, reference points slipping even as they emerge. The quintessential political reference of such texts would thus be the following, from *Abahn Sabana David*: 'il a douté de la politique du Parti dans les camps de concentration de la Judée soviétique' (*ASD*, 130). Soviet communism and the Holocaust are both cited here, and both function powerfully as extra-textual reference points; yet both are woven into a spatial confusion which locates the concentration camps not in Nazi Germany, nor even as gulags in the USSR, but in the impossible 'Judée soviétique', a metaphorical location which invites interpretation (anti-Semitic persecution is by no means limited to the Germany of the Third Reich), while frustrating it by means of the paradoxical intercalation of apparently stable referential groundings. As with all invitations to interpretation in these texts, the gestures they make towards political interpretation are insistently double moves. Miming the resolution of frustration by the provision of extra-textual reference points, they simultaneously half-conceal those reference points, exposing them to the play of intra-textual complication and incomplete signification, doubling the frustration they might have calmed.

The redoubled incomprehension produced by such incomplete gestures towards political interpretation is, however, itself susceptible to a possible political reading, as an enactment of the radical political rejection of rationality proclaimed by one of the discursive strands of Duras's work of this period, and clearly in evidence in the festive politics of May 1968. Thus, the texts' rejection of logic in favour of contradiction and paradox is advocated by certain of the political discourses within the texts, as part of 'la destruction capitale'. The use of paradox to articulate a politics of refusal and negativity is apparent in the 'film-annonce' to *Détruire dit-elle*: 'C'est un film politique? Profondément oui.—C'est un film où il n'est jamais question de politique? Jamais. Non' (Rivette and Narboni, 51). Within *Détruire dit-elle*, the use of oxymoron at times verges on an implicit political significance which clearly recalls the slogans of 1968:

—Et vous? demande-t-il, qu'est-ce que vous enseignez?
—L'histoire, dit Max Thor. De l'avenir.

(*Dd*, 122)

This politics, in which silence gives onto radical refusal and utopian destruction, is formulated in *Abahn Sabana David* as the revolutionary work of the Jew(s):

—Vous venez pour briser l'unité?
—Oui.
—Pour introduire le désordre dans l'unité?
—Oui.
—La division, le trouble dans l'unité?
—Oui.
Elle attend, ils la regardent toujours. Elle, non. Son regard s'absente.
—Pour diviser? briser?
—Oui, dit le juif.
—Et remplacer par quoi?
—Par rien.

(*ASD*, 39–40)

Blanchot—one of the dedicatees of *Abahn Sabana David*—had offered his view of Jewishness in 1962:

Il y a une vérité de l'exil, il y a une vocation de l'exil, et si être juif, c'est être voué à la dispersion, c'est que la dispersion, de même qu'elle appelle à un séjour sans lieu, de même qu'elle ruine tout rapport fixe de la puissance avec *un* individu, *un* groupe ou *un* État, dégage aussi, face à l'exigence du Tout, une autre exigence et finalement interdit la tentation de l'Unité-Identité.[18]

There is a clear constellation in and around Duras's writing of this time, in which the figure of the Jew and the gesture of radical refusal are joined in the rejection of unity, identity—and hence comprehension. Alissa, the force of pure negation (*P*, 21), whose hands will instigate 'la destruction capitale' (*Dd*, 59), and both Sabana (her successor) and Abahn/the Jew(s) of *Abahn Sabana David* are the sites of a radically fragmented agency, any positive action having been dismantled and replaced by the politics of radical refusal. Thus the Jew, in place of a concentration camp serial number, bears on his wrist the tattoo 'NON', the mark of refusal, the sign of destruction *via* radical negativity (*ASD*, 123).[19]

Such a gesture of refusal, of a negativity productive of creative openings (but which remain only possibilities, never realized, in order to avoid themselves becoming a positive system) recalls the politics of 1968 in its rejection of teleology in favour of—nothing, emptinesses, openings. And the teleology primarily targeted is that of a supposedly inevitable path towards revolution, this model itself seen as already incarnating (as in Gringo's Party) the dictatorship it recommends as later necessary. Opposition to the dogmatic, bureaucratic politics of the PCF was already apparent during the May events, and becomes a constant theme in Duras's work and public statements in the aftermath of 1968. In 1977, Duras declares both that 'Toute la politique du P.C.F. depuis vingt ans, trente ans, c'est pour éviter la révolution' (*C*, 113) and that 'Être apolitique, c'est

---

[18] Maurice Blanchot, 'Être juif', in *L'Entretien infini*, 180–91 (184). Discussing *Jaune le soleil*, Duras refers explicitly to these lines: misquoting slightly, she attributes to Blanchot the claim that Jews are 'les premiers à avoir détruit l'unité-identité, c'est-à-dire le rapport de l'individu avec un groupe ou un état' (Duras, 'Remarques générales sur "Les Juifs" de *Jaune le soleil*', 20). An historical account of the construction of this vision of Jewish identity, whose negative pole is embraced by Duras and Blanchot, is provided by Zygmunt Bauman: 'Construed in such a way, the conceptual Jew served a function of prime importance: he visualized the horrifying consequences of boundary-transgression, of not remaining fully in the fold, of any conduct short of unconditional loyalty and unambiguous choice; he was the prototype and arch-pattern of all nonconformity, heterodoxy, anomaly and aberration . . . *The conceptual Jew carried a message: alternative to this order here and now is not another order, but chaos and devastation*' (Bauman, *Modernity and the Holocaust* (Cambridge: Polity, 1989), 39, original emphasis). Duras's treatment of Jewish identity will be discussed further in Chapter 6, below.

[19] This typographical emphasis recalls directly the imperative to be found in Mascolo's discussion of 'Refus inconditionnel' in *Le 14 Juillet*, as seen above, thereby underlining the lineage of these politics: 'Que notre premier et dernier mot soit NON' (Mascolo, *A la recherche d'un communisme de pensée*, 149).

être inscrit au P.C.F.' (*O*, 177); and *L'Amant*, in 1984, contains the astonishing claim that membership of the PCF and wartime collaboration are strictly equivalent, deriving from 'la même débilité du jugement' (*At*, 85). And it is *Abahn Sabana David* that provides this rejection of established communism with its most explicit literary elaboration. The Jew is, according to Abahn, 'un homme différent': 'C'est un communiste qui croit que le communisme est impossible' (*ASD*, 94). This assessment is later borne out by the Jew himself, whose line on communism is that 'Il faudra quand même essayer de ne pas le construire' (103), which turns the culmination of the revolutionary dialectic from a happily inevitable goal to a burdensome fate, to be avoided if at all possible. Indeed, the historical inevitability inherent in the dialectic is rejected by these more radical revolutionaries: in Abahn's words, 'Nous avons cru à l'attente rationnelle, interminable. Maintenant nous croyons qu'elle est inutile' (95). The PCF is, supposedly, concerned to avoid the radical revolution announced in *Détruire dit-elle* and *Abahn Sabana David*; the characters of these texts are concerned to avoid the dictated revolution of the Party. And this chiastic stand-off figures the flat refusal of an orthodox communist line. The classifications of prescribed teleology are thus rejected, in favour of paradox and contradiction, in the very terms in which Duras will herself discuss the significance of May 1968 in 1977 (see *C*, 114–15, as quoted above):

—Le juif croyait que la réussite existait, dit Abahn. Il ne le croit plus . . .
—Il croit que la réussite est l'échec, continue Abahn. Que la réussite la plus évidente est l'échec le plus grave.

(99)

Radical refusal, in its rejection of both communism and fascism, represents the destruction of the dialectical order in which revolution and reaction are complicit in the propagation of oppression. Even a revolutionary project is refused by a politics of paradox which embraces (as does Duras in the long aftermath of 1968) failure and loss as essential. It is perhaps in the light of this politics of the non-rational that the incompletion of the text's political allusions might itself be read as significant. A reference such as that to the 'camps de concentration de la Judée soviétique' does not simply make the point, via the symbolic interpretation of its refusal of spatial limitation, that anti-Semitism is not geographically limited (although it does make this point in this way); it is also productive of a blockage of understanding on the part of the reader in the realm of political understanding. It produces, by its paradoxical juxtapositions, the experience of precisely that refusal of rationality that these texts—and the politics of May 1968—posit as the necessary pre-requisite for a truly revolutionary politics. If the political references in these texts are productive of incomprehension, then this incomprehension may be read as the enactment in the reader of precisely that experience advocated by the texts as politically essential. On the crucial understanding, however, that this understanding here fail, as the decision to posit a good equivalence between incomprehension and its textual enactment inevitably wrecks this incomprehension in its attempted re-symbolization. The notion that the literary enactment of a politics of loss could *work* represents the odd introduction of a moment of success, untainted by paradox, into the failure it supposedly embraces. Rather, as Duras's texts keep the reader hanging between the invitation to interpret and the frustration of this gesture—and between the invitation to interpret this predicament as significant and its own inevitable frustration— so must the attempt to recuperate this suspension as politically symbolic or performative remain frustrated, invited by the texts to the precise extent that it is also rendered uncertain in its fragmented, paradoxical formulation. A politics of incomprehension and failure can exist only insofar as it fails to cohere into a politics; its textual enactment similarly succeeds on condition of its failure quite to realize itself, its hesitation on the verge of (im)possible meaning.

Textual Politics?

Duras's texts of 1969 to 1971 do, then, stand in detailed relation to the politics of May 1968. That this relation succeeds inasmuch as it fails must, however, encourage caution before the confident assertion of the ability of writing to enact negativity even with reference to the political—and this not least because of the nature of the politics here in question. For these politics are often radically site-specific, rejecting assimilation into a positive programme or summary—or enactment—in favour of a multiplicity of heterogeneous interventions. According to Patrick Combes, 'Mai échappe, c'est sa vertu, à la docte saisie définitive, à une glose militante sûre

d'elle-même—à toute synthèse' (Combes, 13). The ragged openness and engulfing fluidity of Duras's texts, when interpreted symbolically as the literary manifestation of the events of May,
produces—paradoxically—an effect of closure, of rigidity. To talk
of the textualization or the staging of these politics is to neglect the
extent to which they are already, in a sense, textual, already theatrical. As well as representing, as Michel de Certeau has it, a 'prise de
parole', they also produce a discursive explosion, their characteristic fabric constituted in large part by a tissue of slogans, tracts, and
graffiti.[20] For Patrick Combes, 'Ce sont ces paroles multiples,
enchevêtrées, qui *écrivent* l'événement' (Combes, 104, original
emphasis); Paris becomes a revolutionary palimpsest, marked by
the inscription of the events.[21] The heterogeneity of the May interventions, their slogans such as 'L'Imagination au pouvoir!', their
unmanageable plurality, their valorization of pleasure, their production of discrete, disordered, non-totalizable effects rather than
well-rounded manifestos: such features already align these politics
with models of ludicity, theatricality, and textuality. A student enters
the fray dressed up as a mediæval soldier, in a costume liberated
from the state-funded Théâtre de l'Odéon (see unpaginated photograph in Seale and McConville); on 15 May, the theatre's manager-
director, Jean-Louis Barrault, declares his support for the protestors
(see Reader and Wadia, 13). There is a limited extent to which, during the events, the theatrical becomes the political, and vice-versa.
Even the barricades, most material manifestation of the political,
are seen as valuable as much for their symbolic evocation of the
Commune as for their (uncertain) tactical usefulness in the Paris of
1968. (See Reader and Wadia, 11.) For Cohn-Bendit, 'la construction des barricades, jusqu'à ce que les flics attaquent, c'était un peu
la fête' (Cohn-Bendit, 33). And de Certeau asserts that the events
represent primarily a *symbolic* revolution (de Certeau, 32). So the
claim that Duras's writing can represent a staging of these politics
foists upon them a primary non-theatricality, a theoretical self-
identity, that they nowhere possess (and everywhere abjure).[22]

[20] See Michel de Certeau, *La Prise de parole et autres écrits politiques* (Paris: Seuil, coll. 'Points', 1994).
[21] A claim for the textuality of the events is made (unsurprisingly) in a contemporary issue of *Tel Quel*: the article 'La Révolution ici maintenant' opens with the phrase, 'L'action qui s'exerce par nous et à travers nous étant ici et maintenant textuelle . . .' ('La Révolution ici maintenant', *Tel Quel*, 34 (1968), 3–4 (4)).
[22] None of this, of course, should distract our attention from the fact that the May events

The gap between the politics of May 1968 and their literary elaboration might be seen in Durassian terms as the gap between a singular experience and its symbolization, its attempted comprehension in a later moment of interpretation. Which gap is also at work in these texts. While producing an experience of incomprehension, as described above, they also suggest that this experience is politically significant. The reader is thus tempted to symbolize the experience of the texts—only to find, of course, that such a move immediately loses this experience, that s/he is—again, with Duras, and here politically—on the verge (but no more) of the meaning of unemployable negativity. The suggestion is there, in this readerly experience, of an impossible realization of the practice of community which runs from *Le 14 Juillet* to the CAEE: the reader is bound to Duras (and to her text) by a connection which is so poor as to fail to constitute itself as such, and in which gesture, of course, it is also constituted. Thus, the ruin of literary architecture apparent in these texts—and the experience of incomprehension this imposes—may be interpreted as the symbolic representation of the loss, destruction, negative community, and 'vacance' proclaimed as politically necessary only on the basis of an equivalence which, in its stability, resurrects the positive architecture supposedly embraced as ruined. At this point, a form of eternal regress offers itself: this oscillation, between an experience and an interpretation, may itself represent an experience (that of undecidability) that may be interpreted as symbolically significant (again, as figuring destruction, refusal, negativity). One is caught, in fact, in a literary version of 'contestation permanente', in which each solution produces its own challenge, reveals itself as inadequate—including, of course, this particular supposed enactment: 'contestation permanente' must, inevitably, also contest itself.

Any conclusion lies (is buried) in the gap of the meaning of radical negativity, in the spiral that keeps us between the meaningless collapse of understanding and the recuperation of this collapse as meaningful. Extending the sublime emblem of the 'mot-trou', *Le Ravissement de Lol V. Stein* offers as the impossible image of the rupture of comprehension 'le chien mort de la plage en plein midi,

also constituted a vast—and also festive—general strike, with the participation of some nine million workers, bringing the government to the negotiating table and then—temporarily—suspending its authority. For the last week of May, Nantes was, apparently, effectively run by strike committees. (See Reader and Wadia, 14).

ce trou de chair' (*RLVS*, 48). And when this image is repeated in *L'Amour*, the painful spiral it imposes becomes graphically apparent:

Elle est seule allongée sur le sable au soleil, pourrissante, chien mort de l'idée, sa main est restée enterrée près du sac blanc.

(*Ar*, 125)

'Pourrissante' is bad enough, shockingly visceral in such wan surroundings; worse still, this rotting 'elle' then joins the very figure of abjection, a dead dog, abandoned, a foul nothingness, 'ce trou de chair'. And still worse: she is not even just rotting, putrefying in the sunshine, recalling Baudelaire's 'Charogne'—she is also a dusty, subterranean corpse ('sa main est restée enterrée'). Dry, crumbling decay ('Ce geste sans elle pour le voir, il meurt de soif, il s'effrite, il tombe, Lol est en cendres' (*RLVS*, 49)) joins with teeming liquefaction, this dreadful whole coming to mean—nothing. For this horrible image is, precisely, the 'chien mort de l'idée': understanding collapses in the face of such accumulated decay so upsettingly deprived of reference points. And this slippage is plainly incapable of symbolizing the failure of understanding, such symbolization requiring the erection of a monument of interpretation on top of this rotting hole, the revival (and thus the double death) of the dead dog it claims to interpret. The symbol is appallingly evocative, but fails quite to mean anything, apart from the failure of meaning in its horror—which means that this meaning, too, fails. The dead dog stays dead. Conclusion here gives way—and so embraces again incomprehension, negativity, the politics of refusal, and so on—and so succeeds—and so fails, in disappointment, exhaustion, success.

And so the spiral of impossible enactment which we have traced throughout these first three decades of Duras's writing is wound right up. The paradox of meaningful meaninglessness, however, takes this spiral to its ultimate degree of tension. At which point, the spiral breaks. *L'Amour* marks the end of an initial phase of Duras's writing career, as, shattered and apparently empty, she moves from this broken writing to spend most of the 1970s working in film.[23] The

---

[23] Marilyn Schuster notes that 'The movement towards a minimalist style in the sixties ended in an impasse that led Duras to abandon writing for film-making during the seventies' (Schuster, *Marguerite Duras Revisited* (New York: Twayne, 1993), xiii). Dramatic evidence of this comes in lines written by Duras to Claude Gallimard: 'Les deux derniers livres ne marchent pas et leur panne me laisse interloquée et épouvantée.' (Cited in Adler, *Marguerite Duras*, 448).

edges of this transition are unclear (*India Song*, for example, is presented generically as 'texte théâtre film', and features figures from *Le Ravissement de Lol V. Stein* and *Le Vice-Consul*, and *La Femme du Gange* constitutes a filmic re-elaboration of *L'Amour*), but 1971 sees Duras's last major publication until 1979 which does not, on publication, accompany or anticipate either a film or a play. When she returns to prose at the end of the 1970s, the writing which lies broken with *L'Amour* will have acquired a new, crumbling grandeur, and will rehearse new ways—beyond impossible enactment—of encountering ethical extremity. It is to the period of transition which prepares for this revival that we will now, briefly, turn.

INTERLUDE

INTERLUDE

LA DAME DU *CAMION*

Non seulement elle ne sait pas qui elle est
mais elle cherche dans tous les sens qui elle pourrait être.
Le Camion

In the early 1970s, Duras begins to concentrate on work for the cinema. While the boundaries between writing and film are not simple to establish, it remains the case that, from 1971 to 1979, the only texts Duras publishes which do not accompany or anticipate a film release are either minor pieces, journalism, or collected interviews. Analysis of Duras's cinema is not part of the scope of this study; consequently, this period, seen from the perspective of Duras's career as a writer, appears as something of a sabbatical. Nevertheless, placing writing on the back burner for a time allows Duras to move on from the virtual impasse of *L'Amour*; in this brief section, I propose to explore some aspects of what this sabbatical brings to Duras, and how it prepares the ground for her reinvigorated move back into writing at the end of the 1970s.

Working for the cinema brings Duras a deal of success, notably with *India Song*, and a new kind of stardom, evident not only in her triumphant appearance at the 1975 Cannes film festival (where *India Song* was shown 'hors compétition' and famously failed to win the Palme d'or), but also in the publication in 1974 and 1977 of two sets of authorized interviews (*Les Parleuses* and *Les Lieux de Marguerite Duras*), the latter having been broadcast on French television. It is during this period that Duras makes the decisive shift in her media presence: from a combination of contributor and object of interest, she becomes an object of such interest that, even in her continuing contributions on other subjects, it is the nature of her intervention that is the principal focus of attention. As *Les Parleuses* demonstrates, this period also sees Duras align herself to an extent with aspects of the French women's movement; more generally, she also continues to develop the politics of refusal and loss which emerged in the aftermath of May 1968. The most striking example of this development is provided by the 1977 film *Le Camion*; this work is also notable for its promotion of Duras's star profile, as, filmed reading the script alongside Gérard Depardieu, she identifies herself utterly with the

enigmatic woman whose story she is more or less telling. This identification provides us with a figure who, in fact, condenses certain of
the principal elements of what Duras gains from her film work of
the 1970s; in order to define these elements, and to discover how
Duras is consequently set for her return to writing, we might spend
some time getting to know 'la dame du *Camion*'.

   This may take a while, however. For the principal characteristic
of this figure is that her identity is confusing and, ultimately,
unavailable. Asked 'Qui est-elle?', Duras all but refuses to reply:

Déclassée.
C'est la seule information.

(*C*, 31)

Beyond the logic of identity ('Votre logique m'échappe. Si on me
demande qui je suis, je me trouble' (62)), the woman has only the
vestiges of a self left: 'Dans *Le Camion* il ne lui reste plus d'autre
référence à une identité possible que cette pratique de l'auto-stop.
Elle n'est plus qu'une auto-stoppeuse' (80). This erosion gives the
woman the Durassian force of radical passivity ('Je n'ai jamais rien
fait' (49)), and a celebrated ordinariness:

Petite.
Maigre.
Grise.
Banale.
Elle a cette noblesse de la banalité.
Elle est invisible.

(65)

The glory of this banality, for Duras, is that it allows the woman's
residual, shaky identity to bypass what is presented as the aggression of fixed identities, in favour of an embrace of vulnerable,
oppressed figures also, in Duras's view, subject to this aggression:

Cette femme, sans visage, sans identité, déclassée, peut-être même transfuge d'un
asile d'aliénés, qui invente d'être la mère de tous les enfants juifs morts à
Auschwitz, qui invente d'être portugaise, ou arabe, ou malienne, qui réinvente
tout ce qu'on lui a appris, cette femme pour moi est ouverte sur l'avenir.

(*O*, 177)

'La dame du camion vit un amour d'ordre général' (*C*, 80): her erosion of any positive identity, refusing all militancy (embodied in the

narrated figure of the truck-driver), opens onto an ethics of inter-connectedness, careful to welcome all those whose identity, threat-ened with destruction, becomes both residual and resistant. In the figure of the woman, Duras finds a way of interlinking all sorts of identities, in order to refuse both the injustices of the world as it is and its positive, militant contestation, weaving together fragile, resistant identities into the familiar negative community based on a shared refusal. In an interview with *Jeune cinéma* on the release of *Le Camion*, she says that 'Partout il n'est question que de l'intolérable du monde et de toutes les classes sociales que je mélange exprès'.[1] Interviewing Duras about *Le Camion*, Michelle Porte cites as the film's particular appeal the fact that 'ça parle de tout, à la fois' (*C*, 136); this interlinking will become a dominant feature of Duras's writing after 1979—and is even, in *L'Amant*, given as the defining feature of worthwhile writing: 'Du moment que ce n'est pas, chaque fois, toutes choses confondues en une seule par essence inqualifi-able, écrire ce n'est rien que publicité' (*At*, 15).

It is primarily the figure of the 'dame du camion', in her residual, eroded identity, that facilitates this practice of interconnectedness. Paradoxically, however, this absolute lack of a positive identity is doubled by Duras's absolute identification with the figure of the woman, which renders this identity both residual and saturated. Hints are given in the script of *Le Camion* that the invisible woman is to be identified with Duras: her childhood, for example, may have been spent 'loin du pays français', in a tropical city; and 'quelque-fois, par exemple, j'écris' (*C*, 35). The reading of one of the film's narrating parts by Duras (which apparently was a case of making a virtue out of necessity, as the two actresses Duras wanted for the part of the woman—who was still to be represented at this time— Simone Signoret and Suzanne Flon, were unavailable (*C*, 85)), the absence of any actual image of the woman, and the similarity between her description and the on-screen image of Duras, all sug-gest an identification between the two.[2] Duras is, moreover, quite

[1] René Prédal, 'Entretien avec Marguerite Duras', *Jeune cinéma*, 104 (juillet–août 1977), 16–21 (21).

[2] To Dominique Noguez, in an interview to accompany the release of her *Œuvres ciné-matographiques* on video in 1983, Duras simply says of the woman, 'La description correspond à moi'. (Cited in Aliette Armel, *Marguerite Duras et l'autobiographie* (Paris: Le Castor Astral, 1990), 76). On Duras's elaboration of her image at this time, in *Le Camion* and elsewhere, see Adler, *Marguerite Duras*, 451–9. That the correspondence between Duras and this image

explicit that this identification is to be made. She states that the film is about 'mon histoire avec la politique' (*C*, 112); and later, in more celebratory mode, she affirms that, 'S'il y a une star du *Camion*, c'est moi.'[3] That Duras catapults herself into stardom by means of an identification with this figure means, however, that this status is paradoxical: for, as she will later recall, this identification depends on a shared ordinariness:

Moi je ressemble à tout le monde . . . Je suis la banalité. Le triomphe de la banalité. Comme cette vieille dame du livre, *Le Camion*.

(*É*, 45)

Undermining the star status she simultaneously claims, Duras is able, with *Le Camion*, to insert herself into her own work.[4] Along with the discovery of the technique of interconnectedness, this constitutes perhaps the key find of her work in film during the 1970s in terms of the subsequent development of her writing.[5] When she comes back to writing in 1979, it will be with both a new desire to write in a way which will interlink multiple concerns, and an enhanced sense of her own significance in her work. And dramatically, this work will, from 1979, display a renewed conviction of the importance of writing. Describing the creation of the film of *Le Navire Night* (an initial prose version of which had appeared in the review *Minuit* in 1978), Duras refers to the moment at which the film became impossible to make, presenting it as a moment of joy: just as her writing had reached a rather cramped turning-point with *L'Amour*, so has she now pushed the cinema to its limits:

Cinéma, fini. J'allais recommencer à écrire des livres, j'allais revenir au pays natal, à ce labeur terrifiant que j'avais quitté depuis dix ans. En attendant, j'étais bien. Heureuse. J'avais gagné cet échec, j'avais gagné. Le bonheur devait venir de là,

---

should be seen as a matter of some complication, however, is indicated for example by James Williams, who sees Duras's practice around this question as pre-empting the 'transferential identification' of her as the woman. See Williams, *The Erotics of Passage*, 45.

[3] Lamy and Roy (eds.), *Marguerite Duras à Montréal*, 72.

[4] As Sanda Golopentia writes, 'L'auteur va désormais se montrer telle qu'en elle-même, avec l'impudeur de l'humilité' (Golopentia, 'De Versailles aux Yvelines', *Romanic Review*, 80/1 (January 1989), 30–49 (32)).

[5] Leslie Hill claims that, in this respect, *Le Camion* 'sets the agenda' for Duras's work of the 1980s (Hill, *Marguerite Duras: Apocalyptic Desires*, 16); Marilyn Schuster writes that 'The films of the 1970s enabled Duras to develop a narrative voice in the feminine signed "Duras"'. (Schuster, *Marguerite Duras Revisited*, 103).

d'avoir gagné. Je me reposais d'une victoire, celle d'avoir enfin atteint l'impossibilité de filmer.

(NN, 13)

While this impossibility subsequently becomes the subject of the
film, forestalling the move back towards the primacy of writing, the
rhetoric Duras is developing here is beginning to inflate the significance of writing *per se* in a way which will characterize her work and
pronouncements from 1979 on. (See, for example, *Les Yeux verts* and
Suzanne Lamy and André Roy's *Marguerite Duras à Montréal* for early
instances of this newly categorical way of talking about writing, also
developed for example in *Les Lieux de Marguerite Duras*, and culminating in the 1993 title, *Écrire*; many of its principal instances will be
encountered in the course of the following chapters).

We may see here a phenomenon which also marks Duras's work
from 1979: her ability to anticipate or to strike a chord with what is
in the contemporary cultural air. For the celebration of writing as
uniquely significant in its own right, as a radically disruptive and
non-totalizable practice whose names—*écrire* and, especially, *écriture*—are nonetheless paradoxically erected as something of a totem,
is of course one of the principal features of French literary thinking
from the 1960s on. With its origins in Blanchot's protracted meditation on the nature of writing, and in Barthes's *Le Degré zéro de l'écriture* of 1953, this vocabulary makes its major breakthrough in the late
1960s, with the publication for example in 1967 of Derrida's *L'Écriture et la différence* and *De la grammatologie* (which includes a section on
'La Fin du livre et le commencement de l'écriture'), in 1971 of
Philippe Sollers's *L'Écriture et l'expérience des limites* (the abridged
reprint of his *Logiques*, originally published in 1968), and in 1973 of
Blanchot's *Le Pas au-delà*, perhaps the key text for the association of
writing and transgression. With Barthes more or less constantly
coining working terminology such as *écrivain/écrivant*, and *lisible/
scriptible*, this rhetoric increases the cultural capital of *écriture* in such
a way that, when Duras returns with some joy to writing at the end
of the 1970s, her increasingly frequent celebrations of the business
and existence of writing find a cultural field well disposed to receive
them.

This harmony between Duras's valorization of writing and its
status within a broader context brings out two features which characterize Duras's work after 1979: her insistence on the unqualifiable

importance of writing, and her ability to chime in with aspects of her cultural environment. This talent for cultural timing sees Duras re-visit many of her earlier concerns, but now with an eye to their public, institutional, social, or historical dimensions less evident in her early work. The interest in mass suffering apparent in *Hiroshima mon amour* and, allusively, in the work of 1969 to 1971 crystallizes (as the reference to Auschwitz in relation to *Le Camion* anticipates) into a sustained exploration of world-wide historical trauma, in which the ethic of interconnectedness developed in *Le Camion* will be vital. Duras's overriding fascination with passion gains a political inflection from her brush with the French women's movement, and the 1980s see her addressing the relations between literature and pornography, and between heterosexuality and homosexuality. And the notion of the residual self first elaborated in the figure of 'la dame du camion' sustains Duras's work on the status of the self during the 1980s and early 1990s. In all of these cases (which Part II of this study will examine in detail), the ethical extremity with which Duras has always been fascinated remains of prime significance; three principal additions—established during Duras's excursion into film—are apparent in the way it is addressed, however. First, as just stated, this extremity is now explored (however idiosyncratically) in its wider context. Secondly, the figure of Duras plays a major role in this exploration. And thirdly, the writing which encounters extremity at this grander level is itself now sufficiently valorized in its own right to abandon the problematic of impossible enactment, and to undergo this encounter on a more *ad hoc* basis, simultaneously confident and uncertain, subtle and declamatory, meeting extremity and mapping its attempts to negotiate this encounter. 'J'allais dans tous les sens?', says Duras in the interview published with *Le Camion*. 'D'accord: je suis allée dans tous les sens' (*C*, 99). This new confidence—in writing and in herself, letting go of the constraining safety net of impossible enactment and seeing what uncertainties arise—is perhaps the overall achievement of Duras's sabbatical in the cinema; her work in film—and specifically *Le Camion*—drives home her concerns to the newly significant 'pays natal' of writing, 'ce labeur terrifiant' which, after some time in the wings, is now ready to re-emerge, to encounter some extremely demanding material.

PART II

Confident Uncertainties

4

WRITING AND HISTORICAL TRAUMA

Au milieu les survivants seront le soleil noir, la cause sans éclat, la
sourde machine au fond du navire.

Un Homme est venu me voir

'La reine des Juifs', 'la femme reine de la Samarie', is captured by a
Roman, 'celui qui avait détruit le temple de Jérusalem' (*NN*, 85).
They return to Rome, and develop an intense, forbidden passion.
This is deemed an unacceptable political risk by the Senate
('Le Sénat a parlé du danger d'un tel amour'), and she is exiled from
her exile, banished from Rome, 'Répudiée pour raison d'État' (88).
She returns to Caesarea in agony, 'Foudroyée par l'intolérable
douleur de l'avoir quitté, lui, le criminel du temple' (87). This ter-
rible suffering is then played out on a massive scale, in the eruption
of Vesuvius:

Dans le ciel tout à coup l'éclatement de cendres
Sur des villes nommées Pompéi, Herculanum.

(89)

It is also evoked in the ruins of Caesarea, as they appear to a modern visitor:

Tout détruit.
Tout a été détruit.

(85)

This intolerable, singular moment of suffering remains, both in its
totality and in its traces—which are both verbal and material:

Il n'en reste que la mémoire de l'histoire et ce seul mot pour la nommer
Césarée
La totalité.
Rien que l'endroit
Et le mot.

(83)

Il ne reste que l'histoire
Le tout.

Rien que cette rocaille de marbre sous les pas
Cette poussière.
Et le bleu des colonnes noyées.

(86)

A transposition into the ancient world of the illicit passion of
Hiroshima mon amour, this tale, which Duras entitles 'Césarée', signals
the beginning of her repeated concentration on a phenomenon
which has previously met with her occasional attention: historical
trauma.[1] 'Césarée' condenses many of the features which will characterize Duras's encounter with this realm: the passion evoked constitutes a moment of radical singularity, irreducible to explanation
or adequate reconstruction; it represents a crisis of unbearable suffering; despite its defiance of adequate reconstruction, it gives rise to
its literary re-elaboration; its key figure is Jewish; the suffering in
question enforces the imbrication of areas which might be thought
to be distinct, be these areas of human experience (passion and politics, for example), or geographically and temporally bound locations (Caesarea, Rome, and the time of the text's writing, a cold,
misty summer in Paris (*NN*, 89)); and the catastrophic singularity is
approached via its ruins, its remains.

Historical trauma offers an exacting instance of the sort of ethical case which so fascinates Duras: while the need to exercise ethical judgement can hardly be greater than it is after the traumatic
event, the possible disruption of the capacity for such judgement by
the events in question is also here at its most evident. This area constitutes, therefore, an important example and testing ground of the
character of Duras's encounter with extreme ethical experience
during this phase of her career. In this chapter, I will explore Duras's

---

[1] By this term I understand: events productive of intense and prolonged personal suffering which are linked to the realms of the political and the world-historical. Claire Cerasi, in
Marguerite Duras de Lahore à Auschwitz (Geneva: Éditions Slatkine, 1993), argues that Duras, in
addition to being the poet of private suffering, has also consistently been concerned with suffering on a public scale. In this chapter, I will provide evidence of a concerted period of such
concern, together with a detailed consideration, perhaps lacking in Cerasi's study, of the
techniques and effects produced by and in Duras's writing as a result of this concern. Kristeva, in 'La Maladie de la douleur', also draws attention to the connection between Duras's
writing and historical trauma. While she does deal with texts which explicitly address such
trauma (particularly *Hiroshima mon amour* and *La Douleur*), Kristeva is mainly concerned to
make connections between Duras's writing in general and widespread Western cultural and
political malaise in the aftermath of a century characterized by large-scale suffering. In contrast, I will here explore the relation between writing and historical trauma with reference
specifically to those of Duras's texts which concern themselves with this area.

treatment of historical trauma in works published between 1979 and 1993. The strategies of writing which characterize this encounter both pick up techniques elaborated during Duras's previous work and, under the pressure of this demanding material, develop new approaches; drawing also on certain of Duras's interviews and occasional journalism published during this period, I will indicate some of the implications of these strategies for the evolution of Duras's work, as well as for thinking about the relation between writing and historical trauma. The particular areas and techniques I will discuss in this chapter are: the presentation of identity in the wake of trauma, by means of the doubling of individual identity; the model presented of the interconnectedness of suffering after the traumatic event; and the status of writing after trauma. By way of introduction, I propose here to indicate the development of Duras's concern for historical trauma out of her earlier work, and the new edge this concern gives to earlier preoccupations; the significance of the Holocaust in Duras's thinking and writing; and some of the general problems posed by the traumatic event to the business of writing.

Duras herself insists that her return in 1979 to full-scale prose publication is sustained by a concern for historical trauma, embodied in the figure of Aurélia Steiner, born in a concentration camp. In *Les Yeux verts*, she writes, 'L'écrit, je le retrouve avec Aurélia' and, crucially, 'Si je ne parle pas avec cette survivante, je perds l'écrit' (*YV*, 20).[2] And Aurélia does indeed accompany Duras's move back towards the primacy of writing, specifically in the third of the texts which bear her name published, along with 'Césarée' and others, in the 1979 volume *Le Navire Night et autres textes*.[3] Found at the end of this volume, this text is bound into Duras's filmic work by its titular, thematic, and tonal links to its two immediate predecessors, in which Aurélia first appears, and both of which were also filmed. But it does not itself accompany a film, and as such may be taken as Duras's

---

[2] See also Lamy and Roy (eds.), *Marguerite Duras à Montréal*, 73: 'C'est vrai que, historiquement, quand je serai morte et qu'on fera l'histoire de mes récits, on verra que j'ai recommencé à écrire avec Aurélia.' Aurélia's origins may also lie further back—and close to the moments of trauma to which she refers: the collection *Romans, Cinéma, Théâtre: Un Parcours*, published in 1997, features a text from the 1940s, 'texte à partir de quoi j'ai écrit Aurélia' (*RCT*, 1553).

[3] The three 'Aurélia Steiner' texts will be distinguished by their supposed place of writing, as 'Aurélia Steiner Melbourne', 'Aurélia Steiner Vancouver', and 'Aurélia Steiner Paris'; they will be referred to as 'ASM', 'ASV', and 'ASP', respectively.

return to a writing not immediately supported by other genres. From 1979 on, then, Duras's work is underwritten by a figure who, as we will see, condenses the problems raised by historical trauma in such fields as identity, survival and testimony. From this moment, her writing rarely allows respite from—at the very least—a nagging awareness of this suffering as a defining (if ghostly) presence in her work, and frequently makes of this haunting guarantee its main concern. If the Holocaust and its echoes in other traumas become of such prominence in Duras's work after 1979, then, this emergence is linked both to an insistence on the urgent necessity of remembrance and to the survival of Duras's very writing.

As discussed above, Duras's return to writing brings new dimensions to her work. Writing itself is increasingly valorized; the figure of Duras herself plays a major role in and around her texts; and earlier concerns are re-elaborated with an added sense of their large-scale historical and social dimensions, this re-elaboration often chiming with or anticipating elements of the cultural context in which Duras is writing. As far as historical trauma is concerned, it will be apparent throughout this chapter that Duras insistently interrogates the status of writing in the face of its catastrophe, attempting ultimately to find a form of writing which could accompany suffering, and frequently implicating her own self in these attempts. The importance of historical trauma in Duras's writing from 1979 provides, moreover, a good example of her raising the stakes of questions already encountered in her earlier work. The germ of a concern with historical trauma is already evident in *Hiroshima mon amour*, as seen in Chapter 2. At this point, however, such a concern is something of an exception, as the texts of this earlier period are primarily concerned with the event on a personal or local scale, as, for example, a moment of criminal or erotic intensity, and are interested above all in the consequences of its irruptive temporality. The return to the event as the moment of historical trauma, on the other hand, addresses it consistently as the painful collision of the personal and the world-historical. We may see here how Duras returns to writing after her cinematic sabbatical with the confidence to raise the stakes of her earlier concerns. In her writing on historical trauma, she combines the interest in the temporality of the event of the period 1958 to 1967 with the nascent concern for the Holocaust, Jewish identity, and Soviet labour camps evident in *Abahn Sabana David* (and, to an extent, *Détruire dit-elle* and *L'Amour*) to produce a sustained period of concentration on mass suffering. This concentration allows Duras to correlate her earlier interests, while addressing them on a more consistently global scale. While the incomprehension which plays such a large part in her work of 1969 to 1971 grows out of the drive to reconstruct the lost event explored from 1958 to 1967, the relation between the temporality of this event and the horrors of world history touched upon in *Abahn Sabana David* remains only implicit. From 1979, marrying these two concerns, Duras is able to address their combined significance, drawing out fully the implications of the event considered as both personal and historical trauma.

As well as facilitating the grander reorchestration of earlier topics, Duras's encounter with historical trauma also demonstrates her ability, in the second phase of her career, to anticipate the concerns of a wider cultural context. As Duras's exploration of historical trauma grows from its scattered earlier manifestations into a concerted encounter, a concern for the Holocaust and the Occupation are becoming increasingly important factors in French cultural and intellectual—not to mention legal—life. It is not only Duras who, around this time, is concerned that the crimes of the Holocaust, for example, are being too easily forgotten or too frequently denied. (See, among many examples, Blanchot's *L'Écriture du désastre* (1980), Lyotard's discussion of the problems imposed by the irruptivity of the event of the Holocaust in *Le Différend* (1983), and Claude Lanzmann's *Shoah* (1985).) Duras's prolonged and more sustained elevation of her earlier concerns to the explicit level of world history is thus part of, and feeds into, a wider public interest in these concerns. We do not have to speculate about relations of cause and effect to be able to say that the desire apparent in Duras's work to address her preoccupations at an increasingly global level is in part realized by the increased receptivity to these concerns of a general cultural field.

In terms of the encounter between Duras's writing and the extreme experiences which it everywhere addresses, the concentration on historical trauma introduces fully a sense of confident uncertainty as the characteristic tone of this encounter. The pain of the material in question already challenges radically any suggestion of aesthetic adequacy (as will be discussed shortly); in the face of extremity which has effectively resolved in advance the problematic of enactment, Duras is as it were freed to explore fully the uncertainties of a writing now big enough to encounter suffering without the possible safety net of the problematic of adequation. It is in this sense that Duras's return to writing is guaranteed by the survivor, Aurélia Steiner: it is the new, concerted concern for historical trauma in Duras's work after 1979 that allows her to come back to writing without having to worry about a problem of enactment which this material simply overwhelms. The new sense of scale which marks Duras's later work produces, moreover, an air of confidence and freedom which frees her writing up from the spiralling coils of impossible enactment. This 'freedom' implies not a positive, happy liberation, however: typically, Duras enjoys this development by presenting the awkward complications of the relation of writing to mass suffering.

During the 1980s, in interviews, as well as in journalistic and autobiographical writings, Duras places increasing emphasis on both her personal horror at the Holocaust and the imperative to remember the suffering of the Jewish people. In 1981, she tells an audience in Montreal,

Je ne me suis jamais remise de ce qui est arrivé aux Juifs durant la Guerre, jamais . . . J'ai perdu un enfant, un frère. J'ai perdu des amis, quatorze amis dans la Résistance, dans les camps, à Ravensbruck, Auschwitz, tout ça, mais je me suis mieux remise de ces pertes individuelles que du sort général des Juifs.

(Lamy and Roy (eds.), *Marguerite Duras à Montréal*, 39–40)

The need to write about the Holocaust is connected by Duras to an inability to come to terms both with its occurrence and with a horrified sense of past ignorance: 'C'est le fait qu'on ne s'est pas rendu compte de ce qui se passait . . . Comment est-il possible qu'il ait eu lieu?' (Lamy and Roy, 27–8). What is more, in a text from 1985, Duras locates the Holocaust as a singular rupture in her personal history:

Dans ma vie—je l'ai dit récemment à la télévision anglaise—il y a d'abord l'enfance, puis l'adolescence, cela en toute clarté. Et puis tout à coup, sans prévenir, comme la foudre, les Juifs. Pas d'âge adulte: les Juifs massacrés, 1944.

(*ME*, 31)

The power of the Holocaust to effect such a rupture is related by Duras to what she presents as its utter singularity; this position is expressed particularly in *Les Yeux verts*, where she writes for example that 'aucune extermination n'a été de la nature de celle des juifs, aucune, dans l'histoire du monde' (*YV*, 177).[4] *Les Yeux verts* and *Le Monde extérieur*, in particular, are notable for their insistent return to the suffering of the Holocaust and to the importance of its remembrance, as in the 1981 piece 'Flaubert c'est . . .', which maintains that 'Ça fait cinq ans, sept ans qu'on ne parle plus des camps. Ceux qui disent que c'est un phénomène admis, assimilé, ce sont les nouveaux antisémites' (*ME*, 28). In the light of this insistence throughout her later work, Duras's writing of this period may be seen as both sustained by a concern with historical trauma (with Aurélia Steiner as its fragile guarantee), and determined to prevent the disappearance of this trauma in general, and the Holocaust in particular, from public debate. The performative value of a prominent *œuvre* which aligns itself so closely with a suffering in danger of both repetition and denial ought not to be underestimated.[5]

Before discussing in detail the encounter between Duras's writing and historical trauma, I now propose to sketch the terms of this encounter, by presenting briefly the essential problem posed by the moment of trauma for the linked businesses of remembrance and writing as they are elaborated by Duras. Specifically, the uncertainties of the encounter between writing and the ethical in the realm of historical trauma stem primarily from what has been seen, by Duras and by others, as the radical unavailability for recuperation of the traumatic event. The questions raised in the wake of historical trauma cannot necessarily be answered by writing, whose attempt to do justice to this trauma may always remain deficient; and this writing itself, for all its desire to address the traumatic event, finds itself unable to attain a stable status from which to do so. Once again, as discussed in Chapter 2, above: the event is radically singular. It exceeds any available frame of reference, and imposes the work of retrospective reconstruction. We may thus say, as we have seen, that historical trauma represents the event produced within an historical and/or political context. As Duras elaborates it, the traumatic event presents the following features: it constitutes a

---

[4] Duras's approach to the capitalization of 'juif' (as a noun) varies, but on the whole she prefers the lower-case 'j', in a move which may be read as performing her insistence on the figure of the Jew as disruptive of stable identity, as encountered in Chapter 3, above. For a full discussion of Jewishness in Duras's work, see Chapter 6, below.

[5] See also, in this context, Duras's rage at the desecration of Jewish graves at Carpentras, which leads to the expression of a murderous loathing for Le Pen, and to the impassioned placing of contemporary anti-Semitism in explicit relation to the Holocaust. (In 'La Mort dans les yeux', in *ME*, 32–3).

radical singularity; it imposes a unique degree of suffering; it is available for contemplation largely—possibly *only*—through its remains; it is exemplified (insofar as exemplification is possible here, as will be discussed) by the Holocaust; and it confronts those who come after or survive it with the dilemma of impossible but vital representation. The traumatic event must be represented if it is not to be forgotten; yet the trauma that imposes such a burden also renders adequate representation impossible.[6] And yet, since the moment is radically unavailable for understanding as it happens, reconstruction—as in the case of the smaller-scale event of Chapter 2—may have a vital role in the attempted understanding of trauma. As Robert Antelme, Duras's husband until just after the war, argues in the 'Avant-propos' to his account of his experience of the concentration camps, *L'Espèce humaine*:

> Cette disproportion entre l'expérience que nous avions vécue et le récit qu'il était possible d'en faire ne fit que se confirmer par la suite. Nous avions donc bien affaire à l'une de ces réalités qui font dire qu'elles dépassent l'imagination. Il était clair désormais que c'était seulement par le choix, c'est-à-dire encore par l'imagination que nous pouvions essayer d'en dire quelque chose.[7]

The imperative to represent the traumatic event remains intact, despite the paradoxes imposed by such representation; in the face of the alternatives of either forgetfulness or revisionism, essential reconstruction may take place in the painful awareness of its paradoxes.

While the traumatic event necessarily forces much thought that comes after it into the corner of paradox, I hope that the model suggested in this chapter of Duras's writing as patient accompaniment to suffering will bring out her attempt to maintain the paradoxes of understanding after trauma principally as humbled entanglements—humbled not least, however, by the occasional failures of this writing under this burden. And with such thoughts in mind, it is

---

[6] As Sidra Dekoven Ezrahi puts it, 'Even the most vivid presentation of concrete detail and specificity, the most palpable reconstruction of Holocaust reality, is blunted by the fact that there is no analogue in human experience' (Ezrahi, *By Words Alone: The Holocaust in Literature* (London: University of Chicago Press, 1980), 3). In terms which underscore the proximity of thinking in this area to the Durassian understanding of the event, Shoshana Felman writes that 'Testimony cannot be authentic without that crisis, which has to break and to transvaluate previous categories and previous frames of reference' (Shoshana Felman and Dori Laub, *Testimony: Crises of Witnessing in Literature, Psychoanalysis, and History* (London: Routledge, 1992), 54).

[7] Robert Antelme, *L'Espèce humaine* (Paris: Gallimard, 1957; édition revue et corrigée, coll. 'Tel', 1978), 9.

now time to consider some of the strategies employed in and the effects produced by Duras's struggle to confront in writing the problems generated by its encounter with the terrible singularity of historical trauma.

Doubling: Identity

Inevitably, the radical singularity of the traumatic event will be reduced in its representation. No one object, no single name can stand adequately for the horror they would figure. In the face of the inadequacy imposed upon it by such singularity, representation falters. And may, in fact, address the question of singularity negatively, by refusing it, and troping it into its opposite. Duras's use of this technique will here be termed 'doubling': the location of the traumatic event in several places (and, indeed, several traumas) at once, its scattering across a range of sites and moments.[8] While still participating to an inevitable extent in the reduction of the event, this technique also tears this reduction open by repeating it. The Durassian doubling of the event produces a hole within synecdochic representation, as several parts come to stand impossibly for the unavailable whole—and so engages itself in the paradoxes and dilemmas of the attempt to represent the unrepresentable.

In part, this approach means that Duras insistently interlinks different events, different locations—a technique already evident in *Hiroshima mon amour*, suggested again in *Abahn Sabana David*. Here, however, I propose to focus on her presentation of the effects of the trauma by which these locations are marked on identity. In this section, I will explore in the light of this Durassian doubling the tension between the unique and the typical in the identity of those who have survived mass trauma; the multiplication of this fragile identity over a range of different sufferers; and the internalization of this fragility within the shattered identities of Duras's characters of this period.

It is within the field of identity that Duras elaborates most extensively the dilemma presented to exemplarity by historical trauma. For Duras, that which attempts to bear witness to the event must be qualitatively both typical and unique, if it is both to signify, and to

---

[8] The significance of doubling ('réduplication' or 'dédoublement') in Duras's work is also stressed by Kristeva, principally with reference to character. (See 'La Maladie de la douleur', 253–4).

signify the singularity of the disaster. And this dilemma may be played out in a location which is far from abstract: it is lived corporeally by those who have been subjected to the experience of trauma. Exposed to unique suffering, they must nevertheless attain typicality if they are to bear witness to this suffering and to insist on its integration into the human. For the identity of the individual sufferer, the consequence of this dilemma is oscillation between the unique and the typical, as his/her singular suffering must be both preserved, and translated into generality if it is not to be reduced to the status of a local accident. Thus, for the narrator of the 'Journal' of *La Douleur*, the individual identity of her husband, 'Robert L.' is most apparent when he is most deprived of his selfhood. On his return from the camps, he presents the spectacle of what remains of a man, reduced to a scrap—but somehow still entirely present:

C'est à ce sourire que tout à coup je le reconnais, mais de très loin, comme si je le voyais au fond d'un tunnel. C'est un sourire de confusion. Il s'excuse d'en être là, réduit à ce déchet. Et puis le sourire s'évanouit. Et il redevient un inconnu. Mais la connaissance est là, que cet inconnu c'est lui, Robert L., dans sa totalité.

$(D, 69)$[9]

Towards the end of the 'Journal', the narrator tells her friend Ginetta

Que c'était là, pendant son agonie que j'avais le mieux connu cet homme, Robert L., que j'avais perçu pour toujours ce qui le faisait lui, et lui seul, et rien ni personne d'autre au monde.

(84)

And yet, if his survival is to translate into an act of testimony, Robert L. still has somehow to bear the weight of the universal significance of his experience. So, the indefinable quality which distinguishes him in his individuality, 'cette grâce à lui particulière', is nonetheless 'faite de la charge égale du désespoir de tous' (84).

Robert L. is unique precisely when his individuality is most threatened. This structure is most powerfully evoked when the narrator quite explicitly imagines his remains. In a mass grave, all

---

[9] 'Robert L.' may also be read as a textualization of such erosion, abbreviating as it does both the surname of the individual to whom this name refers (Robert Antelme) and his resistance pseudonym, Leroy. (See Adler, *Marguerite Duras*, 529.) Antelme's own reflections on his experiences, including his recovery, may be found in a letter to Dionys Mascolo, published in Mascolo, *Autour d'un effort de mémoire* (Paris: Maurice Nadeau, 1987).

individuality lost in death, he remains unique: 'A travers les squelettes de Buchenwald, le sien' (16). There can be no decision between unique and typical; Robert L. simply is both:

Tout le long de toutes les routes d'Allemagne, il y en a qui sont allongés dans des poses semblables à la sienne. Des milliers, des dizaines de milliers, et lui. Lui qui est à la fois contenu dans les milliers des autres, et détaché pour moi seule des milliers des autres, complètement distinct, seul.

(16)

Representing a horror which must be understood at the level of the universal, and yet doing so on the basis of the irreducible singularity of his suffering, Robert L. embodies the problem posed to exemplarity by historical trauma, the impossible synecdoche of the traumatic event.

There is a real problem here, of course, inasmuch as 'Robert L.' necessarily refers to the historical individual Robert Antelme, whose trauma now finds itself reduced to an instance of a generalized technique, an example amongst others (for all that he exemplifies the problems of exemplarity). Duras's approach has no comprehensive answer to this objection: characteristically, her work is marked by techniques which are as reductive as they are generous. For there is indeed a generosity in this elaboration as well, insisting on Robert L.'s 'grâce', the pathos of his fragile smile, and binding him to an important solidarity—which Antelme, of course, also insistently affirms, as we will see—with other sufferers. It is precisely in order to resist the reduction of this suffering, then, that Duras doubles it; while certain of its effects remain questionable, this cannot quite negate the companionship that this process also suggests.

In *Écrire*, for example, the doubling of the traumatic event to include the deaths of Paulo, Duras's brother, and W. J. Cliffe, the 'jeune aviateur anglais', produces further consideration of the fate of the unique individual in death. Like Robert L., imagined dead in a common grave in Germany, so Paulo, also in a common grave, loses his identity among that of his unidentifiable companions in death—only to have it returned to him by those who mourn:

Il était mort, lui, sans sépulture aucune. Jeté dans une fosse commune par-dessus les derniers corps . . . C'est le sien, son corps à lui, jeté dans la fosse des morts, sans un mot, sans une parole. Sauf celle de la prière de tous les morts.

(*É*, 74–5)

156 WRITING AND HISTORICAL TRAUMA

Remains are indistinct, but mourning is unique. As such, however, it will be doubled: and so the mourning for Duras's 'petit frère' is accompanied by that for W. J. Cliffe. And W. J. Cliffe, in the disaster of his death, aged twenty, is, again, both unique and typical:

> Le jeune mort anglais c'était tout le monde et c'était aussi lui seul. C'était tout le monde et lui. Mais tout le monde ça ne fait pas pleurer.
>
> (76)

For those buried in a marked grave, the anonymity of death is qualified by the distinction of a memorial, which may preserve the dead in their individuality:

> Comment faire se rejoindre le petit enfant mort à six mois dont la tombe est dans le haut de la pelouse et cet autre enfant de vingt ans? Ils sont encore là tous les deux, et leurs noms, et leur âge. Ils sont seuls.
>
> (77)

What remains, however, is not quite individuality: 'Ici, on est très loin de l'identité' (78). Death reduces the unique individual to a typical fate: 'N'importe quelle mort, c'est la mort.' Inasmuch as this typicality takes place in particular cases, however, it remains haunted by individuality: 'Ce n'est pas tout à fait la mort de n'importe qui. Ça reste la mort d'un enfant.' And yet: 'La mort de n'importe qui c'est la mort entière' (78). These insistent textual twists strive to capture the paradoxes of death and mourning, in which a unique loss is made uniquely painful by the dissolution of the loved individual into the indistinction of death. Levelled by death, we are however all reduced to the same singularity: 'C'est un roi aussi: c'est un enfant aussi seul dans la mort qu'un roi dans la même mort' (93). At this pitch of pain, uniqueness and typicality become inextricably interwoven, and the mourner (here, the narrating voice of *Écrire*) switches from the one to the other, unable to lay her grief in either.

Just as Robert L.'s incarnation of the dilemma of exemplarity is doubled by the deaths of *Écrire*, so too is his fragile, residual identity doubled in 1980 into the figures of a further case of historical trauma: the devastation of famine. The doubling of the traumatic event also implies the mutual doubling of the identity of the victims of these events, this doubling marking in each case the attempt to preserve what is left of a specific identity in the face of trauma. In *L'Été 80*, televised pictures of famine victims in Uganda recall other traumas—culminating in that embodied by Robert Antelme:

Certes, ceux-ci sont très éloignés déjà dans le voyage de la faim mais nous les
reconnaissons encore, nous avons l'expérience de cette donnée, nous avons vu le
Vietnam [*sic*], les camps nazis, je l'ai regardée dans ma chambre à Paris pendant
dix-sept jours d'agonie.

(*É80*, 44)

Famine victims are likened explicitly to deportees (*É80*, 45); and,
like the Holocaust, the event that has brought about this revelation
defies conceptualization, and even expression:

Je ne pense rien devant l'Ouganda. Au retour des camps de concentration, de
même, je ne pensais rien. Si je pense quelque chose, j'ignore quoi, je suis incapable
de l'énoncer.

(45–6)

Threatened with abolition by the traumatic event, the unique identity of each sufferer, like the singularity of the event itself, is preserved as ineffable by its multiplication into a metonymy of
alternative sites and sufferers. The generosity of this move lies in its
refusal to allow suffering to be limited, in its global alignment of a
chain of real or potential sufferers, liable to share the burden of a
suffering which is too great to be borne by any single site. And so the
young boy of *L'Été 80*, already enchanting in his sad, dreamy isolation, has this suffering written on his body: 'Il a le corps d'un
Ougandais blanc' (*É80*, 47). From Robert L. via Uganda to the child
on the beach at Trouville, suffering doubles itself across the whole of
humanity.[10] *Yann Andréa Steiner*, in large part a re-working of *L'Été 80*,
actualizes the boy's potential suffering, and turns the chain into a
circle: the child is revealed to be Jewish, and—impossibly, given his
age—remembers his sister's (Aurélia Steiner's?) death at the hands
of a German soldier (*YAS*, 112–14). As Duras's re-writing of earlier
texts offers an intertextual version of the chain of repetition along
which suffering multiplies, we are returned to the trauma of the
Holocaust. The uncertainty of identity *in extremis* is located by Duras
in a number of sites and sufferers, whose identities become a series

[10] *L'Amant* embraces this doubling intimately, including in its chain Duras's son, Jean
Mascolo: 'Il est maigre, tellement, on dirait un Ougandais blanc lui aussi' (*At*, 21). At this
point, the risk of Duras's approach is evident: if, as it were, 'Nous sommes tous des Ougandais
blancs', then the multiplication of this suffering, far from preserving its singularity, may crush
it, reduce it to a mere tic. I am not sure that the presence of this risk necessarily undoes the
generosity which motivates this technique of doubling; but it should certainly serve as a
reminder that no writing strategy can provide an uncomplicated (or even entirely successful)
response to mass suffering.

of mutual echoes. Doubling the event across different sites, Duras identifies a residual humanity in these sites, in the shreds of identity which remain in the face of their virtual abolition. After the traumatic event, identity may become uncertain, as sufferers are hollowed, forced to the limit point of the human, and threatened with indistinction. The Durassian doubling of identity in the wake of trauma exaggerates this indistinction, the better (paradoxically) to insist on and preserve the unique identities which remain in the face of this threat. The technique of doubling is, however, itself double: working to preserve identity from absolute dissolution, it achieves this preservation precisely by passing through the risk of such dissolution. Duras's concern with the problems of identity after the traumatic event is also manifest in her presentation of characters whose identity is fragmented by this trauma, figures who show the phenomena of doublings and multiplications taking place *within* individual identity. Thus, via the mantra 'Reste l'enfant' (*É8o*, 46/9), we are moved from the child on the beach at Trouville towards the figure who, as an accidental survivor of the Holocaust, remains, to pose most acutely the problem of the internal doubling of identity produced by historical trauma: Aurélia Steiner.

   The child who remains after the trauma of the Holocaust, Aurélia Steiner, in the films and prose texts which bear her name, represents the return—with the addition of a more insistent link to the Holocaust—of the Jewish figures of Duras's work of 1969 to 1971, disruptive of spatial and personal identity, and especially Abahn/'le juif', come to 'semer le trouble dans l'unité' (*ASD*, 104). Just as Abahn renders Auschstaadt a haunting atopia, so Aurélia is somehow everywhere at once, and yet still present. (See *YV*, 155.) Her name already presents her as the return of earlier Durassian figures: notably, Steiner, the survivor of unspecified concentration camps from the 1968 play *Un Homme est venu me voir* (a further example of Duras's concern in the late 1960s and early 1970s for historical trauma set in a vague, semi-mythical Europe), but also Stein, from *Détruire dit-elle*—and, of course, Lol V. Stein. (In *Les Yeux verts*, Duras states that Aurélia is born from Lol's exhausted, ruined body: see *YV*, 134).[11] Her appearance (at least what little of it is offered to the reader) locates her in a

<hr>

[11] This notion is strengthened if we recall that what Duras calls Lol's 'corps massacré' (*YV*, 134) is also that of the woman of *L'Amour*, Duras's last prose text before her departure into film, and that Aurélia guarantees Duras's return to writing eight years later, figuring the rebirth of Duras's writing from its former, exhausted self.

further intertextual interstice: with her blue eyes and dark hair, she anticipates *Les Yeux bleus cheveux noirs*; in the phrase which presents these features ('Bleu, les yeux, sous les cheveux noirs' ('ASV', 127), she recalls not so much Lol as Lol's double, Tatiana Karl. An initial approach to Aurélia's identity through the intertext of Duras's corpus already indicates the multiplications of identity she will figure. And she may, of course be inserted into something of a Durassian tradition of fragmented characters: such a dismantling of character identity has, after all, been apparent in Duras's writing for some time before the appearance of Aurélia Steiner. We may, perhaps, locate its beginnings somewhere around the début of Aurélia's predecessor, Lol V. Stein, and its apogee in Lol's tattered aftermath, *L'Amour*. Between these two, the link between this fragmentation and a Jewishness thought of as disruptive of identity has already been made in *Détruire dit-elle* and *Abahn Sabana David*. With Aurélia, however, this tendency steps beyond a more generalized significance, and forms part of the attempt to think the problem of identity after historical trauma.

The triple location of Aurélia's letters already reveals her impossibly multiplied identity. 'Elle est partout Aurélia, elle écrit de partout à la fois' (*YV*, 20). Across her three locations, she remains the same—or almost. Her letters all end with variations on the formula which closes the first, 'Aurélia Steiner Melbourne':

Je m'appelle Aurélia Steiner.

Je vis à Melbourne où mes parents sont professeurs.

J'ai dix-huit ans.

J'écris.

('ASM', 120–1)[12]

'Aurélia Steiner Vancouver' and 'Aurélia Steiner Paris' repeat this formula, with the substitution, in both cases, of 'J'habite' for 'Je vis à', and, in each case, of the respective place name for 'Melbourne'. Impossibly, the same figure writes from different locations at the same time while remaining identical. The height of this impossibility

[12] In a piece from 1991, Duras identifies herself utterly with Aurélia, by repeating this mantra: 'Je m'appelle Marguerite Duras. | J'ai seize ans. | Ma mère est institutrice dans les postes du Mékong en Indochine française. | J'écris' (*ME*, 171). This identification had already been suggested less dramatically in *L'Été 80*, in which Duras blends her voice with Aurélia's: 'Il y a un an, je vous envoyais les lettres d'Aurélia Steiner. Je vous ai écrit ici de Melbourne, de Vancouver, de Paris' (*É80*, 63).

is reached in 'Aurélia Steiner Paris', where, in addition to representing the further doubling of an already doubled identity, Aurélia becomes both eighteen (in her closing formula) and seven years old (in the main section of the text). The temptation to reconcile this discrepancy (by imagining an eighteen-year-old Aurélia remembering herself as a seven-year-old) is outstripped by the sense that the galloping multiplication which attends Aurélia renders such psychological interpretation unsatisfactory. Indeed, Aurélia's identity is raised as impossible in part by the irreconcilability of information supplied in connection with this identity. The attempt to reconcile this information would represent the application of a paradigm which is, precisely, in question.

This uncertain process, in which identity is produced, but only as tenuous, is evident in the gradual identification of the seven-year-old girl of 'Aurélia Steiner Paris' as Aurélia. Her origins are unclear, apparently; the only clue to her identity, when she was abandoned by her mother, fleeing the German police, was an initialled name-tag:

Sauf ce petit rectangle de coton blanc cousu à l'intérieur de ta robe, dit la dame, ce premier jour, nous ne savons rien ni toi ni moi. Sur le rectangle blanc il y avait les lettres A.S. et une date de naissance. Tu as sept ans.

('ASP', 158–9)

Even before the arrival of the initials 'A.S.', the connection to Aurélia Steiner has been made—by the image of the 'rectangle blanc'. After 'Aurélia Steiner Vancouver', and the awful image of the death of Aurélia's father in 'le rectangle blanc de la cour' ('ASV', 140), the image creates an immediate link between the two Aurélias.[13] The suspicion produced by the repetition in miniature of this image is confirmed by the provision of the two initials, strengthened by the statement of the girl's Jewishness ('ASP', 163), and finally borne out by the arrival of the full name 'Aurélia Steiner' (170). And yet, of course, the identity that arrives with this name is anything but full: it is the bewildering repetition of an identity already scattered across a range of sites. The child cannot be 'identified' as Aurélia in

---

[13] This image is an insistent one of the Holocaust for Duras: it is the 'rectangle blanc d'Auschwitz' (*YV*, 111), and, while figuring 'une page aussi, une scène', also refers to *La Nuit*, by Elie Wiesel, which Duras locates as the origin of the image of Aurélia's father, too light to hang (*YV*, 178). The image may also be connected to Antelme's *L'Espèce humaine*, where moonlight turns an open wagon door into 'un rectangle de lumière' (Antelme, 28), and the 'Place d'Appel' forms 'un immense rectangle' (24). On this image, see Pierre Saint-Amand, 'L'Abîme et le secret', in Vircondelet (ed.), *Duras, Dieu et l'écrit*, 219–41 (233).

any meaningful sense, since this name poses in the first place a problem for the understanding of identity. Aurélia Steiner's mother, for
example (also, we recall, called Aurélia Steiner), attempted to keep
her safe by hiding her from the German police; she also died in a
concentration camp giving birth to Aurélia Steiner. And Aurélia
Steiner Paris goes on to claim descent from the heroine of 'Césarée',
telescoping history into a mythological genealogy of suffering:

Ma mère elle était la reine des Juifs, dit l'enfant. Reine de Jérusalem et de la
Samarie.
Puis des Blancs sont venus, ils l'ont emmenée.

(164)

The figure of Aurélia Steiner, and her link to the multiplication of
suffering, imply that, after the trauma of the Holocaust, identity
may have to be thought of as fragile and residual. The exemplification of this shift creates a clear problem: no 'character' can embody
the dispersal of identity, and its relocation in traces of the former
self, without suffering fragmentation as a character. The problem of
identity here rejoins that of exemplarity posed by the Holocaust in
general: after the apparent dismantling of the rules of representation by an event with which they are unable to cope, what can stand
for this event? Aurélia Steiner figures the resulting impossible
synecdoche in the field of identity: she represents the disturbance of
this field by the traumatic event in her existence as paradox. In the
face of the Holocaust, she is 'un oubli, un accident' (*TV*, 160): in the
terrible dilemma of the survivor, it is as an exception that she can
represent the exceptional event that has ruined representation.[14]

It is nevertheless hard not to remain uneasy in the face of this
insistence that the only identity available to those who have survived
traumatic events is one defined by fragility and residuality, as this
plainly risks the further silencing of survivors who may well importantly demand the right to speak from a position uncompromised
by such supposed displacements. Equally, the stress on the unrepre-
sentability of the traumatic event and its resultant doubling may
challenge the right of survivors to a representation felt as an urgent
and essential act of testimony. These worries cannot be dispelled by

[14] On the accidental status of the survivor, see for example Primo Levi: in the 'Afterword'
to *The Truce*, for example, Levi ascribes 'the fact that [he] survived and returned un-
harmed . . . chiefly to good luck' (Primo Levi, *If This Is A Man* and *The Truce*, trans. Stuart
Woolf (London: Sphere, 1987), 398).

any of Duras's ways of responding to historical trauma in her writing, and must remain to question the status of this writing in response to the trauma it addresses. They may in part be answered, however, by the acknowledgement that aspects of Duras's responses, while highly individual, are not necessarily unique. A questioning of the possibility of representation is part of significant works of testimony (for example, Lanzmann's *Shoah*); and Lyotard and Ezrahi have both, in different ways, drawn attention to the survivor's having to speak of universalized destruction from a position of paradox, as 'un oubli, un accident' (see Lyotard, *Le Différend*, 16ff., and Ezrahi, 10). Moreover, Duras's emphasis on the metonymic multiplication of suffering argues not that survivors are uniquely restricted to a fragility of identity, but that we are all, opened by our inclusion in chains of suffering, to rethink our identity on the basis of such fragility, precisely so that the specific suffering of the victims of trauma should not be reduced, limited to something in which we are not all intimately implicated.

Interconnectedness

Having explored Duras's elaboration of the dispersal of identity after the traumatic event, we are now in a position to consider some of the ethical implications of this elaboration. Once identity loses an amount of stability, questions of judgement and responsibility become fraught. The traumatic event, which is not available for judgement in any straightforward sense, is presented by Duras at this time as imposing the mutual entanglement of ethical positions that might wish to keep themselves apart. This implies not that ethical positions are simply equivalent, in a laissez-faire relativism, but that, in the face of unbearable suffering, no stable position may be isolated which does not have to address its potential implication in the positions it opposes. Moreover, Duras is also concerned to include writing in this web of implication. Accordingly, this section will explore Duras's presentation of the mutual implication of opposing ethical and political positions in the face of trauma, and her inclusion of writing in such implication.

If identity after the traumatic event has become either fragmented (Aurélia Steiner) or residual (Robert L.), then the question of responsibility is clearly problematized. For who, exactly, would be the subject of this responsibility? One of Duras's answers to this question may be found in *La Douleur*, where it is argued that, if the Holocaust is not to be reduced to the level of a local accident, we must all bear some responsibility for its crimes:

Si l'on fait un sort allemand à l'horreur nazie, et non pas un sort collectif, on réduira l'homme de Belsen aux dimensions du ressortissant régional. La seule réponse à faire à ce crime est d'en faire un crime de tous. De le partager. De même que l'idée d'égalité, de fraternité. Pour le supporter, pour en tolérer l'idée, partager le crime.

(*D*, 65)

We have here a very particular instance of how Duras's writings of the 1980s and 1990s extend elements of her earlier work into major new contexts. For in this claim, Duras takes the notion of impossible responsibility she had first elaborated in her work on the temporality of the event (as in the case of Chauvin, who both is and is not responsible for the events in which he is caught up) and considers it on the scale of world history. Conventional thinking about responsibility—in which responsibility divorced from agency makes no sense—cannot apply, for Duras, after the traumatic event. The delimitation of implication produced by such conventional responsibility in the face of historical trauma (largely along the lines of national identity, as signalled by Duras's confrontational reference to 'l'idée d'égalité, de fraternité') is simply inadmissible to Duras as a response to the Holocaust, which must, she insists, be understood at the level of our concept of what it means to be human. The consequences of this insistence are important—and, to say the least, problematic; we might first approach them by way of consideration of Duras's relationship to the treatment of this question in Robert Antelme's own account of his experiences of the concentration camps.

In *L'Espèce humaine*, Antelme insists that the truth revealed in the concentration camps is that of the indivisibility of the human race. The torturer's power is a human power; his victim dies as a human being. While the individual may be murdered, his humanity may not be abolished—and so the torturer's aim (to separate himself from his supposedly subhuman victim) is ultimately bound to fail. Duras's relationship to Antelme's thesis of the indivisibility of the human race is to say the least complicated.[15] As we have seen, she

[15] Extended discussions of this relationship may be found in Claire Gorrara, 'Bearing Witness in Robert Antelme's *L'Espèce humaine* and Marguerite Duras's *La Douleur*', *Women in*

too insists that the suffering of the concentration camps must be understood at the level of our humanity; but her inflection of this understanding is rather different from Antelme's.

There is an uncomfortable implication in Antelme's thesis that, since the indivisibility of humanity is derived from the situation of torture, to torture is also in some sense bound up with what it means to be human. And it is this side of Antelme's argument that Duras chooses to privilege during the 1980s.[16] Her consistent argument during this period is that the characteristic features of Nazism must be incorporated into any subsequent notion of the human.[17] What is perhaps most consistent in this argument, however, is its formulation in paradox. What links all members of the human race, for Duras, is the shared tendency to deny this very shared humanity. This tendency can be given expression, therefore, only as a result of what Duras presents as a naïveté, a failure to recognize that one's violent desires affirm precisely that unity which their acting-out would seek to deny: 'C'est parce que les nazis n'ont pas *reconnu* cette horreur en eux qu'ils l'ont commise' (*YV*, 179; original emphasis). Referring in her piece 'Le Rêve heureux du crime' to a dream she claims to have had repeatedly during the War, in which Germany was 'exterminated', Duras asserts that only by admitting the universality of this kind of desire can one understand one's tie to a shared humanity:

French Studies, 5 (October–November 1997), 243–51; Colin Davis, 'Duras, Antelme, and the Ethics of Writing', *Comparative Literature Studies*, 34/2 (1997), 170–83; and Martin Crowley, '"Il n'y a qu'une espèce humaine": Between Duras and Antelme', in Andrew Leak and George Paizis (eds.), *The Holocaust and the Text: Speaking the Unspeakable* (London: Macmillan, 2000), 174–92. I am very grateful to both Claire Gorrara and Colin Davis for the opportunity to read their pieces prior to publication. Davis's piece, which follows a very different line of argument in relation to this material, has been especially helpful in my attempts to clarify my thoughts in this area.

[16] As Davis puts it, Duras 'develops a possibility inherent in Antelme's position, but one which remains in the background of *L'Espèce humaine*' (Davis, 'Duras, Antelme and the Ethics of Writing', 176).

[17] Duras's position at this time thus has much in common with the following, from Bataille's 1947 review of Rousset's *L'Univers concentrationnaire*, 'Réflexions sur le bourreau et la victime': 'Nous ne pouvons être *humains* sans avoir aperçu en nous la possibilité de la souffrance, celle aussi de l'abjection. Mais nous ne sommes pas seulement les victimes possibles des bourreaux: les bourreaux sont nos semblables. Il nous faut encore nous interroger: n'y a-t-il rien dans notre nature qui rende tant d'horreur impossible? et nous devons bien répondre: en effet, rien. Mille obstacles en nous s'y opposent . . . Ce n'est pas impossible néanmoins. Notre possibilité n'est donc pas la seule douleur, elle s'étend à la rage de torturer' (Bataille, 'Réflexions sur le bourreau et la victime', in *Œuvres complètes*, xi (Paris: Gallimard, 1988), 262–7 (266)).

La différence n'est pas dans le rêve ou non, elle est entre ceux qui voient et ceux qui ne voient pas que le monde entier est en chacun des hommes qui le composent et que chacun de ces hommes qui le composent est un criminel virtuel.

(*O*, 284)

Now, it is indeed the case that Duras here suggests that this recognition is necessary in order to prevent a *passage à l'acte*, and that the distinction she is making is to be understood at an ethical, not an ontological level (at the level of action, not being, as it were): 'Comme moi je rêve, eux ils ont agi', she writes of the Nazis (*O*, 284). And yet she also states that 'Je crois à la différence ontologique entre les gens' (*O*, 286), which plainly contradicts both Antelme's fundamental argument and her own supposed assertion here of a universal humanity based on a shared virtual criminality. But it is her determination to foreground the negative aspect of Antelme's thesis—in precisely the kind of paradoxical terms she claims in *Les Yeux verts* to have rejected in this area (see *YV*, 39)—that leads to a major realm of difficulty and dispute.

It has been suggested that Duras's writings on this question constitute the betrayal of Antelme's position; and that, for example, details in the 'Journal' of *La Douleur* of the behaviour of 'Marguerite' towards 'Robert L.' on his return—notably, her flight from him on his reappearance, and, especially, her declaration soon afterwards of her intention to divorce him in order to have a son by 'D.'—may be read as a kind of intra-diegetic allegory of this betrayal.[18] And it certainly seems to be the case that many readers do find this declaration an obstacle to anything other than a hostile attitude towards the narrator of the 'Journal'. But, just as there are other dimensions to the behaviour of this figure—her horror on her husband's return would seem properly to call for readerly sympathy, for example, and her care for him is indisputable—so is the relation between Duras and Antelme at the level of their arguments more complex than is suggested simply by a model of betrayal. Certainly, Duras emphasizes the disturbing implications of Antelme's thesis in a way which,

[18] This reading is suggested by Colin Davis: see Davis, 'Duras, Antelme, and the Ethics of Writing', 169–72. Moreover, it should be noted that, according to Adler, Antelme (and those close to him) experienced Duras's depictions of his suffering very much as a betrayal (or as reductive, as discussed above): Antelme reacted to the publication of the *Sorcières* extract (in 1976) 'avec stupeur', and, had he been consulted, would not have allowed publication of *La Douleur* (he was in fact in hospital at the time, and unable to respond to the situation); his wife, Monique Antelme, refused to acknowledge receipt of the copy of *La Douleur* sent to her, with a dedication, by Duras. (See Adler, *Marguerite Duras*, 528–9).

while occasionally apparent in *L'Espèce humaine*, is not developed by
Antelme in his testimony (although he does in fact explore these
implications elsewhere).[19] And yet these implications must also be
addressed if the full import of this thesis is to be understood. For if
we fail to incorporate what Bataille calls 'la rage de torturer'
(Bataille, 'Réflexions sur le bourreau et la victime', 66) into our
understanding of our humanity, then we allow the supposition of an
essential distinction between ourselves and the torturer—which
denies Antelme's thesis. And so we might read Duras's writings in
this area as forcing us to think through the full significance of this
position—extending its consequences into areas which seem at the
very least to test it to the limit, for example by means of a confrontation (as in 'Albert des Capitales') with the distressing spectacle
of bloodthirsty torture in the name of the Resistance.[20]

While this position emphasizes that the unpleasant aspects of
Duras's attitude are less a betrayal than a necessary development of
Antelme's, it nevertheless risks minimizing the distress produced by
these aspects by putting it to work in the service of our ultimate
enlightenment. For Duras's contributions to this debate are not simply useful or thought-provoking: they are also wilfully provocative,
scandal-hungry, and play to a large degree on the upsetting juxtaposition of violent material with the apparent absence—or even the
apparent reversal—of the ethical frame this material would seem to
demand. 'Albert des Capitales' is a case in point here: articulating
the narrative via free indirect discourse, Duras presents an act of torture which explicitly and deliberately dehumanizes its victim (and
which thus represents precisely the situation of torture as it is configured by Antelme), while flirting with the possibility that the text
might be endorsing this dehumanization (and thus apparently
denying Antelme's thesis) by aligning itself with the consciousness of
the torturer, Thérèse.[21] Of the victim of her torture, Thérèse
appears to state that 'Il est devenu un homme qui n'a plus rien en
commun avec les autres hommes' (*D*, 158). Or is this the text speaking? Or 'just' Thérèse, her position ironically qualified? The use of

[19] For this exploration, see Robert Antelme, 'Vengeance?' (1945), in Antelme, *Textes inédits / Sur* L'Espèce humaine / *Essais et témoignages* (Paris: Gallimard, 1996), 17–24.
[20] I have argued this elsewhere: see Crowley, '"Il n'y a qu'une espèce humaine": Between Duras and Antelme'.
[21] This argument is put forward forcefully by Colin Davis, who gives full details of the relevant passages: see Davis, 'Duras, Antelme, and the Ethics of Writing', 179–81.

free indirect discourse implies simultaneously the possible absence and the possible existence of a critical frame through which this violence might or might not be being mediated; and this intermittent or virtual frame must appear, in the face of the material it may or may not qualify, as at best problematic, and at worst obscenely inadequate and complacent.

Two points must be made here, I feel. First: this is the continuation of a technique Duras has been employing since at least the late 1950s, and which has been traced in the preceding sections of this study, in which an ethical response is simultaneously called forth and suspended by the material in question—and in which, at this stage of Duras's writing, this double move is frequently accomplished by the same textual material, often an unstable narrative frame. We find Duras here, then, operating once again at what I have called the elastic limit of the ethical. And yet: all material is not necessarily amenable to the same treatment, and this reading risks effacing what Duras herself presents as the radical specificity of historical trauma in an undifferentiated Durassian sweep. Which means, secondly, that we must remain uncomfortable here. And must, therefore, do everything possible to refuse this discomfort the productive (and profoundly soothing) status of a reminder, an irritant, or a prod to further reflection. Duras's thinking on the relation between historical trauma and a common humanity is both important—in its insistence on confronting questions which put this relation most sorely to the test—and problematic (as this confrontation appears at times—see, especially, 'Le Rêve heureux du crime'—to trade on the scandalous *frisson* it may produce). As 'Albert des Capitales' leaves the question of its approval or otherwise of Thérèse's actions suspended in the undecidability of free indirect discourse—and as this suspension sits painfully alongside Duras's provocative, absolute, apparently genuinely confessional, but also (with an ear for Flaubert) highly literary identification of herself with Thérèse ('Thérèse, c'est moi' (*D*, 138))—so must the question of Duras's position in this area remain, finally, undecided.[22] She asserts a fundamental, shared humanity—but establishes this bond on the basis of its denial; she thereby (albeit paradoxically) affirms Antelme's denial of ontological distinctions amongst members of the human

[22] On the resemblance between Thérèse and the behaviour of Duras around the time of the Liberation, see Adler, *Marguerite Duras*, 201, 214.

race—but affirms also her belief in just such distinctions; she narrates the imposition of these distinctions with a technique indicating
an apparent lack of criticism—which also constitutes, precisely, the
possibility of just such criticism. But note: once again, this openness
is not, in Duras, to be valorized (as the space of a liberal interpretative plurality, or a challenge to carry the debate on, or even as a cyn-
ical or self-indulgent avoidance of the real demands of this debate):
it is an awkward, gaping vacancy, edged about with dilemmas and
real dissatisfaction.

The urge to condemn Duras here is strong: it is not (nor should it
be) easy to encounter this kind of material presented in an apparently indulgent manner. But this appearance is only one half of
Duras's approach, which also suggests the possibility of a critical
position—and so, in fact, demonstrates the painful pull of two possible responses to the kind of violence in question, namely indulgence or resistance. Again, we must not read this as a helpful
dramatization: for its value derives precisely from its genuine collapses, the fact that it may, actually, at times slip into indulging this
violence. But we should, at least, attempt to address its full awkwardness. It may be that the indulgence Duras suggests as one available response to the temptations of violence is held to be too
dangerous to be given house room in these discussions; if this is so,
then Duras's contributions—partly in their insufficiencies, which
means that this is not simply thinkable as their achievement—
would at least have the value of insisting that this denial confront
the scale of its own difficulty.

In *L'Amant*, these complexities produce a potentially scandalous
refusal to condemn collaborators, again on the grounds of the
equivalence between apparently opposing positions. Hosts of a literary salon, the Fernandez are also collaborators. They are remembered, however, for their personal charm, which is explicitly
presented as transcending even historical trauma. The grace of
Betty Fernandez is perfect, untainted, unforgettable (*At*, 82–3);
equally, the laughter of Ramon Fernandez reduces the oppositions
of the war to a humorous equivalence:

Durant le temps de ce rire la plaisanterie devenait la guerre elle-même ainsi que
toute souffrance obligée qui découlait d'elle, la Résistance comme la Collaboration, la faim comme le froid, le martyr comme l'infamie.

(85)

And the autobiographical narrator of *L'Amant* adopts this equivalence, but in the mode of scandal rather than humour:

Collaborateurs, les Fernandez. Et moi, deux ans après la guerre, membre du P.C.F.
L'équivalence est absolue, définitive.

(85)

This scandalous equation functions in part, of course, to produce
Duras's writing as outrageous, as exceeding the ethical demands of
the situation evoked, which both feeds off and furthers the greater
sense of portentousness enjoyed by Duras's writing of this period.
And this scandal clearly suggests, once again, the dangers of Duras's
approach to the ethical questions she addresses. One can hardly be
comfortable with the implication that there is no difference between
members of the Resistance and collaborators, or with the notion
that a torturer's denial of his victim's humanity in fact affirms this
humanity as shared. And to the extent that such suggestions produce Duras's writing as simply scandalous, sustaining the increased
grandeur it attains after 1979, we should certainly, as I have suggested above, be critical. But—and this is the real difficulty—this
scandal is not the whole story. A critical attitude will also tell us that
the extremities of war produce ethical dilemmas in which questions
of right and wrong, ends and means, are not simply distributed
according to moralizing polarizations, and in which the emotional
investments of those caught up in the traumatic events are, as Duras
had already suggested in *Hiroshima mon amour*, contradictory, shameful, scandalous. People sleep with their enemies, and not always in
order to trick them. People torture in the name of justice, and not
always without pleasure. While we should be rightly sceptical of the
self-serving aura of scandal that may attach to such scenes in
Duras's writing, then, we should also recognize that their frequent
equation of apparent moral opposites represents, very straightforwardly, a frank response to the realities of this sort of extreme
experience, in which the ethical is every day lived at its very limit.

Duras is not, I believe, claiming that it is a matter of indifference
whether one join the Resistance or the Gestapo. She is, however,
indicating that, in the situation which makes such a choice necessary, even those opposing the attempt to divide and decimate
'l'espèce humaine' will find themselves confronted by circumstances demanding actions which may be all but indefensible. It
is the dangerous and unstable line of this 'all but' that Duras is,

characteristically, interested in exploring. And it is indeed true that she is more interested in this line as the fragile edge between the overwhelming experience of historical trauma and the ethical categories which grasp after this experience than as a solid bulwark against moral collapse. Moreover, it is also true that her writing may at times encounter this line by slipping over it, into the indefensible. The problem here is partly that Duras's writing needs to be criticized for apparently exploiting these slips to further its own rhetorical drama—while also praised for indicating the dangers of such moments with a degree of lucidity and integrity. Perhaps, as I have suggested, it is just not possible to resolve this; perhaps we simply have to accept that both aspects are, indeed, part of Duras's practice in this area, and that one may not be subsumed into the other. And might this not, in the end, constitute a valuable—precisely because it is also at times rather shabby—example in our attempts to negotiate the demands of overwhelming experience, this line at the edge of the ethical? For an honest exploration of the demanding situations Duras presents can hardly avoid the conclusion that, as she in part implies, this vital margin often represents, painfully, a line drawn in the sand—which means not that it makes no difference where it is drawn, but that it must each time be drawn anew, and uncertainly.

Literature, and writing in general, are far from immune from such implication. The Fernandez's literary salon plays host to authors known as collaborators, such as Drieu la Rochelle and (possibly) Brasillach (*At*, 84), dirtying the hands of literature in the mess of politics. The implication of this memory is that writing may, perhaps, be mixed in with the complications of conflictual positions; demonstrating this implication, Duras's writing of this period becomes the locus of an exploration of interconnectedness which drags the reader into its ethically valorized tangle.

The trope which facilitates this exploration is, generally, that identified above in the technique of doubling, namely rampant metonymy. Referents are packed together to create semantically dense chains which reveal the unpicking they invite as trivial and reductive, and must rather be read symbolically, as gestures of interconnection, picking up the embrace of interconnectedness which first appears in Duras's work in *Le Camion*, as seen above. Emblematic in this respect is Duras's description of Aurélia Steiner in *Les Yeux verts*: 'Elle est le chat lépreux aussi, Aurélia Steiner. Ce juif, ce chat juif' (*YV*, 155). Metaphor (Aurélia *is* the cat) slips into metonymy, as strands here lead to 'Aurélia Steiner Paris' (with its cat), Jewishness, and Duras's own *œuvre*, via *Le Vice-Consul*, in which leprosy is so prominent. Gradually, building up chains of interconnection across intertextual repetition, Duras will implicate her own writing self in these chains. In *L'Été 80*, the events of the Solidarity strike in Gdansk are felt passionately by the author—and so linked to the figure of the child on the beach (who, we may recall, is also linked to the Ugandan famine and thence to Robert L.): 'Gdansk me fait trembler comme me fait trembler l'enfant' (*É80*, 55). This personal entanglement is then intensified, as the only equivalent to Gdansk becomes the writing self's love for the shadowy 'vous' who haunts the text:

Je crois qu'il n'y a rien de plus pessimiste que Gdansk. Sauf cet amour que j'ai pour vous et dont je sais qu'il est illusoire et qu'à travers l'apparente préférence que je vous porte je n'aime rien que l'amour même non démantelé par le choix de notre histoire.

(88)

Duras's exhausting, winding syntax draws the reader towards the dizzy claustrophobia of interconnectedness, relentlessly. From 'Gdansk-l'enfant' and 'Gdansk-vous' there is produced a triangle: 'Gdansk est mortelle, elle est l'enfant aux yeux gris, elle est ça. Comme vous, ça' (89). And this accumulation of interlinked building-blocks ultimately culminates in the imbrication of the writing self, her passion, and Gdansk: 'Sur Gdansk j'ai posé ma bouche et je vous ai embrassé' (97).

In *Yann Andréa Steiner*, this imbrication is doubly exacerbated: the passion of the writing voice for the 'vous' (here explicitly Yann Andréa) is more dramatically present, and this passion (as the title—with its reference to Aurélia Steiner—implies) is interwoven both with Duras's *œuvre* and with the added element of the Holocaust. Asked 'Où est-on', the writing voice replies, 'A S. Thala', inscribing the book's passion in the mythical location of Lol's trauma as it crumbles into *L'Amour* (*YAS*, 70). This mythical location is then replaced by 'le port de Gdansk. Devenu pour le monde entier la souffrance des peuples envahis parce que pauvres et seuls' (103), shifting the intertext to *L'Été 80*. Next, the Jewishness of both the child on the beach and his 'monitrice', revealed in this text, provides the final additional dimension to the scenario of *L'Été 80*, and facilitates the extension of the earlier text's mantra of interconnectedness, to take in the writing self, her passion, Gdansk, Jewishness and (by intertextual repetition) her own writing: 'Sur Gdansk j'ai posé ma bouche et j'ai embrassé cet enfant juif' (129). Metonymy and metaphor are here mutually impacted, as the chaining together of disparate elements is sustained by a rhetorical force which binds them so densely that they may no longer easily be separated out. And this density defies understanding, generating a sense of inextricable interconnectedness within the time of the reading of this extraordinary, breathtaking phrase. The dramatic leaps of the Surrealist metaphor are here rendered moving, by the traumatic content of certain of the enchained terms; and the almost desperate perplexity of the reader who has travelled from 'Gdansk' to 'cet enfant juif' on the force of the writing self's passion runs after the awful force of the traumatic events in question.

This apparently endless accretion of interconnected elements becomes by turns dazzling and dazing; but we should not be blinded to its force. On the one hand, the blockages of understanding it produces gesture towards the incomprehension produced by historical trauma, as its interconnections suggest the mutual implication of positions in the wake of such trauma. On the other hand, they refuse simply to instantiate such incomprehension, insisting on the passionate but uncertain communication of the affective importance of the connected elements. Having already explored the tensions of the attempted textual enactment of incomprehension (in part in relation to historical trauma) in her work of 1969 to 1971, Duras now, impelled by her insistence on the importance of this material, moves beyond this problematic to address in a more overtly emotional writing the interwoven details scattered on the edge between attempted understanding and incomprehension in the wake of the traumatic event. Reading and writing must now themselves be seen, quite simply but very uncertainly, as involved in the difficult attempt to address the ethical implications of the traumatic event; and it is to Duras's presentation of the status of writing after this event that we will now turn.

Writing

In 1963, asked if any particular circumstances decided her to write, Duras cites 'la guerre . . . l'ennui de la guerre'. But, she declares, 'cet événement terrifiant ne m'a jamais servi dans aucun livre'.[23] This denial is almost repeated in her 1980 account of the combined shock of Hiroshima and the discovery of the camps, in which she denies ever having written on the war, 'sauf quelques pages' (*YV*, 41). Writing on the war has become an uncertain business: has it taken place or not? What are these 'quelques pages', this odd remainder? (Answer (perhaps): *La Douleur*). Having seen Duras's implication of writing in the metonymic chains of ethical interconnectedness which form part of her response to historical trauma, we are now in a position to investigate the consequences for writing of this implication. Most notably in Duras's work, these consequences are apparent in the questions about the nature of writing as testimony raised by the problematic status of *La Douleur*.

In the prefatory remarks positioned immediately before the 'Journal' in *La Douleur*, the pages which are to follow are presented as the quasi-mystical irruption of the past into the present. Found in the 'armoires bleues' in Duras's house at Neauphle-le-Château, the text has survived regular winter floods to return unbidden—and unremembered—from the past:

Je n'ai aucun souvenir de l'avoir écrit . . .
Quand l'aurais-je écrit, en quelle année, à quelles heures du jour, dans quelle maison?
Je ne sais plus rien.

(*D*, 12)

Vital to the author ('*La douleur* est une des choses les plus importantes de ma vie'), the text is presented as thoroughly excessive, even beyond writing: 'Le mot "écrit" ne conviendrait pas' (12). The text is being positioned as a mystical object, far greater than the sum of its parts. The lack of certainty over its composition problematizes its

---

[23] Pierre Hahn, 'Les Hommes de 1963 ne sont pas assez féminins', 34. In the 'Avant-propos' to *Outside*, Duras nevertheless states that she wrote *during* the war, for material reasons: 'Il y a aussi tous les romans que nous avons fait pendant la guerre, une bande de jeunes, jamais retrouvés non plus, écrit pour acheter du beurre au marché noir, des cigarettes, du café' (*O*, 12). Curiously, Duras does not mention here (in 1981) that she had, two years earlier, found a novel written during the war, as stated in an interview in *Libération* in 1979: 'Hier, j'ai retrouvé un roman. Peut-être le premier que j'ai fait. Pendant la guerre. Et je croyais l'avoir brûlé. Il n'est pas brûlé. Il est là. Il est de 44' (Patrick Duval, 'En effeuillant la marguerite', *Libération*, 22 mars 1979, 15–16 (16)). This 1944 text, found in 1979, cannot be *La Douleur*, since a section of this was published in 1976 (as will be discussed below); and it can hardly represent her first novel, since this (*Les Impudents*) was of course published in 1943. (Although, if Duras is mistaken about the date, it may perhaps represent *Les Impudents*, particularly as the text was out of print at this time). The most one can conclude, it would seem, from this puzzling claim is that Duras's return to writing in 1979 is accompanied by more than one miraculous find.

status as authentic autobiography, but its autobiographical qualities point to an authenticity beyond fictionality. Confronted by this relic, and its traumatic recollections, Duras is as it were paralyzed:

> Je me suis trouvée devant un désordre phénoménal de la pensée et du sentiment auquel je n'ai pas osé toucher et au regard de quoi la littérature m'a fait honte.
>
> (12)

All six texts in *La Douleur* are in fact organized around an opposition between the fictional (literature, which may be re-written) and the real (which shame literature, and are presented as ultimately authentic). 'La Douleur' (the 'Journal'), 'Monsieur X. dit ici Pierre Rabier', 'Albert des Capitales' and 'Ter le milicien', which open the volume, comprise the second group; 'L'Ortie brisée' and 'Aurélia Paris' (the text of a slightly revised theatrical version of 'Aurélia Steiner Paris') the first. In addition to the claims to authenticity of the 'Journal', 'Monsieur X.' is called 'une histoire vraie jusque dans le détail' (90); such insistence culminates in the portentous declaration which precedes 'Albert des Capitales' and 'Ter le milicien': 'Apprenez à lire: ce sont des textes sacrés' (138). In contrast to such writing of suffering and passion beyond reason, literature becomes trivial: 'L'Ortie brisée', declared as 'inventé', bears the dismissive tag, 'C'est de la littérature' (194).

Beyond literature, the 'sacred' texts of *La Douleur* impart a traumatic truth; in the case of the 'Journal', this truth is supposedly manifest in the text's very existence. The devastating memories offered by the piece are allegedly doubled in its continued presence; like Aurélia Steiner, it bears witness to disaster by its accidental escape, while also, in its belated arrival, enacting what has been described as the necessary temporality of testimony.[24] The status of the 'Journal' as the authentic irruption of the past into the present,

---

[24] As Hill puts it, 'The diary not only tells of catastrophe, but, by its miraculous and unexpected survival, also alludes to the possibility of catastrophe which it has itself just narrowly escaped' (Hill, *Marguerite Duras: Apocalyptic Desires*, 125). This status, which recalls as a possible prototype the diary of Anne Frank, as well as texts and images found buried in concentration camps, appears also to have specifically Jewish connotations for Duras; she will return to it, for example, with the biblical 'livre brûlé' of *La Pluie d'été*. On the belated temporality of testimony, see Dori Laub, who argues (in terms which strongly recall Duras) that the traumatic event itself so overwhelms all available frames of reference that it cannot truly be witnessed as it takes place, and that testimony is therefore necessarily articulated around an 'historical gap' (which in no way invalidates the testimony in question). (See Felman and Laub, *Testimony*, 84.)

as claimed in the text's preface, is, however, complicated (if not compromised) by the numerous alterations which have in fact been
made to it. In contrast to the declaration that the diary has not been
touched ('auquel je n'ai pas osé toucher' (12)), the versions of the text
which precede its 1985 publication reveal it as having undergone
considerable rewriting. In 1981, for example, *Outside* offers a text
entitled 'Pas mort en déportation' (*O*, 288–92), which had already
been published in the review *Sorcières* in 1976 (and which represents,
in all probability, the 'quelques pages' referred to in *Les Yeux verts*). At
this point, the text is already presented as excessive, as 'Sans qualification', and as the forgotten relic of the past: 'Je l'ai retrouvé dans un
cahier, une sorte de journal intemporel que je tenais pendant la fin
de la guerre' (*O*, 288). It corresponds to the closing pages of the
'Journal' as published in *La Douleur* (*D*, 71–85), with considerable
omissions and alterations. Large amounts of the text as published in
1985 are absent from the version published in 1981; these absences
are mostly marked in the earlier text by 'points de suspension'.
(Although more than three pages of text (*D*, 81–5) are omitted with
no such marking.) Confusingly, the 1981 text occasionally includes
omission marks where none of the later text has been omitted, raising the possibility that the later text has also excluded sections, but
without marking this as its earlier incarnation had done. In any
case, the considerable and detailed alterations between the two versions (of which the most minute example is the increase in Robert
L.'s height from 'un mètre soixante-dix-sept' in 1981 (*O*, 289) to 'un
mètre soixante-dix-huit' in 1985 (*D*, 72)) must cast significant doubt
on Duras's claim in both cases that the text is presented as found.[25]

For Duras, the text's authenticity is also guaranteed by her signature: 'Je reconnais mon écriture' (*D*, 12). (A claim which may now
be tested, given the presence of the original 'cahiers', containing
this handwriting, in the Duras archive at L'IMEC in Paris). And yet
the marks of style in the text, its particular signature, produce a less
than watertight guarantee of its status. When the 'Journal' switches
from apparently contemporaneous, dated entries (although Duras

---

[25] On the basis of analysis of the original notebooks in the Duras archive at L'IMEC in
Paris, Laure Adler states that a first version of the text was written in 1945, with subsequent
rewrites taking place in 1975 and prior to its publication as the 'Journal' of *La Douleur* (Adler,
Marguerite Duras, 187). Some sense of the detailed changes made to the original version may
be gained from the volume *Romans, Cinéma, Théâtre*, which reproduces a small amount of text:
see *RCT*, 141. (The passage in question corresponds to *D*, 42).

acknowledges that these could not have been written at the time
they describe (12)), the style becomes noticeably that of the later
Duras, featuring a degree of staccato parataxis not generally evident in Duras's other writing of the 1940s: 'Les autres sont restés sur
la plage. Ils jouent au ballon. Sauf Robert L. Pas encore' (82). The
movements of the text's style, its internal signature, may indicate
not so much its authenticity as its problematic status somewhere
between the authentic and the fictional.[26]

Elsewhere, Duras acknowledges the changes made to the text of
the 'Journal' prior to its publication. In Marie-Pierre Fernandez's
Travailler avec Duras (a 'Journal de la création par Marguerite Duras
de *La Musica deuxième*' in 1985), she declares this process of rewriting—and even imbues it with some of the excessive qualities associated with the notion of the text as irruption:

> En ce moment, je viens de finir—ça me rend malade, d'ailleurs—, j'ai écrit pen-
> dant trois mois, j'ai ré-écrit, j'ai remis sur pied, le journal de la guerre, le journal de
> l'attente d'un déporté politique, Robert L.[27]

Even while admitting to its contingency (by declaring her alterations), Duras preserves the text in its excessive status (by stressing
its damaging effects). Similarly, in another interview from 1985,
published in the 1987 version of *Les Yeux verts*, she insists that any
alterations have been minor ('Je n'ai presque pas corrigé'), and that,
in any case, the overwhelming power of the text remains substan-
tively unaltered: 'Je n'ai pas triché sur la douleur' (*YV*, 238). And
indeed, one might argue that the problems produced by the rewriting of what is presented as beyond writing constitute, in fact, its particular brand of authenticity. For what the 'Journal' presents,
according to this argument, is less a mystical irruption or a sacred
relic than the problem of the possibility of authenticity in the field of
remembered trauma. The text poses the problem of the aftermath
of the traumatic event less by incarnating this aftermath physically
than by elaborating, in its contradictory status, the ambiguities

---

[26] In addition to these indications of the text's uncertain composition, we should note the
alteration discussed by Leslie Hill: the change from 'R.A.' to 'Robert L.', and the occasional
shift between the earlier and the later text from first to third person (*Marguerite Duras: Apocalyptic Desires*, 125).

[27] Duras, in Marie-Pierre Fernandez, *Travailler avec Duras* (Paris: Gallimard, 1986), 157.
Elsewhere in 1985, Duras states that the alterations made to the journal return it to its *original*
status: 'Ici c'est la version totale, celle des cahiers de la guerre. L'autre version était très
courte, trois pages, celle parue dans *Sorcières*' (*YV*, 236).

imposed in the wake of trauma. Slipping between involuntary memory and retrospective reconstruction, the undecidable text suggests the difficulties of remembrance after the event; drawing together evidence (the text as a fragment of the past) and recollection (the text as a version of the past), it raises—but is a long way from resolving—the problem of testimony in relation to writing.[28]

It would be particularly generous, however, to decide that *La Douleur* represents simply a thoroughgoing interrogation of the possibility of exemplary testimony. On the one hand, the text plainly does present itself as just such an interrogation (including markers such as '(*sic*)' (*D*, 22) and a footnote (26) to mime an historical veracity), remaining after the event in such a form that its status (and thus its ability to represent the event) is radically uncertain. *La Douleur* does raise the question of testimony both performatively and constatively, and its inconsistencies (notably, the disparity between the claim that it is presented as found and the reality of its re-writing) are a part of this questioning. On the other hand, however, the text's relation to this uncertain status is somewhat duplicitous. Those in the know (notably attentive readers of *Sorcières* and/or *Outside*) will spot the text's claim to unedited testimonial authenticity as spurious; but it would be perfectly possible to read the text and to be deceived into thinking that it is what it says. This

---

[28] Such inconsistencies raise a set of ethical questions relating to the status of the text as historical document. Notably, both Jeanine Parisier Plottel and Lawrence D. Kritzman have argued that the gap between the time of the events narrated and the time of writing compromises the authenticity of Duras's text and, more seriously, allows her to produce historically inaccurate and even offensive implications. (See Plottel, 'Memory, Fiction, History', *L'Esprit Créateur*, 30/1 (Spring 1990), 47–55, and Kritzman, 'Duras' War', *L'Esprit Créateur*, 33/1 (Spring 1993), 63–73.) Duras was subject to similar criticism at the time of the publication of *La Douleur* from those involved in some of the events she describes: see Adler, *Marguerite Duras*, 530. It should be said, however, that the specific charge made by Plottel and Kritzman that Duras juxtaposes de Gaulle and the Holocaust in order to imply, disgracefully, that de Gaulle was somehow complicit in the crimes of the camps, is not borne out by attentive reading of the passage in question, which, while far from kind to de Gaulle, in fact accuses him quite precisely of a disturbing alienation from the suffering of some of the people whose fate he would champion. (See *D*, 60: 'Maintenant que de Gaulle est au pouvoir . . . C'est là qu'on les pleure'). The instabilities of Duras's testimony need not lead one to see offensive insinuation in a cry of protest over the elision of grief. Moreover, the notion that such criticism of de Gaulle could hardly have been written immediately around the Liberation, which Plottel uses to argue that the 'Journal' was written years later (Plottel, 52), is contested not only by Duras's statement in December 1985 that the phrases in question were present *telles quelles* in the 1945 version of the text, but also by the presence of similar criticism of the effacement of grief over Jewish suffering in Sartre's *Réflexions sur la question juive*, itself written in 1944 and published in 1954.

deception may, it is true, be turned into a point about the possibility of testimony *per se*, in which the trickery of *La Douleur* asks questions of the limits of acceptable artistry within testimonial literature; but this argument (which introduces a rather airless kind of eternal regress familiar from countless other instances of twentieth-century art, in which any objection to the object is immediately recuperated within the object's goal of provocation) draws no distinction between deception and problematization, content with its dose of scandal. But in the case of testimonial literature, is it really enough to claim that a text which deceives many readers into thinking it possesses one particular kind of authenticity (although it may continue to be authentic in other ways) already constitutes a valuable interrogation of the possibility of authentic testimony, without it needing to do anything more than simply deceive in order to deserve this accolade?

We do not need to recuperate the occasional descents of *La Douleur* into misleading self-aggrandizement by making them its supposed virtue in order to recognize its many important features. The portrait of Robert L.'s suffering and eventual return to some kind of health is memorable in the extreme, combining a stark challenge to our understanding of the limits of the human with the virtuoso tracing of the emotions of the narrator. The interconnectedness of ethical positions after the extremity of trauma, and the impossibility of dismissing the violence which creates such trauma from any notion of 'l'espèce humaine', are dramatized to genuinely extraordinary effect. And the question of testimony is raised and addressed with some passion and delicacy, especially in the suggestion of a possible, partial doubling in Paris of Robert L.'s experiences elsewhere, which bears witness to these experiences not by representing them, but by marking their absence in the narrator's distress. And these do not exhaust the text's many achievements. It is a remarkable text indeed which, as we have seen, manages to present such suffering so carefully, while addressing with similar passion the compulsion to violence also born of the very situation that has caused this pain. *La Douleur* offers an unflinching gaze on the appalling demands of war at its margins, and insists on presenting a considerable range of resulting difficulties. To convert the occasional deception which accompanies this presentation into a useful point (an interrogation of the possibility of writing about this kind of material) is, in effect, to neutralize

precisely the kind of difficulty in question. As I argued above in relation to Duras's position on violence as part of a shared humanity, if
La Douleur does represent an important and awkward inquiry into
the possibility of writing about the kinds of suffering it evokes so
movingly, then it does so in part—and this may not be counted in
any way to its credit—on the basis of its irrecuperable, self-serving
lapses; and on condition, therefore, that we accept these extravagant moments as deserving a deal of criticism, as part of a determination to read all of *La Douleur* with the attention and passion of
which, in its best moments, it provides such an important example.

Doubling, Impossibility, Despair

The reciprocity implied in *La Douleur* between war-time Paris and
the concentration camps recalls the technique I have here been calling 'doubling', which may perhaps serve as a focus for the various
strategies offered in Duras's writing as responses to the traumatic
event, and which have been explored in this chapter. For it touches
on: the status of the individual, whose suffering must become both
unique and typical in order that its significance should not be lost;
and thence the question of identity, in which it responds to the
dilemma of what it means to survive the traumatic event by preserving by multiplication fragile identities; and it also leads to the
trope of interconnectedness, in which doubling is multiplied into
great, impacted metonymic chains of ethical implication. Moreover, doubling would appear to have something essential to do with
writing: it is one of Duras's favourite metaphors for the mysterious
process in which she is involved. In 1982, she writes, 'Il n'y a rien de
plus mystérieux que ça, ce dédoublement de l'être humain dans
l'écrit' (*ME*, 24). And in 1993: 'Ce n'est même pas une réflexion,
écrire, c'est une sorte de faculté qu'on a à côté de sa personne, par-
allèlement à elle-même, d'une autre personne qui apparaît et qui
avance, invisible, douée de pensée, de colère, et qui quelquefois, de
son propre fait, est en danger d'en perdre la vie' (*É*, 64–5). If writing
is essentially a doubling, a mysterious accompaniment to the business of life, and if doubling appears in Duras as a frequent response
to historical trauma, perhaps writing may similarly be seen as an
appropriate response to the traumatic event?

Inasmuch as it is a doubling, however, writing may not be known:

Pourquoi on se double de ça, on se double d'une autre vision du réel, pourquoi tout le temps ce cheminement de l'écrit à côté de la vie, et duquel on ne peut absolument pas s'extraire? J'ai beaucoup parlé de ça, et puis . . . Je ne sais pas ce que c'est, d'écrire, je ne sais pas.[29]

If writing is to accompany life, Duras implies, then it must do so negatively, as a shadow which will not quite be known. In relation to the writing of historical trauma, this negative accompaniment may find itself raised to the power of impossibility. Writing of and after the traumatic event will inhabit its own impossibility, as that which cannot (but) take place. The event both must and cannot be represented, and neither of the poles of this paradox will be resolved into the other. For Duras, then, the record of trauma will accompany suffering *impossibly*, as she demonstrates with reference to the film of 'Aurélia Steiner Vancouver', made precisely inasmuch as it was impossible:

Le film est admirable parce qu'il n'essaie même pas de corriger l'impossibilité. Il accompagne cette impossibilité, il marche à son côté.

(*YV*, 135)

This statement offers the image of the aesthetic as a patient accompaniment to trauma, at its side, bound to give support in the full knowledge of the impossibility and inadequacy—and yet the necessity, the generosity—of this gesture. And that this image should not become too comfortable, and hence radically at odds with the uncertainties of Duras's writing in this area, we should give full weight to the suffering implied in the *patience* of writing. We may think, perhaps, of Adorno:

If thinking is to be true—if it is to be true today, in any case—it must also be a thinking against itself. If thought is not measured by the extremity that eludes the concept, it is from the outset in the nature of the musical accompaniment with which the SS liked to drown out the screams of its victims.[30]

In the wake of historical trauma, thought must think against itself, and—somehow—according to the suffering that escapes conceptualization. Which is to say: thought must think (in) its own impossibility, without subsuming this impossibility into a moment in the

---

[29] Interview with Duras by Bernard Pivot on *Apostrophes*.
[30] Theodor W. Adorno, *Negative Dialectics*, trans. E. B. Ashton (London: Routledge and Kegan Paul, 1973; originally published in German in 1966), 365.

kind of dialectical totalization Adorno is contesting here. In the distress of thought after the traumatic event, Duras's writing produces impossible combinations, say between moving attentiveness (such as the delicate, fleeting attention paid to the suffering of 'la petite juive du faubourg du Temple' in *La Douleur* (see *D*, 72)), and conceptual overload (as in those dense, metonymic chains in which the various elements—e.g. Gdansk, Jewishness, childhood, passion, writing, famine, the Holocaust—are mutually impacted in a cry of ethical interconnectedness). There is no thinking through these combinations: they ruin thought, but maintain these ruins in the attempt to respond to the catastrophe, to accompany its awful consequences.

The writing of historical trauma somehow sustains itself in its own impossibility. The book that writes the mourning imposed by the event attempts—impossibly—to evade its inadequate status as any kind of literature:

Ce livre n'est pas un livre.

Ce n'est pas une chanson.

Ni un poème. Ni des pensées.

Mais des larmes, de la douleur, des pleurs, des désespoirs qu'on ne peut pas encore arrêter ni raisonner.

(*É*, 90)

Straining away from itself, telling its own impossibility, writing both effaces itself before grief and just fails to disappear, in order to record this grief:

Ce qu'il faudrait dire là, c'est l'impossibilité de raconter ce lieu, ici, et cette tombe. Mais on peut quand même embrasser le granit gris et pleurer sur toi. W. J. Cliffe.

(95–6)

Recording suffering, writing records its own inadequacy; it may, even, predict its eventual eclipse in favour of the pain it struggles to accompany:

Et puis un jour, il n'y aura rien à écrire, rien à lire, il n'y aura plus que l'intraduisible de la vie de ce mort si jeune, jeune à hurler.

(100)

But this day has not arrived; and writing is bound always to strain, never to break free, to continue, in its painful inadequacy. That writing is here impossible allows it no transcendental relief: there is just—awkward, exhausted—accompaniment.[31] 'Écrire quand même malgré le désespoir. Non: avec le désespoir' (35). Whereas Camus argues in *L'Homme révolté* that a writing which instantiated the despair of which it spoke would be a contradiction in terms, Duras is suggesting that writing can neither *be* despair nor leave this despair behind in its successful communication. Writing remains snagged on the very suffering that provokes its desire for self-effacement. Just as the dilemmas produced by historical trauma cannot be resolved by writing, so writing cannot resolve the question of its own status, and continues to stumble along, unable either to disappear or to achieve an existence that could be adequate.

From *Aurélia Steiner* to *Yann Andréa Steiner* and *Écrire*, Duras's later work brings writing *per se* into an encounter with historical trauma, confident enough to dispense with the problematic of enactment; established enough, indeed, to wonder about the possibility of its own effacement before the suffering it accompanies. Far too confident, at times; for we have also seen how this effacement can be reversed into self-promotion and scandal, mere 'publicité'. Without converting these excesses into a positive success, and while remaining critical of them, it is still possible to see them, along with the more humbled and generous aspects of Duras's work in this area, as part of the slippages of a writing which is bound to accompany the suffering it encounters uncertainly. As has been apparent more than once in this chapter, it is simply too neat to say that Duras is using the discomfort produced by her taste for provocation to intensify our awareness of the issues at stake. But conversely, this discomfort does not simply rule out the extent to which Duras is exploring the

---

[31] While she generally implies an adequation between Duras's writing in this area and the material it confronts which is ultimately, as I am arguing here, untenable in the light of the details of Duras's textual practice, Kristeva's more nuanced stress on the absence of a cathartic impulse in Duras's writing is relevant here: 'il s'agira cette fois de suivre le malheur pas à pas, cliniquement presque, sans jamais le surmonter' ('La Maladie de la douleur', 232). Jacques-Pierre Amette brings out the sublime aspect of this tendency in Duras, linking it to the figure of the edge: 'Duras essaie de donner forme à un dialogue d'après le cataclysme comme si chaque mot devenait une caresse, une manière de toucher un blessé sans l'offenser, d'exprimer un inexprimable, de marcher au bord de l'abîme, comme le font les somnambules' (Amette, 'La Duras qui nous touche', *Le Point*, 9 mars 1996, 63).

important paradoxes of her distressing material. While she at times flaunts the paradoxes of thinking and writing after the traumatic event, in other words, and risks the fetishistic reduction of the suffering she addresses, this is far from the whole story; and the bulk of this story, I would argue, is represented by Duras's striving, which I have attempted to trace in this chapter, to produce a writing which, neither reducing nor ignoring the grave difficulties presented by mass trauma to writing, nevertheless tries, constantly, to walk alongside its suffering. There is here, then, the blossoming of the notion of writing as an uncertain accompaniment to ethical extremity whose origins we have traced in Duras's early work. We have seen in this chapter how the minutest details of Duras's writing in the area of historical trauma work compellingly to explore the limits of their possible response to this trauma: whether it is in the twists of mourning in *Écrire*, or in the lyrical interconnectedness of *L'Été 80* and *Yann Andréa Steiner* ('Sur Gdansk j'ai posé ma bouche et j'ai embrassé cet enfant juif'), this writing has the assurance to force its most delicate machinery into an encounter with suffering, and then to map compassionately the unstable, moving results. Duras insists that the pain of historical trauma remain at the forefront of our awareness, that it be intimately written into each of our lives, and that we recognize that it imposes dilemmas which, at the very limit of our ethical competence, demand a writing which attempts to respond patiently, carefully, and with an occasionally wild generosity— which is to say, awkwardly, walking the line of uncertainty and occasionally slipping off into mere scandal—to 'the extremity that eludes the concept'.

One element of Duras's presentation of historical trauma that has frequently been apparent in the above discussion, but which I have not examined in detail, is its constant connection, in Duras, to erotic passion. Aurélia Steiner, the *monitrice* and the child on the beach, the narrator of 'La Douleur', 'Thérèse', 'la reine des Juifs': these and many other characters find their experiences of historical trauma tightly wound into their erotic experience. The painful line between public and private is here traced by Duras in a way which reminds us that her concern for historical trauma begins with the French actress and the Japanese architect of *Hiroshima mon amour*. Just as Duras progresses from this isolated instance of an interest in the problems of mass suffering, via a relatively brief address to these problems in and around *Abahn Sabana David*, to their full-scale engagement in her later work, so does her interest in passion—consistently at the very heart of her work—move, in this later phase, to acquire new, more large-scale institutional and social dimensions (without Duras's extraordinary talent for the intensities of erotic drama being at all diminished). It is, accordingly, this new inflection of longstanding pre-occupations that we will now explore.

5

WRITING AND SEX

Je vous aime comme il n'est pas possible d'aimer.

Agatha

La différence sexuelle représente une des questions ou la question qui est à penser à notre époque. Chaque époque—selon Heidegger—a une chose à penser. Une seulement. La différence sexuelle est probablement celle de notre temps. La chose de notre temps qui, pensée, nous apporterait le 'salut'?[1]

If Irigaray is right, and the question of sexual difference is *the* question of our time, then Duras is one of our foremost questioners. The whole of her work is shot through with memorable examples of relations between the sexes *in extremis*, which invariably manage to present the gap of sexual difference as both an absolute given and an overwhelming questioning. During the first phase of her writing career, Duras hardly leaves off from presenting the question of heterosexual relations. From young women finding their way in the machinations of the sexual world (Maud, Françou, Suzanne), via slightly older women, mostly married, engaged in reconstructing and/or repeating the lost event as part of a network of heterosexual relationships (the French actress, Anne Desbaresdes, Maria, Lol, even, to an extent, Claire Lannes), to pale figures who announce a valorized loss of identity (Alissa, Sabana, 'elle'), the principal concerns of Duras's writing as traced in Part I, above, have repeatedly been hooked up to her presentation of striking figures of female desire surrounded by men who struggle to gain some purchase on their extraordinary fascination.

From the 1940s to the 1970s, the enigmatic qualities of these women are increasingly to the fore. During Duras's sabbatical from prose writing in the 1970s, this fascination with a femininity construed as primarily mysterious receives a political inflection. In the early 1970s, Duras was relatively close to aspects of the French women's movement: notably, she provided a 'postface' for Erica Lennard's *Les Femmes et les sœurs*, published in 1970 by the recently

[1] Luce Irigaray, *Éthique de la différence sexuelle* (Paris: Minuit, 1984), 13.

established *des femmes*, the publishing house set up by the group 'Psychanalyse et Politique'; and, in April 1971, she signed the 'Manifeste des 343', in which 343 women declared that they had had abortions, and demanded free and legal access to contraception and abortion. This proximity (also expressed in *Les Parleuses* and in Duras's contributions to the review *Sorcières*) allows Duras to respond to the ongoing politicization of sexuality by building on established aspects of her work. For example, she develops the disruptive force within figures such as Anne Desbaresdes and Alissa into Isabelle Granger, who, in *Nathalie Granger* (1973) presents a feminist version of Duras's politics of loss and refusal by burning her electricity bill, *Le Monde*, and her daughter's report cards, and by reducing Gérard Depardieu's washing-machine salesman to tears with her elusive, unfathomable silence and flat refusal of his patter. The silence and enigma by which Duras's women have increasingly been characterized finds a ready home in much French thought on femininity of the 1970s, concerned to celebrate the disruptive power of the feminine 'blanc', or aporia. (It is in 1975, for example, that Cixous, in 'Le Rire de la Méduse', cites Duras as the only living French female exponent of an *écriture féminine*; and in 1977, two psychoanalytically influenced readings of Duras's treatment of femininity—Marcelle Marini's *Territoires du féminin*, and Michèle Montrelay's *L'Ombre et le nom*, both of which were published by the Éditions de Minuit—provide clear evidence of Duras's importance to thinking in these areas.) As seen in Chapter 3, above, however, the politics of refusal which, for Duras, results from the celebration of silence, incomprehension, and so on, is not containable within any political project; and so Duras's relationship with feminism deteriorates from that of a cautious fellow-traveller to outright hostility.[2] The political force of femininity for the Duras of the 1970s derives from what she calls a 'passivité *avertie*', 'une passivité qui est complètement informée d'elle-même' (*P*, 146, original emphasis); and, while Duras does speak exceptionally at this point of such passivity inaugurating 'une politique féminine' (*P*, 146), such a force poses substantial problems for a feminism understood as a positive political project.[3] It is by no

---

[2] A good overall account of Duras's relation to feminism is given in Stephanie Anderson, *Le Discours féminin de Marguerite Duras: Un Désir pervers et ses métamorphoses* (Geneva: Droz, 1995), 7–8.

[3] Verena Andermatt Conley, for example, observes that 'the generalized loss and negativity [of Duras's work] are incompatible with a feminism read as the sociality of a

means clear that the silence and negativity which Duras valorizes can, even in her terms, inaugurate anything other than loss and destruction, a destruction to be replaced 'Par rien' (*ASD*, 40), Duras's dreamed of 'programme politique entièrement négatif' (*P*, 108). While Duras continues to espouse feminist positions during the 1980s, then (stating for example in *La Vie matérielle* that 'Les femmes sont renseignées sur elles-mêmes depuis des siècles par l'homme qui leur apprend qu'elles lui sont inférieures' (*VM*, 44–5)), this espousal is accompanied by the vociferous rejection of the project of feminist politics. 'Je n'ai milité dans aucun mouvement de femmes', writes Duras in *Les Yeux verts*: 'l'idée me fait encore fuir' (*YV*, 183). Already in *Le Camion*, 'le cinéma . . . des femmes' was one of a list of positive interventions rejected in favour of a politics of loss (*C*, 73); in 1981, after a screening of *Le Camion*, Duras declares: 'On me demande si la proposition féministe est pourrie? Je dis oui . . . . Parce que toute proposition militante est infirme' (Lamy and Roy (eds.), *Marguerite Duras à Montréal*, 33).

Something of the political inflection which touched her work of the 1970s remains in Duras's treatment of sexuality in the 1980s, however. As we have seen, when Duras returns to prose writing, her work is marked by a three-fold sense of renewed grandeur: the figure of Duras herself plays an increasingly important role both within her texts and as a commentator on them; writing *per se* is repeatedly trumpeted as an overwhelming, incomparable phenomenon; and questions addressed during the early part of Duras's career are re-examined with an eye to their larger-scale social, historical, and institutional aspects. Accordingly, Duras's work on sexuality during the 1980s moves from the presentation and valorization of fascinating, enigmatic female figures to an investigation of the social structures and discourses in which such figures are caught up (but which they may also exceed). In this chapter, I will be considering three texts—*L'Homme assis dans le couloir, La Maladie de la mort*, and *Les Yeux bleus cheveux noirs*—which, preeminently among Duras's work of this period, examine questions of sexuality in exacting relation to the political discussions which have emerged to form their contemporary context. Partly in the aftermath of the slew of micro-political challenges generated by the explosions of 1968, this

community' (Conley, ' "L'Affaire Grégory" and Duras's Textual Feminism', *L'Esprit Créateur*, 30/1 (Spring 1990), 69–75 (71)).

context offers, for Duras, an ideal contradiction: an insistence on understanding what is for her the incomprehensible wildness of desire in terms of the worldly structures this desire also shatters. (It is for this reason that the question of sexuality, notably plural and ramified in this context of debate and upheaval, is relentlessly understood by Duras in terms of what she sees as the absolute of sexual difference: as will be seen, it is this supposedly sublime gulf that, for Duras, alone guarantees the extremity of genuine desire, and so allows this contradiction to emerge). Engaging as ever with the key debates of her time, Duras thus finds in this area an opportunity to trace dramatically the line of the edge of the ethical, and to draw this line all the more emphatically with the newly available *chiaroscuro* of sexual politics. And this is nowhere clearer than in the three texts I will be discussing here, in which this new, more institutional focus takes in pornography, homosexuality, and the realm of the homosocial, adding a new dimension of resonance to Duras's longstanding fascination with the extremity of passion.[4]

It is important to recognize that these institutional dimensions do not enter Duras's work in the form of critique, however; rather, as I have suggested, they constitute a new, more ambitious way of sketching the edges of ethical extremity. With her return to writing, Duras is determined to avoid reduction to what she generally terms 'procès', namely didacticism or militancy; writing is increasingly conceived of in terms of an intransitivity which carries it beyond polemic—but which remains, as we shall see, awkwardly hooked into the worldly, ethical questions it encounters. *L'Homme assis dans le couloir* presents a violent heterosexual encounter, and a form of writing which may or may not be pornographic: in its encounter with extremity, the status of writing is rendered uncertain, as the instabilities of its operation leave open the question of whether it constitutes the critical staging or the fascinated reproduction of the violence it represents. With *La Maladie de la mort* and *Les Yeux bleus cheveux noirs*, the extremity in question is that of desire, with which Duras's writing has long been concerned, but which is now explored in relation to the larger structures which serve to articulate it. Edging the

---

[4] Establishing an important reading of these three texts—which I will nevertheless have reason to question, as will be seen—Kate Ince links them under the sign of what she calls 'a deconstructive erotics' (Ince, '*L'Amour la mort*: The Eroticism of Marguerite Duras', in Alex Hughes and Kate Ince (eds.), *French Erotic Fiction: Women's Desiring Writing, 1880–1990* (Oxford: Berg, 1996), 147–73 (148)).

irruption of passion about with the oblique intimation of such social dimensions as the realm of the homosocial, Duras's writing strives to avoid collapsing into a merely contingent denunciation or social critique, and so becomes perhaps especially allusive and ambiguous; precisely this ambiguity means that writing cannot, however, quite maintain itself beyond the contingent structures it addresses, and which it may, therefore, reconfirm. Characteristic of this new three-fold Durassian encounter between writing, sexuality, and social institutions is, then, an uncertainty which cuts both ways, keeping each of these texts between two antagonistic readings. What these texts have in common is not only a determination to address questions of sexuality in relation to newly emergent social debates, but also, crucially, a signature twist in the status of Duras's writing as a result of the demands placed on it by the nature of this address. Keen to maintain her writing as radically intransitive while also implicating it in urgent polemic, Duras runs this writing through with a line of uncertainty as to its own status which it never quite resolves—and which, perhaps, constitutes the considerable fascination of these particular texts for readers interested in these questions.

These are texts, then, which present excellent elaborations of the quintessentially Durassian combination of extremity and fragility; and which, opening up and maintaining incompatible interpretations, offer dramatic examples of the line of uncertainty which characterizes this period of her work. In the second half of this chapter, I will discuss the operation of this line in relation to *La Maladie de la mort* and *Les Yeux bleus cheveux noirs*. First, I propose to examine *L'Homme assis dans le couloir*. A woman is beaten, loves it, may be left for dead. The writing which presents this may be offering a critical staging of the pornographic enjoyment of such scenes—or it may not. We are, here, at a new, and possibly more savage stage of the Durassian encounter with ethical extremity; one which will, ultimately, leave us with little more than discomfort.

'Inclassable dans le genre pornographique'

For Duras, everything begins with sex and violence—specifically, with the obscure conjunction of the two which, in *Les Impudents*, she calls 'le pire'. While Duras's subsequent work occasionally evokes the violence of sexuality, the closest Duras comes over the next thirty years to sexualized violence in her major publications is the symbolic repetition by Anne and Chauvin of the *crime passionnel* of *Moderato cantabile*. In 1962, however, a short text called 'L'Homme assis dans le couloir' had appeared in *L'Arc*; eighteen years later, a revised version was published by the Éditions de Minuit. Any reader who had been waiting for Duras to produce a concerted exploration of eroticized violence would have had this wait amply rewarded by either of these texts, but especially by the later, more lithe and lyrical version, which extends its frame of reference to the business of writing about such brutal material, thereby also engaging with resurgent cultural debate about the nature and effects of pornography.

L'Homme assis dans le couloir is a powerful, disturbing text, which has produced some of the most intense and detailed debate in Duras criticism. It (at the very least) flirts with the categories of pornographic representation, and its combination of brutality and obscenity makes it unique in Duras's *œuvre*. The question all readers of this text must sooner or later confront is a classificatory one: Is this text pornographic? In order to address this question, I propose first to present summaries of the events it presents, and of the arguments generally put forward to support the position that, so far from representing an example of pornography, the text in fact elaborates a *critique* of the genre. These arguments invariably rely on the function of the particular writerly devices employed by the text, claiming that these devices in fact displace the pornographic and facilitate its critique. I will present them in some detail, as they are on the whole accurate and persuasive.[5] They are also, I believe, limited. For while attending to the critical disturbance of pornographic clichés operated by the text, they fail to consider the possibility of the re-inscription of the text within the genre it attempts to displace. If it is true that this text offers a trenchant critique of pornography, then one is tempted to ask: so why all the fuss? Can the distress produced by *L'Homme assis dans le couloir* be completely resolved by the claim that, although the text may look like pornography, this resemblance is in fact the result of a critical repetition, and not of collusion? I suspect that our affects are not to be tidied away quite so

[5] For key examples of these arguments, see Cohen, *Women and Discourse in the Fiction of Marguerite Duras*, and Hill, *Marguerite Duras: Apocalyptic Desires*.

comprehensively, and that traces of the pornographic will remain to haunt its supposed critique. The reasons for this suspicion will form the final part of my discussion of this troubling work.

There are, then, two extant versions of *L'Homme assis dans le couloir*. The first was published in the October 1962 edition of *L'Arc*; the second, more familiar version in 1980 by the Éditions de Minuit, having initially been destined for Duras's special edition of *Les Cahiers du cinéma* (itself published in 1980 as *Les Yeux verts*). The most significant alterations made to the text during the intervening process of re-writing consist in the increased significance given to the act of narration in the presentation of the scene, and the sharpened focus which Duras thus brings to the question of the relation between writing and the erotic. The 1980 text is far more sexually explicit than its predecessor (and represents the peak of sexually explicit writing in Duras's work), although it remains within the tradition of Duras's writing by employing substitutions and ellipses to important effect in the presentation of passion (recalling, for example, *Le Marin de Gibraltar* and *Les Petits Chevaux de Tarquinia*), as will be seen below. But in addition to this greater (and shocking) candour (not to say obscenity), a subtler narrative frame is provided for the scenario. In *Les Yeux verts*, Duras presents her alterations in the following order: first, the attention paid to the landscape is extended; secondly, love is factored into the relationship (although, in contrast to Duras's 1980 claim, it is not entirely absent from the first version: indeed, the only words spoken in this version are the man's 'C'était donc ça, t'aimer' ('HACa', 74)); thirdly, a narrating spectator is introduced, framing and complicating the earlier third-person narrative; fourthly, the characters' orgasms are explicitly related. (See *YV*, 60–1.) As a development of the third of these additions, we should also mention the re-casting of much of the narrative in the conditional perfect tense, displacing the narrative into a hypothetical fantasy frame Duras had already begun to explore in *Le Camion*. The changes in the text over the course of its development thus take place in the intersection of writing and the erotic. As the text is rendered far more explicit, its explicitness is simultaneously displaced by the introduction of a set of framing devices. The new version is, thus, both more obscene and more subtle. And it is at this particular crossroads that our discussion of the text may begin.

This is a text which distresses. It narrates obscene and brutal events, and moreover eroticizes these in a manner which (to say the

least) recalls the practices of various forms of pornography. A standard critical approach to the text would be two-fold, comprising
first a summary of the diegesis (to demonstrate the proximity of the
text to a pornographic narrative), and then the re-introduction of
the properly literary qualities of the writing (to recuperate the text
by illustrating its critical—or at least defamiliarizing—*staging* of
such narrative). And indeed, a summary of the events recounted in
the text does present primarily its similarities to models afforded by
both soft- and hard-core pornography. (Such a summary will also
make clear the increase in sexual explicitness in the 1980 text compared with its predecessor). A man sits in a corridor in the shade,
watching a woman lying in the sun. Neither is named. The woman's
dress is torn at the front, 'qui la laisse voir' (*HAC*, 8). She clenches
her legs together. She opens her legs and spreads the lips of her
vagina. She chews the already-torn sleeve of her dress, and cries
out, apparently to the man. He stands over her, and urinates on her,
from her mouth, face, and hair, over her breasts to her vagina. He
rolls her body around with his foot. 'Le corps est docile, fluide, il se
prête à ces traitements tout comme s'il était évanoui' (17). He places
his foot on her chest. He speaks. 'Je t'aime. Toi' (18). He presses
down with his foot. She cries out, and he returns to the shadows of
the corridor. The woman continues to cry out. The woman enters
the corridor, and speaks to the man: 'Je t'aime.' He replies: 'Oui'
(23). She crouches between his legs, removes the clothing which surrounds his genitals, and performs fellatio on him. The man's pleasure begins to turn into agony. She releases his penis, licks his anus,
and returns to performing fellatio. The man cries out. The man
pushes her over onto the floor and penetrates her, while she weeps.
They have both reached orgasm. He tells her that he would like to
stop loving her, and that one day he will kill her. She tells him that
she wants to be beaten, and asks him to do it. She says she would like
to die. He beats her, starting with her face. 'Elle dit que oui, que c'est
ça' (34). His beating intensifies, and moves to her breasts, her body.
'Elle dit que oui, que c'est ça, oui' (34). He accompanies his blows
with insults. Her head flops around on her neck 'comme chose
morte' (35). There are cries, then silence. He lies over her, weeping.
She does not move. She may be asleep.

Such a summary reveals both the awful force of this text, the horror it can provoke, and the relation of this force to models of female
degradation, submission and humiliation to be found across the

gamut of pornographies.[6] *L'Homme assis dans le couloir* does not, however, simply represent a collection of pornographic scenes: it is written in such a way as to render its inclusion in this genre at least problematic.[7] What the above plot summary reveals, then, is *both* the proximity of the action of the text to pornographic models and the reductions which one must perform on the text in order to emphasize and present this proximity as unproblematic. And what must be reduced is the *writing*, the complexities of which are unlike any of the particular tropes characteristic of the properly pornographic.

For much of the writing of *L'Homme assis dans le couloir* seems to be dedicated to the dismantling of the clichés on which a good deal of pornography is founded. The figures involved in the scene are never, for example, allowed the fixity of identity which might be associated with representations more simply called pornographic. The man is anything but in command of the scene, a far cry from the dominant figure one might expect in a straightforwardly pornographic rendering of the events in question: he is devastated by his desire, trembles, is frightened. And he is, crucially, reduced to tears by the explosion of his violence in the final scene. (Which again recalls both the original event and the climax of its symbolic repetition in *Moderato cantabile*). Pornographic cliché, of course, is generally seen as working diligently to shore up masculinity against such devastation; in psychoanalytical terms, this work takes place most clearly in the desire to master and to stabilize the field of vision as it is invested with libidinal significance, and in so doing to deny the threat of castration. Visual pornography may be interpreted as an attempt to guarantee the gaze of the masculine viewer as the metonymic bearer of phallic authority, both by presenting and representing the phallus itself as powerful and valorized, and by

---

[6] Marcelle Marini summarizes Nancy Huston's list (in her *Mosaïque de la pornographie*) of the main features of these models, and adds some of her own: 'Nancy Huston souligne, à propos de *L'Homme assis dans le couloir*, comment il est fidèle aux thèmes classiques de la pornographie: abdication par la femme de son propre corps, jouissance qu'elle y prend, fétichisation du sexe masculin, confusion entre cri de plaisir et cri de douleur. On pourrait ajouter: assimilation de tout désir sexuel, chez la femme, à la prostitution, avec racolage, exhibitionnisme, séduction provocatrice, coups et mort considérés comme punition inévitable (juste? souhaitée?) de l'érotisme féminin, etc.' (Marini, 'La Mort d'une érotique', *Cahiers Renaud-Barrault*, 106 (1983), 37–57 (44)). Anderson states boldly that 'le texte est pornographique, il faut le dire sans réticence' (*Le Discours féminin de Marguerite Duras*, 19).

[7] On this, see Cohen, *Women and Discourse in the Fiction of Marguerite Duras*, 114; and Ince, '*L'Amour la mort*', 152.

presenting those who are defined by their lack of the phallus as eager for its supplementary benefits—even if these benefits are only to be supplied metonymically by the viewer's gaze.[8] Against this attempt to provide reassuring guarantees of masculine visual mastery, *L'Homme assis dans le couloir* presents the inadequacy of the scopic drive before its objects, precisely inasmuch as this drive is structured by desire. As the woman presents her spread sex to the man, her exhibitionism presents a challenge, performing the ability of her 'lack' to exceed his gaze, always to present (to secrete) something *more*, this excess producing an effect of disgust: the woman presents herself to the man so that he might see

plus encore que son sexe écartelé dans sa plus grande possibilité d'être vu, qu'il voie autre chose, aussi, en même temps, autre chose d'elle, qui ressorte d'elle comme une bouche vomissante, viscérale.

(15)

The woman's performance makes a mockery of would-be mastery.[9] Projective (and protective) fantasies of 'lack' blind the man to what he sees—'Il regarde toujours sans voir ce qui se présente à ses yeux' (19)—and condemn his desire always to be exceeded by the object it seeks to master.

To accompany this dismantling of the traditional masculine visual mastery promoted by the vast bulk of pornography, the text also continually stresses the constructed nature of identity, even stretching the process of construction out over several clauses and even tenses to exaggerate still further its uncertainties: 'Elle est devenue laide, elle est devenue ce que laide elle aurait été. Elle est laide' (12). These uncertainties are, moreover, written into the structure of gender identity within the text, most spectacularly by the feminization within the narrative discourse of the man's body. Inasmuch as the man inhabits a sexed body, he inhabits a body whose gendering is uncertain. His anus is 'cette autre féminité' (28), and,

---

[8] Linda Williams offers a definition of hard-core pornography, driven by the desire for visual evidence of female orgasm (the desire that, in the face of what is read as castration, there should still be something to see)—a desire generally displaced into the figure of male ejaculation—as a 'frenzy of the visible'. (See Williams, *Hard Core* (London: Pandora, 1990), 50.)
[9] One may think, at this point, of Bataille's Madame Edwarda (whom Duras discusses in her 1958 piece on Bataille: see *O*, 34–6), who accompanies such a parade (itself a pornographic cliché) with the declaration that she is God, provoking in the narrating male spectator the reaction 'Je suis fou' (Georges Bataille, *Madame Edwarda* (Paris: Jean-Jacques Pauvert, 1956), 41).

together with his genitals, constitutes 'ce qu'il ignore de lui' (29), the hole in a masculinist delusion of wholeness. And, audaciously, this femininity becomes, in the text, the only mark of the phallus which the projections of castration anxiety are supposed to preserve. As has often been noted, the text never names the man's penis; it is only ever referred to pronomially—and, crucially, the pronoun in question is 'elle' (or the accusative 'la'). The phallus is rendered problematic, uncertain, tentative; it must be conjectured out of pronomial opacity by the reader's production of an absent, obscene verbal referent ('la verge'? 'la bite'?). The penis is allowed to exist textually only inasmuch as it is feminized. And it is feminized, crucially, inasmuch as it participates in sexual acts. The penis becomes feminine in the very moment of its becoming phallus (sexual, potent). The man is not simply castrated: rather, he is feminized to the precise extent that he is sexual. This is no simple inversion, no straightforwardly vengeful symbolic chop: rather, it is the dismantling of a phallic masculinity by the teasing out of its anxieties and their complicating re-location within the very figure from which they had been projectively banished.[10]

And in this complication, the function of the narrator, of the 'moi qui regarde' (9), is vital. Perhaps the key alteration made to the text between 1962 and 1980 is the introduction of this third figure, a narrator-cum-observer. Duras stresses the importance of this intervention in *Les Yeux verts*:

Puis j'ai trouvé que les amants n'étaient pas isolés mais vus, sans doute par moi, et que cette vue était, devait être mentionnée, intégrée aux faits.

(*YV*, 60)

The typically Durassian triangular structuration of the field of vision which had surprisingly been absent from the first version of the text is restored in its later rewriting, providing a displacing frame for its aping of the brutalities of pornography. It is the narrator who presents the scene as a fantasy, oscillating between the hypothetical conditional perfect and the banal present, placing in

---

[10] Anderson, however, suggests that this play around the edges of sexual identity fails to disturb the fundamentally sado-masochistic economy of the text, arguing that, ultimately, 'Les valeurs attachées aux signes masculins et féminins ne sont pas mises en cause' (*Le Discours féminin de Marguerite Duras*, 99). While this is not quite accurate—the description of the phallus as a desperate source of overwhelming agony, for example, would appear to constitute precisely such a questioning—Anderson's stress on the possible reinscription of the text in its pornographic context is as necessary as it is rare. I will pursue this argument below.

question the status of the events described; this questioning is, more-over, itself rendered uncertain by the narrator's repeated ignor-ance, recalling that of Chauvin and Jacques Hold. Narratorial observation is generally characterized by indecision, from the open-ing scene—'On ne peut pas dire si ses yeux sont ouverts ou fermés' (*HAC*, 8)—to the indeterminacy of the final paragraph:

Je vois que l'homme pleure couché sur la femme. Je ne vois rien d'elle que l'immo-bilité. Je l'ignore, je ne sais rien, je ne sais pas si elle dort.

(36)

Moreover, even events which are qualified as neither conditional nor indeterminate are rendered (paradoxically) questionable by their introduction with the phrase 'Je vois'. Readers of Duras are, by 1980, well aware that vision, as structured by desire, is no guarantee of secure knowledge; they may recall, for example, that 'Je vois' is also the mantra of Jacques Hold, in whose usage it demonstrates the vain grasping after knowledge in fantasy, and who even, therefore, equates it with 'J'invente'. (See *RLVS*, 56, and Chapter 2, above.) We are denied any confidence in the attribution of responsibility for the telling of this tale; the crucial interposition of the narrator both frames the events and shakes this frame, a self-conscious challenge to the pornographic tendency to naturalization.[11]

For pornography may perhaps in part be characterized by a frequently determined avoidance of the implication of the frame within the images presented. Duras's parade of the frame in the narrative structure of *L'Homme assis dans le couloir* thus functions as an effective commentary on the structural denial in which pornography is caught, in which the constructedness of its material is disavowed, and this knowledge displaced into a faith in the authenticity of the enactment. On the basis of this instability, the brutality of the text, its style of confrontation ('cette pose obscène, bestiale' (12)) and shock-ing tropes (the woman's vagina likened to a 'bouche vomissante, vis-cérale', for example (15)) may be read as a staging of the brutalities of pornography, and its eroticization of these brutalities interpreted as a critical repetition of the incessant pornographic link between the

[11] As Marcelle Marini states, 'Si Marguerite Duras arrive à ébranler quelques fondaments du genre pornographique, c'est à la fois en accentuant son caractère de théâtralisation pour détruire sa prétention à la fidèle mimesis d'une réalité indiscutable, en déroulant les com-mentaires et enfin en jouant sur l'équivoque des relations entre récit et discours' (Marini, 'La Mort d'une érotique', 53).

erotic and the violent. Furthermore, *L'Homme assis dans le couloir* actively works to position a pornographic reading as a violent reading. In order to force the text to resemble conventional pornography in any straightforward way, the reader must strip away the writing, lay bare the action as if it could exist independently of the text as it is. Any reading of *L'Homme assis dans le couloir* as simply a reproduction of pornographic violence is thus forced to reveal *itself* as a violent reading, one which violates the text by dispensing with the intricacies of the frame.[12] And thus, the text may be read as revealing the violent aesthetic disavowals of pornographic reading *per se*, in order to emphasize the distorting violence which is the condition of possibility of the supposed mimesis of the pornographic genre.

And yet, and yet. Genuine doubt must surely remain as to whether this text is in fact so clearly concerned to displace the pornographic. Were matters so straightforward, we could hardly account for the trouble it arouses. We must, surely, wonder whether the line between critique and collusion is so easy to establish; we must, in other words, ask the question so well formulated by Susan Rubin Suleiman: 'To what extent are the high-cultural productions of the avant-gardes of our century in a relation of complicity rather than in a relation of rupture vis-à-vis dominant ideologies?' (Suleiman, 'Transgression and the Avant-garde', 83). What if Duras (Bataille, Robbe-Grillet, Buñuel, 'Pauline Réage', and so on) were, in subverting certain ideologies, reinforcing others? (One need hardly specify that here, pornography is viewed as consonant with, not disruptive of, dominant ideology inasmuch as this is marked as misogynistic.) What if *L'Homme assis dans le couloir* were— here and there, but in ways which could not be erased by reference to framing techniques—pornographic? The kind of summary of the action of *L'Homme assis dans le couloir* provided above, and which represents a key stage in the argument that it is the particularities of the writing of the text that allow it to inhabit critically the realm of the pornographic, strips the text of more than just its narrative and stylistic subtleties. It also reduces the disturbing erotic charge which the writing carries. By laying bare the pornographic content of the work, in order to show the displacing framing of this content by the writing, critics who wish to redeem *L'Homme assis dans le couloir* as

---

[12] For a similar point, made within a careful criticism of this type of reading of literary pornography, see Susan Rubin Suleiman's response to Andrea Dworkin's reading of Bataille's *Histoire de l'œil*, in Suleiman, 'Transgression and the Avant-garde'.

anti-pornographic in fact distort certain key features of this writing—features which render this displacement less secure. Summarizing the text, one says 'urinates', 'anus', 'fellatio': not terms from
the pornographic repertoire. The text itself refers to these terms by
periphrasis and ellipsis. While this is not typically pornographic,
nor, crucially, is it as definitively removed from the pornographic as
the critical completion of circumlocution and lacunæ by latinate
vocabulary might suggest.[13] (We may perhaps recall from
Chapter 1, above, that the ellipsis is a decidedly slippery figure in
Duras). Critical vocabulary may represent a hygienic, neutralized
version of the text's own, more obscene discourse; as is the case, for
example, with the text's marked term for sexual bodily fluid, 'foutre'
(*HAC*, 16). The text is, in fact, producing obscenity and complication in the same places, which refuses their separation into content
and frame, as the example of 'foutre' makes clear. This obscenity is
invariably understood in readings of *L'Homme assis dans le couloir* as
meaning 'sperm' (another polite substitution)—yet it may well in
fact represent the actualization of a virtually invisible meaning
(found in Sade, but generally neglected), referring to the secretions
of the woman's vagina, as they mix with the man's urine: 'Lorsqu'il
[le jet] atteint le sexe il a un regain de force, il s'écrase dans sa
chaleur, se mélange à son foutre, écume, et puis il se tarit' (*HAC*, 16).
There might be here, then, a play on gender identification within
obscenity, as Duras relocates a term overwhelmingly associated
with the masculine to the most intimately feminine site, without
altogether removing the traces of this more habitual sense (as the
conventional critical understanding of the term demonstrates); that
this ambiguity is found in Sade, and also allowed within certain
equivalent terms in some English pornography, should warn us not
firmly to distinguish the text from the pornographic on the basis
of such complication.[14] Translating the text into the mode of

---

[13] Kate Ince notes that ellipsis may in fact be 'typical of erotic writing'—but insists that
here, this figure 'in fact has more marked deconstructive effects' ('*L'Amour la mort*', 149). My
concern, however, is that the recuperation of textual instability in such positive, productive
terms (heightened when Ince talks of the text as offering 'a free circulation of sexual signifiers'
(150)) may obscure the extent to which these same features also operate to keep the text
bound into the very genre supposedly being displaced.

[14] On the other hand, we need not assert unconditionally that Duras's ambiguity is easily
resolved by this kind of context. Stephanie Anderson (unusual among critics in spotting
Duras's possible use of the Sadean (vaginal) sense of 'foutre': see *Le Discours féminin de Marguerite Duras*, 97) insists that this simply *is* the sense of the word, and so misses the point that

summary, in order to separate out diegesis (pornographic) from writing (anti-pornographic), one may, then, efface the pornographic features of this writing. While the general force of the text is towards a general displacement of the pornographic, there are exceptions to this, and to elide these exceptions is to reduce the full force of the text—a force which is the product, ultimately, of its disturbing ambiguity. There can be little doubt that this is a troubling work. I hope to show now that the attempt to reduce the anxiety it provokes by the provision of a stabilizing, critical frame depends on readings which are, precisely, reductive. As liberal readers, we feel compelled to insist on the text's creation of a safe, ironic distance between itself and the pornography it so resembles, to distance ourselves from our first impressions. These critical distances may, however, be maintained only on the basis of distortions and inconsistencies in our readings; the text is, ultimately, unwilling to allow us so completely to sublimate our affects.

In order to stabilize this unsettling text, we must be able to provide a fixed point, a locus of certainty beyond the text's fluctuations, in which to ground our interpretations. If the perspective offered by this fixed point is one which is critical of the conventional structures of pornography, then the text's apparent complicity with a supposed pornographic hegemony may be shown to be an illusion. Textual ambiguity may be converted from a distressing into a progressive force, and presented as working to undo this hegemony. That work of this kind does indeed take place in the text seems fairly clear, as seen above. But I hope now to show that the ambiguity on which this critical textual working is based will not finally allow itself to be adequately stabilized, and that it in fact returns to upset the very structure thought to secure it.

This structure is provided by the text's narrative frame. As seen above, the displacement produced by this frame of the conventions of pornography enables the text to be read as a disruptive staging of these conventions, and so as a critique of the genre. The recuperative reading of *L'Homme assis dans le couloir* requires that the narrative frame remain stable, to guarantee the ironic distance between the text and the pornography it may then be said to mime. (Ironically,

Duras might in fact be using the term to hint at this meaning, while never quite effacing the impression that she might also have been conjuring up the physiologically unlikely image of simultaneous male ejaculation and urination—as Anderson in fact confirms by stating elsewhere that 'il urine et éjacule sur elle' (28).

the requirements of the 'anti-pornographic' reading of the text here resemble those of the pornographic genre, inasmuch as the frame must in both cases remain safe). Such stability may, for example, be provided by the use of the conditional tense for much of the narrative, declaring the events reported as fantasy, and encouraging an interrogation of the relation between fantasy, writing, and reality; or by the identification of the narrative voice as a non-alienated female position, exhorting the female protagonist and (crucially) the reader to a critical understanding of the scene being played out. This identification is partially encouraged by Duras's remark in *Les Yeux verts* that 'les amants n'étaient pas isolés mais vus, sans doute par moi' (*YV*, 60, my emphasis). The narrator may thus be read as an authorial proxy, gendered as female, and so (it is assumed) critical of the assumption of eroticized suffering presented by the female protagonist.[15]

The scene is quite explicitly staged, the narrative manipulates tenses in order to comment on its presentation of this staging as a fantasy, and this frame insulates the text from the threat of an uncritical repetition of the genre it resembles. Is the frame really so stable, however? It is, we may recall, important for the reading of *L'Homme assis dans le couloir* that seeks to redeem it from the charge of inhabiting the pornographic that the narrative position should *not* be stable. The frame is established, according to this reading, in order to display its own inconsistencies, its uncertainty, its unreliability. The text is displaced from the pornographic not solely by the indication of its frame, but, significantly, also by the tendency of this frame to indicate itself as problematic. The naturalizing omniscience which the pornographic attributes to its hidden frame is dismantled in this text, it is argued, by the parade of a frame which is unstable, plural, and ignorant. Quite explicitly, as everywhere in Duras's work, the narrator is not in possession of the truth of the scene s/he narrates. And yet, if this narrative voice is to serve as the fixed point which will anchor a critical position, it is also read (according to a recuperative model) as representing a non-alienated female subject-position, in full possession of its knowledge. The recuperative reading of the text needs to argue that its narrative frame is both radically unstable and finally fixable, that it both adopts a variety of positions and adheres definitively to one.

[15] See, for example, Cohen, *Women and Discourse*, 231, n. 5.

Duras's statement about the structure of the scene is that the lovers are *probably* seen by her: '*sans doute* par moi' (*YV*, 60, my emphasis). The narrator *may* be an authorial delegate—but then again, s/he may *not* be. (Nowhere in the text is the gender of the narrator indicated, for example. We may suspect, from certain of the identifications made by the voice, from Duras's extra-textual comments, that this position is that of a woman; but this suspicion remains awkwardly residual, both encouraging and frustrating a recuperative reading). Even if we decide that the narrator is a woman, we still have no firm grounds for identifying her with a position of non-alienation. The crucial passage in the debate over this aspect of the text is the following:

Je lui parle et je lui dis ce que l'homme fait. Je lui dis aussi ce qu'il advient d'elle. Qu'elle voie, c'est ce que je désire.

(*HAC*, 16–17)

Is this the voice of a woman who wishes to help another out of her alienation? Quite possibly. But this conclusion depends on an equation between vision and knowledge which Duras's entire *œuvre* works to problematize, especially in the realm of desire. As seen above, it is vital to the claim that *L'Homme assis dans le couloir* offers a critique of traditional pornography that the man's supposed visual mastery be dismantled by the function of desire in the field of vision. The link between vision and knowledge figured in two of the senses of 'voir' is rendered thoroughly unstable by the operation of desire, which permeates the scopic with the fantasmatic. We may think of *Hiroshima mon amour*, of *Moderato cantabile*, of *Le Ravissement de Lol V. Stein* (especially), and of so many others: everywhere Duras works to demonstrate the difficulties that beset a phrase such as 'Qu'elle voie, c'est ce que je désire'. And these difficulties are to the fore in *L'Homme assis dans le couloir*, of course, in which knowledge is constantly questioned by desire, and narratorial certainty is hinted at, but—and in this very gesture—refused. Travelling the link from desire to the woman's knowledge to the knowledge of the narrator, even the solidarity between the narrator and the woman may work to undo the knowledge necessary for consciousness-raising. It is in their shared knowledge that the narrator and the woman are explicitly joined:

Elle sait qu'il la regarde, qu'il voit tout. Elle le sait les yeux fermés comme je le sais moi, moi qui regarde.

(9)

Yet the saturation of knowledge with desire ('Qu'elle voie, c'est ce que je désire') renders this certainty precisely uncertain, illusory, unstable and so unsettles a woman-to-woman identification which might have recuperated the text as instructive. *L'Homme assis dans le couloir* cannot be saved from the pornographic by both narratorial ignorance and narratorial insight. Can we really decide that the narrative voice is lucid and insightful at this point in the text, and ignorant and partially sighted at that, without this ignorance disturbing any overall assumption of lucidity? In respect of the question of generic classification which *L'Homme assis dans le couloir* poses so dramatically, this may represent its awkward, unsettling interrogation. Is this text pornographic? Is it not? Can we really decide?

This really is a distressing text. While it does employ stylistic and structural devices to introduce instability into the pornographic model it reproduces, this very instability also prevents these devices from producing the text as simply a critique of this model. The metaphors of framing, of staging, which attempt to isolate the text from the pornography its mime would displace, cannot ultimately stabilize the ironic distance necessary for such isolation. The frame is not safe; its prophylactic function cannot be assured of complete reliability. Inasmuch as the text's writing exceeds the pornographic model, this excess also maintains it beyond a recuperative reading. We are faced, then, with a text which oscillates. While it contains large amounts of material which would encourage us to read it as critical of the clichés of mainstream pornography, such material is juxtaposed with other moments during which we have no way of knowing that the assumptions which underpin such clichés are not being espoused. When the text, in its penultimate paragraph, broadens its focus to include an historical dimension (specifically that of a women's history), our interpretations must remain uncertain:

Je vois que d'autres gens regardent, d'autres femmes, que d'autres femmes maintenant mortes ont regardé de même se faire et se défaire les moussons d'été . . .

(35–6)

Does this ancient female gaze frame the woman's masochism, constituting a protest against the repeated brutalization of women throughout history (and the repeated internalization by women of this experience of brutalization)? Or does it, on the contrary, with its link to the cyclical rhythms of the surrounding landscape, naturalize this masochism, present it as inevitable, immemorial? Does history represent the frame of desire, or desire the beyond of history? A similar evocation of the weight of historical time is made around the figure of the phallus:

De même que son cœur elle bat. Forme des premiers âges, indifférenciée des pierres, des lichens, immémoriale, plantée dans l'homme autour de quoi il se débat.

(23)

Is this fetishization ironic? Quite possibly. But nothing in the text allows us finally to conclude that this is the case. The anxiety provoked by the proximity of the text to the phallocentrism of a pornographic idiom will not quite be resolved by attempts to frame this proximity as critical reproduction, as moments of irreducible ambiguity also bind the text into the idiom they simultaneously displace.

Such ambiguities may, if desired, be resolved by critical readings. But resolution will here be bound to parade its arbitrariness, unable fully to justify itself by reference to the text. It is clear why such resolution should be desirable: at its most extreme, the text unsettles by imposing ambiguity at moments of the most disturbing brutality. We may wish, for example, that the female protagonist be shown submitting to the man's imposition of violent domination, and that the text present a critique of the masculine sadism which desires, enforces, and enjoys such submission. But the text will not grant our wish. The woman asks to be beaten, and what the text presents is in fact the following scene:

Et puis elle dit qu'elle désire être frappée, elle dit au visage, elle le lui demande, viens. Il le fait, il vient, s'assied près d'elle et la regarde encore. Elle dit: frappée, fort, comme tout à l'heure le cœur. Elle dit qu'elle voudrait mourir.

(32-3)

The woman's desirous participation in her brutalization could hardly be clearer:

La main gifle la naissance des lèvres puis, de plus en plus fort, elle gifle contre les dents. Elle dit que oui, que c'est ça. Elle relève son visage afin de l'offrir mieux aux coups, elle le fait plus détendu, plus à la disposition de sa main, plus matériel.

(33-4)

La main descend, frappe sur les seins, le corps. Elle dit que oui, que c'est ça, oui.

(34)

(And here, the man's synecdochic reduction to his beating hand, as well as confusing his gender, also works to reinforce the brutal participation, as 'elle gifle contre les dents' slips into 'Elle dit que oui, que c'est ça'). The power relation presented by *L'Homme assis dans le couloir* is not just one of domination and submission: it is one of complicity. This complicity may be the result of a masochistic female internalization of male brutality, and its presentation may consequently represent the liberatory lament of this internalization—but this interpretation must remain a critical projection onto the ambiguous text. The first version of the text describes the woman in the following terms:

> Mais la forme reste immobile dans son dernier état, ordonnée, consentante de toute sa sagesse au risque qu'elle court, unie à celle de l'homme par un même désir, dans une inversion d'une vertigineuse adéquation.

('HACa', 75)

Moreover, the woman's explicit request to be beaten is one of the additions made to the text before its 1980 publication, further emphasizing the strength of the collusion, the depth of the 'vertigineuse adéquation'.

Reference to the symbolic transposition of this interaction in *Moderato cantabile* would remind us that the category of 'will' (and hence questions of complicity) may not be fully operative here—but this fact cuts two ways. First, it indicates that, given the presence of desire in the equation, the man's beating of the woman is not justified simply because she requests it. Subject to her desire, she is not simply responsible for her request—her complicity may represent, for example, the internalization of oppression. Secondly, however, the operation of desire also emphasizes that the man is similarly removed from the realm of simple responsibility, equally disabled by the violence of his passion. And so complicity returns without the will, as sublime parity before desire. As with both Chauvin and Jacques Hold (see Chapter 2, above), responsibility becomes a trembling residue, neither fully attributable (because of the operation of desire), nor happily absent (how can we remove questions of responsibility from such a scene?); and so the question of collusion *versus* critique simply cannot (quite) be answered.

To the view that this collusion is simply staged, representing a critical exposition of an alienated female internalization of the eroticized role of victim, the answer remains—if only. For the distance established by the provision of a safe frame for the text is, we may recall, double: it is operative both between the text and the pornographic, and between the anguished impressions of our first readings and our later, critical recuperation of the text by means of this ironic distance. The frame is there as much to protect distressed readers as to recuperate the text. But, however much we would wish to sublimate our pornographic distress into anti-pornographic critique, the text insists that an amount of this distress remain, an unsettling, ambiguous residue that will not be removed by the strength of our wish. There remain elements of the text which may be reclaimed by the pornographic without the text having to be violated any more than it is by the critical reading which presents these elements as part of the text's critique of pornography. The very force of the text derives from its refusal quite to allow its ambiguities to be resolved in the direction of critique rather than collusion, and from the insertion of this refusal into a readerly experience of some of the most upsetting subject matter. Even as it is suggested, recuperation-in-critique is prevented by the text from quite realizing itself, as precisely those features which suggest a reading as critique also remove the certainty on which this reading might be founded.[16] Ambiguity, in fact, here produces two incompatible readings, and denies both final priority. Accordingly, any response which is settled in its adequacy—any response which realizes itself, for example by recuperating the text as a critique of the pornographic—can remain so only by effacing the textual operations on which it thinks to base itself. Moreover, according to Duras, writing-as-critique— useful writing—would itself be an instance of that which it would here think to critique: in a rare use of the term 'pornographique', she declares (in the very year in which *L'Homme assis dans le couloir* is published): 'Or l'écriture est jaillissement intransitif, sans adresse, sans but aucun que celui de sa propre finalité, de nature essentiellement inutile. Ou bien elle est pornographique'.[17] We may look where we will—to Duras (or 'Duras'), to the writing as opposed to the diegesis, to narrative structure—nowhere can we find a

---

[16] Ince, for example, states that 'Although the conventional power relations of a sado-masochistic scene are broadly respected, Duras contorts and reworks the figures one might expect to accompany them' (*'L'Amour la mort'*, 151). This position may be inverted, however, and still make perfect sense: one might also claim that, while Duras 'contorts and reworks' the conventional figures of a sado-masochistic scene, its usual power relations 'are broadly respected'. Or even (worse): that certain of the features supposed to effect this reworking also function to maintain this respect.

[17] Roland Thelu, 'The Thing', *Gai pied*, 20 (novembre 1980), 16.

guarantee that the text's apparent complicity is only a simulation, merely an insulated and insulating *performance* of the pornographic. Indeed, the evidence of instability we need to rescue the text from the pornographic eventually works to undo the certainty needed for this rescue to take place. And perhaps this lack of final, decisive evidence should tell us something about the nature of this shifting, inconsistent text.

L'Homme assis dans le couloir is not (simply) pornographic. It contains far too many elements which disrupt generic conventions to inhabit this genre comfortably. Yet nor is it (simply) anti-pornographic, since many of the elements which disrupt the pornographic also disrupt the frame which would ensure its position as a critical inhabitant of this genre. The unstable text may be recuperated neither for pornography nor for anti-pornography; and it may particularly not be recuperated as critique on the impossible basis of its instability. Marcelle Marini terms the work 'inclassable dans le genre pornographique' (Marini, 'La Mort d'une érotique', 45), indicating that its textual complexity prevents it from being classed as simply pornographic. But by exploring a little further the subtleties of her felicitous phrase, we may perhaps glimpse the paradox which constitutes the core of the problem around this text. *L'Homme assis dans le couloir* is, in some senses, 'dans le genre pornographique'. Not simply, nor solely, but occasionally, and (at times) forcefully. But, within this genre, it is an awkward, unusual, uncomfortable inhabitant. Its complications mean that it resists ultimate assimilation to the generic norm, rendering it 'inclassable'. It is both within the pornographic and unclassifiable within this genre. The text remains caught on the edge of the genre, implicated in the banal, worldly conventions of a vast industry, while also slipping away from the snags of such generic limitation. Its generic status remains, ultimately, undecidable. On the first page of the 1980 edition of the text, we read, 'Après, très loin, et jusqu'à l'horizon, il y a un espace indécis' (*HAC*, 7). There is, as far as *L'Homme assis dans le couloir* is concerned, nothing beyond undecidability. We may believe that such ambiguity is inappropriate in the face of a genre sustained by systematic violence and degradation; but, for all that we might like it to, the strength of this belief will not convert uncertainty into recuperation, will not turn the text into something it is not.

The Sickness unto Death

Ambiguity in *L'Homme assis dans le couloir* works, then, both to subvert the conventions of pornography, and, inasmuch as it is ambiguous, to subvert this subversion. This ambiguous ambiguity is not to be resolved: the text is caught between two antagonistic readings, in a stand-off which traces the line of uncertainty characteristic of this later phase of Duras's work. A similar duality is evident in two of Duras's other principal treatments of sexuality in the 1980s, *La Maladie de la mort* and *Les Yeux bleus cheveux noirs*. In these texts, Duras is concerned to lament what she sees as the sterility of men without women; but she also wants to keep her writing from collapsing into the merely useful by simply denouncing this sterility. Accordingly, she relies heavily on ambiguity and ellipsis, to lift her writing away from the contingent, and towards the mythic; the ambiguity in question, however, also works to keep the texts hooked into the contingencies they strive to surpass in their 'jaillissement intransitif' (Thelu, 16). The tensions between Duras's rather incompatible aims for these texts generate the fault-line along which they are located, both surpassing and bound up with the worldly structures which serve to articulate the explosions of passion. As in *L'Homme assis dans le couloir*, two antagonistic readings are produced: specifically, these texts are caught by their defining ambiguity between the contingent and its transcendence. In *La Maladie de la mort* and *Les Yeux bleus cheveux noirs*, the line of uncertainty between incompatible readings which defines so much of Duras's later writing is created by the strategies she employs to address the ethical edge where the extremity of passion meets the structures of the world—in the particular form of the relationship between heterosexuality, homosexuality, and the homosocial.[18]

---

[18] Eve Kosofsky Sedgwick provides the following definition of the homosocial: '"Homosocial" is a word occasionally used in history and the social sciences, where it describes social bonds between persons of the same sex; it is a neologism, obviously formed by analogy with "homosexual", and just as obviously meant to be distinguished from "homosexual". In fact, it is applied to such activities as "male bonding", which may, as in our society, be characterized by intense homophobia, fear and hatred of homosexuality' (Eve Kosofsky Sedgwick, *Between Men: English Literature and Male Homosocial Desire* (New York: Columbia University Press, 1985), 1). In a specifically French context, Elaine Marks and George Stambolian claim that the revelation of homosocial desire constitutes one of the key features of the MLF. (See Marks and Stambolian (eds.), *Homosexualities and French Literature* (London: Cornell University Press, 1979), 27).

Same-sex desire really emerges in Duras's work in the late 1960s and early 1970s, where it is a question of desire between women, presented as part of a disruptive, valorized feminine proximity to madness. First, Alissa's declaration to Élisabeth Alione, 'Je vous aime et je vous désire', is met by the horrified response 'Vous êtes folle' (*Dd*, 101–2). Then, the 'voix brûlées' of *India Song* and *La Femme du Gange* repeat this Durassian link between lesbian desire and madness: in *India Song*, where 'les voix de ces femmes sont atteintes de folie', the first voice 'se brûle à l'histoire d'Anne-Marie Stretter', while the second 'se brûle à sa passion pour la voix 1' (*IS*, 11); in *La Femme du Gange*, their passion is mutual: 'Elles sont liées par le désir. Se désirent' (*NG*, 105).[19] From the mid-1970s, however, passion between women fades from Duras's work, reappearing only in the adolescent desire of the narrator of *L'Amant* for Hélène Lagonelle— and even this is, crucially, mediated through the figure of her (male) lover. More than lesbian desire, it is the question of male homosexuality that interests Duras in the later stages of her writing career; from 1974 to the late 1980s, the figure of the male homosexual (the latest addition to Duras's list of fascinating marginal figures) makes frequent appearances in her interviews and journalism, as well as in the literary works I will discuss shortly.

In *Les Parleuses*, Duras is mostly positive about male homosexuality. While she does present it as a deviation from the implicitly natural path of heterosexuality ('Il y a toujours eu, au départ de l'homosexualité masculine, un accident qui a fait que la voie, la voie de l'hétérosexualité a été abandonnée, hein, toujours' (*P*, 28)), she is also keen to align male homosexuals and women in their opposition to the 'para chez tout homme' (33): 'Il y a une donnée commune, là—mettons, dans l'oppression de la classe phallique' (153). In 1980, interviewed in the paper *Gai pied*, Duras repeats this comparison. Stressing the institutional dimension to the link she is making, she embraces homosexuality within the politics of refusal she has, by now, championed for over a decade:

Q: Crois-tu qu'il existe une parole commune aux femmes et aux homosexuels?
—Si elle est commune, elle est de l'ordre que j'ai essayé de dire plus haut. L'homosexualité est un refus en soi.

[19] James Williams cites Sue Ellen Case (in her 'From Split Subject to Split Britches: The Metonymically Displaced Subject', in Enoch Brater (ed.), *Feminine Focus: The New Women Playwrights* (Oxford: Oxford University Press, 1989), 129–46) as the only critic to have identified the voices as linked by a specifically lesbian desire (Williams, *The Erotics of Passage*, 174).

Q: Un refus par rapport aux valeurs établies?
—Oui. Par rapport au postulat phallocratique de tout pouvoir et conséquemment aux valeurs proposées par celui-ci, à ses institutions, à sa programmation minutieuse de l'interdit majeur, celui de la liberté.

(Thelu, 16)

This embrace allows Duras joyfully to align herself—in the gay press, which gives this statement no small significance—with the figure of the homosexual in a shared victimization by the upholders of a certain macho aggressivity, marked by her parodic perversion of a favourite term of homosocial identification, 'mec':

Cette semi-clandestinité dans laquelle je me tiens encore—comme dans ma famille—rejoint naturellement celle des homosexuels. Le boycottage fantastique dont j'ai été l'objet de la part des mecs hommes et des mecs femmes, tu vois, ici, dans ce journal, j'en parle avec joie, avec gayté. [*sic*] (*rires*)

(Thelu, 16)

Happy to ridicule the locker-room aggressions of the 'classe phallique', Duras thus valorizes both femininity and homosexuality—with herself as the link between the two, and with femininity not yet defined as exclusively heterosexual—as resisting the dominance of the homosocial.

In 1981, however, Duras begins to be less enthusiastic in her comments on male homosexuality, restricting desire to heterosexuality (and thereby, incidentally, limiting femininity to female heterosexuality), and banishing homosexuals to what she calls their 'exil'. Her position on the compulsory heterosexuality of desire is blunt: whereas in *Les Parleuses* it had been seen simply as 'un mouvement vers l'autre' (*P*, 182), by 1981 this other is limited to a member of the opposite sex: 'Pour moi le désir ne peut avoir lieu qu'entre le masculin et le féminin, entre des sexes différents' (*ME*, 13). Increasingly, for the Duras of the 1980s, homosexuality is so much masturbatory narcissism, 'le prolongement de la pratique masturbatoire' (*ME*, 13), in love only with itself, as she emphasizes in 1987: 'La passion de l'homosexualité c'est l'homosexualité. Ce que l'homosexuel aime comme son amant, sa patrie, sa création, sa terre, ce n'est pas son amant, c'est l'homosexualité' (*VM*, 41).

In contrast to this supposed self-sufficiency, Duras describes heterosexuality as a glorious, sublime, impossible gulf, yawning with irreducible difference:

Dans l'hétérosexualité il n'y a pas de solution. L'homme et la femme sont irréconciliables et c'est cette tentative impossible et à chaque amour renouvelée qui en fait la grandeur.

(VM, 40)

As the exclusive possession of heterosexuality, and the cause of its monopoly on desire, difference is here erected on the basis of the gap of sexual difference. Blurring object-choice and the operation of desire per se, Duras conflates the movement of desire with its object, and expels the internal rupture of desire into the gap of anatomy (which may then be re-internalized—by a female morphology): 'Là où nous sommes atteintes par le désir de notre amant, c'est dans cette cavité du vagin qui résonne comme un creux dans notre corps. Un endroit duquel la verge de notre amant est absente' (VM, 41). Lesbian desire seems to have been entirely forgotten: Duras's scenario has women defined anatomically by their embodiment of their difference from the object of their desire, namely men; who may, it is true, desire each other—but only in a kind of counterfeit, bad faith version, a denial of the nature and locus of authentic desire. Within this binary schema, the female sex comes, then, to incarnate the desire based on anatomical difference: discussing homosexuality with the writer Denis Belloc, also in 1987, Duras defines 'la dialectique homosexuelle' as 'croire que quelque chose à quoi tu n'as jamais pensé existe quand même. Le sexe qui est le désir, ne jamais y penser...'[20] It is this 'ignorance' that homosexuality represents for Duras—which disbars male homosexuals from creative or significant thought or writing:

Là où l'imaginaire est le plus fort c'est entre l'homme et la femme.

(VM, 39)

L'écrivain qui n'a pas connu de femmes, qui n'a jamais touché le corps d'une femme, qui n'a peut-être jamais lu des livres de femmes, des poèmes écrits par des femmes et qui croit cependant avoir fait une carrière littéraire, il se trompe.

(VM, 41)

Banished from both desire and creativity, male homosexuals are, for Duras in 1988, 'dans un exil plus profond que les autres hommes'.[21] This is a continuum, however: for Duras uses homosexuality to represent the self-sufficient sterility of the homosocial, of men

---

[20] Duras, 'L'Exacte Exactitude de Denis Belloc', Libération, 19–20 septembre 1987, 32–3 (32).

[21] Pierre Bergé, 'Duras est sexy!', Globe, 30 (juillet–août 1988), 78–83 (80).

without women. Her statement that 'les hommes sont des homosexuels' (*VM*, 38), far from revealing the homosocial desire that underpins the fraternizing which also serves to repress it, is in fact designed to equate homosexuality (exiled from desire defined by Duras as heterosexual) with the homosocial, as merely the most dramatic instance of a sterile male bonding which excludes women (and therefore, for Duras, desire): 'Si vous êtes un homme, votre compagnie privilégiée dans l'existence, celle de votre cœur, de votre chair, de votre race, de votre sexe, c'est celle de l'homme' (*VM*, 45). All men are homosexual, for Duras, because they are exiled from desire (from women); male homosexuals are just more exiled than most ('dans un exil *plus profond* que les autres hommes'). Duras has thus moved, over fourteen years, from seeing the male homosexual as disruptive of the homosocial 'classe phallique' to seeing him as its most perfect representative; and from aligning women and gay men in their opposition to this class to insisting on an absolute stand-off between the sexes, in which the homosocial and the male homosexual (by now the only kind, for Duras) are conflated in order the better to underscore their supposed estrangement from 'le sexe qui est le désir', a femininity which now relates only negatively to this monolithic masculinity. In *La Maladie de la mort* and *Les Yeux bleus cheveux noirs*, Duras addresses these questions in literary form. This means, in part, that she is determined to avoid simple denunciation or critique of the deathliness with which she is concerned; the ambiguity that is the product of this determination may in fact, however, demonstrate as much the awkwardness as the supposed necessity of using the male homosexual as a synecdochic figure of the homosocial.

According to Duras, *La Maladie de la mort* was born of a moment of doubt in her enthusiastic promotion of heterosexuality as the sole locus of desire. (See *YV*, 232–3.) Given the faith placed by Duras in the radical divide of sexual difference as guarantee not only of desire but also of the imaginary (and hence of writing), we may imagine the importance of such a moment of doubt. The literary elaboration of this potentially traumatic question is to be found in the encounter between male homosexuality and the absolute of sexual difference (figured in a woman) in *La Maladie de la mort* and its 1986 re-working, *Les Yeux bleus cheveux noirs*. An alternative interpretation of this encounter (represented for example by Blanchot's reading of *La Maladie de la mort* in *La Communauté inavouable*) would see it as a critique of the deathly self-sufficiency of the homosocial, and an appeal for the opening of the self to the other in love, as the possible site of an impossible lovers' community. The interpretative conflict between these two readings—between the homosexual and the homosocial—establishes the possible area of confusion of the texts: do they represent a critique of the death-dealing homosocial, or of male homosexuality, or is any dimension of critique inevitably clouded by their ambiguity? As we shall see, Duras insists that these texts remove themselves from the field of polemic; it may be the case, however, that this self-exemption also renders itself uncertain, allowing the texts to collapse back not only into polemic, but even into reconfirmation of that which they would lament. Confronting the sublime gap of sexual difference, Duras's writing may always—in its ambiguity—reconfirm the contingent banalities which edge it about.

The location of the events of *La Maladie de la mort* in the frame of homosocial exchange is encouraged by the nature of the encounter presented: it consists quite explicitly of a contract, agreed according to specific conditions and dependent upon remuneration. It is, moreover, the body of the woman—the stock object of homosocial exchange—that is the subject of the contract, framed in fantasy terms which insert this negotiation into the supposedly centuries-old history of such exchange:

Vous dites qu'elle devrait se taire comme les femmes de ses ancêtres, se plier complètement à vous, à votre vouloir, vous être soumise entièrement comme les paysannes dans les granges après les moissons lorsque éreintées elles laissaient venir à elles les hommes.

(*MM*, 10)

This, then, is the realm of the homosocial, in which women figure as objects of male exchange, and which is founded on the certainty of sexual difference. Across this gulf, there is no possibility of male understanding of the women who are exchanged; woman, in fact, constitutes (in Irigarayan terms) the blind spot of the 'knowledge' which is content simply to inhabit one side of the divide, this ignorance figured repeatedly here in the woman's apparently inexhaustible sleep: 'Vous rentrez dans la chambre. Elle dort. Vous ne comprenez pas' (28). And this ignorance is at its most profound in that area in which woman's status as exchange-object is most profoundly inscribed, namely her sexuality:

Je ne sais pas non plus si vous percevez le grondement sourd et lointain de sa jouissance à travers sa respiration, à travers ce râle très doux qui va et vient depuis sa bouche jusqu'à l'air du dehors. Je ne le crois pas.

(15)

As in *L'Homme assis dans le couloir*, the woman's sexuality, embodied by Duras in her genitals, represents the point at which male 'knowledge' (as it extends itself over the field of vision) breaks down:

Votre main est sur le dessus du sexe, entre les lèvres qui se fendent, c'est là qu'elle caresse. Vous regardez la fente des lèvres et ce qui l'entoure, le corps entier. Vous ne voyez rien.
Vous voudriez tout voir d'une femme, cela autant que puisse se faire. Vous ne voyez pas que cela vous est impossible.

(39)

Doubly blind, the man cannot see that he cannot see the whole of a woman—that the valorization of visible evidence as a guarantee of presence has *as its aim* the impossibility of seeing a woman as present. The absence so created inevitably becomes fascinating, however; and so the attempt to shore up masculinity as the home of certainty is always haunted by the lack against which it defines itself, by the suspicion that there must always be something more to see. (And the above excerpt would, thus, present to perfection the classic scene of castration anxiety, which shifts from the anatomical to the symbolic via the hinge of ambiguity in 'Vous ne voyez rien'.) The disturbance of a masculinist fantasy of mastery as it projects itself into the field of vision is here also indicated by a pronominal uncertainty again reminiscent of *L'Homme assis dans le couloir*: the man is represented synecdochically by his hand, which is marked of course as feminine: 'c'est là qu'elle caresse'.

Such failure to master the woman's otherness is compensated for by the production of fantasies, in which this mastery may be assured—this assurance being guaranteed by the projection of these fantasies onto just those areas in which this mastery falters. Thus, the mysterious interiority of the woman's vagina is stabilized by the production of common knowledge, introduced by the Durassian formula of everyday common-sense 'wisdom', 'on dit': 'On dit que ça résiste plus encore, que c'est un velours qui résiste plus encore que le vide' (10). And in the face of this projected 'wisdom', the woman remains ignorant, alienated: 'Elle dit qu'elle n'a pas d'avis, qu'elle ne peut pas savoir' (10). It is, moreover, an important part of this fantasy 'knowledge' that the woman's body be permanently available, permanently sexually open:

Curieusement les seins sont bruns, leurs aréoles, presque noires. Vous les mangez, vous les buvez et rien dans le corps ne bronche, elle laisse faire, elle laisse.

(26)

The woman plays her role to perfection, as had been agreed in the contract. But this perfection produces an uncertainty: in the fantasy of permanent availability, how is consent to be ascertained?

Elle serait toujours prête, consentante ou non. C'est sur ce point précis que vous ne sauriez jamais rien. Elle est plus mystérieuse que toutes les évidences extérieures connues jusque-là de vous.

(19)

Even the compensatory fantasy fails to stave off the anxious awareness of its inadequacy. And it is in this resistance to projection, in its opaque refusal simply to fulfil appropriate fantasies—even if this refusal is produced in their *too perfect* fulfilment—that Duras locates the woman's power:

Vous regardez cette forme, vous en découvrez en même temps la puissance infernale, l'abominable fragilité, la faiblesse, la force invincible de la faiblesse sans égale.

(31)

Inasmuch as it exceeds the projections of masculine epistemophilia, the woman's body provokes the displacement of this drive into fantasies of brutalization:

Le corps est sans défense aucune, il est lisse depuis le visage jusqu'aux pieds. Il appelle l'étranglement, le viol, les mauvais traitements, les insultes, les cris de haine, le déchaînement des passions entières, mortelles.

(21)[22]

The consequences of this displacement in the man's imaginary are clear: 'Elle vit toujours. Elle appelle le meurtre cependant qu'elle vit. Vous vous demandez comment la tuer et qui la tuera' (37).

---

[22] Blanchot argues (in a Levinasian reading of this figure of woman) that it is precisely her vulnerability which *exceeds* the fantasies of brutalization it provokes, and which renders its destruction ethically impossible by means of its imposition of an irreducible responsibility for the vulnerable other: see Blanchot, *La Communauté inavouable*, 63. The link between *La Maladie de la mort* and Levinas is also made by Ince: see *'L'Amour la mort'*, 156.

In addition to facilitating the self-subversion of such masculine compensatory fantasies, the woman also reveals the truth of the self-sufficient masculinity of the homosocial. First, she allows its ignorance to become apparent:

Jusqu'à cette nuit-là vous n'aviez pas compris comment on pouvait ignorer ce que voient les yeux, ce que touchent les mains, ce que touche le corps. Vous découvrez cette ignorance.

(22)

This ignorance is the result, of course, of the gulf of sexual difference, hitherto unacknowledged by the man in his self-contained isolation within one pole of this difference. It is this isolation that constitutes 'la maladie de la mort', the refusal impossibly to embrace 'la frontière infranchissable entre elle et vous' (25). There is no suggestion that this gulf might be bridged; the man's failure is, rather, the failure to welcome and to love this impossibility. As the narrative closes, he remains isolated in the face of the abyss:

Quand vous avez pleuré, c'était sur vous seul et non sur l'admirable impossibilité de la rejoindre à travers la différence qui vous sépare.

(56)

The gap of sexual difference may not be closed; but it may be embraced, in a moment of tragic, passionate recognition. The man, however, prefers to return to the realm of the homosocial, reducing the possible impossible experience of otherness to an anecdote:

Le soir de son départ, dans un bar, vous racontez l'histoire. D'abord vous la racontez comme s'il était possible de le faire, et puis vous abandonnez. Ensuite vous la racontez en riant comme s'il était impossible qu'elle ait eu lieu ou comme s'il était possible que vous l'ayez inventée.

(54–5)

The 'admirable impossibilité' missed by the man in this non-encounter is recuperated in its blokeish retelling into a cheery fiction—yet the deadpan breathlessness of Duras's syntax suggests that this narrative recuperation has failed—miserably—to see the glorious impossibility which represented the only escape from deathly complacency.

Thus, *La Maladie de la mort* may be read as a critique of the homosocial by means of the staged encounter between this realm and the figure of woman it positions as its other and so attempts to reduce. This reading has yet to address the question of the man's sexuality, let alone the consequences of this question for the critique elaborated above. For Duras suggests, and the text confirms, that the man is homosexual.[23] This homosexuality is mostly implicit, never unequivocal—but the accumulation of hints is strong. The woman clearly identifies the man's 'knowledge' as the product of a deathly self-sufficiency which is the result of a failure to love—a failure, therefore, impossibly to embrace feminine otherness:

Elle dit: Je ne voudrais rien savoir de la façon dont vous, vous savez, avec cette certitude issue de la mort, cette monotonie irrémédiable, égale à elle-même chaque jour de votre vie, chaque nuit, avec cette fonction mortelle du manque d'aimer.

(50)

This failure to love is, quite explicitly, the failure to love a woman; and it is this failure that represents deathliness:

Elle demande: Vous n'avez jamais aimé une femme? Vous dites que non, jamais.
Elle demande: Vous n'avez jamais désiré une femme? Vous dites que non, jamais.
Elle demande: Pas une seule fois, pas un instant? Vous dites que non, jamais.
Elle dit: Jamais? Jamais? Vous répétez: Jamais.
Elle sourit, elle dit: C'est curieux un mort.

(34–5)

The man's preferred realm is that of corporeal semblance, 'la grâce du corps des morts, celle de vos semblables' (37). The woman's body is, for him, an anomaly, a bewildering departure from which he will turn away:

De ce corps [i.e. that of the woman] vous voudriez partir, vous voudriez revenir vers le corps des autres, le vôtre, revenir vers vous-même et en même temps c'est de devoir le faire que vous pleurez.

(16–17)

The woman's bodily challenge pushes the man to close in more securely within this deathly sameness: 'Vous fermez les yeux pour vous retrouver dans votre différence, dans votre mort' (36). That this realm of sameness is also the locus of the man's sexuality—that

[23] For Duras's implicit confirmation of the man's homosexuality, see *Les Yeux verts*, 232–3. Dominique Noguez claims that, as she was finishing it, Duras announced *La Maladie de la mort* as 'un texte sur l'homosexualité' (Noguez, 'Notes sur Marguerite Duras (1975–1983)', *Nouvelle Revue Française*, 542 (mars 1998), 41–53 (52)). See also Adler, *Marguerite Duras*, 490 ff.

the negative information of his failure to have loved a woman is to be converted into the positive knowledge that he has loved men—is indicated rather coyly by the text, in its reference to his familiarity only with a penetration which is not vaginal:

Elle sourit, elle demande: Vous voudriez aussi de moi?
Vous dites: Oui. Je ne connais pas encore, je voudrais pénétrer là aussi. Et aussi violemment que j'ai l'habitude.

(9–10)

The man is, then, gay; he is 'dead' inasmuch as his sexuality refuses to embrace in its impossibility the radical gulf of sexual difference.

At this point, the text is open to a critical reading, according to which it would reconfirm the deathly order it also denounces. The general force of the text's critique of masculine fantasies of mastery (for example in the field of vision) may undermine itself: there is a possible implication that any man who *has* desired a woman is *not* dead, and does not need to construct compensatory fantasies of mastery as a defence against what is now a beloved difference. The only way in which the more radical possibility of the critique of the homosocial may be kept open is by the belief in the maxim that 'Les hommes sont des homosexuels', inasmuch as they are radically unable to know a woman (a position proposed, incidentally, by Duras in *Les Yeux verts*: see *YV*, 233). This position, however, conflates the homosexual and the homosocial in a manner which ignores the foundation of the latter on the repression of the former. The homosexual will not serve as representative of the homosocial, since it does not simply inhabit this space, but, rather, both inhabits and disrupts it, as its repressed term. Duras *does* argue that the homosexual is the repressed of the homosocial (*VM*, 38), and that its status as the latent truth of this realm may be revealed accidentally. But from this she concludes not that its relation to this space is potentially disruptive (as one might expect of a repressed term), but that its manifestation in fact simply *confirms* the order of (masculine) same and (feminine) other by which this space is structured. In fact, rather than reducing the other to the same, by the love of the anatomically identical, as Duras would have it, the movement of desire between such bodies in the homosexual may be read as producing the same as the other, thereby *disrupting* the order of the homosocial, which is that of the binary separation of same and other.

Within the Durassian staging of this confused realm, otherness is, of course, figured as a woman. It is clearly the case that, within the homosocial, otherness is indeed figured in this way. And Duras's text may be read as a critical staging of this figuring, as I have shown above. The conflation of the homosocial and the homosexual, however, may also suggest reliance on a model of difference which is anatomically determined. Beyond social mediation, this morphological rigidity is governed by a binaristic logic which, therefore, forces it in fact to reconfirm that the other is, simply, the other of the same. And the two halves of this model are, then, complementary: vaginal penetration represents, for the man, his arrival at an awaited home, 'le logement nocturne' (*MM*, 43). The narrative structure of the text places such penetration as the final interaction between the two protagonists, and the narrative voice marks it with a variant of the Durassian formula of culmination:

Elle dit: Prenez-moi pour que cela ait été fait.
Vous le faites, vous prenez.
Cela est fait.
Elle se rendort.

(53)

After this moment of perfected penetration, the woman departs. Heterosexuality thus becomes the text's catastrophic climax: the argument of the structure of the text is that heterosexuality (vaginal penetration) is unavoidable. The claim that all men are homosexual is conflated with its opposite, in the adoption of heterosexuality as an inevitable narrative *telos*. *La Maladie de la mort* thus suggests that heterosexuality-as-Truth can be revealed by the encounter of a gay man and a woman, even if this encounter takes place in the only way permitted by the gulf of sexual difference, i.e. negatively, in its failure. By excluding desire from homosexuality, Duras is able to claim both that heterosexuality is the latent truth of homosexuality and that homosexuality is the latent truth of heterosexuality. In *La Maladie de la mort*, the homosexual man denies the truth of difference in his preference for the homosocial; in *La Vie matérielle*, heterosexual men are denying the truth of their mutual homosexuality. So: the denial of difference constructs the homosocial; the denial of homosexuality within the homosocial constructs heterosexual masculinity; but heterosexual masculinity is one of the poles of sexual difference, which has constructed the homosocial. These contradictions ensue not from a blurring of the boundaries between the homosocial and the homosexual, in order to emphasize the repression of the latter in the former (a gesture which depends on the notion of homosocial *desire*), but rather from the attempt to use the homosexual as a synecdochic figure of the homosocial, which may be critiqued as imploding precisely because of its exclusion of this desire, and its consequent inability to address this repression. If Duras's definition of desire as exclusively heterosexual is rejected (as it is by Blanchot, for example), then the relation of the homosexual to the homosocial cannot be figured synecdochically, since the former term does not simply inhabit the latter, but is rather—as its repressed term—both within and without it, disrupting its margins rather than confirming its selfsame identity. (At which point, the synecdoche becomes, as Blanchot says, 'un peu factice' (Blanchot, *La Communauté inavouable*, 84)). The attempted use of this figure would, then, constitute an impossible synecdoche based on anatomical difference as the sole ultimate criterion of desire. This model may, then, reconfirm masculine self-identity and feminine otherness—which is the law of the homosocial, and so the very deathliness the text would like to critique. So far from a critical staging of the death-dealing homosocial, then, *La Maladie de la mort* may, possibly, be read in the manner sketched here as the reconfirmation of the presuppositions of this realm—and may, then, be afflicted by the very deathliness it laments.[24]

This reading remains an external critique of Duras's position, however; this position, whether one agree with it or not, is at least internally coherent. It is not binary gender difference that troubles Duras, but the failure to love this difference in its sublime

---

[24] This point is made by James Williams, in 'A Beast of a Closet: The Sexual Difference of a Literary Collaboration in the Work of Marguerite Duras and Yann Andréa', *Modern Language Review*, 87/3 (July 1992), 576–84 (584). See also Williams, *The Erotics of Passage*, esp. 174. Ince ('*L'Amour la mort*', 160) gives a careful account of the flickering presence of the homosexual in the text: 'Homosexuality is insufficient explanation for the failure of desire (the text has something to say to all men), but remains the possible motivating factor *La Maladie de la mort* and its imperious narrating voice most obviously point to.' Referring in an excellent image to 'the trace of homosexuality' in the text, Ince claims that this ambiguity 'maintains the encounter in an undecidable space between the two types of relation' (160). The notion of undecidability, however, here risks effacing the extent to which Duras is positioning the encounter not *between* the homosexual and the homosocial, but squarely *within* the homosocial on the problematic basis of its homosexual coding. Overall (and recalling *L'Homme assis dans le couloir*), it would seem that undecidability in this period of Duras's work means less 'either/or', than (impossibly) 'both/and'.

impossibility. That she reconfirms this binarism is fine, from her perspective: indeed, she needs to reconfirm it, in order both to denounce its sterile, banal version, and to glorify its sublime version. Thus, to read Duras as *apparently* faithful to a framework of compulsory heterosexuality, while *in fact* working textually to unsettle the untroubled identifications on which this framework depends is to miss this Durassian distinction: Duras addresses heterosexuality not just as the banal and compulsory way of the world (and thus something that one might be in a position to subvert), but also (and most emphatically) as an overwhelming, splendid, non-negotiable abyss.[25] Her disruption of masculine erotico-epistemological mastery may accordingly represent not the dismantling of this structure, but rather an emphasis on the inadequacy of this supposed mastery before the sublime force of a still exclusively heterosexual passion. She may well be reconfiguring masculinity (in terms of vulnerability, weakness, tearfulness, and so on); she is doing so, however, in the name of the further glory of her particular, and thoroughly binaristic, vision of gender relations.

It is moreover vital to Duras that, as the articulation of this vision, her text should not represent mere denunciation, should not slip back from intransitivity into usefulness. She insists, therefore, that, 'Contrairement à ce que l'on croit, il n'y a pas de procès dans *La Maladie de la mort*' (*YV*, 231). And it is in order to remove the text from the vulgarity of mere denunciation that Duras keeps it resolutely ambiguous at key points, relying on ellipsis and allusion to create a degree of coy, poetic confusion about the man's actual sexuality. That he is familiar with non-vaginal penetration is indicated by the oblique 'Je voudrais pénétrer là aussi' (*MM*, 9–10), which imposes a series of assumptions: that 'là aussi' refers to the woman's vagina (half-confirmed by the rumour 'que c'est un velours qui résiste encore plus que le vide' (10)); that the form of penetration with which the man *is* familiar would therefore be anal; and that this would mark the man as homosexual. Each of these connections depends on conclusions which are almost (but not quite) necessary; resting on a weight of implication, the text nudges the reader towards the realization of the man's homosexuality. There is no trial; this is a matter less of contention than of elegant innuendo.

---

[25] Such a reading is proposed by Emma Wilson: see '"Mon Histoire de Lol V. Stein": Duras, Reading, and Amnesia', esp. 189.

But such textual nicety may also tip ambiguity in the opposite direction and whisper that the man may (also?) *not* be homosexual. Echoing an earlier exchange, the woman returns to the failures of his love-life:

Elle dit: L'envie d'être au bord de tuer un amant, de le garder pour vous, pour vous seul, de le prendre, de le voler contre toutes les lois, contre tous les empires de la morale, vous ne la connaissez pas, vous ne l'avez jamais connue?
Vous dites: Jamais.
Elle vous regarde, elle répète: C'est curieux un mort.

(45)

'Un amant': might deathliness stem also from a failure of *homosexual* love, or of love undifferentiated between homosexual and heterosexual? Suddenly, the possibility that the man might be heterosexual rushes back in, through the relentless gendering of French grammar. As the woman conflates classically in her grammar the masculine and the universal, the man comes to hover between the heterosexual and the homosexual, becomes—a man. Straight or gay? 'C'est selon, semblerait-il', concludes Duras (*YV*, 232).

And this equivocation is essential for Duras, for two reasons. First, she needs the man to be just a man, so that there may be no exceptions to her simultaneous denunciation and celebration of the gulf of sexual difference. Secondly, as we have seen, ambiguity around the man's sexuality provides the prime textual locus of an uncertainty which, for Duras, helps the text to transcend polemic. This very ambiguity, however, also keeps the text involved in such polemic, as it is precisely this equivocation (the use of the homosexual as representative of the homosocial) that is contested by the critical reading described above. The two incompatible readings produced by *La Maladie de la mort*—Duras's celebration of sexual difference and the critique of the terms of this celebration—are thus produced out of the same ambiguity. Ultimately, *La Maladie de la mort* suggests that it is the very intransitivity of writing that keeps it caught on the edge of the transitive, polemical world.

Despite Duras's insistence that *La Maladie de la mort* surpasses denunciation, it seems that she was in fact dogged by some sense of its continuing implication in the contingencies of polemic. For four years after its publication, she produces *Les Yeux bleus cheveux noirs*. This later text re-works the encounter of *La Maladie de la mort*, with added complications: the woman is now involved with two men, one (with whom the repeated encounter takes place) gay, the other straight; the text is punctuated by hypothetical staging instructions from 'l'acteur'; it includes a deal of discussion about the necessity or otherwise of heterosexuality; and it at times declares its provenance by quoting from *La Maladie de la mort*. There is thus observable here a similar process of complication from *La Maladie de la mort* to *Les Yeux bleus cheveux noirs* as was apparent between the 1962 and 1980 versions of *L'Homme assis dans le couloir*, with the later text both repeating and exceeding its earlier version. And, as in this earlier case of intertextual repetition, the framing techniques of the later text are both more prominent and more unstable than those of its predecessor. This additional framing instability appears designed to lift *Les Yeux bleus cheveux noirs* out of the polemic in which *La Maladie de la mort* remained enmeshed. Only two years after having insisted that *La Maladie de la mort* avoided all 'procès', Duras states that, 'Si on a l'esprit à faire des généralités, on peut dire que *La Maladie de la mort* est un premier état des *Yeux bleus cheveux noirs*. Mais *La Maladie de la mort* c'était un procès et ici, il n'y a rien de pareil, en aucun sens' (*VM*, 38). To Alice A. Jardine, Duras declares, 'I believe writing is beyond all . . . contingency'.[26] And *Les Yeux bleus cheveux noirs* serves here as an example of this absolute: 'I write outside all polemic. You see, *Blue Eyes Black Hair* is outside any polemic' (Interview with Duras by Jardine, 73). Might *Les Yeux bleus cheveux noirs* represent a re-elaboration of *La Maladie de la mort* that frees itself from its predecessor's snags and finally does move beyond polemic?

If *Les Yeux bleus cheveux noirs* is to make such a move, it will have to offer a suspension of the earlier text's binary schema which, as seen above, collapses into contingency and polemic in the very gesture towards intransitive ambiguity. And *Les Yeux bleus cheveux noirs* does present a model of sexual relations which appears both to reaffirm and to complicate the masculine-feminine binarism of *La Maladie de la mort*. Before considering the operation of complicating critical distance within this model, we will need first to consider three of its principal binaristic aspects: the woman's desire; the supposed inevitability of heterosexuality; and the text's presentation of a discourse of homophobia.

---

[26] Interview with Duras by Alice A. Jardine, in Jardine and Anne M. Menke (eds.), *Shifting Scenes* (New York: Columbia University Press, 1991), 71–8 (71).

The first two of these three take up the binary logic ultimately elaborated by *La Maladie de la mort*. While the sexual scenario of *Les Yeux bleus cheveux noirs* is complicated by the split of the heterosexual/homosexual man of *La Maladie de la mort* into his two component parts, so that the woman is now in contact with one homosexual and one heterosexual man, this complication continues to espouse the earlier text's anatomical fixity. The woman's desire remains grounded in the certainty of masculinity, regardless of fluctuating sexualities. The multiplication of the man of *La Maladie de la mort* into his two constituent selves fails to disturb the earlier text's binarism, as the poles of masculine and feminine remain stable within the woman's desire. The circulation of men within the other term of this desire, rather than complicating its heterosexuality, may in fact reconfirm it, as the woman's object-choice is determined in both cases by anatomical difference.

Moreover, the inevitability of heterosexuality is displayed even more clearly in *Les Yeux bleus cheveux noirs* than it had been in *La Maladie de la mort*. It is posited by the woman as part of an on-going debate with the homosexual man, in the following terms (which recall, initially, the vocabulary of *La Maladie de la mort*):

> Elle lui demande de venir voir ça, que c'est une chose infecte, criminelle, une eau trouble, sale, l'eau du sang, qu'un jour il devra bien le faire, même une fois, fourrager dans ce lieu commun, qu'il ne pourra pas l'éviter toute sa vie.
>
> (*YB*, 51)

And, as in *La Maladie de la mort*, the narrative structure of *Les Yeux bleus cheveux noirs* positions heterosexuality as unavoidable *telos*, thereby espousing these ideas. The man is indeed unable to avoid 'ce lieu commun', this 'chose infecte, criminelle' (which recalls *L'Homme assis dans le couloir*'s 'bouche vomissante, viscérale' (*HAC*, 15)): he does, eventually, penetrate her vagina, and is subject to the agony of the impossible reconciliation of the binary terms of desire, in which anatomy is indeed destiny:

> Il se retournera. Il recouvrira son corps avec le sien, il le ramènera vers lui, dans l'axe du sien, et lentement il s'enlisera dans la vase chaude du centre.
> Là il reste sans bouger. Il attendra sa destinée, le vouloir de son corps. Il attendra le temps qu'il faudra.
> Le temps d'y penser, l'idée se déclare, brutale, dans un cri d'agonie. Elle cesse.
>
> (132)

There is here a clear repetition of the equivalent scene from *La Maladie de la mort*:

> Vous le [son corps] recouvrez complètement du vôtre, vous le ramenez vers vous pour ne pas l'écraser de votre force, pour éviter de le tuer, et puis ensuite vous le faites, vous revenez vers le logement nocturne, vous vous y enlisez.

(*MM*, 42–3)

Les Yeux bleus cheveux noirs goes beyond *La Maladie de la mort*, however, in that this man continues to desire the woman after their encounter, as a result of this revelatory experience. (See *YB*, 136.) Translated into the world of heterosexuality, the man is frightened by the sudden prospect of futurity, in contrast to the supposed sterility of homosexuality, 'ces hommes sans descendance' (31).[27] And the force of this new desire also propels the narrative towards the telos it presents as inevitable. Both repeating and exaggerating the structure of *La Maladie de la mort*, the narrative structure of the later text is marked throughout by a model of homecoming. The town in which the action takes place is the man's home town, to which he has just returned: 'Il était parti de cette ville-ci, très jeune, à l'âge où il ne pouvait pas encore savoir. Il était resté longtemps absent' (70–1). (We may recall, perhaps, the explanation of male homosexuality offered by Duras in *Les Parleuses*, where it is presented as determined by a childhood trauma: 'Il y a toujours eu, au *départ* de l'homosexualité masculine, un accident qui a fait que la voie, la voie de l'hétérosexualité a été abandonnée, hein, toujours' (*P*, 28, my emphasis)). A return home, then, for the formerly ignorant homosexual prodigal, from his deviant path to his true sexual home, the 'logement nocturne' (*MM*, 43), the 'lieu commun' (*YB*, 51), the *telos* of both narrative and desire.

In the face of this inevitability, homosexuality finds itself reduced to a combination of sterility and misogyny, as the text presents a discourse of homophobic cliché. The man is, apparently, familiar only with one-night stands ('il n'a jamais eu d'histoires que très courtes,

---

[27] In 1990, Duras locates in this heterosexual, fertile futurity the essential difference between *La Maladie de la mort* and *Les Yeux bleus cheveux noirs*: 'Dans le deuxième partie des *Yeux bleus cheveux noirs*, quand la chose a été vécue le désespoir est beaucoup plus grand que dans *La Maladie de la mort*, seulement il est fécond. Il rejoint les désespoirs de l'amour, tandis que l'homosexualité de *La Maladie de la mort* reste aride, solitaire.' This leads her to a particularly extreme declaration, which efface les ambiguïtés de *La Maladie de la mort*: 'L'homosexualité, c'est peut-être la mort. C'est ce que je crois, moi, très fort et je l'ai tout de même montré' (Aliette Armel, ' "J'ai vécu le réel comme un mythe" ', *Le Magazine littéraire*, 278 (juin 1990), 18–24 (24)).

sans lendemain' (*YB*, 98)), as opposed to what is presented as the extension over time of heterosexuality. His misogyny appears to be produced out of the frustrated wish for the woman's death, which might have allowed him to desire her (although this precondition is later revealed as unnecessary): 'Mais il eût fallu pour ce faire qu'elle soit morte, et, lui, il avait oublié de la tuer' (58). In this sterile misogyny, the homosexual rejoins the deathly homosocial already familiar from *La Maladie de la mort* (and the figure of murder underscores this recollection): the heterosexual man is also able to feel only 'un certain sentiment, facile et sans lendemain' (127). Homosexuality is distinguished by characteristics which render it indistinct, and accedes to justification as natural only inasmuch as it is marked by a misogyny which reconfirms the gulf of sexual difference—and so effaces homosexuality as locus of desire: 'Votre détestation de moi, elle ne me regarde pas. Elle vient de Dieu, il faut l'accepter comme telle, la respecter comme la nature, la mer' (49). Natural inasmuch as it is indistinguishable from the deathly homosocial, homosexuality is the figure around which *Les Yeux bleus cheveux noirs* repeats the worldly binarism of *La Maladie de la mort*.

Such, then, are the text's moments of reliance on a masculine-feminine schema inherited from its predecessor. As has already been fleetingly apparent, however, this presentation of a compulsory and inevitable heterosexuality takes place in the context of the unsettling of its polemical bent, as gender positions are complicated in a manner reminiscent of *L'Homme assis dans le couloir*. While a certain stability is established between the two poles of the sexual relation, this stability is also complicated by the mutual interference of masculine and feminine terms. The woman's mystical knowledge of the man's gaze is located (behind closed eyes) in her body, and is thus marked with a masculine pronoun: 'Que ce corps dorme ne signifie pas qu'il soit sans vie aucune. C'est le contraire. Et à ce point qu'à travers le sommeil il sait quand quelqu'un regarde' (24). Similarly, the man is feminized, linked to a feminine *mascarade* by the trace of make-up around his eyes (25). And beyond this fairly standard feminization of the figure of a homosexual man, the woman's heterosexual lover, a more straightforward member of 'la classe phallique', finds his phallus both fetishized and feminized in the manner by now familiar from both *L'Homme assis dans le couloir* and *La Maladie de la mort*. Here, the phallus is both ancient, 'un objet du début du monde' (recalling the 'Forme des premiers âges, indifférenciée des pierres, des lichens, immémoriale' from *L'Homme assis dans le couloir* (*HAC*, 23)), and, in its status as phallus, 'toujours pleine et dure', likened to the crude, stereotypical image of the vagina, 'pénible comme une plaie' (*YB*, 131).

On the basis of such complication, might *Les Yeux bleus cheveux noirs* be read as a critical staging of the terms of compulsory heterosexuality? The question is certainly debated explicitly in a manner absent from *La Maladie de la mort*:

> Elle demande:
> —Jamais cela ne vous est arrivé?
> —Jamais.
> Elle ne lui demande pas s'il sait d'où vient cette difficulté dans sa vie.
> —Jamais avec une femme, vous voulez dire.
> —C'est ça. Jamais . . .
> —Comment en être sûr à ce point?
> —Pourquoi vouloir à ce point que je n'en sois pas sûr?
>
> (28–9)

The man, moreover, is allowed to argue that homosexuality is inevitable, thereby contesting the teleology of the narrative:

> Elle le lui dit:
> —Non. Il aimait être avec des femmes.
> Il dit la phrase de la prédication:
> —Tôt ou tard il serait venu à nous, ils y viennent tous, il suffit d'attendre le temps qu'il faut.
>
> (92)

It is also possible that the woman's hostility to homosexuality, including the notion of its supposed sterility, is being staged within the text for critical inspection: challenged to justify her desire for a flaw in the man's homosexual desire, she reveals the blockage of her thought on this question—and hence, possibly, a failure within heterosexuality, blinded by its own pseudo-necessity:

> —Pourquoi vouloir à ce point que je n'en sois pas sûr?
> Elle le regarde comme elle regarderait son image en son absence. Elle dit:
> —Parce que on ne peut pas faire autrement.
> Elle le regarde encore avec cette fixité. Elle dit:
> —On ne peut pas le comprendre.
>
> (29)

We might recall here that 'On' is the name given to the voice of platitude and gossip throughout Duras's work. There might be found in such passages, then, the belated working-out of the doubt about the necessity of heterosexuality which Duras gives as the origin of *La Maladie de la mort* (*YV*, 232). The question is certainly debated openly, both sides held up for inspection, the woman's motives questioned: when the homosexual man asks her if his sexuality is 'aussi terrible que de ne pas croire en Dieu', the text answers:

Elle le croit. C'est le fait de l'homme indéfiniment présent à lui-même qui effraie. Mais ce doit être là qu'on est le mieux, le plus à l'aise pour vivre le désespoir, avec ces hommes sans descendance qui ignorent être désespérés.

(31)

In addition to interrogating the motives of the woman's horror of homosexuality, the text also complicates the heterosexuality affirmed in her choice of masculine objects of desire. When the homosexual man and the woman first kiss, he kisses through her his absent male object—and this is her desire:

Elle lui donne sa bouche à baiser.
Elle lui dit qu'il l'embrasse, lui, cet inconnu, elle dit: Vous embrassez son corps nu, sa bouche, toute sa peau, ses yeux.

(20)

Her desire is for his homosexuality: for him as a man among men, then, and so (again) a reaffirmation of heterosexuality; but also for herself as a (proxy) man, upsetting the poles of absolute sexual difference. That they share a desire for this absent male object establishes an erotic chain passing through them both and reversing their polarities: he is feminized (by his make-up), and she—crucially, and beyond this stock effeminacy—becomes his homosexual lover: 'Elle a cette couleur d'yeux et de cheveux des amants qu'il désire; ce bleu-là des yeux lorsque les cheveux sont de ce noir' (46). Homosexuality even comes to articulate the violent heterosexual relations between the woman and her straight lover, becomes itself the gulf between the sexes, imposing a frantic passion: after she confesses her growing passion for the homosexual man,

Elle dit que l'homme criait, qu'il était perdu, que ses mains étaient devenues très brutales à toucher le corps. Que la jouissance avait été à en perdre la vie.

(100)

Such scenes offer a complication of the binarism to which *La Maladie de la mort* reduces in its very effort to escape such reduction. Just
as the explicit intervention of the 'acteur' in *Les Yeux bleus cheveux noirs*
exaggerates the implicit drama of *La Maladie de la mort*, so the critical
staging of the earlier text's crucial schema suggests a displacing
force which troubles the return to worldly polemic.

And yet: the above scene may just rehearse another brutal
moment of heterosexual desire, heightened by the man's straightforward jealousy before the figure of another man. Again, a binarism remains in its potential complication. Which should remind us
that, in Duras, techniques of staging never quite assure the critical
distance they promise. The staging is affected by the very ambiguity it introduces, to the extent that it ceases to be thinkable as staging, and comes to be juxtaposed with the material it might be
thought to qualify. Thus, rather than displacing the discourses it
presents, a narrative structured by ambiguity may simply suggest
plural readings—without citing any within any other. Take, here,
the use of 'style indirect libre' in *Les Yeux bleus cheveux noirs*, at critical
moments in the debate over the necessity of heterosexuality, such as
the man's question to the woman about the true extent of the supposed lapse that is homosexuality:

Il demande si c'est aussi terrible que de ne pas croire en Dieu.
Elle le croit. C'est le fait de l'homme indéfiniment présent à lui-même qui effraie.

(31)

The impossibility of distinction between character and narrative
voice also collapses the distance between espousal and staging:

Elle demande:
—Jamais cela ne vous est arrivé?
—Jamais.
Elle ne lui demande pas s'il sait d'où vient cette difficulté dans sa vie.

(28)

'Elle ne lui demande pas s'il sait d'où vient cette difficulté dans sa
vie': is homosexuality ('ce nom qui n'est jamais prononcé' (Blanchot, *La Communauté inavouable*, 84)) a difficulty for the woman, or for
the narrative voice? 'C'est le fait de l'homme indéfiniment présent
à lui-même qui effraie': is just the woman frightened? Or also the
text? These examples condense the ambiguity of *Les Yeux bleus cheveux
noirs* regarding the simultaneously sublime and banal binarism of

La Maladie de la mort: this binarism is *both* adopted *and* qualified. The uncertainty introduced into its fixity by its textual staging also affects this staging, which may or may not be taking place, both is and is not operative. *Les Yeux bleus cheveux noirs* may be read as unsettling a model of desire grounded solely in sexual difference; and it may be read as reconfirming this model. Would *this* (meta-) ambiguity mean that *Les Yeux bleus cheveux noirs* has finally reached a point beyond polemic, in the absolute intransitivity proper (according to Duras) to writing?

The way of the world is never absent from *Les Yeux bleus cheveux noirs*. And the way of the heterosexual world might be one of self-perpetuation by a generalized coercion which at times (at least) touches on the abusive. In its ambiguity, the text may suggest that a thirteen-year-old girl's accession to womanhood takes place at the hands of a man, thus:

Ç'avait été très lent, avec ses doigts d'abord il avait pénétré et puis avec sa verge ensuite. Dans le désir il parlait de Dieu. Elle s'était débattue contre. Il l'avait tenue entre ses bras.

(102–3)

This encounter represents the shift from youthful folklore to rite of passage: recalling the 'loi pourtant impérieuse . . . de-se-faire-découvrir-le-corps' of 'Le Boa' (*DJ*, 114–15), the text introduces the experience thus (again mobilizing free indirect discourse):

Les filles de la classe parlaient des masses de pierres et des gens qui y allaient la nuit. Certaines filles y étaient allées pour se faire toucher par les hommes . . . Celles qui y étaient allées, une fois revenues de là, ne pouvaient plus jamais être pareilles à celles qui ne savaient pas.

(102)[28]

Wondering the next day whether to tell her mother about the incident, the woman (as girl) realizes that the mother is already aware— and that she accepts what has happened, with what is presented as a worldly female wisdom:

[28] Similar scenes throughout Duras's writing cumulatively suggest just an experience as the Durassian accession to womanhood, a paradoxical structure in which adolescent girls/young women actively seek a passive experience as the rite of passage into adult sexuality, this paradox marked by the repetition of the construction 'se faire . . .'. See, in addition to *Les Yeux bleus cheveux noirs* and 'Le Boa', *L'Amant*, *L'Amant de la Chine du nord*, and the section 'Le Train de Bordeaux', from *La Vie matérielle*. Adler (*Marguerite Duras*, 82) gives a good account of this structure of active passivity.

Ce que l'enfant n'avait pas su avant ce soir-là, c'était si cette femme avait elle aussi franchi cet équateur de l'autre versant. C'était au regard de la mère sur son enfant, ce soir-là, à ce silence entre elles, à ce rire caché qui traversait le regard de connivence inavouable qu'elle l'avait appris. Elles étaient les mêmes sur le point de ce qui se passait à cet endroit de la nuit.

(103)

The woman has, then, acceded to a female continuum which recalls the watching women at the close of *L'Homme assis dans le couloir*, and as in this earlier text, this female gaze (here explicitly one of connivence) *both* naturalizes what it watches *and* implies at least the possibility of a critical staging of such naturalization.

Ambiguity in *Les Yeux bleus cheveux noirs* thus rests on three possible positions: an espousal (and naturalization) of the contingent structures by which sexuality is articulated in the world; the critical staging of these structures; and their glorification, their elevation to a passionate point beyond the contingent, where their naturalization gives onto mythification beyond qualification. *Les Yeux bleus cheveux noirs* provides justification for all of these readings (often within the same textual moment), and allows none priority over the others. The ambiguity at work between the three may emphasize the third, in that it begins to align the text with the intransitivity beyond contingency. This gesture of beginning fails quite to complete itself, however. For the ambiguity in question lies in the uncertain opposition between transitivity (espousal/critique) and intransitivity (passion, myth)—and so, by virtue of the ambiguity by which it reaches beyond critique, writing is detained in the between, intransitive inasmuch as it can but gesture towards intransitivity. The beyond remains beyond, and writing traces its edge.

Which returns us to the Durassian ethical. For, in a gesture which rigorously accompanies the move towards the absolute, the instances of sublime passion offered by Duras in these texts both exceed the categories of knowledge and judgement in which an ethical evaluation would be founded, and provide cases in which such suspension is intolerable:

—Si vous n'étiez pas revenu, je serais allée de nouveau avec les gens des masses de pierre, la nuit, pour être avec eux, aller sans savoir, revenir pareil. Les regarder mettre leur verge dans la main de la petite fille et pleurer les yeux fermés.

(122)

These invisible (hypothetical, nocturnal) tears recall those of the maid of *Le Square*; again, they trace the line at the edge of the world where writing and the Durassian ethical uncertainly meet. Like all Durassian characters in the grip of passion, these abusive men (who include the woman's heterosexual lover) are not simply responsible for their actions, are overwhelmed by their terrible desire. And yet, again, the scene which suspends an ethical response cannot avoid evoking it. What *Les Yeux bleus cheveux noirs* adds with its constant suggestion of critical staging to this classic Durassian ethical scenario is the possibility of a qualifying frame; this addition hardly makes matters any clearer, however. For the frame may provide a critical distance on the events presented, inviting a critical ethical response; or it may work to naturalize them, to elevate them to a point beyond mere critique. Throughout this chapter, we have seen that Duras's work on sexuality from the 1980s employs ambiguity to relentlessly ambiguous effect. *L'Homme assis dans le couloir* confronts its eroticized violence with a writing which both is and is not pornographic, both qualifies and buys into the clichés it stages; *La Maladie de la mort* denounces the sterile homosocial, using an ambiguity to lift it beyond polemic which keeps it caught in precisely such contingent arguments; and *Les Yeux bleus cheveux noirs*, attempting to resolve this problem, provides a critical frame which makes it both an undecidable disruption of heterosexual gender relations and, at the same time, their ultimate, naturalizing glorification. As her later work views passion through the lens of broad social and institutional frameworks, Duras's writing maintains itself on the very edge of these frameworks, both challenging and espousing them, slipping away from them without this slippage itself being fixable as subversion. The edge between the world and its loss traced so passionately in Duras's earlier work is here explored again, but with inflated significance. For the world is now manifest in large-scale structures and institutions, lending a new level of drama to its mooted suspension. And the writing in which this suspension almost takes place is itself elevated, striving for the status of pure 'jaillissement intransitif'. It is the line on which these two developments in Duras's work meet that produces the constant ambiguity in these works on sexuality: as the world is addressed at a more architectural level, so the writing making this address exaggerates the drama of its gesture beyond the world. The fault line produced by this tension is the line of ambiguity which Duras's later writing, as it attempts to accompany the articulation of passion in the world, insistently walks. If Duras does think the question of sexual difference, as Irigaray urges, then this thinking certainly brings no salvation: for it produces nothing beyond uncertainty.

Even Duras's own words provide no protection from this uncertainty, as we have seen. Writing Duras into her work primarily draws attention to the shifts by which she is, awkwardly, neither here nor there, written in as she is written out; or, alternatively, produces a twilight, somewhat shameful sense of intrusion, if we wish to read these texts as more or less oblique transcriptions of the conflagrations of Duras's private life. And, as the Durassian corpus gains in both prominence and self-assurance in this later, post-1979 period of her work, so the question of the identity of the self—national, linguistic, autobiographical—comes to the fore; and it emerges with a pathos beyond a mere play of presence and absence. As writing is located on the ethical edge of the world, the question arises: how are we constituted, who also live on this edge? It is, accordingly, to Duras's elaborations of the status of the self that we will now, finally, turn.

6

WRITING AND THE SELF

Toi qui es nommée toi qui es douée d'identité
je t'aime d'un amour indéfini.

Les Mains négatives

Throughout Part II of this study, we have seen the increased importance of the figure of Duras in her work after 1979. Born during her
sabbatical from prose writing, notably in *Le Camion*, this figure
implicates herself in the writing of historical trauma, as seen in
Chapter 4, and suggests herself as a possible narrative frame for her
1980s work on sexuality, as discussed in Chapter 5. Beyond this
prominence of the writing self, the status of the self *per se* emerges as
a prominent question in Duras's later work, particularly the status
of the individual in relation to collective political discourses and
national identity. This interest again allows Duras to re-visit earlier
concerns (particularly the status of the dispossessed and a politics of
loss), while taking a new look at these interests through the triple
lens of an increased attention to their social implications (the issues
of immigration and racism, for example, come to the fore of Duras's
fiction for the first time during this period, and the status of the individual is insistently related to its threatened totalitarian abolition),
an explicit championing of the writing in which they are addressed,
and the dramatically inflated importance of the writing self, the figure of Duras. And, again as we have seen throughout her writing
after 1979, this re-elaboration produces double, ambiguous effects,
marked by the line of uncertainty characteristic of Duras's later
writing. It will be the aim of this chapter to trace Duras's work during this period on the status of the self, in order ultimately to bring
out the operation in this context of the line of uncertainty, and to
suggest its possible significance to Duras's writing in general. By
way of an introduction to its ambiguities in relation to the self, we
could do much worse than to consider the fate after 1979 of the figure of Duras herself.

It is in the period of her writing career after 1979 that Duras
enters the public field of ridicule and adoration that she will make

her own. During these years, she develops her already considerable public figure into a powerful media presence, providing dazzling television performances, scandalous *ex cathedra* judgements, and even interviews with the President.[1] Such interventions demonstrate the increasing importance of the figure of Duras within her non-literary work; in contrast to a more workaday journalistic approach, evident in Duras's earlier contributions to this medium, the figure of the writer refuses self-effacement before the object of the piece, instead sustaining the argument in question in part by means of self-dramatization. And, in addition to such interventions, Duras begins, as we have seen, to produce work which calls attention to the presence of her writing self, from texts which resemble diary entries or collections of fleeting thoughts (for example *L'Été 80* and *Les Yeux verts*), via others which both flirt with and question the most intimate autobiographical interpretations (*La Maladie de la mort, Les Yeux bleus cheveux noirs, Yann Andréa Steiner*), to still others which present themselves as autobiographical (*L'Amant, L'Amant de la Chine du Nord*). This work is, moreover, accompanied by interviews and occasional pieces in the press which continue to inflate the significance of the figure and private life of Duras, mostly in declamatory rather than explanatory mode.[2] Proof of the force of Duras's presence in the media at this time may be found in the barbed compliment of spoof and parody, testifying to the remarkable prominence attained by the figure of Duras during the 1980s.[3] As she soars to ever greater fame, sustained largely by the huge success of *L'Amant*, Duras finds her public figure met by a corresponding degree of scepticism and impatience. To many critics, Duras's career from the 1980s on becomes a torrent of self-serving *provocation* from a literary empress whose vanity is naked. It is not solely a matter of self-promotion, however. For the majority of the texts and interventions mentioned here do not simply vaunt the figure of the

---

[1] I refer here to Duras's appearance on *Apostrophes*, on Antenne 2, 28 September 1984; her 1985 article on the case of Christine Villemin, 'Sublime, forcément sublime Christine V.' (*Libération*, 17 juillet 1985, 4–6); and her 1986 interviews with her wartime Resistance colleague François Mitterrand in *L'Autre Journal*.

[2] See, for example, Yann Andréa, 'C'est fou c'que j'peux t'aimer'; Marguerite Duras, 'Moi' (*ME*, 74–5), and 'La Pute de la côte normande' (*Libération*, 14 novembre 1986, 30–1; published as *La Pute de la côte normande* (Paris: Minuit, 1986)).

[3] See Michel Bergain, 'Duras, de gauche complètement', *Globe*, 13 (janvier 1987), 29–33; and 'Marguerite Duraille', *Virginie Q* (texte présenté par Patrick Rambaud) (Paris: Balland, 1988).

writer; they also, by elevating this figure to star status, explore its tensions, seductions, contradictions, and effects. The description of this move as self-dramatization may recall the instabilities identified above in the phenomenon of *staging* in Duras's work: far from providing insulation for the object staged, Durassian dramatization exposes this object to an uncertain encounter with its outside. Thus, the Durassian staging of the writing self is also a passionate investigation of the several inflections which the representation of this figure can undergo. Which is perhaps less than a critical analysis of the field, but more than mere publicity. Duras is laying her self on the line; and she facilitates, by means of such a display, the exploration of substantial and moving concerns whose common thread is the status of the self, specifically the connections between the fluctuations of this self in a range of contexts and the business of writing. This may be read as the pleased interference of a noisy ego in areas demanding quiet; but it may also be read as the attempt by a writing self passionately to accompany her reader through the demands of the material in which her writing is caught. Over the course of its career, Duras's writing self builds up a considerable momentum; during its later years, this self exaggerates this momentum, both relishing its freewheeling grandeur, and putting it to work as the motor of a focused concern with the various inflections of selfhood. The Durassian gesture of self-dramatization is, then, characteristically ambiguous: while it does undeniably produce wearing effects of narcissism, it also possesses a more generous, enabling function, serving as the focus of a passion which sustains the reader through the detailed investigation of the field of the self.

This investigation has, moreover, inevitable ethical implications. For etymologically, *ethos* refers to 'moral character'; and the identification of the self as the locus of ethics is both as old as philosophy and as recent as the later Foucault. From the fundamental 'How should I live?' to Kant's autonomous moral agent, Hegel's situating of this agent in concrete social networks, and the Kierkegaardian individual's progress from the aesthetic via the ethical to the religious life, for example, ethical thought in a Western tradition has been inseparable from notions such as agency, will, and responsibility, all of which imply a self. Even Levinas's reversal of the ethical and ontological hierarchy, in which I am preceded and questioned by the vulnerable other, plainly depends on my remaining a moral agent, albeit exceeded by the responsibility to which I am called.

Duras's characteristic interest is also in ethical extremity which exceeds those it affects—but in a slightly different sense. For, as we have seen, Duras is everywhere fascinated by cases in which an ethical category such as responsibility is both exceeded and somehow still in place. The edge of the ethical also implies the ethical as residue—and therefore, possibly, the residual self, no longer quite a moral agent (Chauvin, for example, is not simply responsible for the orchestration of Anne's symbolic death), but still not free of the demands of the ethical (nor is he simply not responsible for this repetition). Seen in this light, Duras's simultaneous inflation and offering-up of the self thus both situates the questions it embraces within the traditional ground of the ethical and, in the same gesture, interrogates this ground. For if the self is understood as the conventional locus of the ethical, then the move—which we have now traced through almost the entirety of Duras's career—to the edge of the ethical must be understood as questioning the limits of the self. One question to the ground of ethics raised by Duras's attempt to write on the edge of the beyond is: what kind of self is implied in this attempt? Accordingly, much of Duras's later writing—which will be examined in this chapter—concerns itself with what is left of the self after the interrogation of its limits, developing extensively the figure of the residual self first sketched out as such in *Le Camion*.

What is more, this questioning, and the residuality which serves to articulate it, also constitute major contributions to their literary and philosophical context. For the development of these contexts during this period of Duras's career moves away from the apparent dismissal of the subject as a fleeting, bourgeois illusion, and towards some kind of residual subjectivity, remaining to form the fragile site of various forms of ethical thought. From Foucault (whose dismissal of the humanist subject at the end of *Les Mots et les choses* is among the most poetic, and yet who comes to interest himself in a quasi-classical ethics of selfhood), to Nancy's development of Heideggerian finitude in the direction of community defined as shared exposure, and with the influence of Levinas increasingly to the fore, this context has in part moved from the implicitly ethical liquidation of a confident humanism (too ready to ignore the other, and thus, in Levinas's formulation, insufficiently human) to investigate the kind of selfhood that could serve as the locus of this new, heteronomous responsibility. And in literary terms, an analogous movement may be traced: from the evacuation of the supposedly bourgeois, humanist presuppositions of narrative convention advocated for example in Robbe-Grillet's *Pour un nouveau roman*, and a generalized interest in the ludic, reflexive, and properly formal qualities of literary textuality, it has more recently been possible to observe a growing interest in ways of relating writing to subjectivity: in the resurgence of autobiography (exemplified not least by Robbe-Grillet), in the notion of life writing (which explicitly reworks the autobiographical in the light of this itinerary), in the importance of notions of testimony, in the explosion of personal narratives of intimate suffering.

That Duras is part of this context is evident, and well enough recognized (for example with reference to her practice of autobiography). What I would like to emphasize, however (and what has perhaps been less well documented) is that the model of selfhood she elaborates during this period, and the writing strategies which constitute this elaboration, have major contributions to make to these debates. Quite simply, the kind of selfhood which is to form the locus of our contemporary ethical and political thought is, plainly, a matter of enormous importance. If no simplistic return is possible to the arrogance of a humanism oblivious to its obligations to encounter others as more than just a secondary problem to be negotiated along my self-centred way; and if, at the same time, the notion of 'otherness' is not simply to become an empty fetish (the danger to which Derrida, of course, draws attention in 'Violence et métaphysique'), then an extremely subtle, fragile thinking of the self may well be necessary. And such a thinking, I will argue, may be found in Duras, whose definition of selfhood in terms of residuality seems to offer a way of approaching the line of minimal contact (between the minimally present other and the already-exposed self, as described in my Introduction, above) at the heart of the ethical. In this way, then, Duras's contribution to these debates—which must, as ever, be followed in the detailed patterns of her texts, and not just in her declarations or their thematics—may well prove to be among the most vital.

In this chapter, then, I will explore the various inflections of the status of the self presented by Duras after 1979, focussing particularly on the significance to her work of the notion of the residual self. Again, however, this interrogation produces an ambiguity characteristic of Duras's later work: while the residual selfhood she elaborates at this time has, as will be seen, its generosity and its pathos, it also risks—as discussed in Chapter 4, above, in the case of those caught up in mass trauma—the mere fetishization of residuality. In Duras's exaggeration of her own persona and in her work on self-hood in general, then, a similar ambiguity is apparent: between self-promotion and an enabling implication of the self in the first case, and between reductive fetishization and a generalized, mutual residuality in the second. The incompatibility of the two poles of this ambiguity (its generosity and its reductions) produces its own residual sense of self, however, as the two irreconcilable aspects of Duras's treatment of selfhood erode each other, to leave us simply with the uneasy sense that some kind of self is important to Duras at this time, but that we cannot quite decide which. The following chapter will, accordingly, explore Duras's elaboration of a residual selfhood in her writing after 1979. (It will, it should be noted, be a matter here less of an encounter with extreme ethical experience than of the status of the self who undergoes this experience). I will introduce this exploration with a brief account of Duras's move to a valorization of the individual, before discussing the relation between the identity of the self and racial identity, including a general account of Duras's treatment of Jewish identity, and the constitution of the writing self. When we have followed Duras through the turns of her encounter with these issues, we will find that some kind of self—and some kind of ethics, therefore—is left; and the importance in Duras's work of a self (and an ethics) thought of as residual may allow some overall conclusions about the line of uncertainty which characterizes this later phase of Duras's writing.

The Valorization of the Individual

Duras is not, of course, without her assertions of a self—and particularly a writing self—that seem to represent anything but a nuanced exploration of the complexities of the field of selfhood. In pieces from the late 1980s, for example, she claims that she alone represents 'le héros principal' of her work, and that 'Écrire, c'est écrire pour soi' (*ME*, 203); or that her ultimate goal is to write 'sur moi seule à travers les siècles' (*VM*, 53). And in *Les Yeux verts*, a rather bullish independence comes to the fore: 'On ne pourra jamais faire voir à quelqu'un ce qu'il n'a pas vu lui-même, découvrir ce qu'il n'a pas découvert lui seul' (*YV*, 28).

The self asserted in these declarations is not a strong, individual-istic presence, however. Rather, it comes into being only inasmuch as its status is uncertain. The centuries-old self with which Duras proclaims her writing to be preoccupied is an odd presence, both narcissistic and a ghostly echo; and, crucially, the figure of self-discovery is used by Duras in contexts which reveal the self in question as a by-product. It is already clear in the 1970s, for example, that the individual is championed primarily as the site of a fragile resistance to any totalizing or collective discourse. In *Les Parleuses*, Duras resorts to an assertion of individual independence in response to Xavière Gauthier's advocation of all-women consciousness-raising groups (*P*, 150–1); and in 'La Voie du gai désespoir' (an interview to accompany the release of *Le Camion*), the resurgence of the individual is important to her as an escape from the suffocating equivalence of all positive political programmes. (See *O*, 175–6).

Residue of and resistance to the equivalent oppressions of all positive political claims, through the turbulent journey of Duras's own left politics from 1958 to 1985, the individual is the weak and ruined site of the politics of loss elaborated along this itinerary. And it is in this capacity that this figure is glorified by Duras: the residual individual is championed precisely on the basis of this humility, which—just as Robert L.'s identity is most evident for the narrator of 'La Douleur' when it is most threatened, and just as, for Antelme, the unity of 'l'espèce humaine' is revealed in the moment of its attempted abolition—allows the self to escape its attempted destruction. Speaking in Montreal in 1981, Duras states: 'Je ne crois plus à rien du tout, seulement à l'individu et à sa propre survie, à sa propre liberté, à sa propre sauve-garde, et à sa propre grâce, à sa propre immensité' (Lamy and Roy (eds.), *Marguerite Duras à Mon-tréal*, 47). Duras is not alone in this move to the valorization of the resisting individual: both *Tel Quel* and Foucault operate similar moves around this time, for example, and the entry onto the Parisian intellectual stage of the *nouveaux philosophes* is marked in part by their denunciation of Soviet labour camps (a denunciation present in Duras's work since the late 1960s) and championing of the figure of the dissident.[4] Her use of paradox to articulate this move

[4] See, for example, Julia Kristeva, 'Un Nouveau Type d'intellectuel: Le Dissident' (*Tel Quel*, 74 (Hiver 1977), 3–8); and the account of both Foucault's political activities of the 1970s and the rise in this context of the *nouveaux philosophes* in David Macey, *The Lives of Michel Foucault* (London: Vintage, 1994).

(speaking of the 'immensité' of the individual, for example) signals that she is, however, particularly attuned to the complexities of its residuality. If the surviving self is all that is left, then, for Duras, it cannot be possessed, cannot be known, even as it is invaluable; self-confidence, for example, becomes an absurd leap of faith: 'Il faut faire confiance à cet inconnu, soi' (*ME*, 22).

The residual self is, necessarily, fragile; it is by definition weak, at risk, threatened for example by the totalitarian discourses whose aggressions it attempts to resist. Offering resistance to positive politics, this self also remains (just) within the political. Solidarity with the struggles of groups whose identity approaches that of the residual, resistant self may thus entail an amount of violent protest, in a passionate alignment in which Duras's literary and political concerns with the vulnerable individual may be seen to meet. The Oxford English Dictionary lists a usage of the term 'residuum' from 1897 as 'applied to persons of the lowest class'; the *Grand Larousse de la langue française* gives a sense of 'résidu' as 'être méprisable ou abject';[5] and Duras's elaboration of a residual selfhood has always been accompanied by a vociferous vindication of the rights of groups—particularly immigrant communities—whose scorned identities resist their threatened abolition. Examples of Duras's early journalism testify to a determination to focus attention on the problems faced by immigrant workers in Paris, confronted by a racism that is both banal and institutional (see in particular 'Les Fleurs de l'Algérien', 'Racisme à Paris', and 'Les deux ghettos'); one of the exhortations to be found in Duras's 1969 'film-annonce' for *Détruire dit-elle* is that in favour of a general alignment with 'le dernier coolie' (Rivette and Narboni, 51), and Duras's alignments with racially marginalized groups are constant.[6] Her denunciations of the Front National during the 1980s are frequent and vociferous, and represent the strongest example of this solidarity which survives the loss of politics. Insistent support for the victims of exclusionary aggression also marks Duras's literary and filmic work, of course;

[5] *Oxford English Dictionary*, 2nd edn. (Oxford: Clarendon Press, 1989) (I am grateful to Ingrid Wassenaar for this particular bit of linguistic residue); *Grand Larousse de la langue française*, 7 vols. (Paris: Larousse, 1977).
[6] See, for example, Duras's participation in 1970 in a protest against the death of five immigrant workers in a 'Foyer de solidarité franco-africaine' in Aubervilliers. A group of two to three hundred seized the premises of the Conseil National du Patronat Français; one hundred and sixteen (including Duras and Jean Genet) were arrested. (See Jean Genet, *L'Ennemi déclaré* (*Œuvres complètes*, vi) (Paris: Gallimard, 1991), 338).

and while repeatedly refusing any project based on a positive understanding of group identity, Duras continues to embrace the identities of the oppressed, to celebrate these identities inasmuch as they open onto a radically empty future in a view of the self as both fragile and resisting its oppression.

The key figure for Duras in this model, as the particular identities associated with 'la femme du *Camion*' ('qui invente d'être portugaise, ou arabe, ou malienne' (*O*, 177)) suggest, is that of the immigrant. The immigrant is by definition displaced, and on the border between at least two national identities; an original identity becomes positioned as to some degree residual, as that which remains of home. Duras's embrace of the residuality of the self in the figure of the immigrant represents the condensation in her later work of the political and literary fascination of this residuality traced here from the late 1950s; in order to explore the details of this embrace, I will now discuss the role of this figure in Duras's writing of this period *via* a reading of *La Pluie d'été*.

Many of the concerns of *La Pluie d'été* recall those established during Duras's writing of 1969 to 1971, as discussed in Chapter 3, above, thus underscoring the provenance of the residual immigrant self in Duras's work. Ernesto's rejection of his schooling—'je retournerai pas à l'école parce que à l'école on m'apprend des choses que je sais pas' (*PE*, 22)—grows in part out of the valorization of incomprehension inaugurated during this earlier period. (*Ah! Ernesto*, the text in which this figure makes his début is, for example, published in 1971). Moreover, once the increasing notoriety of Ernesto's phrase has earned him the attention of the national press, his sister makes clear how far removed this refusal is from the jargon of a conventional oppositional politics:

Le journaliste: Excusez-moi . . . On peut se tromper . . . Alors il s'agirait d'une forme de révolte . . . de la découverte de l'injustice . . . immanente . . . du fait social en quelque sorte . . .
Jeanne: Je crois pas que ça intéresserait mon frère ce que vous dites.

(115)

In addition, the figure of Jewishness is woven through the text as a figure of the instability of identity, in what is by now a typical Durassian gesture, established in the works of 1969 and 1970. In *La Pluie d'été*, however, Jewishness (the significance of which in Duras's work will be discussed below) is doubled by the figure of the immigrant self as the locus of the uncertainty of identity, and the renewed politics of refusal which flows in the wake of May 1968 is now presented within a field of explicitly contemporary urgency.

Defence of immigrant communities has been an integral part of Duras's politics from the 1950s, as seen above; in the 1980s, she begins to insist on a vision of France as exemplarily open to a welcome flux of immigration. In 1981, she interprets the nation as just having voted 'pour le Salvador, pour le Nicaragua, et pour le prolétariat colonial chez elle émigré, ces gens de l'Afrique et de l'Europe pauvre qui depuis trente ans construisent ses autoroutes, ses parkings, le gros-œuvre de son habitat';[7] in 1985, she praises what she calls 'l'internationalisme de l'idée française'.[8] As an immigrant family living in a Paris suburb, Ernesto's family weld questions of selfhood to the concrete of this politics in 1990s France. Duras's elegiac fable could hardly be more real; and the links between Duras's interest in the fragile, residual self and the contemporary politics of racial identity are apparent throughout the work. In her coda to the text, in which its setting is declared, she makes clear the links between the Vitry of the text and its extra-textual counterpart: 'le port s'appelle vraiment le Port-à l'Anglais. La Nationale 7 est la Nationale 7. L'école s'appelle vraiment l'école Blaise Pascal' (*PE*, 150). And yet, as one might expect, these links are rendered unstable even as they are established: 'Vitry est une banlieue terrifiante, introuvable, indéfinie, que je me suis mise à aimer. C'est le lieu le moins littéraire que l'on puisse imaginer, le moins défini. Je l'ai donc inventé' (149). *La Pluie d'été* may not be reduced to simple transcription; yet nor may it be removed from the milieu within which its exploration of the position of the immigrant self is also lived.

The scenery against which this exploration takes place is evoked quite precisely as that of the post-industrial Parisian suburb; and the position of the immigrant self within this scenery is sketched with a deft parodic calm. When the 'vieille autoroute de ciment noir' is to be demolished, the arrival of immigrant workers 'de l'Afrique du

---

[7] Marguerite Duras, 'Un Pays du nord', *Des Femmes en mouvements hebdo*, 48 (3–10 juillet 1981), 25.

[8] Marguerite Duras, 'L'Internationalisme de l'idée française', *Globe*, 23 (décembre 1987), 36. Denouncing the Front National in 1992, Duras repeats this vision of an open France, in terms which recall her disgust in *La Douleur* at what she saw as de Gaulle's elision of grief after the Holocaust: 'Ils ont souillé la France, qui est la terre sainte de l'Europe, la terre de l'accueil et de la liberté, qui a pleuré pour les Juifs' (Jean-Louis Ezine, 'Vive Cresson et la lutte des classes!', *Le Nouvel Observateur*, 2–8 avril 1992, 65).

Nord, de la Yougoslavie, de la Turquie' is flatly stated (119); and the quotation of the Mayor's fleeting dismissal of the homes of the town's immigrant community in favour of housing designed as municipal self-justification produces a deadpan, ironic denunciation:

[Le maire] avait annoncé l'essor de la ville, sa compétitivité prochaine. Les voies ferrées seraient déplacées afin d'agrandir la surface de la nouvelle zone industrielle. La ville, du même coup, allait être débarrassée des bidonvilles du bord de Seine, ainsi que des troquets et des maisons closes qui faisaient la honte des populations laborieuses de la région.

(119–20)

The constant displacement of immigrant workers by a political discourse which excuses itself by a well-worn rhetoric of the deserving versus the undeserving poor ('qui faisaient la honte des populations laborieuses de la région') is clearly marked. In relation to this indifferent municipality, the family of the text becomes both an irritant and resistant: 'Dans tous les rapports de la mairie les concernant il était fait état de la mauvaise volonté de ces gens et de l'obstination étrange qu'ils mettaient à s'y tenir' (11–12). Of course the family's 'obstination' is described as 'étrange': the irritation they introduce is that of a foreign body. The judgemental 'on' that is the Durassian voice of petty prejudice here becomes the fount of faltering racist platitudes:

On parlait d'eux dans Vitry, les femmes surtout, les mères: ces gens-là, un jour ou l'autre, ils abandonnent leurs enfants. On disait: c'est dommage, des enfants aussi beaux . . . pas d'école . . . pas d'éducation . . . rien . . . ces gens-là, les allocations, ils en vivent, vous m'avez comprise . . .

(70)

This, then, is the scenery of irritated prejudice against which the immigrant self presents the complications of residual selfhood as Duras sees them. Indeed, racist irritation is presented quite straightforwardly as the result of the disturbance introduced by the immigrant presence into assumptions about native identity. Turning a racist logic back on itself, Duras valorizes this disturbance, and celebrates what she presents as its enigmatic beauty. Returning from late-night drinking sessions, the mother and father of the family (but especially the mother) sing *La Neva*, evoking a specifically Russian cultural origin even as this origin is washed away, as the song becomes 'très beau, sans plus de paroles' (108). This residual cultural marker then becomes free-floating, and draws non-immigrant identity into its instability, until 'c'était impossible de savoir d'où elle pouvait bien venir' (108). Mobilizing the ready-made figures of childhood and music, Duras implicitly contests a racist discourse on its own terms, presenting the residual cultural identity of the immigrant self as a primary model of enchanting loss and displacement whose ungovernable, confusing spread is to be welcomed.

Duras's embrace of what she sees as the complications of immigrant identity is demonstrated in part by the fluctuations of naming within the text. We may recall the swirl of complexity which attends naming in 'Aurélia Steiner Vancouver' (see Chapter 4, above); here, such complexity repeats the instabilities of this earlier, Jewish figure of unstable identity with reference to the immigrant self. The father is relatively simply named, and his origin stated: he is Emilio Crespi, from Italy (57). And yet within a matter of lines, the mother switches from using this name to calling him Enrico. To have only two names may represent a relative stability of identity for a prominent figure in this text, however. Ernesto, in addition to 'Ernesto', is named by its diminutive, Ernestino (23/91)—ironically, in the second instance, since he is being described as 'immense'—and Vladimir (23). And quoting from the biblical 'livre brûlé', he speaks in the voice of David (111). But—as in the case of Aurélia Steiner—it is with the mother that the questions of naming and national identity become especially exacerbated. Most usually, she is named Natacha (28 *et passim*); in addition, she is called Eugenia (65), Emilia (98), and Ginetta (96). When her origin is revealed, it is claimed that her true name is none of these: 'Elle s'appelait Hanka Lissovskaïa' (58). As this profusion suggests, the mother's national identity is a matter of generalized confusion: 'Personne, ni dans son entourage ni dans Vitry, ne savait d'où venait la mère, de quel côté de l'Europe, ni de quelle race elle était' (44). Emilio alone has some idea, and even he is unsure: 'Elle, du Caucase, enfin . . . de ce côté-là . . . ' (66). The revelation of her origin, accordingly, reveals it as a non-origin:

Elle était née avant le départ de ses parents pour la Pologne, elle n'avait jamais su où, un village avait dit sa mère, quelque part dans le fatras des populations entre l'Ukraine et l'Oural.

(58)

In her obscure provenance, the mother is also located in the region of the Escaut (25), and, recalling the atopia of *Abahn Sabana David* and 'Aurélia Steiner Melbourne', in 'la Sibérie Centrale' (45).

In *La Pluie d'été*, then, the techniques of confusion in relation both to geography and identity which have been a politically significant feature of Duras's work since *Abahn Sabana David* in 1970, are related to the residual identity of the immigrant self. This self becomes the site of obscure echoes, traversed by a forgotten past:

Il lui reste de son passé des consonances irrémédiables, des mots qu'elle paraît dérouler, très doux, des sortes de chants qui humectent l'intérieur de la voix, et qui font que les mots sortent de son corps sans qu'elle s'en aperçoive quelquefois, comme si elle était visitée par le souvenir d'une langue abandonnée.

(27)

The father, too, is as it were given over to what remains of his former linguistic identity, seized intermittently by a strange, unrecognizable version of Italian,

qui sortait de lui comme si c'était la fin de sa vie et qu'il se vidait de ce qui lui restait encore de cette autre vie qu'il avait eue avant cette avalanche d'enfants.

(69)

The residual identity of the immigrant self is thus here represented linguistically, as the textual avalanche suggests its engulfing return. Producing a disturbance in the field of identity which extends beyond its own limits, the figure of the immigrant self offers, in this text, an exploration of the self as residual that is intimately linked to a contemporary identity politics. The valorization of the figure of the immigrant self against the platitudes of racism represents not (simply) the celebration of a different identity, but rather the elaboration of a different model altogether, in which the self is presented and embraced as fragile, residual and resistant.

Racial Identity

It comes as no surprise to Duras's reader that these qualities of the immigrant self also produce its tentative qualification as Jewish. When the lost words to *La Neva* eventually return to the mother— 'sans qu'elle s'en rende compte'—they are displaced from an expected Russian origin into a mixture in which a Jewish element introduces a tone of mourning: 'Ce n'était pas du russe les paroles retrouvées, c'était un mélange d'un parler caucasien et d'un parler juif, d'une douceur d'avant les guerres, les charniers, les montagnes de morts' (*PE*, 142). Ernesto insists to his brothers and sisters that their parents are 'les derniers rois d'Israël, à Vitry' (57) and, emphasizing this residuality, reads from the biblical 'livre brûlé' which (recalling the claims made for *La Douleur*) suggests a miraculous survival of the conflagrations of a traumatic history. Throughout Duras's work since 1969, the figure of Jewishness has been the paradoxical emblem of unstable identity, a celebrated fragile selfhood embraced in its resistance to its attempted destruction. The weaving of Jewishness into the fabric of *La Pluie d'été* heightens the sense that questions of residual identity are considered largely during this period by Duras through the lens of national/racial identity. From the immigrant self, figuring Duras's valorization of the fragility of identity, we may, therefore, move to a consideration of questions of racial identity in general. Shortly, I will consider the tensions in Duras's work between fixity and instability in this field, and the characteristic double, ambiguous reading these tensions produce. First, however, I propose to begin discussion of this area with reference to Duras's treatment of Jewish identity.

The emergence of Duras's characters as explicitly Jewish coincides with their emergence as dispersed, residual figures: the first appearance of such characters comes with *Détruire dit-elle*, and the link between Jewishness and the dismantling of unified identity is explicit in *Abahn Sabana David*. As her concern with the presentation of Jewish identity intensifies in the early 1980s, Duras backdates this emergence to *Le Ravissement de Lol V. Stein* and *Le Vice-Consul*, despite the lack of textual indication (see *YV*, 157); despite this, it remains the case that only in 1969 does Jewishness begin to play a significant part in her work, initially related to the events of May 1968, and presented as radically exceeding Western social structures. The embodiment of this disruptive force comes in the figure(s) of Abahn, in *Abahn Sabana David*; the particular revolutionary position elaborated in this work in relation to this view of Jewish identity has already been discussed in Chapter 3, above. After this intense development, the figure of Jewishness recedes from Duras's writing, and undergoes a double transformation. First, the question of Jewish identity re-emerges dramatically in 1979 with the *Aurélia Steiner* texts, now a major locus of elegiac and troubling representations. Secondly, Jewishness becomes the most consistent element in the

chains of interconnectedness which come to characterize Duras's
work after 1979, a development announced in 1977 by the presentation of 'la femme du *Camion*' as 'la mère de tous les enfants juifs
morts à Auschwitz' (*O*, 177). And with *Les Yeux verts*, Duras inaugur-
ates both a period of intense concern with the trauma of the Holocaust, as discussed in Chapter 4, and a determined privileging of the
question of Jewishness across the range of her writing. Having
already discussed the function of the figure of the Jew as revolutionary agent in Chapter 3, above, I will now concentrate on Duras's use
of Jewishness during the 1980s as a model for identity in general.

The unique trauma suffered by the Jewish people in the
Holocaust means, for Duras, that this identity can no longer be
comprehended:

> Non, le lieu juif, je ne peux pas arriver à le résoudre, à le rattacher, même de très
> loin à une donnée de notre vie . . . La mort d'un juif à Auschwitz, quant à moi
> peuple l'histoire tout entière de notre temps, toute la guerre.

> (*YV*, 177)

After this catastrophe, which attempted to erase the identity of an
entire people, Duras claims that it is impossible to *be* Jewish: 'Moi je
me demande comment on peut être juif aujourd'hui, comment un
Juif peut accepter d'avoir subi ça' (*ME*, 28). Duras appears to be
placing Jewishness in a double bind here, by arguing that the only
Jewish identity available is, precisely, the lack of an identity. And this
double bind might, in turn, be accused of repeating anti-Semitic
aggressions, by excluding Jewish identity from consideration as fully
human, or accepting that it has been destroyed. (It is interesting,
for example, to note the equation between 'être juif aujourd'hui'
and 'accepter d'avoir subi ça.') For Duras, however, the model is
reversed: as in the case of the immigrant self, the calling into question of the identity of the Jewish people is valorized, as paradigmatic
of an identity founded problematically in displacement. The otherness ascribed to Jewishness, by virtue of its history of exclusion and
exile, is thus, for Duras, to be understood as the model for a new
understanding of Western identity in general: 'L'Occident est juif.
Cette faculté de l'homme européen d'être l'autre et lui-même à la
fois, c'est juif.'[9] 'Nous sommes tous des juifs allemands': if we—any
of us—are to think our identity, it must, Duras maintains, be on the

[9] Marguerite Duras, 'Africa, Africa', *L'Autre Journal*, 19–25 mars 1986, 24–33 (31).

basis of a non-self-identity for which Jewishness supposedly provides the privileged model.

Duras provides examples of such thinking in her presentation of her own moments of identification with Jewishness. Anticipating the return of Robert L., possibly with Jewish deportees, the narrator of 'La Douleur' wonders, if he is to return, then 'Pourquoi pas avec les juifs' (*D*, 36). This phrase might well serve as a motto for Duras's many alignments of herself with Jewishness in a range of interviews and writings. We have already encountered (in Chapter 4) her emphasis on the Holocaust as a personal trauma; according to *Le Monde extérieur*, her identification with Jewish friends began even before awareness of the full horrors of their persecution, in a confused desire for complete resemblance, which produced the idea that she, too, might wear the yellow star—unaware, as too were they, 'que c'était pour les dénombrer afin de les déporter et les gazer' (*ME*, 28). In the face of the shock of the removal of this ignorance, Duras's identification is not abandoned, however; rather, it becomes total: 'L'Histoire des Juifs, c'est mon histoire' (Lamy and Roy (eds.), *Marguerite Duras à Montréal*, 73).

The drama of such identification plainly suggests some of the dangers involved in Duras's treatment of Jewish identity, however. By arguing, for example, that a supposedly 'European' capacity to integrate otherness into the self is 'Jewish', or by asserting outlandishly her own 'Jewishness', Duras risks robbing these terms of any historical or cultural specificity, and reducing them to a self-serving metaphorical tic. This is certainly the view taken by Charlotte Wardi, writing in 1979 (and hence about the figure of the Jew in *Détruire dit-elle* and *Abahn Sabana David*).[10] Wardi sees Duras as presenting in novelistic form the ideas on Jewishness elaborated by Blanchot in *L'Entretien infini*, and criticizes both these ideas and what she sees as their novelistic repetition in Duras. There are, certainly, good reasons for this association (although Wardi does not make them explicit); the extent of Blanchot's influence on Duras's view of Jewish identity has already been seen in Chapter 3, above. Wardi argues against these ways of thinking about Jewishness, claiming that they reduce Jewish identity to 'quelques formules faciles', and constitute only arbitrary philosophical speculation (Wardi, 8).

[10] Charlotte Wardi, 'L'Oubli du génocide dans le roman français de 1945 à 1970', *Les Nouveaux Cahiers*, 58 (Automne 1979), 4–9.

Blanchot's position (and, by extension, Duras's) is dangerous, argues Wardi, 'dans la mesure où elle déshumanise le génocide et le transforme en un symbole dont l'abstraction appelle toutes les déformations' (7). Acknowledging the dangers of ahistorical abstraction, Blanchot had defended his highly metaphysical discussion of Jewishness on the grounds that it is precisely within metaphysics that the full significance of Jewishness is to be located—and that the attempt to deny this metaphysical import (the relationship to otherness presented by Judaism) is a common feature of anti-Semitism (Blanchot, 'Être juif', 190, n. 1). To refuse 'abstraction' in this debate would, for Blanchot, mean refusing the full gravity of the historical meaning of Jewishness.[11] Wardi appears not to acknowledge Blanchot's acknowledgement, doubtless seeing it as a caveat which fails to alter the highly speculative nature of his thesis. Describing Duras's writing as the fictional form of this dangerous thesis—albeit adapted to Duras's 'mythologie personnelle'—Wardi argues that, in Duras, 'Le juif, homme de la rupture, est l'antithèse de la société occidentale capitaliste et se réduit à une entité, à une notion' (Wardi, 8).

Wardi's criticisms are indisputably pertinent, even to the bulk of Duras's writing on Jewishness, produced after Wardi's article. In this writing, Jewishness represents the key term in Duras's ethic of interconnectedness, and as such is linked to all sorts of figures and places, from Melbourne to Vancouver, Poland to Duras's room at Trouville, a cat to Yann Andréa (who, in reference to *Yann Andréa Steiner*, says 'Avec ce nom, elle m'a judaïsé').[12] While this interlinking

---

[11] Part of Blanchot's aim in this argument is to contest Sartre's presentation of Jewish identity in *Réflexions sur la question juive*. As Blanchot points out, Sartre defines Jewishness negatively, as the product of non-Jewish projection: 'Ce n'est ni leur passé, ni leur religion, ni leur sol qui unissent les fils d'Israël. Mais s'ils ont un lien commun, s'ils méritent tous le nom de Juif, c'est qu'ils ont une situation commune de Juif, c'est-à-dire qu'ils vivent au sein d'une communauté qui les tient pour Juifs' (Sartre, *Réflexions sur la question juive* (Paris: Gallimard, 1954), 81). Against this definition, Blanchot insists that any definition of Jewishness takes place against 'un fond de réalité et d'authenticité "historiques" préalable, fond que l'on doit appeler le judaïsme et qui définit, de manière implicite, le rapport de tout homme à lui-même. Être juif ne peut donc pas être le simple revers de la provocation anti-juive . . . Être juif signifie davantage et sans doute quelque chose d'essentiel qu'il importe de mettre au jour' (Blanchot, 'Être juif', 182). Far from being abstract, then, Blanchot's thesis is, in his terms, a defence of the historical *and* metaphysical specificity of Judaism *against* abstraction.

[12] Philippe Lançon, 'Le Survivant', *Libération*, 18 mars 1996, 44. This identificatory tendency is identified by Kristeva as a generalized post-War phenomenon: 'Une fascination pour le judaïsme, pour ne pas parler de flirt, s'imposa dans cette voie, révélant la culpabilité de toute une génération d'intellectuels face à l'antisémitisme et à la collaboration des premières années de la guerre' (Kristeva, 'La Maladie de la douleur', 231).

serves, for Duras, to stress both the irreducibility of Jewish identity to any fixed position and the importance of a constant, expanding sharing of suffering, it also, plainly, risks collapsing into a mere fetish, and comes dangerously close to emptying the term of any specific meaning.

Inversely, however, other instances of Duras's treatment of Jewishness also fill the term with potential meanings and associations that are to say the least disquieting. Aurélia Steiner, for example, is quite definitely identified as Jewish. And in the most intimate manner: this name, in its German form, with inevitable shuddering intimations, is bestowed upon Aurélia by the sailor, the substitute for her father, just as he penetrates her:

> Il dit: Juden, Juden Aurélia, Juden Aurélia Steiner.

> Il se tient à l'entrée du corps d'Aurélia Steiner, reste là, toujours dans le soin extrême de mener le supplice jusqu'à son terme. Puis il entre dans le corps.

('ASV', 146)

The ambiguities here are multiple. The disquieting name given to Aurélia is plural ('Juden'), and repeated, almost shattered, questioning its ability to name its object; written inside her body, moreover, this name both profoundly identifies Aurélia and escapes her understanding (*YV*, 110). A disturbing scenario emerges: perhaps there does, after all, exist a stable identity for Aurélia, and perhaps this identity would be racial, named in a word inextricable from its traumatic history, and imposed upon her in a way that is beyond her understanding? The paradox that Duras claims to find within this identity resides, however, in the fact that its stability exists precisely inasmuch as it is unknowable. The sailor is no more in possession of Aurélia's name than she is: when he uses the 'name' 'Juden',

> il ne s'agit pas d'une insulte, il se laisse prendre, emporter par la force de la malédiction qui règne sur la race, le corps d'Aurélia Steiner, il ne s'aperçoit pas qu'il ne la nomme plus mais qu'il l'appelle par le mot qui dit sa race et ce faisant, il entre dans le vertige du désir fou . . .

(*YV*, 111)

Linking the use of the term 'Juden' to the sailor's passion, Duras removes the act of naming from possible condemnation as simply abusive: the sailor is not, as the racist thinks s/he is, imposing by a hateful name the 'truth' of the person or group named. The sailor is carried beyond himself by his use of this word; if this logic is extended even to consciously anti-Semitic uses of the term, the supposed insult may be seen to turn back on its user with the full force of the horror it evokes. Jewishness, for Duras, presents an identity which escapes stable definitions as such; the anti-Semitic attempt to stabilize this fluidity as an insult would, then, collapse under the weight of its own impossibility. 'Juden'—as an insult— names nothing, no one.[13]

And yet: this scene focusses the worry that Duras is fetishizing Jewishness, and (here) eroticizing anti-Semitism. The equation of the sailor's powerlessness before the maledictory force of the history of the term 'Juden' with his desire, for all that it reveals the extent to which anti-Semitism is exceeded by an historical force it thinks it can control, also removes anti-Semitism into the realm of the passions, thereby potentially absolving the anti-Semite of responsibility for his/her brutalities. Clearly, the sailor's use of the term is not simply abusive; but nor is it simply subversive of its abusive use. Is such ambivalence appropriate here? Granted, Duras insists on reading Jewishness under the sign of ambivalence—but then, this ambivalence itself might be abusive. Again, the Durassian notion of residual responsibility (as seen with reference to Jacques Hold and Chauvin in Chapter 2, and *L'Homme assis dans le couloir* in Chapter 5) emerges, with worrying implications, as the sailor might be excused from what may be his anti-Semitism on the grounds that he is not fully in control of his behaviour. This is not quite what Duras is doing, since for her the fascination of this kind of residual responsibility lies in the fact that even as judgement is cut through, it remains necessary—but this agonizing ambiguity at the edge of the ethical might well be seen as an inadequate, paralysed response to the obscenity of anti-Semitism.

Duras's use of the figure of Jewishness touches, then, on the ethical consequences of situating the self at the limit of its coherence. For this liminal position keeps the fragile residue of selfhood bound into the aggressions of the political, both calling forth these aggressions in its troubling vulnerability, and apparently removing from the self the agency by which they might be positively resisted. The

---

[13] This implosion of meaning is returned to in *Écrire*: 'Le mot juif est "pur" partout mais c'est quand il est dit dans la vérité qu'il est reconnu comme étant le seul vocable à exprimer ce qu'on attend de lui. Et ce qu'on attend de lui, on ne le sait plus parce que le passé des juifs, les Allemands l'ont brûlé' (*É*, 134).

valorization of fragility may thus perpetuate its oppression. Characteristically, Duras celebrates the oppressed term of a hierarchy in the very terms in which it is oppressed, and so risks the repetition of this oppression rather than its displacement.[14] It should be stressed, however, that Duras's embrace of the residual self (both immigrant and Jewish) seeks less to invite its continued persecution than to refuse and to confuse the terms on which this persecution is possible. While further aggression remains a danger, such danger is called forth only inasmuch as it is, supposedly, exceeded by the fragility it attempts to master.[15]

Some kind of political agency must remain, however, if brutalization is to be resisted, for all that any positive politics may become the locus of brutalization. Duras's negative utopian appeals to refusal will not themselves forestall the violence of a racist or an anti-Semitic politics, for example—which is why they are part of a double move, the other phase of which comprises the forceful denunciation of such violence. We cannot, however, simply remove the unease of Duras's aestheticization of oppressed identity by pointing to her extra-literary condemnation of its oppression. Nor, conversely, can we remove the upsetting force of the valorized residual self in relation to an aggressive politics of stable identity. The ambiguity which marks Duras's later writing thus characterizes her presentation of immigrant and Jewish identity: on the one hand, she vehemently resists racist aggression, in part by celebrating residual, threatened identity as the basis for a generalized shift in thinking about identity; on the other hand, this celebration inevitably fetishizes this residuality, and thus perpetuates the exclusion it supposedly explodes. Duras's increasingly contentious writing, in equal parts generous and reductive, committed and self-aggrandizing, bears the new social and historical weight of its concerns both impressively and clumsily, and invites a reading which must, necessarily, be both enthusiastic and critical.

Such a double reading is, moreover, also necessitated by Duras's treatment of questions of racial identity in general. In this field as a

[14] Marilyn Schuster writes that Duras 'still encloses Jewish identity within terms set by the oppressor . . . Again, the line between sympathy with an oppressed group and appropriation of their story, between empathetic representation and fatalism, remains problematic' (Schuster, *Marguerite Duras Revisited*, 103).

[15] The comparison is unavoidable here with Duras's visions of a femininity which would exceed masculine mastery precisely by its silence, what *La Maladie de la mort* calls 'la force invincible de la faiblesse sans égale' (*MM*, 31).

whole, Duras's figures often seem poised between stereotype and uncertainty; again, on the line between the reconfirmation and the refusal of racist discourses. Examples of the use of racial stereotypes are not hard to come by in Duras's texts. In *L'Amant de la Chine du Nord*, for example, the young girl's elder brother refers to her Chinese lover as 'Sale Chinetoque' (*ACN*, 164). Such examples imply no espousal by the text's narrative voice of the position in question, and can be read straightforwardly as its critical staging. It is not always thus, however. In *Emily L.*, the couple from the Isle of Wight whose story is reconstructed in hypothesis by the text's 'je' and 'vous' figures are said to drink 'les boissons des alcooliques anglo-saxons: la Pilsen noire pour lui et pour elle le double bourbon' (*EL*, 17).[16] In this case, there is no safe distance between simplistic position and narrative voice (recalling the instabilities between narrative voice and interior monologue in *Un Barrage contre le Pacifique*, discussed in Chapter 1, above). When other, more serious racial stereotypes are invoked elsewhere in Duras's work, this unstable critical frame can become disturbing. Such images are in plentiful supply in *Emily L.*, in the perceptions of the narrating 'Je' of a group of Koreans who have inexplicably appeared in Quillebeuf. On their first, enigmatic appearance, the group all look alike:

Je regarde autour de nous et voici qu'il y a des gens, là-bas, au fond de cette place, à la sortie du chemin abandonné, là où il ne devrait y avoir personne. Ils sont arrêtés et ils regardent vers nous. Ils sont une quinzaine, tous pareillement habillés de blanc. Il s'agit d'une même personne indéfiniment multipliée. Je cesse de regarder.

(*EL*, 11)

Her presentation of these figures appears relatively content to dehumanize or at least patronize them:

Plusieurs d'entre eux s'étaient mis à courir, à jouer à s'attraper, d'autres étaient arrivés du chemin abandonné le long du fleuve, ils étaient identiques aux premiers. C'étaient des hommes ronds, précocement atteints par l'obésité. Quand ils couraient, ils rebondissaient sur le sol, ils étaient légers comme des ballons, des gros bébés.

(49)

---

[16] Both *Emily L.* and some of the difficulties raised by Duras's encounter with racial difference during this period are discussed in essential detail in Williams, *The Erotics of Passage*, 125–32. The narrator's attitude towards the Koreans is also discussed in Raylene Ramsay, 'Through a Textual Glass, Darkly: The Masochistic in the Feminine Self in Marguerite

And the terror inspired in the narrator by these figures is linked, apparently, to a visceral conviction of their innate cruelty:

J'ai montré les Coréens.
—Regardez-les. Tout à l'heure j'ai cru qu'ils allaient encercler le café et procéder à notre extermination. Comme je vous ai dit, ces gens sont très cruels. Ce sont les plus cruels que porte la terre.

(55)

Such crude generalizations are justified by the narrator on two grounds. First, she invokes a model of scandal, according to which offensiveness may serve as a mark of truthfulness: as in Duras's 1985 piece on Christine Villemin ('Sublime, forcément sublime Christine V.'), refrains such as 'J'ai dit ce que je crois' and 'C'est ce que je crois' (14) affirm the blunt nature of the belief in question as evidence of its value. More subtly, perhaps, the narrator also justifies her feelings by reference to her colonial past, which, she claims, has afforded her insights into an 'Asiatique' mentality:

J'ai dit que je connaissais les Asiatiques, qu'ils étaient cruels, que sur les routes ils s'amusaient à écraser les chiens moribonds de la plaine de Kampot avec leurs voitures.

(47)

J'ai encore parlé des Asiatiques. J'ai dit qu'ils étaient cruels et joueurs de cartes et hypocrites, et fous, que je me souvenais bien des animaux en Indochine, tous squelettiques et pleins de gale comme dans le sud de l'Espagne et en Afrique noire.

(64)

In such pronouncements, the fragile self resisting racist aggressions seems to have returned to the position of the other of a discourse of racial certainty. Not all immigrants, apparently, are equally valorized. With the second of these examples, however, the invocation of a colonial past which serves primarily to justify a position based on the fixity of national and racial identity begins to tip over into the complication of just such a position. The comparison with other geographical contexts inevitably destabilizes the claim being made for the particular cruelty of the 'Asiatiques'. (Although it remains within the prejudices of northern Europe). Elsewhere, the narrator's colonial past is also invoked in order to provide evidence of her own complicated national identity: even as she is describing more

Duras's *Emily L.'*, in *The French New Autobiographies* (Gainesville: University Press of Florida, 1996), 165–88 (185).

examples of Indochinese cruelty, the narrator concludes in a phrase which necessarily complicates the simplistic model she is espousing:

Dans la plaine de Kampot, quand ils tuaient les chiens à coups de baton, ils restaient souriants, comme des enfants. Ils regardaient mourir les chiens avec des rires frais, ils regardaient en s'amusant les grimaces et les gesticulations d'agonie des chiens squelettiques. Je dis que je ne pouvais pas être pareille aux Français de France après cette enfance.

(53)

No stable qualification, however: the narrator may be claiming that her childhood has removed her from perhaps the more liberal presuppositions of 'les Français de France'. But the distinction certainly appears to introduce a slippage within national identity, with the narrator claiming for herself a residual immigrant identity.[17]

Where there may be simple espousal of a fixity of national/racial identity, there may also be the qualification of this fixity, then. So, while the narrative adopts the narrator's ignorance of the identity of the Koreans on their first appearance, and so enforces an alignment (however temporary) with her position, it also incorporates the dismissive criticism of this position by her companion: 'Espèce de raciste à la gomme' (14). Moreover, the narrator herself presents her fear of the Koreans as a kind of pathological condition ('On m'a dit que c'était probablement les colonies, l'enfance là-bas et l'alcool' (50)) and as pathetic, this judgement itself presented as a prophecy fulfilled in its writing: 'j'étais toujours, je le dirais plus tard dans un livre, aussi lamentable, désespérante d'idiotie' (15). There is, then, also a displacing frame around the narrator's racism; and the self-fulfilling *Emily L.* explicitly asks to be read as a critical staging of her position. As with both *L'Homme assis dans le couloir* and *Les Yeux bleus cheveux noirs*, however, (see Chapter 5, above) the frame is not safe, the position in question is not simply denounced by its staging. Rather, a potential frame is juxtaposed with material it may or may not qualify. Again, the unease created by this (un)framed material will not quite be removed by its possible framing; the text presents both the stereotype and its critique, without allowing the latter quite to

[17] For an evocative description by Duras of her displaced national identity and her Vietnamese childhood, see *L*, 60–1. Elsewhere, Duras presents her displacement from Indochina as a liberation from the baggage of national identity: 'A dix-sept ans, quand je suis allée à Paris pour faire l'université, j'ai été définitivement nettoyée de l'appartenance à une quelconque patrie.' This then enables the provocative statement, 'Je suis créole' (Thelu, 'The Thing', 16).

qualify the former. Residuality may, then, here operate to propagate rather than to refuse a racist position—but, necessarily double, it may also operate in the opposite direction. The narrator, who may or may not be deluded, who may or may not see herself as 'la Française', declares that this ambiguity is in fact proper to writing: 'Écrire, c'est aussi ne pas savoir ce qu'on fait, être incapable de le juger' (58). Writing is not *simply* beyond judgement: it is *also* beyond judgement. The very ambiguity that gestures beyond polemic also keeps writing caught on the edge of the polemical world, in Duras's double gesture here performed in relation to national identity. There are racist positions here; and there is their qualification. There is a celebration of the perceived residuality of Jewish and immigrant identity; and there is the reduction of this residuality to an empty mannerism. I would like to put off drawing conclusions about this inconclusive stand-off (which, as we have seen, runs through Duras's later work in a range of areas) until the end of this chapter; for there remains one vital area in which the role of the residual self should first be considered: Duras's autobiographical writing.

The Writing Self

In Duras's more or less autobiographical works, the authorial voice is simultaneously risked and inflated, both produced as the source of a hyperbolic interpretative truth and at the same time rendered unstable by the manner of this production. The figure of the writing self thus both completes the reader's hermeneutic venture (as its glorious guarantee) and comes to worry this venture, as an elusive, passionate chimera. And this situation is exacerbated by the problematic referential status of these texts: this 'je' both is and is not Marguerite Duras, this both is and is not her adolescence, her life with Yann Andréa, and so on. As the public figure of 'Duras' is performed with increasing exaggeration during this period, and her various attributes (the voice! the glasses! the skirt! the cooking tips!) become so many metonymic fetishes, this self comes to saturate the work in a way which, oddly, ends up emptying itself out, and binding the reader something altogether more delicate, a classically Durassian relation of separation and connection—which here gives importantly onto the notion of residuality. In this transferential uncertainty, some sort of self remains; and it is the nature of this

residual self that I propose to explore here. In this section, I will discuss the constitution of the writing self across two particular grids
from Duras's later work. Shortly, I will explore its production in
those texts that are structured as it were dialogically, between a 'je'
and a corresponding 'vous'. First, however, I will present its uncertain position in Duras's most explicitly autobiographical works,
L'Amant and *L'Amant de la Chine du Nord*, where—as it were in internal
anticipation of the relation between the writing self and the public
figure yet fully to be generated by the success of this writing—it is
suspended between the figures of 'je' and 'elle'.

The writing of autobiography inevitably splits the self it presents:
between the writing self and the self written.[18] Externalizing this
split, Duras offers it in the celebrated passage in which the voice of
the writing self contemplates her aged face, offering an exemplary
autobiographical reading of the *figure* of her self (see *At*, 10). Immediately after the conclusion of this passage in devastation ('J'ai un
visage détruit' (10)), the narrative voice instigates the shift into the
remembrance of the key period in her adolescence which will form
the text's focus: 'Que je vous dise encore, j'ai quinze ans et demi'
(11). This shift—paradoxically presented as a repetition—enacts for
the first time in the text the split which constitutes its autobiographical marking as reminiscence, namely that between the writing 'je'
('Que je vous dise encore') and the self written ('j'ai quinze ans et
demi'), this split rendered fractious by the use of the historic present.
The text accentuates this split still further, however, as the written
self also moves into the third person, as 'elle' (43 *et passim*), 'l'enfant',
(46 *et passim*), 'la fille' (50 *et passim*), and so on. This doubling appears
as the result of the encounter with the Chinese lover which will be
the text's main concern: the presentation of the written self as 'elle'
intervenes for the first time with the scene of the first meeting
between the future lovers: 'Elle lui dit qu'elle ne fume pas, non
merci' (43). The gap here opened up within the self may, moreover,
represent a basic element of the accession to womanhood and
desire as narrated by the text. Reconstructing the moment at which
she first tried on the fedora which is such a striking part of her image
in the encounter with the lover, the narrator presents this scene as a
determining moment of existential self-assumption—in which the

[18] Lejeune splits this writing three ways: into author, narrator, and character, the unity of
these three being the defining feature of autobiography. (See Philippe Lejeune, *Le Pacte autobiographique* (Paris: Seuil, 1975), 15).

self assumed is a self which has acceded to otherness, to the status of an object to be exchanged:

Soudain, je me vois comme une autre, comme une autre serait vue, au-dehors, mise à la disposition de tous, mise à la disposition de tous les regards, mise dans la circulation des villes, des routes, du désir.

(20)

The writing self appears to confirm the learning of this early lesson: womanhood, as it is negotiated by this older figure, clearly entails the moulding of the self to the desire of others:

Ce que je veux paraître je le parais, belle aussi si c'est ce que l'on veut que je sois, belle, ou jolie, jolie par exemple pour la famille, pour la famille, pas plus, tout ce que l'on veut de moi je peux le devenir.

(26)

And the desire felt by the young written self before her sexual initiation is quite explicitly to be allowed to become an other, in a classically Durassian assumption of otherness as feminine self-discovery:

Elle lui dit: je préférerais que vous ne m'aimiez pas. Même si vous m'aimez je voudrais que vous fassiez comme d'habitude avec les femmes.

(48)

As commodity, the autobiography becomes a condensed enactment of this process, and perhaps the apotheosis of the written self's successful assumption of her self-as-other: this self, in part alienated into an 'elle' whose sexual initiation is told in the text, circulates (with incredible success) in the marketplace, and becomes the dominant figure of the writing self, of 'Duras'.

This alienation is neither naïve nor simple, however. For the writing self also criticizes a female alienation which would mould itself to its vision of male desire, represented by the exquisite figures of the colonial wives of Saigon. She rejects a vision of femininity as masquerade, and claims that her younger self already knew that desire was not to be provoked by stereotypical trappings (26–7), moreover,

Ce manquement des femmes à elles-mêmes par elles-mêmes opéré m'apparaissait toujours comme une erreur.
Il n'y avait pas à attirer le désir. Il était dans celle qui le provoquait ou il n'existait pas.

(28)

And in the arousal of desire lies considerable power, along with an indefinite elusiveness, as the young written self, in the third person as self-as-other, already knows:

Tout à coup elle sait, là, à l'instant, elle sait qu'il ne la connaît pas, qu'il ne la connaîtra jamais, qu'il n'a pas les moyens de connaître tant de perversité . . . C'est à elle à savoir. Elle sait . . . Il lui plaît, la chose ne dépendait que d'elle seule.

(48)

The otherness to which the written self accedes in becoming a woman would thus be neither a pre-critical alienation into a stereotypical femininity, nor powerless; it is, rather, presented as a sublime force which displaces attempts to seize it. But what of this, in an autobiography? If the written self's lover is not sufficiently a man of means to know her, is the reader—however gendered—similarly impotent? The turns of this contradictory figure of 'perversity' may well absent her from our knowledge—for she is not simply to be located at any single textual point. Both 'je' and 'elle', she is clearly neither.

Displaced from knowledge, she may temporarily be located (in all her elusiveness) in the field of desire, however. For it is here that the oscillation between 'je' and 'elle', and the relation between this oscillation and the constitution of selfhood are displayed most openly: in the scene in which the young written self loses her virginity. As she (in one sense) becomes a woman, the written self briefly vacillates. For the passionate ballet of foreplay to the very moment of penetration, she is 'elle'; with her penetration, she is effaced, replaced by the extraordinary paradox of an 'il y a' that hymns passion; then memories, images, thoughts; and then, in a bloody afterglow, she becomes 'je'. (See *At*, 49–50.) She becomes herself, then—becomes 'je', and (classically) becomes a woman—inasmuch as this moment is one of the complication of identity, not its resolution. And the moment itself is lost, somewhere in the gulf between the pronouns, in the impossible symbolism of 'La mer, sans forme, simplement incomparable' (50).

Derrida remarks upon the ambiguity of the hymen in the following terms:

L'hymen, consumation des différents, continuité et confusion du coït, mariage, se confond avec ce dont il paraît dériver: l'hymen comme écran protecteur, écrin de la virginité, paroi vaginale, voile très fin et invisible, qui, devant l'hystère, se tient *entre* le dehors et le dedans de la femme, par conséquent entre le désir et l'accomplissement.[19]

Taking place via a moment of willed passivity, the Durassian accession to womanhood is marked traditionally in *L'Amant*, at the very moment when the written self becomes herself (again), is returned by this moment to 'je': 'Je ne savais pas que l'on saignait' (*At*, 50). But the marking of this moment only in its residue robs it of stability; there is, as it were, no place in which it might take place:

> Ce qui compte ici, c'est l'*entre*, l'entre-deux de l'hymen. L'hymen 'a lieu' dans l'*entre*, dans l'espacement entre le désir et l'accomplissement, entre la perpétration et son souvenir.
>
> (Derrida, 'La double séance', 240; original emphasis)

The moment is lost: when does the written self become herself/a woman? The structure which separates her virginal self ('elle') from her adult self ('je') by the brief evocation of fleeting but intense memories and images refuses to answer this question, displacing its answer into precisely the abyss of these images, *between* desire and its fulfilment, from the rush towards pleasure to the blood of what was the hymen—with nothing (and everything) in between. The written self becomes her self—becomes the self-as-other who will become the writing self—somewhere about the hymen. And writing about the hymen, the text so structures her accession to selfhood and womanhood that the writing of these positions retains the impossible moment in which they are constituted, precisely by letting go of this moment, lost in the sublime gulf of its eventhood, 'sans forme, simplement incomparable'.

And as it is re-elaborated in *L'Amant de la Chine du Nord*, this moment also becomes the moment of the accession to writing. As the writing of this crucial scene in *L'Amant* is remembered in the later text, the later writing self arrives in the text for the first time—in the third person, as 'elle':

> Elle se souvient. Elle est la dernière à se souvenir encore. Elle entend encore le bruit de la mer dans la chambre. D'avoir écrit ça, elle se souvient aussi, comme le bruit de la rue chinoise. Elle se souvient même d'avoir écrit que la mer était

[19] Jacques Derrida, 'La Double Séance', in *La Dissémination* (Paris: Seuil, coll. 'Tel Quel', 1972), 199–317 (241); original emphasis.

présente ce jour-là dans la chambre des amants. Elle avait écrit les mots: la mer et
deux autres mots: simplement, et le mot: incomparable.

(*ACN*, 78)

This doubled doubling—in which the writing self writes her self
into her text as an other, and in which she remembers both the loss
of her virginity and the writing of this moment in the earlier text—
introduces the figure of the writing self as a remembering figure:
when she returns in the text, it will frequently be in the phrase 'Elle
se souvient' (e.g. 185/218). This is, however, not quite the figure of
the writing self from *L'Amant*, as the first-person pole of its oscillation
has virtually disappeared: this text is no longer distributed around
'je' and 'elle'.[20] This difference is signalled in part by the explicit
rejection of the figure which had known such success from *L'Amant*
(itself inflated, celebrated as 'le livre'), in favour of the younger, written self:

La voix qui parle ici est celle, écrite, du livre.
Voix aveugle. Sans visage.
Très jeune.
Silencieuse.

(17)

This is autobiography as self-*effacement*: in the drive to supply the
truer truth about the earlier work (11), the self removes her self (as
'je') from her story, which therefore becomes a novel (12)—and yet
is paradoxically signed with her full name, rather than the lapidary
'M.D.'.[21] The self is both displaced and affirmed, as the text glories
in its authorial return ('Je suis redevenue un écrivain de romans' (12))
and erases the figure with which this self had achieved such successful public circulation precisely as an author. The removal of the first
person (caught up in the text as residual: 'Je suis restée dans l'histoire

---

[20] This disappearance is anticipated towards the end of *L'Amant*, in the brief appearance
of the writing self as 'Elle': see *At*, 140–1.
[21] We might perhaps also recall that the figure of 'la dame du *Camion*', with whom Duras
identifies herself (see 'Interlude', above), is described as 'sans visage' (*O*, 177). The affectivity
of this model of autobiography as self-effacement—in which, radioactively, the self is never
quite eroded, while all the time vanishing, leaving its moving trail—might mark a quiet difference from the bolder claims of de Man's terminologically similar 'Autobiography as De-
Facement', in which, for example, 'death is the displaced name of a linguistic predicament'
(Paul de Man, 'Autobiography as De-Facement', in *The Rhetoric of Romanticism* (New York:
Columbia University Press, 1984), 67–81 (81)). (I have derived this image of radioactivity
from 'The Rest of Radioactive Light', a paper given by Robert Smith to the 'Side-effects, By-
products, Residues' Seminar, Oxford University, on 1 March 1996).

avec ces gens et seulement avec eux' (12)) allows a multiplication
of third-person figures, beginning with the affirmative signatory,
'Marguerite DURAS' (12). This signatory implicitly questions the
status of the Marguerite Duras who became a star thanks to the now
apparently incomplete *L'Amant*, and so both usurps this position
and renders it untenable for herself, since the position of successful
autobiographical writing self is clearly open to subsequent
challenge. The capitalized author thus gives way textually to a triad
of 'elle' figures: the young written self of the story; the writing self;
and the self who has lived the life between these two moments. The
appearances of this last figure are rare, but when she does arrive,
she ties together all of these positions into a kind of angry, compassionate unity: 'Toute sa vie, même vieille, elle avait pleuré sur la
terrible injustice dont leur mère avait été victime' (100).

But this unity—as trinity—is fragile: for it also represents the dispersal of the self across the years, a fragility attested to in the writing
self's arrival, where she is immediately introduced as residual: 'Elle
est la dernière à se souvenir encore' (78). Towards the end of a writing life, here is its summary—what is left:

Des années après la guerre, la faim, les morts, les camps, les mariages, les sépar-
ations, les divorces, les livres, la politique, le communisme, il avait téléphoné.

(231)

It has perhaps always been too late, however ('Très vite dans ma vie
il a été trop tard' (*At*, 9)): for this summary repeats (and extends) that
given at the close of *L'Amant*:

Des années après la guerre, après les mariages, les enfants, les divorces, les livres, il
était venu à Paris avec sa femme. Il lui avait téléphoné.

(*At*, 141)

The life of the writing self will always have been what is left; and this
self accordingly fragile. Residual perhaps: not known (we know that
she cannot be known, even her lover is—again—impotent here),
but loved? ('Je connais Lol V. Stein de la seule façon que je puisse,
d'amour' (*RLVS*, 46)). Right at the end, he returns: and the passion
remains. The writing self will not have been located—but who is not
moved by her tears?

Il avait dit que pour lui, c'était curieux à ce point-là, que leur histoire était restée
comme elle était avant, qu'il l'aimait encore, qu'il ne pourrait jamais de toute sa vie
cesser de l'aimer. Qu'il l'aimerait jusqu'à la mort.

Il avait entendu ses pleurs au téléphone.

Et puis de plus loin, de sa chambre sans doute, elle n'avait pas raccroché, il les avait encore entendus. Et puis il avait essayé d'entendre encore. Elle n'était plus là. Elle était devenue invisible, inatteignable. Et il avait pleuré. Très fort. Du plus fort de ses forces.

(*ACN*, 232)

She is not present; and what is left is the passion. Whom does he love? This very figure, the self who is not to be located, who removes herself—and yet who remains there, utterly, in his tears. No more moving self remains; what is more tender, more fragile, than the residual self, and what more affecting than the writing self who lays her self on the line, slopes away into this residual position, gives her self to be loved even as she fades? Narcissism? (His tears are, after all, her fantasy, as she is no longer near the telephone). No doubt. And this is still (just) the self who declared her chameleon abilities: 'Ce que je veux paraître je le parais' (*At*, 26). But the pathos of this scene renders its possible vanity part of, not the end of, a dramat-ization of the self which is self-aggrandizing to the precise extent that it also punctures this inflation on an irreducible affectivity. The self displayed here is both narcissistic and impoverished, both glorious and weeping, strong and residual. And these two elements rub against each other until a further residue is left: a weak, moving sense that the grandeur and the pathos of some sort of self are what we are being left with, as a writer erodes her self from 'je'/'elle' to 'elle'/'elle' to a disappearance, this gradual loss marked in the invis-ible path of these Durassian tears.

This path necessarily leads us back to *Le Square*; and so Duras writes the span of her literary career (which receives the briefest of mentions: 'les livres') into this scenario, typically invoking a sus-tained presence, a record of achievement—not least the constant achievement of tremendous, delicate scenes such as these—in the very moment of unworking the self to whom this might all belong. And the reader, again, is bound into this drama to the precise extent that these bonds are also loosened by their constitutive, moist-eyed pathos. Not just the scene itself, but also the subtle evocation of these grander dimensions even in the midst of this fragility, are productive of this pathos, in which the figure of Duras, her intimate emotional life, her career as a writer, and her reader, are joined the more urgently by the poignant impossibility of this union.

And yet: Duras apparently regretted this scene in *L'Amant* on the grounds that it was a travesty of the truth—which might reduce this poignancy to a different, cheaper kind of impossibility: what if I have just been manipulated, drawn into a pathos which is a mere confection? This is, of course, part of Duras's habitual effacement of an earlier text by its later repetition: for the remark is made in the context of the beginnings of *L'Amant de la Chine du Nord*, which thus finds itself promoted as making good the supposed insufficiencies of its predecessor (albeit, here, by developing them!). More importantly, however, the telephonic drama of the scene is not simply removed by reference to biography: for Duras was also apparently told in May 1990—by telephone—that the lover had been dead for some time.[22] The articulated pathos of connection and separation with which Duras infuses this scene, figured in the workings of telephonic technology, might also characterize the relation between these scenes and Duras's lived experience, a relation which seems caught between fiction and displacement, slipping away from the real only to find the real returning as its unavoidable referent. What Duras manages to achieve here, then, is more than a complacent neutrality, a knowing nod to the reader who acknowledges the necessary artifice of all this, and walks away unscathed from the frustration of an unfulfilled transferential promise: for classic Durassian undecidability means not 'neither/nor', but, impossibly, 'both/and', and so these scenes remain caught on both Duras's life and the reader's emotions by their awkward, over-determined, indeterminate relation to the life which itself remains, somehow, despite the unquantifiable amount of fiction through which it has been mediated, that of the vulnerable self whose erosion they expose.

Also at this time, however, Duras is building an alternative edifice for this fragile self: not only strung out between 'je' and 'elle', her self is also, importantly, constructed as part of a dialogue. It is, moreover, this dialogue that, according to Duras, enables her to begin writing again in 1979. As seen above, it is with Aurélia Steiner that Duras becomes primarily a writer again; and the Aurélia Steiner texts were, apparently, brought about by a dialogic urge which, in their address to an unnamed 'vous', they continue to mark:

[22] For details of Duras's attitude to these scenes, and of the telephone call which brought her belated news of the lover's death, see Adler, *Marguerite Duras*, 563.

A l'origine d'*Aurélia Steiner*, il y a une lettre adressée à quelqu'un que je ne connais pas . . . Avec cette lettre, tout à coup, j'ai recommencé à écrire.

(YV, 10)

This letter, (re)produced in *Les Yeux verts*, presents the drama of Duras's return to writing as a move into dialogue suggested at the moment of Duras's abandon of the written text, in the voices of *India Song*. Upon her return, the writing voice ('je') is now sustained by its passionate interlocution: 'Vous écrire, pour moi, c'est écrire' (*YV*, 12). The future path of writing is spelled out: 'Je vais peut-être faire ça, vous écrire des lettres' (13).

The 'vous' who underwrites the return to writing comes in time to figure in this writing as more than the distant destination of unsent letters. His entrance as a figure comes in *L'Été 80*, in which he functions initially as an addressee: 'Il y a un an, je vous envoyais les lettres d'Aurélia Steiner' (*É80*, 63). This arrival allows two confusions: first, between the figure of the writing self and that of Aurélia Steiner (an identification discussed in Chapter 4, above). Secondly, between the figure of the 'vous' and the reader: for, until this figure becomes more substantial, 'vous' may still be read as an appeal to a general addressee, to a reader. This reader may, then in turn become self-aggrandizing and humble, as s/he is now the very guarantee of Duras's writing—inasmuch as s/he will correspondingly risk residuality, welcome effacement in favour of the occupation of a vacant structural position. As *L'Été 80* draws on, however, the figure of the 'vous' gradually acquires more substance. He becomes the support for invocations of the scenery and the weather (still possibly the reader at this point, the text is still being written to me): 'Venez voir, tout est clair tout à coup, la mer, le ciel, la mer s'était déchaînée à l'aurore, elle était devenue méchante et sombre et la voici maintenant heureuse' (*É80*, 89). As the text closes, this figure becomes present: still shadowy, but unequivocal: 'Je suis dans la chambre noire. Vous êtes là. Nous regardons dehors' (91). His status as guarantee of this writing is explicitly declared: 'La jeune fille et l'enfant sont seuls. Je les regarde en votre présence. Vous qui connaissez l'histoire, vous sans qui je n'en dirais rien' (92). And finally this figure becomes the source of the text's vision—and it is within this vision ('Vous dites') that the text closes (102).

Here then, by the end of the summer of 1980, is the 'vous', installed as the guarantee of the writing self's writing ('vous sans qui je n'en dirais rien'). This presence is accentuated during the 1980s, as this mode of narrative address becomes established as a regular Durassian technique. And these texts take us to the verge of auto-biography: as Duras's companion, Yann Andréa, plays an increas-ingly prominent part in her public life (accompanying her on her trip to Montréal in 1981, for example, interviewing her for *Libération* in 1983, or editing and prefacing the texts included in *Outside*), the apparent parallels grow between the situations evoked in these dia-logic texts and that of Duras's life as it is glimpsed through the prism of her publications and appearances. This movement is given con-siderable impetus by Andréa's *M.D.*, published in 1983, in which the dialogue is reversed, and the writing self becomes the 'vous'. This reciprocity is alluded to in *Emily L.*, in which the 'vous' declares, 'Ce que nous préférons, c'est écrire des livres l'un sur l'autre' (*EL*, 61). And 1992 sees the apogee of this tendency, as Yann Andréa is writ-ten explicitly into Duras's *œuvre*: as *Yann Andréa Steiner*.

The re-elaboration and extension of *L'Été 80*, *Yann Andréa Steiner* provides the origin of the encounter between the 'je' and the 'vous' which has structured much of Duras's writing of the previous decade.[23] It offers a letter, for example, written from the writing self to the 'vous'—the first such letter, although not that presented in *Les Yeux verts*—in which the 'vous' and 'Yann Andréa' are explicitly in apposition (see *YAS*, 9–11). This then allows the presentation of the scene of Yann's arrival (16–18), and the explicit link between this and *L'Été 80* offers this as the grounding of the obscure arrival of the 'vous' in the earlier text:

C'était l'été 80. L'été du vent et de la pluie. L'été de Gdansk. Celui de l'enfant qui pleurait. Celui de cette jeune monitrice. Celui de notre histoire. Celui de l'histoire ici racontée, celle du premier été 1980 l'histoire entre le très jeune Yann Andréa Steiner et cette femme qui faisait des livres et qui, elle, était vieille et seule comme lui dans cet été grand à lui seul comme une Europe.

(17–18)

This originary encounter has its own origin, however, in the very

---

[23] This paradoxical structure—in which a repetition provides an origin—is already famil-iar from Chapter 2, above; and (as with the question of the telephonic drama at the end of both *L'Amant* and *L'Amant de la Chine du Nord*) it is characteristic of Duras's autobiographical writing. Thus *L'Amant de la Chine du Nord* trumps *L'Amant*, and writes the truth of the original family drama (*ACN*, 11); but *L'Amant* itself had already trumped *Un Barrage contre le Pacifique* (and other works referring to this setting, such as *L'Éden cinéma*) in similar style (*At*, 14).

first meeting between the two. And this has been almost lost: it has to be supplied to the writing self by the 'vous' (7). The provision of origins is kept uncertain, then, by this fragility of the forgotten—and (hence) original—origin. Moreover, the letter to the 'vous' which is at the origin of Duras's return to writing is not the same in *Yann Andréa Steiner* as it had been in *Les Yeux verts*: the arrival of the origin casts some doubt on the validity of the reconstruction of such moments. What is not in doubt, however, is the vital nature of the writing which is produced out of this possibly lost moment. Guaranteeing her writing, the 'vous' is the guarantee of the very life of the writing self in *Les Yeux verts*: 'Quand j'écris je ne meurs pas. Qui mourrait quand j'écris?' (*YV*, 13). Reciprocally, the writing self is also the guarantee of the existence of the 'vous': their meeting comes as the prelude to his suicide, but the writing of this testifies to the deferral of this decision (see *YAS*, 22–3). The ongoing passion of writing allows the self to remain, fragile and uncertain, reciprocally complicated but somehow still there.

The 'je' and the 'vous' are written across Duras's *œuvre*, in the scenery of the coastline around Trouville which becomes their setting—and the elements of Duras's writing which locate themselves in this scenery, particularly when structured around this dialogue, are imbued with a potential autobiographical quality. Thus *Emily L.*, for example, established as such a dialogue, and set in Quillebeuf, is potentially grounded by this revelation from *Yann Andréa Steiner*:

C'est après, encore après, dans les terres alluvionnaires du Marais Vernier que se trouve Quillebœuf [*sic*] où Emily L. a été vue par vous et moi pour la première et la dernière fois de sa vie.

(*YAS*, 71)

The nature of this writing is, however, to gesture towards such grounding whilst simultaneously questioning its possibility. For these figures are not necessarily any less textual than Emily L. The writing self declares that, before Yann's arrival, she had lived for years with certain of her characters (19–20); and, asked where they are, she displaces their Trouville coastline into the ruined beachscape of *L'Amour*:

Vous me demandez:
—Où est-on?
—J'ai dit: A S. Thala.

—Et après S. Thala.

J'ai dit qu'après S. Thala c'était encore S. Thala.

(70)

Referring with a combination of passion and self-referential wit to the words of the 'fou' of *L'Amour* (see *Ar*, 19–20), the writing self places her self and that of her interlocutor within the devastated space of her work, thereby simultaneously implying an autobiographical dimension to elements of this work and undermining the distinction on which this dimension could be founded.[24] The constitution of the writing self and her companion in the dialogic space of the works in which they predominate thus presents the same combination of apparent autobiographical openness and the complication of just this openness as is evident in the constitution of the writing self in the autobiographical writings which refer to her adolescence. In the dialogue of these texts, the writing self becomes residually autobiographical: the simultaneous provision and undermining of autobiographical interpretation means that this reading cannot quite be grounded—but that the considerable affective charge it carries (particularly for a reader who may still be clinging to the vestiges of the 'vous' position from which s/he has been displaced by Yann Andréa) will not quite be neutralized. Again, then, as the writing self comes to be constituted, it is the passion which remains, beyond the complications, in a moving accompaniment. As the following tender evocation of the fading and glorious survival of the figure of the 'vous' makes clear, when the self begins to be placed in question, its affectivity remains—and it is here that the residual self ('je', 'vous'— in which the reader is also caught) may be located:

Votre souvenir est déjà là, en votre présence, mais déjà je ne reconnais plus vos mains. Il semblerait que vos mains, jamais encore je ne les ai vues. Reste vos yeux peut-être. Et votre rire. Et ce sourire latent, toujours prêt à sourdre de votre visage fantastiquement innocent.

(*YAS*, 61)

---

[24] The reference to *L'Amour* also produces a tragic echo between the figures of Yann Andréa and the 'voyageur': Andréa has apparently come to Trouville/ S. Thala in order to know Duras before committing suicide; and the 'voyageur' has come to S. Thala with a similar aim in mind (see *YAS*, 22, and *Ar*, 80).

The Residual Self

Through the complications and uncertainties by which it is beset in its erosion and its dramatization, then, something of the self remains; and this something is its affectivity, 'sa propre grâce', 'sa propre immensité' (Lamy and Roy (eds.), 47). Which brings us back to where we came in, with the valorization of the individual. For by the time of *Écrire* (1993), what remains is the individual writing self, gloriously alone. The 'vous' has apparently faded, as have the totalitarian discourses of collectivity against which this individual self had previously been valorized; there are no more third-person guises; just the solitary writing self, meditating on the solitude which is, she claims, the prerequisite for all writing. This realization was apparently brought on by the writing of *Le Ravissement de Lol V. Stein* and *Le Vice-Consul*: 'J'ai compris que j'étais une personne seule avec mon écriture, seule très loin de tout' (*É*, 16). Without this solitude, there is no writing (no true writing), and the vital link between writer and text is severed:

La solitude de l'écriture c'est une solitude sans quoi l'écrit ne se produit pas, ou il s'émiette exsangue de chercher quoi écrire encore. Perd son sang, il n'est plus reconnu par l'auteur.

(17)

This is no writing in a café; this is a solitude which alone can allow the intensity of true writing. This intensity is dangerous, however, and puts even the life of the writer at risk from the very suicide against which writing can also protect:

Il y a le suicide dans la solitude d'un écrivain. On est seul jusque dans sa propre solitude. Toujours inconcevable. Toujours dangereux. Oui. Un prix à payer pour avoir osé sortir et crier.

(38)

Not only suicide, but also madness lie within the writer's solitude: 'La solitude est toujours accompagnée de folie. Je le sais' (54). The very intensity of the experience of the solitary writing self begins to erode this isolated self, then, as this is in fact a solitude which carries the self beyond its own limits. This isolation is looking less splendid, and more devastating.

If the self is rent precisely inasmuch as it is constituted and valorized as alone, is this figure of solitude still valid? Just who would be left to be alone? Pointing to this ambiguity, Duras refers in the same piece to 'Cette illusion qu'on a—et qui est juste—d'être le seul à avoir écrit ce qu'on a écrit, que ce soit nul ou merveilleux' (31). Recalling an image she had used in 1977 of the writing self as a 'passoire' (*L*, 98), and her frequent references to writing as a 'doubling', Duras insists that the writing self is also not alone inasmuch as she writes: 'Tout écrivait quand j'écrivais dans la maison. L'écriture était partout' (*É*, 28). The writing self also becomes a porous figure, not so much isolated with her writing as traversed by a generalized writing; alone perhaps in terms of human company, but with only permeable borders between her self and the writing world by which she is surrounded: 'Autour de nous, tout écrit, c'est ça qu'il faut arriver à percevoir' (55).

And yet the writing self is perhaps not even alone in human terms: even *Le Ravissement de Lol V. Stein*, the supposed inauguration of the experience of radical writerly solitude, was apparently composed in company:

J'ai fini *Lol V. Stein* ici, j'ai écrit la fin ici et à Trouville devant la mer. Seule, non, je n'étais pas seule, il y avait un homme avec moi pendant cette époque-là.

(21)

And there is, apparently, even no such thing as solitude: 'On n'est jamais seul. On n'est jamais seul physiquement. Nulle part' (46). From suicidal solitude, writing becomes again a defence against suicide—and not solitary:

Il y a ça aussi dans la fonction d'écrire et avant tout peut-être se dire qu'il ne faut pas se tuer tous les jours du moment que tous les jours on peut se tuer. C'est ça l'écriture du livre, ce n'est pas la solitude.

(39)

The paradoxes abound. Inasmuch as writing is not solitary, it is a defence against suicide—and so the guarantee of the existence of the writing self, whose writing is guaranteed by her solitude, which is suicidal. Any salvation which writing might offer, any hope, is perhaps itself residual—what is left after the risk of abolition to which writing also subjects the writer. And fragile—since this risk may always return, in the twists of these contradictions.[25]

---

[25] One further contradiction, from the realm of the biographical: from *Écrire* on (i.e. *Écrire*, *C'est tout*, *La Mer écrite*), Duras's texts are, apparently, not written by her in a physical sense: they constitute, according to Adler, 'des propos rapportés, des conversations transcrites, des

We are left with a figure, the site of a powerful investment; a voice, a style: not quite a presence, but much more than a name. That the self exposed through Duras's writing is residual tends to question whether self-disclosure is simply a matter of revelation. The extremity of the gesture of exposure also removes the self it reveals into simultaneous impoverishment (the self is spent in the passion of disclosure) and performance (this disclosure is high drama), giving the self as that which is left, not that which was, like the stripper's flesh, waiting to be revealed.[26] A self who writes her madness, her banality, the extraordinary minutiæ of her everyday life, who contradicts her self and so opens her self up to our love of the multitudes within. The refusal of self-effacement in Duras's extra-literary work of this period may thus be read not merely as self-indulgence or as ridiculous egotism; it is also an extravagant cry which, precisely by courting mockery, demands a passionate response and thereby blocks its own path to control. That there exist in these cries vanity and self-promotion is undeniable; but this ought not to blind us to their implosive dynamic, which also sustains a gentler, more generous move, as noisy self-affirmation also, bizarrely, implies a quiet gesture of solidarity with the impoverished.[27]

Thus it is, paradoxically, that the saturation which characterizes the presence of 'Duras' in and around the texts of this period also, in part, constitutes a version of the articulated relationship (here, between author and text, and, through this, author and reader) which I have presented as typical of Duras's work in general. The ridiculous passion which spins out of this saturation necessarily disbars the author-figure from the authority she also claims: and so she is left in a kind of limbo, both all too present and, strictly, unlocatable. And the reader's investment in this figure—even if, as often,

décryptages de films' (Adler, *Marguerite Duras*, 571). Which means that 'writing' simply cannot be a matter of solitude in anything other than a figurative sense.

[26] A description of Duras's self-disclosure as the dramatic revelation of the self is given by Dennis Porter: 'Committed to the ethic of hiding nothing and sparing no one, [Duras] performs a kind of moral and emotional striptease' (Porter, 'Marguerite Duras: Autobiographical Acts, Celebrity Status', in *Rousseau's Legacy* (Oxford: Oxford University Press, 1995), 217–37 (233)). The force of Duras's commitment to this gesture, however, empties the self that might have been revealed into the residue of its affectivity—which may also imply, as we shall shortly see, an alternative ethic.

[27] A positive reading of this extravagant self-promotion is provided for example by Jean-Claude Lamy, writing after Duras's death: ' "La Duras", personnage incontrôlable, n'aura jamais cessé d'interroger le monde, quitte à se caricaturer elle-même' (Lamy, 'Marguerite Duras, l'éternelle rebelle', *Le Figaro*, 4 mars 1996, 26).

and not only among her detractors, this is one of annoyance—cannot but reconfirm this structure, as I find myself held in the bear-hug of this exaggerated presence, which I may reject, but which I cannot deny. Indiscreet as ever, Duras pushes her self to the fore; but the urgency of this move also suggests its own discretion, the erosion of the ridiculous self, a hint of the residuality we are encouraged to valorize from this most irritating of authors, loitering noisily around her own delicate works.

This structure, however, depends on the emphatically non-redemptive status of this move. Duras remains (a different sort of residuality, here) infuriating, even disgraceful. The offensiveness of certain of her interventions cannot be tidied away in the name of some sort of literary right to scandal, a quasi-divine entitlement to rewrite the world as part of some sort of generalized poetry. Oddly, the generosity of Duras's self-exposure only works if we refuse to allow it to justify such moments: for only this cycle of non-redemption keeps the possibility of exposure, and hence generosity, open. This does not have to be a problem; it is only a problem, indeed, if we want a total answer to what we might call the Duras question. Her work is sometimes disgraceful; this disgrace is also part of a more generous move; but this generosity does not remove or justify the occasionally disgraceful work. There is, surely, no need to resolve this.

Throughout this chapter, we have encountered Duras's delineation of the limits of identity, where self brushes against other—from the residual individual, via the immigrant self and racial identity, to the edges of the autobiographical self, caught between identity and alienation ('je' and 'elle') in the space of a dialogue ('je' and 'vous'). And, crucially, the encounter between self and other in Duras's later work is neither simplistically explosive nor naïvely optimistic. The self is neither exuberantly despatched nor happily open—rather, at its edge, it is fragile and uncertain. And this delicacy is nowhere more apparent than in Duras's autobiographical writing, in which we may glimpse the ethics implied by this impassioned embrace of residuality. The author is left as the traces of an affectivity—and so in a residual alignment with the impoverished in the name of compassion, a self-sacrificial challenge to deal with the fragile provocation of residuality, which she is also concerned to champion in the cases of the resisting individual and (problematically) racial identity. Which moves us from the valorized individual self—the traditional seat of ethics, as discussed above—to the limit of this ground, to a ground which is itself moving, the compassionate writing which attempts to embrace the left-over self. There is here, in the passion which invites derision as mere vanity, an attempted patient accompaniment which we have already met in *Le Square* and in Chapter 4, above; at the edge of the ethical, there is left an ethos which is, generously, a pathos, a delicate affective line which, while picking up the line between the world and its beyond with which Duras has always been fascinated, also suggests that the ethical self which lives on this uncomfortable line might best be understood as tender, impassioned, and uncertain.[28]

Refusing all positive identification other than the small line of an indefinable solidarity, this punctured humanism (in which what is shared is precisely what is not known, an irreducible residue) resists oppression and injustice in the name of an unlimited friendship for all that is weak, uncertain, and endangered, marked only by the agitated questioning it locates as the gnawing heart of the human.[29] By Levinas out of Bataille (with Blanchot as the midwife), this ethics demands a responsibility towards the poor, weak other which manifests itself in part in my refusal of anything other than an eroded, self-contesting, irreducible humanity revealed in its resistance to its threatened abolition. (Mascolo and Antelme are also on hand here).[30]

---

[28] Paul Thibaud points to this view of the remainder as what I have called above (see Chapter 4) *patient accompaniment* in his discussion of Duras's 'Être de gauche': 'Le refus de l'honnête résignation conservatrice semble ici déborder non sur des pulsions terroristes mais sur une maladroite et balbutiante patience' (Thibaud, 'Marguerite Duras: Les Ambiguïtés de la compassion', *Esprit*, 116 (juillet 1986), 75–7 (77)). The evolution from the dissolution of the self to a form of compassion is well traced in Aurore Diet *et al.* (Collectif d'étudiants), '*L'Amant*, intertexte sacré', in Vircondelet (ed.), *Duras, Dieu et l'écrit*, 163–75 (174–5).

[29] Renate Günther identifies this move throughout much of Duras's work: 'From 1964 onwards, Duras's work became a progressive movement towards emptiness, a movement which reveals lack and absence as the paradoxically hollow core of existence' (Günther, 'Alcohol and Writing: Patterns of Obsession in the Work of Marguerite Duras', in Sue Vice, Matthew Campbell, and Tim Armstrong (eds.), *Beyond the Pleasure Dome: Writing and Addiction from the Romantics* (Sheffield: Sheffield Academic Press, 1994), 200–5 (200)).

[30] Ingrid Safranek reads Duras's work overall as offering 'une référence-clef pour tous les sujets politiques nouveaux, pour tous ceux qui cherchent une troisième voie post-bipolaire, post-guerre froide, un nouvel humanisme qui affirme les différences' ('Textes des origines, origines du texte', in Rodgers and Udris (eds.), *Marguerite Duras: Lectures plurielles*, 57–75 (58)). While such an insistence on the philosophical and political importance of Duras's configuration of subjectivity is enormously welcome, to see this configuration as affirmative of a new humanism is surely to proceed rather too rapidly. The compassionate alignment which Duras's residual self allows with the dispossessed loses its necessary fragility if it founds anything so confident, so accomplished; it must, if it is to maintain its distinctive ethical potential, remain at the level of ruination, dispersal, loss: in a word, residuality.

Such would be some of the implications of Duras's embrace and production of a residual selfhood. But Duras also, of course, trumpets her self, attracts huge derision for her fits of extraordinary egotism. And this self-promotion cannot entirely be recuperated as part of the generous erosion of the self—although its exorbitance does also contribute to this erosion. Equally, Duras's treatments of immigrant, Jewish, and racial identity are all marked by a similar ambiguity: on the one hand, Duras produces a generous uncertainty, resisting oppression in the name of complex, shifting, but defiant residual identity; on the other hand, she turns this residuality into an abstraction, the repetition of the exclusionary aggressions it resists. And the uncertainty between these two readings cannot, again, be counted simply as a positive achievement, since one of its incompatible poles consists of a critique, not an explication, of Duras's practice.

Still grappling with the edge of the ethical (in the shape of ungraspable trauma, passion and violence, and the status of the residual self who might experience this extremity), and doing so on a more ambitious scale, Duras now marks this edge as the slippery line between ethical extremity as it is almost articulated through the architecture of the world and a shifting, ambiguous writing, responding to this twisting articulation with both a nuanced, delicate attention and exaggerated, wild assertion, constituting itself as a relentlessly uncertain accompaniment. By the end of her writing career, then, Duras—in her extravagances, passion, subtleties, and outrages—continues to demonstrate the drama, pathos, and problems of writing on the edge of extremity. While the effects of this spectacle may not always be to her credit, it remains a compelling and remarkable attempt to bring writing into an encounter with the intractable, vital demands of the ethical.

CONCLUSION

Comment faire pour vivre un peu, encore un peu.

C'est tout

It is 14 March 1996. Duras has been dead for eleven days. *Paris Match* opens a twelve-page tribute with a photograph, taken in 1993 by Hélène Bamberger, of Duras working at the desk in her room at Trouville. This is, in the imaginary universe woven around her writing, the 'chambre noire' of *L'Été 80*, the source of Aurélia Steiner's letters; the effect of seeing into this previously invisible, textual space is unsettling, the more so from its complete banality. For this is, after all, just Duras at her desk, in a room which she had evoked in some of her texts. On a small table placed next to the desk, half-hidden in this photograph by a vase-cum-lamp, is a telephone, modern, flat, white. And I cannot stop thinking that this is the telephone through which the writing self of *L'Amant de la Chine du Nord* heard the voice of her lover for the first time in decades, through which he in turn perhaps heard her tears, as she shrank from his overwhelming voice back into this room, away from the desk, towards the bed perhaps, here strewn with paper and with linen fresh from the laundry.

Elle n'était plus là. Elle était devenue invisible, inatteignable. Et il avait pleuré. Très fort. Du plus fort de ses forces.

(*ACN*, 232)

The pathos of this scene—already considerable—is now heightened: for 'elle' is indeed 'invisible, inatteignable', no longer here. And only now that she is definitively gone has the setting of this earlier fading away been revealed. After Duras's death, the shifting chiaroscuro which marks her autobiographical writing self is suddenly extraordinarily stark: where is she now, as we read any of the texts from the 1980s which feature this setting, and which already play hide-and-seek with the reader? In one sense, Duras's death only confirms what we all know about the death of the author: if she is now uncertainly present in and around her texts, this serves as a brusque reminder that it was ever thus, that she was never really there in the first place, was already just a collection of passionate, pathetic, at times even ridiculous readerly investments, and already marked by death.[1] And in any case, as we now know, this scene was just so much fabrication, so much writerly artifice, my relentless imaginings just the product of my overheated transferential identification, played on by an author busily cloaking whatever the truth might have been in swathes of melodramatic fiction, the better to disappear into an absence which prefigured the death by which she has now been claimed. And yet it is not the same. There is no symmetry between the living writer who is also marked by death inasmuch as she writes and the dead writer who lives on in her writing. For the fragility of this new situation is of a different quality, redoubling that already present in the work with the fact of death, invoking a brute reality which, even as it is invoked, cannot quite be made sense of. (Which should also, incidentally, give us pause before confident proclamations that Duras 'lives on' in her writings: the survival here, if this term is at all appropriate, and not just a noisy metaphor, is—as Duras always thematizes it— entirely fragile, chancy, precarious). If this is the same old play of presence and absence, it is a game now played with a far greater intensity, for the absence now really does mean the end of the line, no more books. Although there have, of course, already been posthumous publications, if only to make good the prediction of *Les Yeux verts* :

Le reste, les choses qui traînent dans les armoires bleues de ma chambre, de toutes façons elles seront publiées un jour, soit après ma mort, soit avant, si une fois, de nouveau, je manque d'argent.

$(YV, 11)^2$

The awkward pathos produced by Duras's death (awkward partly in the difficulty in distinguishing it by other than slippery, affective reasons from her uncertain textual presence when alive) may offer some sort of position from which to conclude this discussion of the ways in which her writing addresses the ethical questions with

---

[1] Thus Duras in 1979: 'Écrire c'est n'être personne. "Mort", disait Thomas Mann' (*NN*, 11). See also, for example, Roland Barthes, *Sade Fourier Loyola* (Paris: Seuil, coll. 'Tel Quel', 1971); and Blanchot, *Le Pas au-delà*.

[2] I am afraid that I have no room to consider here *La Mer écrite*, Duras's first posthumous publication; I will just note, in passing, that its odd temporality (published as scheduled shortly after Duras's death, accidentally posthumous) works to split any final moment: *C'est tout*, which (as will be seen) also worries at this split, thus both is and is not emptied of the finality it appears to promise (and which it also, of course, fails to deliver).

which it is confronted. For here we meet dramatically the edge between the world and its loss, and the uncertain operation of this edge within writing. In October 1995, Duras published *C'est tout*, a sparse anticipation of her imminent death, by turns amusing and distressing. Here, it is quite explicitly a question of writing on the edge of beyond, tracing the line of uncertainty which Duras's work presents as the fragile position of the ethical. As a way of beginning to conclude, then, I propose now to read these last words.

That's All

Around the time of her return to writing in 1979, Duras begins to suggest that writing may in some sense cheat death. We may recall that this return is guaranteed by the figure of Aurélia Steiner as survivor; and writing becomes, for Aurélia, a way of denying death its due. Citing the multiple rumours surrounding the death of her addressee (who is most often her father), she writes,

Je vois que ce n'est pas vrai.
Que lorsque je vous écris personne n'est mort.

('ASM', 107)

This generalized, redemptive prosopopœia is made specular in *Les Yeux verts*, as writing becomes for Duras a form of self-preservation: 'Quand j'écris je ne meurs pas. Qui mourrait quand j'écris?' (*YV*, 13). And in a text written for *Des Femmes en mouvements hebdo* in 1981, this challenge to death's hold is given as a defining feature of both writing and reading: 'L'écrit est enlevé à la mort. La mort est mutilée à chaque poème écrit, lu, à chaque livre.'[3] Well over a decade later, *C'est tout* provides the ultimate realization of this position in the form of paradox, as its writing voice pretends at

---

[3] Marguerite Duras, 'Le Noir Atlantique', *Des Femmes en mouvements hebdo*, 11–18 septembre 1981, 30–1 (31); collected in *ME*, 14–17. Madeleine Borgomano reads these lines as a symbol of the redemptive qualities of Duras's work; I will be suggesting, however, that such confidence may be as misplaced as the Kristevan myth of adequation it seeks to challenge, and that declarations such as this need to be interpreted in the context of Duras's career-long struggle with the *question* of the redemptive or otherwise capacities of writing. To resolve this question, as I will attempt to show, diminishes greatly the value of Duras's work—which is just what Borgomano wants to protect, here. (See Borgomano, 'Que sont les oiseaux devenus . . . ?', 165, n. 3).

times to speak from beyond the grave, leaping into her own death and thereby denying it:

Ça y est.
Je suis morte.
C'est fini.

(*CT*, 45)

The text is set up in this mode from the very beginning, its forget-me-not dedication anticipating the coming death, introducing the text as an address already supposedly *d'outre-tombe*: 'Dépêche-toi de penser à moi' (7). The writing voice mimes a posthumous position to suggest her survival of the death she tries to cheat by anticipation, the text an epitaph which speaks out against the end it also announces.

As well as crystallizing the motif of uncertain survival present throughout Duras's later writing (in Aurélia Steiner, Théodora Kats, Robert L., the figure of the residual self, and so on), this final challenge to death represents the culmination of Duras's tendency to self-aggrandizement, the voice that would escape even her own mortality assuming a still further inflated status. The last word on the identity of this writing self, who has been simultaneously fêting and eroding her self during the 1980s, is that she is, finally, just herself, in a divinely tautological self-definition:

Y.A.: Que diriez-vous de vous-même?
M.D.: Duras.

(8)

At times, this explicitly terminal book comes to resemble the apparent vanity of Nietzsche's *Ecce homo*, itself written on the verge of an imminent collapse, with sections entitled 'Warum ich so klug bin' ('Why I am so clever') and 'Warum ich so gute Bücher schreibe' ('Why I write such good books'), as Duras explicitly, and with a sense of some defiance, courts the egotism of which she has so often been accused:

Y.A.: Êtes-vous très douée?
M.D.: Oui. Il me semble bien.

(15)

Il se trouve que j'ai du génie.
J'y suis habituée maintenant.

(39)

And this skill would be total: just as she is what she is ('Duras'), what she does is—simply—literature:

Y.A.: Vous êtes qui?
M.D.: Duras, c'est tout.
Y.A.: Elle fait quoi, Duras?
M.D.: Elle fait la littérature.

(26)

Not 'de la littérature': 'Duras' (who is everything) *makes literature.* Which also gives her the right to tear this institution down, to write it off in favour of a biblical thundering, to elevate herself (as she had done in the prefatory remarks to the 'Journal' of *La Douleur*) beyond mere literature, by writing her own work into a biblical weave. As an angry, irruptive messiah ('Je suis l'écrivain sauvage et inespérée' (30)), Duras speaks in the voice of Ecclesiastes, repeating the phrase which first fascinated her writing in *La Pluie d'été*, and suggesting a religious undertone in the mantra of *Le Camion*:

Vanité des vanités.
Tout est vanité et poursuite du vent.
Ces deux phrases donnent toute la littérature de la terre.
Vanité des vanités, oui . . .
Que le monde aille à sa perte.
Vanité des vanités.
Tout est vanité et poursuite du vent.

(30–1)[4]

This preacher's voice binds together Duras, her work, the Bible, and the citation of the Bible in Duras's work (including itself, therefore, this implosion heightening the mystical tone) into a potent, dramatic arrangement; this voice on the edge of death, both anticipating and speaking from beyond the grave, writes her self into the beyond, echoing through the universe: 'Dites donc, ça se confirme Duras, partout dans le monde et au-delà' (38).

All of this inflation is, however, obviously punctured. Once again, Duras is doubling up: while she conflates her writing with biblical pronouncements, she also writes that 'toute la littérature de la

---

[4] Compare Ernesto, also speaking in this biblical voice: 'Et puis, dit Ernesto, j'ai considéré tous les ouvrages que mes mains avaient faits et la peine que j'avais eue à les faire. | — Et voici: j'ai compris que tout est vanité. Vanité des Vanités. Et Poursuite du Vent' (*PE*, 55). Ernesto is both quoting from and paraphrasing Ecclesiastes, particularly Chapter II, v.11.

terre'—her own, therefore, including this text—is as nothing beside these pronouncements, a mere gloss. The self who affirms herself in the beyond deprives her self of a glorious status twice over: first, by disappearing into a mystical realm ('au-delà') where she can no longer be assured of any earthly glory, and which she explicitly anticipates as nothingness (10); secondly, by suspending her self between this disappearance and earthly success, 'partout dans le monde et au-delà'. Again, Duras's self-promotion is caught on the hooks of the very paradoxes which also produce its rhetoric. Her divine self-definition as simply 'Duras' is also resoundingly banal, an 'I am what I am' marked as much by the dullness as by the mysticism of tautology. There are countless biblical phrases which a writing voice might parrot in order to elevate itself beyond the humdrum; that Duras cites the other-worldly relegation of earthly concerns to mere vanity immediately ruptures the egotism of this ventriloquism. For this elevation is also, and dramatically, just vanity; and so it spoofs itself as it goes along, both egotistical and mocking this narcissism both humorously and pathetically. The straightforward declaration that 'Je n'ai jamais été prétentieuse' (39) is instantly self-subverting, in its self-congratulatory humility; for pretension to be deflated, subtler means are necessary. Thus, the grand declaration that Duras 'fait la littérature' is immediately transformed into a 'gong vide' (*RLVS*, 48) by the small, almost despairing mumble which creeps into the resulting silence:

Y.A.: Elle fait quoi, Duras?
M.D.: Elle fait la littérature.

Silence, et puis.

Trouver quoi écrire encore.

(*CT*, 26)

And what is it worth, this lifelong occupation of making and remaking literature?

Toute une vie j'ai écrit.
Comme une andouille, j'ai fait ça.

(38)

The writing which is relied upon to preserve this voice after her death may in fact have no such redemptive power, may just have been a foolish (if lovable) waste of time, itself afflicted with the banal tautology which marks the writing self: 'Écrire toute sa vie, ça apprend à écrire. Ça ne sauve de rien' (39). What if it has all just been vanity, after all? There is a sense here that this is indeed all there is, that her writing, for all its paradoxical self-aggrandizement, cannot ultimately guarantee that anything will remain of this voice after her death. Anticipating—and prescribing—the happy memories she will leave behind her, Duras strikes a note that is both smug and pleading, invoking a tenderness whose instability (she can have no control over her memory, after all) makes its arrogance also pathetic:

Y.A.: Et après la mort, qu'est-ce qui reste?
M.D.: Rien. Que les vivants qui se sourient, qui se souviennent.

(10)

This statement is potentially self-fulfilling, as an indulgent, nostalgic smile at Duras's characteristic vulnerable egotism may well play across the reader's lips; but it also questions the status of her voice, reminding us that she is speaking (in anticipation, but also—now—in fact) from beyond the grave, from nowhere. And the book which records this voice, and which may or may not be sustaining it beyond death, also registers this uncertainty. It may be evoked in a joke, as when Duras tells Yann that the title of 'le prochain livre'—this one, or maybe the next one (called *La Mer écrite*, however—so maybe the one after that, if there is another one?)—will be 'le livre à disparaître' (11), both book and writer envisaging their ambiguous posthumous existence; or it may be stated quite simply, as when Duras contemplates the writing of this future book: is she discussing the book we are reading, or some apparently unrealized further project? Has this book been written, 'enlevé à la mort', or is it too late?

C'est une question de temps. Je ferai un livre.
Je voudrais mais ce n'est pas sûr que j'écrive ce livre.
C'est aléatoire.

(9)

There is a delicate strain of tragedy in the modulation from 'Je ferai un livre', through the more realistic 'Je voudrais mais ce n'est pas sûr' into the bright-eyed but tentative subjunctive, telling of both future promise and threatened failure, culminating in the blunt

'C'est aléatoire'. The implied heroism which would result from this being the book whose writing was uncertain, Duras having conquered uncertainty to bring out this final offering, is plainly undercut by the sense that this may always be only the book in which this future book is predicted, and thus (possibly) only the record of a failure to write—although future publications may always turn this failure back into a realized promise.

Such are the oscillations which result from this final attempt to write on the edge of beyond, to speak both in front of and from within the grave. This book is always finishing, either with repeated expressions of nauseous exhaustion—

Je voudrais continuer à divaguer comme je le fais par certains après-midi d'été comme celui-là.
Je n'en ai plus le goût ni le courage.

$$(22)—$$

or with promises of renewal which limp into a feeble silence:

Je vais arrêter là ce texte pour en prendre un autre de toi, fait pour toi, fait à ta place.

Silence, et puis.

Alors, ce serait quoi, ce que tu veux entendre écrire?

$$(42–3)$$

'C'est tout' is never the truth; as often as it is spoken, it is contradicted by yet more words, including, quite possibly, 'C'est tout' again. The declaration that

C'est tout.
Je n'ai plus rien à dire.
Pas même un mot.
Rien à dire.

$$(37)$$

is immediately contradicted, as words continue to come; and the declaration that 'C'est tout' is repeated a further six times before the end of the text—whose last words are not 'C'est tout'. As Duras says here, 'Il n'y a pas de dernier baiser' (36): these statements of finality are never quite the end, there's always something—however slight—still to come. Now that Duras is actually dead, however, they may after all be true—or rather, they become both true and false in different perspectives. When we read that

Ça y est.
Je suis morte.
C'est fini.

(45)

we are reading the truth: Duras is dead, it is all over. But inserted into a running collection of dated entries, this statement is also plainly false, a premature announcement of the end which will not come for ten pages yet.

But it is coming, this end, and, guaranteed only by this unstable, contradictory book, the writing self begins to slide out of view, recording her descent into a creeping death:

Quelquefois je suis vide pendant très longtemps.
Je suis sans identité.
Ça fait peur d'abord. Et puis ça passe par un mouvement de bonheur. Et puis ça s'arrête.
Le bonheur, c'est-à-dire morte un peu.
Un peu absente du lieu où je parle.

(8)

'Je ne sais plus très bien qui je suis' (14); 'C'est plus moi maintenant. C'est quelqu'un que je ne connais plus' (48): this is the actualization of the dilapidation of the writing self which Duras has frequently discussed over the years—which also, of course, contradicts these earlier statements, in that the self is still around to be eroded, and this erosion is taking place not by writing, but by death, whose work writing is recording. This is more than a shadow-play of presence and absence; more even than some twisting and intricate elaborations of the paradoxes of speaking on the edge of beyond— although it is both of these things. It is also, however, the record of a confrontation with death, which, in addition to its more stoical moments, includes a deal of pain and anguish. There is a sense in which we can read this absolutely straight, in which we should take its scenes seriously, and feel their extremity.

Je me sens perdue.
Mort c'est équivalent.
C'est terrifiant.

(25)

The statements of fear (of, for example, 'une peur immédiate de la mort' which is followed by 'une fatigue immense' (43)) throughout the text have their raw affectivity: these *are* the words of a woman about to die, and terrified. The pathos is at times immense, as in the following declaration of endless ability, whose brash optimism is just very difficult to read in the knowledge of its utter uselessness: for Duras, there are no more tomorrows, no more moments, and this faith will not have preserved her against death:

Moi, je peux tout recommencer.
Dès demain.
A tout moment.
Je recommence un livre.
J'écris.
Et hop, voilà!

(37)

The rabbit fails to emerge from the hat; the trick of salvation has not worked. ('Ça ne sauve de rien'). The poignancy of this is increased still further by the actual end, when it does come: in the text's final entry, on the first day of August, it is, finally, all over, and Duras writes her self into the beyond by once again effacing the figure of her glory, just as she had done in *L'Amant de la Chine du Nord*: the face of *L'Amant*, there celebrated in its devastation, here slips away as part of a distressing final disintegration. The appeals which punctuate the entire text, and which again (as in *L'Été 80*, for example) ring out somewhere between the reader and Yann Andréa, here mark both of us with a dreadful uselessness, powerless in the disappearing face of this loss:

Je crois que c'est terminé. Que ma vie c'est fini.
Je ne suis plus rien.
Je suis devenue complètement effrayante.
Je ne tiens plus ensemble.
Viens vite.
Je n'ai plus de bouche, plus de visage.

(54–5)[5]

[5] Again, as discussed in Chapter 6, this spectacle features an affectivity not immediately apparent in de Man's sleek elaboration of 'Autobiography as De-Facement'. Duras exemplifies well de Man's point about autobiography as a strange inversion of prosopopœia (the more she writes about herself, the more she rubs away her face), but introduces an explicit and surely essential emotional dimension into this scene, snagging the elegance of rhetoric on the mess of pain and upset: death is not just a trope.

It is important to read *C'est tout* naïvely, to feel the poignancy of these scenes, to take seriously the claim that these are Duras's last words; for she is dying, she is disappearing, and this situation is evoked with a terrible frankness. The naïve reading is far from the whole story; but it cannot quite be reeled back in as if the feelings it registers were somehow only preparing the way for their intellectual recuperation. The whole story is that there is this affective dimension, raw, poignant pathos; and there is also its complication. For *C'est tout*, of course, also set off a considerable debate about the possible authenticity of this type of text, not in fact written by Duras, but transcribed by Yann Andréa—indeed, apparently, Andréa's brainchild, designed to catch the still-precious words sparkling through Duras's last mumblings, as she teetered between life and death.[6] Recalling the blend of confession and artifice which marks *L'Amant* and *L'Amant de la Chine du Nord*, this is a text which manages to be both utterly mediated (Duras's brief phrases arranged, dated, spaced by Andréa) and utterly immediate (but they are still her words, still the final snatches from one of our century's most important wordsmiths) at once, in one and the same place, in the characteristic gesture of impossible undecidability which marks Duras's later work. This is not *either* literature *or* not: it is *both* literature *and* not literature. On the one hand, the artful orchestration of what is still, just about, lived experience; on the other, the awful, astonishing incursion of this uncontainable experience into the emotional world of the reader of expensive, beautifully crafted literary *objets*. Equally: this is not *either* by Duras *or* not: it is *both* her text (her signature, a recognizable voice, picking up repeatedly the concerns of her *œuvre*) *and* not by her in any straightforward sense (this voice might easily be the result of pastiche or ventriloquism, for example). There is, here, little beyond complication.

This complication is such, however, that it refuses quite to clean up the affective mess which forms one of its poles: the real pathos here is that we are caught between pathos and its recuperation, stumbling. We know, of course, that this is not the end, Duras is not about to die—there is no equivalence between text and extremity, as she shows us again here, *in extremis*. The final entry, in which the

---

[6] On this, see Adler, *Marguerite Duras*, 575; Alain Vircondelet, 'Marguerite Duras, libre et captive: des voix de l'écriture à la voie fatale', in Vircondelet (ed.), *Duras, Dieu et l'écrit*, 125–46 (144)); and Marini, 'Fortune et infortune de l'œuvre durassienne', in Rodgers and Udris (eds.), *Marguerite Duras: Lectures plurielles*, 169–83 (172).

writing self falls apart, is dated seven months before Duras's death. Her life is not over. This is not an unmediated transcription of her last words, then, as the repetition of the figure of self-effacement from *L'Amant de la Chine du Nord* makes plain. This is artifice, staging the flood of pathos as part of—what? A meditation on the approach of death? A subtle display of the investments and reactions produced by the spectacle of the end of a writer's life? A dramatization of the impossible status of the writer, already between life and death in any case, neither here nor there, and so who, on dying, has nowhere else to go? Yes, yes, all of these: but how dull they are, how far they fall short of the feelings they attempt to bracket. For, to reiterate, she is dying, really. This is the apotheosis of Duras's relentless, double ambiguity: she is provoking emotional reactions in her reader; these reactions are qualified, staged for inspection; and this qualification cannot quite remove their residual importance. There is no resolution of this stand-off in favour of any of its elements, not even the affective remainder which just exceeds its artful frame. *C'est tout* is caught on Duras's life as on ours by this snagged uncertainty: it is not simply a record of authentic emotional experience, naïve in the manner of a homily; it is both garishly true, unutterably blunt, and playful, manipulative, tricky. It is hooked into both her emotional life and ours—but the exact nature of this catch is hard to discern. The impossibility of resolving the text as either true nakedness or just the empress's final, deceptive suit means, however, that we are obliged to fumble on, accompanying the pain marked in the text while trying to hold both of these interpretations at the same time, which may well get us precisely nowhere:

Venez avec moi dans le grand lit et on attendra.
Rien.

(52)

'Silence, et puis'

For over half a century, Duras kept speaking and writing in order to map just this edge. It is, moreover, where she located the ethical. The ethical in Duras is found at its limit; the passion, violence, and loss with which she was fascinated both burst the coherence of its terms and continue to evoke their necessity. This vision of the ethical presents it as characterized by an extremity which both suspends and is inevitably caught up in the world. In her earlier writing, it is the local truth of this inextricability that is principally apparent: Sara's adulterous passion is debated by her and her friends; Anne's symbolic death is her social disgrace, she is both within and beyond the world of the café; the passionate loss of self embodied in Alissa is disruptive of a particular social order. Later, ethical extremity is addressed at the more architectural levels of history and social structures and institutions, with reference for example to the Holocaust, the homosocial, and the politics of immigration. In all of these areas, Duras raises questions which are recognizably those of the ethical (inevitably linked to notions of judgement and responsibility, for example), but also denies a safe ethical purchase on the material she confronts. When a woman is beaten by a man, and both appear to derive erotic pleasure and a rending loss of self from this experience, the situation demands an ethical response it simultaneously challenges; the indeterminate frame with which this scene is supplied suggests both that it remains within the field of judgement, and that this judgement cannot quite get a hold on its extremity. Duras's characteristic concerns all gain their considerable valency from their location at the point where ethical categories are both cut through and still unavoidable.

This point is marked in Duras's writing in two ways. First, in her work from 1943 to 1971, her writing gestures towards the textual enactment of its encounter with ethical extremity, but demonstrates the impossibility of such enactment, thus drawing uncertainly the line on the edge of beyond where it locates the ethical. Then, from 1979, as Duras's writing extends its scope and its ambitions, it becomes both more confident and more delicate, abandoning the problematic of enactment in favour of a more general marking of the uncertainties resulting from the textual encounter with ethical extremity. At this time, Duras's writing also becomes notably more contentious, drawing a further line of uncertainty between the incompatible, ambiguous readings generated by her texts. Throughout her career, the encounter between this writing and the ethical is forever undecided, always to be re-negotiated in a snagged openness that is less a happy utopia than an essential, exhausted residue, all that is left us at the limit of our understanding.

Reading Duras's work in terms of its fascination with the edge of the ethical offers a new perspective to Duras criticism that is both intrinsically and more generally significant. Simply in its own right, an acknowledgement that Duras's work has always dealt with ethical questions allows the recognition of an aspect of her achievement for which she has received little credit. Duras's writing explores the most intimate and overwhelming areas of our ethical experience, not to tease out their nice complications, but rather to confront us with their fascinating, inextricable extremity. An approach to Duras by way of the ethical also begins to suggest the scale of her accomplishments. For, while such an approach need make no claims to a total appraisal of Duras's work, it does at least have the advantage of bringing out a constant thread which runs through most of the principal areas of her work, thereby reminding us of the range and intensity of this extraordinary *œuvre*. Reading Duras in the light of the ethical shows both the scope of her various concerns—gender relations, erotic violence, mass trauma, racial identity, left politics, mourning, criminality, and also boredom, love, drink—and the constant fascination with the ethical edge of beyond by which these and other concerns are linked.

Moreover, an appreciation of the operation of this edge in Duras's work allows a re-assessment of the model of writing as excess, transgression, and violence through which she is so insistently read. Both Duras's own rhetoric, which often invites this model, and the strategies of her writing indicate in their love of paradox that its application is far from self-evident, thus pointing up the essential pain of the line of transgression, effaced in its triumphant (or even, incredibly, just habitual) critical embrace. Taking us closer to a less exuberantly subversive, more exhausted, patient, wan understanding of transgression (such as we also find in Blanchot and Bataille), Duras allows us no respite from the awkwardness of her writing on this line, which by definition also refuses the elevation of this irritation into a further critical category if such a move does not immediately stumble on its inherent paradox. Far from simply meaning that it is impossible to write critically about Duras (which would collapse awkwardness into a premature and redemptive despair), this dogged spiral forces the discussion of writing in terms of excess, transgression, violence, and so on, to realize—by means of close reading—that it exists as a discourse to the precise extent that it is impossible, and that even this impossibility needs to be embraced as a constant and genuine disruption, not a stick-on critical battle scar. Any attempt to make Duras's writing coincide with the excess with which it is fascinated must ignore its subtle work on the problems of just such adequation—which reveals the programmatic conservatism of a supposedly radical critical model when it fails to read. The brilliance, patience, and exorbitance of Duras's writing all suggest that the excessive, violent transgressions of writing are a good deal quieter—which is to say, more disturbing, more upsetting, and more significant—than their noisy proclamation in fact allows.

What is truly excessive in Duras's writing is its awkwardness, its constant worrying at just what sort of writing could be possible in the face of ethical extremity. Duras works with the desperate, exhausted movements of our ethical experience, and keeps the sometimes exorbitant attempt to write alongside this experience going, to insist that we do not turn away from the unbearable demands which confront us at the limits of our ethical life. (Although this insistent provocation may always result in precisely nothing.) As she suggests, certain aspects of our ethical experience do take place as it were beyond the elastic limit of the ethical, where we both cannot and yet still must respond ethically; the anguish of this confrontation with an irreducible ethical responsibility which is neither coherent nor suspended is registered in Duras's work with a rare attentiveness. We are buttonholed by Duras's writing in the middle of our most private upsets; but this invasive writing intrudes into our lives in order to accompany the pain of our ethical experience in a way that is at the same time halting, irritating, fascinating, and generous.

If we were to attempt to define in one phrase the essence of the ethical, a certain contender would be the question, 'How should I live?' That Duras has no answer to this question does not stop her asking it—almost, in Alissa's whispered 'Comment vivre?' (*Dd*, 107). But this question may have nothing to do with the ethical, may just be a moment of existential perplexity. Duras leaves us not quite with nothing, but with precious little, with the line of ambiguity within Alissa's phrase, the edge of the ethical. Which is to say: with everything, with a delicate and sublime concern for the sick sense that it is all too much. 'Comment vivre?' As we ask this lonely question, struggle to move out of the silence, it is perhaps something to know that Duras's writing, at least, will not leave us alone, is always impertinent and always supportive, is always trying.

Silence, et puis.

Pour adoucir la vie?
Personne ne le sait. Il faut essayer de vivre. Il ne faut pas se jeter dans la mort.
C'est tout.
C'est tout ce que j'ai à dire.

                                                                (CT, 48–9)

Making the Broken Whole

Which, after all, is something. It is via this question of the redemptive or otherwise status of the literary text in relation to the extremity it addresses that we may be able to grasp something of what
Duras offers us, now. Having been around the loop of the fetishization of textuality (to rid us of referential naïveté), addressed by a
range of urgent political and, indeed, ethical claims, our current
critical climate finds itself faced by the returning demands of some
sort of relation to the real, and, consequently, by the question of how
this relation might be configured. (Often, indeed, the notion of 'the
ethical' is invoked to suggest precisely this question). Duras's work,
I would argue, suggests that this relation may well be thought along
the lines of the ethical—a very particular notion of the ethical, that
is, and as long as this analogy is recognized as impossible. Recalling
the Blanchotian formulation of the Levinasian ethical relation as a
'rapport sans rapport' (Blanchot, *L'Entretien infini*, 104), I would say
that precisely this structure—that of a connection which is also a
separation—is, as I have tried to show, at work throughout Duras's
peculiar implication of her work in its overwhelming concerns. And
the debate (in response to Kristeva's reading in *Soleil noir*, and given
renewed vigour after Duras's death) over the possibility of seeing
her work as possessing redemptive qualities in relation to these concerns offers an initial approach to this structure, which may help to
bring out its significance.

    On the one hand, then, Duras's work would be as one with the
negativity it explores—dangerously blocked below the level of
symbolization, as Kristeva has it, a 'littérature non cathartique'
(Kristeva, 'La Maladie de la douleur', 233). Thus, works on forgetting themselves enact this very forgetting, a text on violence
becomes (in the familiar chiasmus of critical rhetoric) a violent text,

and so on. I have tried to show throughout this study that this kind of identification between text and subject matter represents a glaring contradiction in the case of the particular subjects habitually addressed by Duras, and that this is demonstrated in the details of their textual elaboration. On the other hand, Duras (inasmuch as she is—and she is—a great writer) must be defended against this apparently sub-aesthetic immersion; and thus it is claimed that the properly accomplished, artistic qualities of the work raise it above this kind of identification. (This is, in a sense, a variant on the position that assumes that the provision of framing material around explosive subject matter is enough to insulate author, text, and reader from the dangers of contamination—whereas, in Duras's case, it is in fact anything but, as we have seen). This elevated Duras (restored to her rightful grandeur as The Artist) would, then, offer us an antidote to the various dubious substances which flood her work.[7] Or perhaps Duras just suspends us between the two, leaving us habitually in the perhaps uncomfortable, but profoundly comforting space of liberal undecidability.

The decision to answer the question in one direction or another (to agree with Kristeva, and posit an equivalence between writing and extremity; or to disagree, and argue for some kind of aesthetic, redemptive sublimation) may not, in fact, represent the most appropriate response. For, as I have been arguing, Duras's writing is in fact characterized by its impossible occupation of the non-space of the line which divides these two answers; to answer the question would be to answer the work, constituted as it is as gnawing, inviting, worrying, offering the suggestion of resolution, futurity, attainment (the beyond in its redemptive, eschatological aspect) without ever allowing us the confidence of arrival—including, therefore, the

---

[7] See Madeleine Borgomano, *contra* Kristeva: 'Kristeva dénonce le poison sans voir que Duras offre en même temps le contre-poison' (Borgomano, 'Que sont les oiseaux devenus...?', 165, n. 3). The position developed by Emma Wilson (whose relation to Kristeva's argument I have discussed in Chapter 2, above) in her *Sexuality and the Reading Encounter* is also relevant here—principally since it appears to wish to maintain the disruptive text as in some sense redemptive (a formative part of a project of subversion) on the basis of the traumatic (mis)identifications it offers (and which remain, therefore, unredeemed). (See, for example, the claim that 'those texts which strive to disrupt, frustrate, and mispresent their readers may have the greatest force in changing the world they appear to reflect' (Wilson, 195)). While it does seem to retain certain problematic recuperative moments, then, Wilson's reading—positive potential maintained, perilously, by uneffaced negativity—is, as will be seen, of considerable significance to the argument I am developing here about the relation of Duras's texts to the extremity they confront.

confidence of a positive embrace of 'undecidability'. From its impossible non-position, then, Duras's work asks us whether we think it is in fact possible to get anything out of (or even, sometimes, just to get out of) the experience of extremity. Such would be the stakes of trying to read Duras; they are, plainly, considerable, and are situated within the ethical space (of care, concern, fellow-feeling; or judgement, condemnation, rejection, to name but a few) which is perhaps the secular inheritor of the eschatology by which the encounter with overwhelming negativity is still, here, structured.

In fact, as I have been suggesting, Durassian undecidability has nothing comforting about it—not least because it also refuses the conventionally avant-garde heroism of the irritant, the reminder, the nagging call to some lost authenticity. In relation to the awful material it encounters, her work allows us no sense that it might be redemptive. We have seen this many times, from the lost head of Marie-Thérèse Bousquet (make it meaningful if you will, redeem its loss—and so lose it again) to the unstable frame around *L'Homme assis dans le couloir*, Duras upsetting both the hygienic displacements demanded by the conventions of polite literary criticism and the naïve myths of adequation which sustain those enamoured of heroic, subversive, useful transgression. This also means, however, that she is at the same time not prepared to abandon the notion of redemption: she keeps on (especially in the later texts) insisting that her work is still bound into the suffering it addresses, even though it can do nothing; it remains, stubbornly, there, alongside.

In Duras's universe, the notion that art might save us is no longer a viable option, this art having proved itself over and over either useless or complicit in the face of the horrors of this century. And the political versions of this faith, Sartrean *engagement*, for example, or socialist realism, receive nothing but scorn from the later Duras, for whom they simply fail to notice the empty grandeur of unworking proper to writing. What is left, then, for a writer who nonetheless refuses to give up on the idea of her work as in some sense *engaged*? Neither active nor isolated; both intransitive and urgently concerned: while she may not be able to save us by her work, Duras nonetheless (with Seamus Heaney, for example, with Beckett, with Camus, in his less heroic moments) implicates this work in our efforts to make it through the mess of our unredeemed world.

Caught up in our ethical life, yet also necessarily separated from it, Duras's work may thus be characterized by its *articulated* relationship to this life, which constitutes this relationship, in fact, and in a figure I have used more than once over the course of these pages, as one of accompaniment. There is a growing critical sense of the importance in Duras's work of the notion of accompaniment; glimpsed above principally in Chapters 4 and 6, in relation to her work on historical trauma and the residual self, it has its roots at least as far back as *Le Square*, which traces with such hesitant compassion the lonely, tearful path of 'les derniers des derniers'.[8] While this vision of writing as an accompaniment to the extremity of our ethical life draws on the model (familiar from much ethical criticism, and most extensively developed by Wayne C. Booth, in his *The Company We Keep*) of an encounter, characterized by a particular ethos, between text and reader, it also qualifies this model somewhat. First, our relationship with Duras's writing is not really all that well described by the rather cosy Boothian image of a potential friend knocking at the door and offering a particular quality of experience. With what is perhaps a particularly Durassian temporality, Duras's texts give the impression that they have somehow already found their way in, are already rubbing up here and there against the intimacies of our ethical experience even before we have decided whether or not to let them in. And once they are in, their behaviour is again perhaps less than civilized: rather than proposing a particular quality of ethical conversation, they seem to be neither here nor there, too close and then suddenly nowhere. This strange, intrusive, and residual presence suggests that this is not quite an encounter which I may calmly evaluate; the encounter between Duras's writing and our ethical experience is, in fact, an encounter that may already have started, or may even not be taking place at all. Her writing stumbles alongside the extremity of the ethical which it addresses, and offers (intermittently) its own idiosyncratic, fascinated kind of support. It *touches on* our ethical lives; rather than instructive or enlightening conversation, it offers an attempted gesture of loving companionship which has no certain

[8] Examples of this emerging view of Duras have been cited above; they include, in particular, Kristeva's view of Duras as attempting to 'suivre le malheur pas à pas, cliniquement presque, sans jamais le surmonter' ('La Maladie de la douleur', 232); Jacques-Pierre Amette, 'La Duras qui nous touche'; and Paul Thibaud, 'Marguerite Duras: Les Ambiguïtés de la compassion'. See also Danielle Bajomée's excellent 'C'est par ce chat maigre et fou que je vous atteins, ou la compassion chez Marguerite Duras', in Vircondelet (ed.), *Duras, Dieu et l'écrit*, 103–23.

grasp on what it touches, which might always be getting it wrong. Duras is just (awkwardly, and according to a faltering rhythm we can hardly discern) there, sometimes getting it hopelessly wrong, sometimes movingly right. And every now and again, her inconstant hand is on our shoulder, as her writing hooks awkwardly and intricately into the extremities of our ethical experience.

If Duras's work has an overall model to offer, then, it might be this presentation of writing as an obscure accompaniment to our ethical life, 'ce cheminement de l'écrit à côté de la vie, et duquel on ne peut absolument pas s'extraire' (Interview with Duras by Pivot on *Apostrophes*). In this accompaniment, writing is marked by what we might see as a tangential referentiality, brushing against the texture of our lived experience, without this encounter ever quite constituting itself, remaining as fragile as it is vital. (At which point, the notion of Duras's 'survival' in her writings returns: for this figure, if it takes itself at all seriously, cannot but suggest the most hesitant of encounters, absorbing inasmuch as it may always also not be taking place; the chaotic haunting which Duras herself liked to use as an image of this delicate yet impassioned referential relation). And yet this fleeting touch contains so much. For in it, Duras takes us to the edge of our ethical experience, refuses a ready grasp of the demands of this experience, and thereby insists (in part, of course, by falling short of this) on an absolute openness to the demands of the unknowable beyond—which we might also, after Levinas, Blanchot, and Derrida, call the wholly other, demanding a justice which is always still to come;[9] while also thematizing these demands, inasmuch as they burst into our lives, engaging her writing messily in our attempts to negotiate them; while also simply offering her writing as some sort of companion (faithful, helpful or otherwise) in this process; and also just managing to hold this writing back from the confident, successful assumption of this status, which would wreck the delicacy by which it is alone maintained. (Which is why, incidentally, any sense of Duras's work as redemptive negates the patience and the pathos by which, at its best, it is characterized—while also conveniently forgetting the slippages and self-serving distortions of which, at its worst, it is eminently capable).

---

[9] On this, see Caputo, *The Prayers and Tears of Jacques Derrida* (Bloomington: Indiana University Press, 1997), 118ff.

Duras offers, then, no less than a suggestion as to the way in which we might go about thinking the relationship between the aesthetic and the real, between art and life, at the end of a century whose criticism has thought of little else. An appropriately modest suggestion, perhaps, for a century of dereliction, which has seen the withering of various redemptive aesthetics, but which is yet left with its sufferings, and its art, which still refuses to leave these sufferings alone. In the midst of an apparent return of the ethical within literary criticism, the tentative nature of this Durassian accompaniment might serve to remind us that a return is always in part in the business of re-creating the home it comes back to. If literature really is one place where we can learn the surprising quirks and painful pressures of ethical experience, then the relationship between literature and this experience—if it is not to deny precisely these elements—can hardly be other than odd, oblique, tangential. For over fifty years, Duras took her writing and its readers to the limit of the ethical, and provided some sort of accompaniment to the extremity located there. It is a rare body of work indeed which can be so insistently caught up in the world of ethical experience, and at the same time so utterly unsure about the nature of this relationship. Duras spent her writing life mapping the limit of the ethical as a way of accompanying its inexpressible passions and agonies in the only consistent way possible: uncertainly. Silence alone will not do: for what could come of that? For all that these passions, these agonies may exceed our understanding, we cannot but speak of them; what matters, for Duras, is finding a way of speaking, of writing which would mark their demands in part by letting their silence resonate *within* the stubborn, inadequate attempt somehow to carry on—which also means carrying on speaking, writing.[10] If we want to take the extreme demands of the ethical seriously, and if we want to bring them into an encounter with the business of literary criticism,

---

[10] Sylvie Germain expresses this quasi-Beckettian position extremely well, while also marking its difference from the famous conclusion to Wittgenstein's *Tractatus*: 'Ce dont on ne peut parler, justement, c'est quoi? C'est ce néant du monde, cette absence de Dieu, cette absence de sens et d'espérance, cet échec total de la communication, ce désert de l'amour. Elle n'a écrit que là-dessus. On ne peut pas en parler, on ne peut pas le communiquer, ni même vraiment le vivre et pour survivre à ça qu'est-ce qu'on fait on écrit. Donc "ce dont on ne peut parler, il faut le taire", mais on a envie de continuer avec Duras, en disant "oui, mais on va écrire"'. (In Aliette Armel, 'Marguerite Duras et l'absence de Dieu', in Vircondelet (ed.), *Duras, Dieu et l'écrit*, 13–45 (43)). The reference is to Ludwig Wittgenstein, *Tractatus Logico-Philosophicus* (London: Routledge and Kegan Paul, 1949), which concludes with the sentence, 'Whereof one cannot speak, thereof one must be silent' (189).

then Duras's faltering, generous accompaniment may offer a vital counsel—not least in its suggestion that, confronted by these demands, our ethical conversation may have to find a way of speaking while at the same time falling silent.

Comme une peur immédiate de la mort.
Et après une fatigue immense.

Silence, et puis.

Viens.
Il faut qu'on parle de notre amour.
On va trouver les mots pour ça.
Il n'y aurait pas de mots peut-être.

(*CT*, 43–4)

BIBLIOGRAPHY

Editions given are those to which reference is made above. Where more than one date is given, the first refers to the original date of publication. In all cases, the latest date given refers to the edition used. Generic classification is largely secure, but inevitably, at times, provisional. Such works are given as have been consulted during the writing of this study. For supplementary information, the reader is referred to the excellent bibliography in Leslie Hill, *Marguerite Duras: Apocalyptic Desires*, and to Harvey and Volat, *Marguerite Duras: A Bio-Bibliography*.

I. WORKS BY DURAS

1.i Prose

Les Impudents (Paris: Plon, 1943; Gallimard, coll. 'folio', 1992) (*I*).
La Vie tranquille (Paris: Gallimard, 1944; coll. 'folio', 1993) (*VT*).
Un Barrage contre le Pacifique (Paris: Gallimard, 1950; coll. 'folio', 1992) (*BCP*).
Le Marin de Gibraltar (Paris: Gallimard, 1952; coll. 'folio', 1994) (*MG*).
Les Petits Chevaux de Tarquinia (Paris: Gallimard, 1953; coll. 'folio', 1973) (*PC*).
Des Journées entières dans les arbres (Paris: Gallimard, 1954, 1990) (*DJ*).
Le Square (Paris: Gallimard, 1955; coll. 'folio', 1993) (*S*).
Moderato cantabile (Paris: Minuit, 1958, 1988) (*MC*).
Dix heures et demie du soir en été (Paris: Gallimard, 1960; coll. 'folio', 1991) (*DH*).
L'Après-midi de M. Andesmas (Paris: Gallimard, 1962) (*AMA*).
Le Ravissement de Lol V. Stein (Paris: Gallimard, 1964; coll. 'folio', 1992) (*RLVS*).
Le Vice-Consul (Paris: Gallimard, 1966; coll. 'L'Imaginaire', 1991) (*VC*).
L'Amante anglaise (Paris: Gallimard, 1967; coll. 'L'Imaginaire', 1991) (*AA*).
Détruire dit-elle (Paris: Minuit, 1969, 1987) (*Dd*).
Abahn Sabana David (Paris: Gallimard, 1970, 1990) (*ASD*).
L'Amour (Paris: Gallimard, 1971, 1992) (*Ar*).
L'Homme assis dans le couloir (Paris: Minuit, 1980, 1989) (*HAC*).
L'Été 80 (Paris: Minuit, 1980, 1990) (*É80*).
Outside (Paris: Albin Michel, 1981; P.O.L., 1991) (*O*).
L'Homme atlantique (Paris: Minuit, 1982).
La Maladie de la mort (Paris: Minuit, 1982, 1986) (*MM*).
L'Amant (Paris: Minuit, 1984, 1986) (*At*).
La Douleur (Paris: P.O.L., 1985; coll. 'folio', 1993) (*D*).
Les Yeux bleus cheveux noirs (Paris: Minuit, 1986, 1987) (*YB*).
La Pute de la côte normande (Paris: Minuit, 1986).
Emily L. (Paris: Minuit, 1987) (*EL*).

298 BIBLIOGRAPHY

Les Yeux verts, nouvelle édition augmentée (Paris: Cahiers du cinéma, 1987) (*YV*).
La Vie matérielle (Paris: P.O.L., 1987, 1989) (*VM*).
La Pluie d'été (Paris: P.O.L., 1990; Gallimard, coll. 'folio', 1994) (*PE*).
L'Amant de la Chine du nord (Paris: Gallimard, 1991, 1992) (*ACN*).
Yann Andréa Steiner (Paris: P.O.L., 1992) (*YAS*).
Écrire (Paris: Gallimard, 1993) (*É*).
Le Monde extérieur (Paris: P.O.L., 1993) (*ME*).
C'est tout (Paris: P.O.L., 1995) (*CT*).
La Mer écrite (with Hélène Bamberger) (Paris: Marval, 1996).
Romans, Cinéma, Théâtre: Un Parcours (Paris: Gallimard, 1997) (*RCT*).

1.ii Theatre

Les Viaducs de la Seine-et-Oise (Paris: Gallimard, coll. 'le manteau d'arlequin', 1960) (*VSO*).
Théâtre I (*Les Eaux et forêts* (1965); *Le Square* (1965); *La Musica* (1965)) (Paris: Gallimard, 1965).
'Pièce russe', *Cahiers Renaud-Barrault*, no. 52 (1965), 76–90.
Théâtre II (*Suzanna Andler* (1968); *Des Journées entières dans les arbres* (1965); *Yes, peut-être* (1968); *Le Shaga* (1968); *Un Homme est venu me voir* (1968)) (Paris: Gallimard, 1968).
L'Éden cinéma (Paris: Mercure de France, 1977; coll. 'folio', 1992).
Agatha (Paris: Minuit, 1981, 1987).
Savannah Bay (Paris: Minuit, 1982; nouvelle édition augmentée, 1990).
Théâtre III (*La Bête dans la jungle* (French version of James Lord's stage adaptation of Henry James's 'The Beast in the Jungle') (1962; revised 1981); *Les Papiers d'Aspern* (French version, by Duras and Robert Antelme, of Michael Redgrave's stage adaptation of James's 'The Aspern Papers') (1961); *La Danse de mort* (French adaptation of Strindberg's 'Dödsdansen' (1970)) (Paris: Gallimard, 1984).
La Musica deuxième (Paris: Gallimard, 1985).
La Mouette de Tchékhov (adapted by Marguerite Duras) (Paris: Gallimard, 1985).
'Home' (French adaptation of play by David Storey), in *L'Avant-scène du théâtre*, 792 (15 juin 1986) (copyright Gallimard, 1973).
Éden cinéma (nouvelle version scénique) (Paris: Actes Sud-Papiers, 1988).
Le Théâtre de l'Amante anglaise (Paris: Gallimard, coll. 'L'Imaginaire', 1991).

1.iii Screenplays

Hiroshima mon amour (Paris: Gallimard, 1960; coll. 'folio', 1991) (*HMA*).
Une aussi longue absence (with Gérard Jarlot) (Paris: Gallimard, 1961).
India Song (Paris: Gallimard, 1973; coll. 'L'Imaginaire', 1991) (*IS*).
Nathalie Granger, suivie de: La Femme du Gange (Paris: Gallimard, 1973) (*NG*).
Le Camion, suivi de: Entretien avec Michelle Porte (Paris: Minuit, 1977) (*C*).

Le Navire Night, suivi de: Césarée; Les Mains négatives; Aurélia Steiner; Aurélia Steiner; Aurélia Steiner (Paris: Mercure de France, 1979; coll. 'folio', 1992) (*NN*).

Véra Baxter ou les plages de l'Atlantique (Paris: Éditions Albatros, coll. 'ça/cinéma', 1980).

1.iv Journalism and Occasional Writings

'Une Pièce involontaire', *L'Express*, 14 septembre 1965, 15.

'Les Travailleurs contre le gouvernement' (with Jacques-Francis Rolland), *France-Observateur*, 18 avril 1957, 10–11.

'La France à l'italienne', *France-Observateur*, 27 juin 1957, 13.

'L'Internationale Tintin', *France-Observateur*, 4 juillet 1957, 13.

'Le Dimanche des héros', *France-Observateur*, 11 juillet 1957, 10.

'Travailler pour le cinéma', *France-Observateur*, 31 juillet 1958, 20.

'Deschamps, Simone', *France-Observateur*, 16 octobre 1958, 14.

'Le Repos du guerrier', *France-Observateur*, 27 novembre 1958, 18.

'Uneuravek', *L'Express*, 22 janvier 1959, 27–8.

Interview with Jeanne Moreau, *Afrique-Action*, 17 octobre 1960, 23–4.

'L'Homme assis dans le couloir', *L'Arc*, octobre 1962, 70–6 ('HACa').

'Pourquoi?' (with Gérard Jarlot), *L'Avant-scène du théâtre*, 1 janvier 1963, 9.

'Le Vice-Consul' (extract from *V-C*), *Cahiers Renaud-Barrault*, 52 (1965), 57–75.

'Les Recalés de l'écriture', *Le Nouvel Observateur*, 22 avril 1965, 22–3.

'Vivre seule', *Le Nouvel Observateur*, 29 septembre–5 octobre 1965, 18–19.

'Gugusse, c'est moi!', *Le Nouvel Observateur*, 12–18 octobre 1966, 45–6.

'La Femme d'Evreux', *Cahiers du cinéma*, février 1967, 43.

'Melina la superbe', *Arts-Loisirs*, 1–7 février 1967, 20–3.

'Les Hardes de Salonique', *Le Nouvel Observateur*, 8–14 novembre 1967, 46–7.

'*Un An après*: Le Comité d'action écrivains-étudiants', *Les Lettres nouvelles*, juin–juillet 1969, 143–88.

'Le Tombeau de l'impossible', *Le Quinzaine littéraire*, 1–15 décembre 1971, 26–7.

'Comment, pourquoi *India Song*', *Le Monde*, 5 juin 1975, 17–20.

'Notes sur *India Song*', in Barat and Farges (eds.), *Marguerite Duras*, 12–20.

'*India Song* (découpage)', in Barat and Farges (eds.), *Marguerite Duras*, 21–74.

'La Soupe aux poireaux', *Sorcières*, janvier 1976, 36.

'Les Enfants maigres et jaunes', *Sorcières*, janvier 1976, 37–8.

'Seyrig-Hiss', *Sorcières*, mars 1976, 32.

'Le Cinéma ouvert', *Le Quotidien de Paris*, 3 juin 1976, 11.

'Bleu le ciel, le matin, soleil', *Libération*, 15 juin 1976, 14.

'Mothers', *Le Monde*, 10 février 1977, 17.

'Le Navire "Night"' (first version), *Minuit*, mai 1978, 2–14.

Les Yeux verts, special edition of *Les Cahiers du cinéma*, juin 1980. (Expanded and republished in 1987 as *YV*.)

'*Agatha* est le premier film que j'écris sur le bonheur', *Les Cahiers du cinéma*, mai 1981, 64–5.

'Un Pays du nord', *Des Femmes en mouvements hebdo*, 48 (3–10 juillet 1981), 25.
'Le Noir Atlantique', *Des Femmes en mouvements hebdo*, 11–18 septembre 1981, 30–1.
'Je n'ai rien à justifier', *Le Quotidien de Paris*, 8 octobre 1981, 33.
'Les Rendez-vous manqués: après 1936 et 1956, 1981?', petition signed by Duras *et al.*, *Libération*, 15 décembre 1981, 18.
'Sur le pont du Nord un bal y est donné', interview by Duras with Jacques Rivette, *Le Monde*, 23 mars 1982, 15–16.
'Le Château de Weatherend', *L'Arc*, octobre 1983, 100–2.
'Le Décor de *Savannah Bay*', interview with Roberto Plate, *Cahiers Renaud-Barrault*, 106 (1983), 7–12.
'Pascale', *Libération*, 30 novembre 1984, 30.
'Work and Words', *Marguerite Duras: œuvres cinématographiques. Édition vidéographique critique* (Paris: Minstère des relations extérieures—Bureau d'animation culturelle, 1984), 63.
'Sublime, forcément sublime Christine V.', *Libération*, 17 juillet 1985, 4–6.
'Avec ou sans les amitiés de M.D.', *Libération*, 23 juillet 1985, 33.
'Le Scandale de la vérité', *Cahiers du cinéma*, juillet–août 1985, 13.
'Elle a sorti la France de ses gonds', *Le Quotidien de Paris*, 1 octobre 1985, 25.
'Écrit pour tous les temps, tous les carêmes', *L'Autre Journal*, novembre 1985, 73.
'Le Bureau de poste de la rue Dupin', interview with François Mitterrand, *L'Autre Journal*, 26 février–4 mars 1986, 31–40.
'Le dernier pays avant la mer', interview with François Mitterrand, *L'Autre Journal*, 5–11 mars 1986, 33–40.
'Le Ciel et le terre', interview with François Mitterrand, *L'Autre Journal*, 12–18 mars 1986, 26–34.
'Africa, Africa', interview with François Mitterrand, *L'Autre Journal*, 19–25 mars 1986, 24–33.
'La Nouvelle Angoulême', interview with François Mitterrand, *L'Autre Journal*, 7–13 mai 1986, 24–34.
'Être de gauche', *Esprit*, 116 (juillet 1986), 78.
'La Pute de la côte normande', *Libération*, 14 novembre 1986, 30–1. (Published as *La Pute de la côte normande*.)
'Ils veulent continuer à lire *Le Matin*', including contribution from Duras, *Le Matin*, 13–14 juin 1987, 26–7.
'L'Exacte Exactitude de Denis Belloc', *Libération*, 19–20 septembre 1987, 32–3.
'Remarques générales sur "Les Juifs" de *Jaune le soleil*', 'Note de tournage sur *Jaune le soleil*', *Cahiers du cinéma*, 400 (octobre 1987), 20–1.
'L'Internationalisme de l'idée française', *Globe*, 23 (décembre 1987), 36.
'Écrire', *L'Esprit Créateur*, 30/1 (Spring 1990), 6–7.

1.v Prefaces, Translations, Adaptations

Gibson, William, *Miracle en Alabama* (*The Miracle Worker*), pièce en trois actes par William Gibson, texte français de Marguerite Duras and Gérard Jarlot (Paris: L'Avant-scène du théâtre, 1963).

Lapoujade, portraits et compositions, preface by Marguerite Duras (Paris: Galerie Pierre Domec, 1965).

Dallet, Jean-Marie, *Les Antipodes*, preface by Marguerite Duras (Paris: Seuil, coll. 'Écrire', 1968).

Lennard, Erica, *Les Femmes et les sœurs*, postface de Marguerite Duras (Paris: des femmes, 1970).

Chillida, Eduardo, *Adoración*, trois eaux-fortes par Eduardo Chillida; version française par Marguerite Duras (Paris: Imprimerie Fequet–Baudier/Morsang, 1977).

Kuroda, Aki, *Ténèbres*, texte de Marguerite Duras (Paris: Galerie Adrien Maeght, 1980).

Wittig, Monique, *L'Opoponax*, avec une postface de Marguerite Duras (Paris: Minuit, 1983).

Choukroun, Henri, *Pour une nouvelle économie de la création*, preface by Marguerite Duras (Paris: H. Choukroun, 1985).

Yves Saint Laurent et la photographie de mode, preface by Marguerite Duras (Paris: Albin Michel, 1988). (Reprinted in Yves Saint Laurent, *L'Esprit du temps*, textes de Françoise Sagan, Bernard-Henri Lévy et Marguerite Duras (Paris: Movida, 1989)).

Niepce, Janine, *France*, texte de Marguerite Duras (Arles: Actes-Sud, 1992).

Lennard, Erica, *Maisons d'écrivains*, textes, Francesca Premouli-Droulers; prologue, Marguerite Duras (Paris: Éditions du Chêne, 1994). (Extracts from *Écrire*).

2. INTERVIEWS WITH DURAS

2.i Books

Duras, Marguerite and Gauthier, Xavière, *Les Parleuses* (Paris: Minuit, 1974) (*P*).

Duras, Marguerite and Porte, Michelle, *Les Lieux de Marguerite Duras* (Paris: Minuit, 1977) (*L*).

Lamy, Suzanne, and Roy, André (eds.), *Marguerite Duras à Montréal* (Montreal: Éditions Spirale, 1981).

Marguerite Duras: Œuvres cinématographiques. Édition vidéographique critique (Paris: Ministère des relations extérieures—Bureau d'animation culturelle, 1984).

2.ii Various

'Le "Barrage" est mon histoire', *L'Express*, 8 mai 1958, 22.

André Bourin, 'Non, je ne suis pas la femme d'Hiroshima', *Les Nouvelles littéraires*, 18 juin 1959, 1/4.

Interview by Denise Bourdet, *La Revue de Paris*, novembre 1961, 129–32. (Reprinted in Bourdet, *Brèves rencontres* (Paris: Grasset, 1963), 65–71).

Interview by Madeleine Chapsal, in Chapsal, *Quinze écrivains* (Paris: René Juillard, 1963), 57–64. (Originally in *L'Express*, 30 juin 1960, 36–8).

J.-C. Kerbourc'h, 'Marguerite Duras cherche la liberté et la vérité dans le crime', *Combat*, 16–17 février 1963, 9.

'François Billetdoux, Agnès Capri et Marguerite Duras font le portrait de Katharina Renn', *Arts*, 6–12 mars 1963, 5.

'L'auteur d'"Hiroshima mon amour" vous parle', *Réalités*, mars 1963, 90–5. (Includes pre-publication extract from 'Le Vice-Consul de France à Calcutta').

Anne Germain, 'J'ai peur, j'ai très peur . . .', *Les Nouvelles littéraires*, 13 août 1963, 3.

Pierre Hahn, 'Les Hommes de 1963 ne sont pas assez féminins', *Paris-Théâtre*, 198 (14 septembre 1963), 32–7.

Interview with Duras in Pierre Dumayet, *Vu et entendu* (Paris: Stock, 1964), 105–9.

Charles Silvestre, 'La Confidence n'est jamais privée', *Humanité–Dimanche*, 21 novembre 1965, section 'Télé H.D.', 2.

Sonia Lescaut, 'Quand Marguerite Duras joue de la *Musica*', *Arts*, 26 janvier–1 février 1966, 6.

Anne Cappelle, 'Pourvu que ça marche!', *Arts*, 27 juillet–2 août 1966, 38–40.

Pierre Montaigne, 'Marguerite Duras: Oui . . . mais . . .', *Le Figaro*, 9–10 septembre 1967, 16.

Hubert Nyssen, 'Un Silence peuplé de phrases', in Nyssen, *Les Voies de l'écriture* (Paris: Mercure de France, 1969), 125–41. (Originally in *Synthèses*, 254–5 (août–septembre 1967), 42–50.

Jacques Rivette and Jean Narboni, 'La Destruction la parole', *Cahiers du cinéma*, 217 (novembre 1969), 45–57.

Interview by Bettina L. Knapp, *The French Review*, 44/4 (March 1971), 653–9.

François Marie-Banier, 'Duras l'étrangère', *L'Express*, 24–30 janvier 1972, 86.

Interview by Suzanne Horer and Jeanne Socquet, in Horer and Socquet (eds.), *La Création étouffée* (Paris: Pierre Horay, coll. 'Femmes en mouvement', 1973), 172–87.

Jean-Louis Ezine, 'Ce que parler ne veut pas dire . . .', *Les Nouvelles littéraires*, 15–21 avril 1974, 3.

Xavière Gauthier, 'Marguerite Duras', in Barat and Farges (eds.), *Marguerite Duras*, 75–92.

P. Bregstein, 'Parce que le silence est féminin', *Cinématographe*, mai–juin 1975, 22–4.

Pierre Montaigne, 'D'"India Song" à "Véra Baxter": Marguerite Duras et les vertus de l'ellipse', *Le Figaro*, 28 avril 1976, 29.

Interview by Claire Clouzot, *Écran*, 15 juillet 1976, 62–3.

'Rencontres des Cahiers Renaud-Barrault', *Cahiers Renaud-Barrault*, 91 (1976), 3–26.

Jack Gousseland, 'Le Feu d'artifice de Marguerite Duras', *Le Point*, 14 février 1977, 83–5.

René Prédal, 'Entretien avec Marguerite Duras', *Jeune cinéma*, juillet–août 1977, 16–21.

Pierre Montaigne, 'La Nuit sur le navire de Marguerite Duras', *Le Figaro*, 2 août 1978, 13.

Patrick Duval, 'En effeuillant la marguerite', *Libération*, 22 mars 1979, 15–16.

Roland Thelu, 'The Thing', *Gai pied*, 20 (novembre 1980), 16.

Yann Andréa, 'C'est fou c'que j'peux t'aimer', *Libération*, 4 janvier 1983 (supplément 'livres', unpaginated).

Marianne Alphant, 'J'avais envie de lire un livre de moi', *Libération*, 4 septembre 1984, 28–9.

Gilles Costaz, 'Ce qui arrive tous les jours n'arrive qu'une seule fois', *Le Matin*, 28 septembre 1984.

Hervé Le Masson, 'L'Inconnue de la rue Catinat', *Le Nouvel Observateur*, 28 septembre–4 octobre 1984, 92–4.

Interview by Bernard Pivot, *Apostrophes*, Antenne 2, 28 septembre 1984. (Released on video: *Apostrophes: Bernard Pivot rencontre Marguerite Duras* (Paris: Seuil, 1990)).

Interview with Duras in Michèle Manceaux, *Éloge de l'insomnie* (Paris: Hachette, 1985), 31–44.

Pierre Benichou and Hervé Le Masson, 'Duras tout entière', *Le Nouvel Observateur*, 14–20 novembre 1986, 114–17.

Michel Bergain, 'Duras, de gauche complètement', *Globe*, 13 (janvier 1987), 29–33.

Didier Eribon, 'Comme une messe de mariage', *Le Nouvel Observateur*, 16–22 octobre 1987, 140–1.

Colette Felous, 'Duras dans les régions claires de l'écriture', *Le Journal littéraire*, 2 (décembre 1987–janvier 1988), 126–7.

Pierre Bergé, 'Duras est sexy!', Globe, 30 (juillet–août 1988), 78–83.

Colette Mazabrard, 'J'ai toujours désespérément filmé . . .', *Cahiers du cinéma*, 426 (décembre 1989), 62–5.

Jean-Marcel Bouguereau, 'Duras 89–90', *L'Événement du jeudi*, 1–7 février 1990, 84–7.

Frédérique Lebelley, 'Marguerite retrouvée', *Le Nouvel Observateur*, 24–30 mai 1990, 129–33.

Aliette Armel, '"J'ai vécu le réel comme un mythe"', *Le Magazine littéraire*, 278 (juin 1990), 18–24.

Gilbert Guez, 'La Lanterne magique de Marguerite Duras', *Le Figaro*, 7 février 1991, 29.

Interview with Duras by Alice Jardine in Jardine and Menke (eds.), *Shifting Scenes* (New York: Columbia University Press, 1991), 71–8.

Jean-Louis Ezine, 'Vive Cresson et la lutte des classes!', *Le Nouvel Observateur*, 2–8 avril 1992, 65.

Jean-Louis Ezine, 'Les Nostalgies de l'amante Duras', *Le Nouvel Observateur*, 25 juin–1 juillet 1992, 109–11.

3. CRITICISM: WORKS ON DURAS

3.i Books Wholly Devoted to Duras

Adler, Laure, *Marguerite Duras* (Paris: Gallimard, 1998).

Alazet, Bernard, *Le Navire Night de Marguerite Duras: Écrire l'effacement* (Paris: Presses Universitaires de Lille, 1992).

Alleins, Madeleine, *Marguerite Duras: Médium du réel* (Lausanne: Éditions L'Âge d'Homme, 1984).

Ames, Stanford S. (ed.), *Remains to be Seen* (New York: Peter Lang, 1988).

Anderson, Stephanie, *Le Discours féminin de Marguerite Duras: Un Désir pervers et ses métamorphoses* (Geneva: Droz, 1995).

Armel, Aliette, *Marguerite Duras et l'autobiographie* (Paris: Le Castor Astral, 1990).

Bajomée, Danielle, *Duras ou la douleur* (Brussels: De Boeck-Wesmael, 1989).

Bajomée, Danielle and Heyndels, Ralph (eds.), *Écrire, dit-elle* (Bruxelles: Éditions de l'Université de Bruxelles, 1985).

Barat, François, and Farges, Joël (eds.), *Marguerite Duras* (Paris: Éditions Albatros, coll. 'ça/cinéma', 1975).

Bernheim, Nicole-Louise, *Marguerite Duras tourne un film* (Paris: Éditions Albatros, coll. 'ça/cinéma', 1974).

Blot-Labarrère, Christiane, *Marguerite Duras* (Paris: Seuil, coll. 'Les Contemporains', 1992).

Borgomano, Madeleine, *Duras: Une Lecture des fantasmes* (Paris: Cistre, 1985).

—— *L'écriture filmique de Marguerite Duras* (Paris: Editions Albatros, 1985).

Cerasi, Claire, *Du Rythme au sens: Une Lecture de L'Amour de Marguerite Duras* (Paris: Archives des Lettres Modernes, 1991).

—— *Marguerite Duras de Lahore à Auschwitz* (Geneva: Éditions Slatkine, 1993).

Cismaru, Alfred, *Marguerite Duras* (New York: Twayne, 1971).

Cohen, Susan D., *Women and Discourse in the Fiction of Marguerite Duras* (Basingstoke: Macmillan, 1993).

Cranston, Mechthild, *Beyond the Book—Marguerite Duras*: Infans (Potomac: Scripta Humanistica, 1996).

L'École des Lettres, second cycle, 6 : Marguerite Duras, de Vinh-Long à Calcutta (Paris: École des Lettres, 1987).

Fernandez, Marie-Pierre, *Travailler avec Duras* (Paris: Gallimard, 1986).

Glassman, Deborah, *Marguerite Duras: Fascinating Vision and Narrative Cure* (London: Associated University Presses, 1991).

Guers-Villate, Yvonne, *Continuité/discontinuité de l'œuvre durassienne* (Brussels: Éditions de l'Université de Bruxelles, 1985).

Harvey, Robert, and Volat, Hélène, *Marguerite Duras: A Bio-Bibliography* (Westport: Greenwood Press, 1997).

Hill, Leslie, *Marguerite Duras: Apocalyptic Desires* (London: Routledge, 1993).

Hofmann, Carol, *Forgetting and Marguerite Duras* (Niwot: University Press of Colorado, 1991).

Lebelley, Frédérique, *Duras ou le poids d'une plume* (Paris: Grasset, 1994).

Lemaître, Maurice, *Marguerite Duras: pour en finir avec cet escroc et plagiaire généralisée* (Paris: Centre de créativité, 1979).

Ligot, Marie-Thérèse, *Marguerite Duras: Un Barrage contre le Pacifique* (Paris: Gallimard, coll. 'Foliothèque', 1992).

Limam-Tnami, Najet, *Roman et cinéma chez Marguerite Duras: Une Poétique de la spécularité* (Tunis: Faculté des sciences humaines et sociales/Alif-Les Éditions de la Méditerranée, 1996).

Marguerite Duras: Vérité et légendes (Photographies inédites, Collection Jean Mascolo; Texte, Alain Vircondelet) (Paris: Éditions du Chêne-Hachette Livre, 1996).

Marini, Marcelle, *Territoires du féminin. Avec Marguerite Duras* (Paris: Minuit, coll. 'autrement dites', 1977).

Murphy, Carol J., *Alienation and Absence in the Novels of Marguerite Duras* (Lexington: French Forum, 1982).

Papin, Liliane, *L'Autre Scène: Le Théâtre de Marguerite Duras* (Saratoga: Anma Libri, 1988).

Pierrot, Jean, *Marguerite Duras* (Paris: Librairie José Corti, 1986).

Ricouart, Janine, *Écriture féminine et violence: Une Étude de Marguerite Duras* (Birmingham, Alabama: Summa, 1991).

Rodgers, Catherine, and Udris, Raynalle (eds.), *Marguerite Duras: Lectures plurielles* (Amsterdam: Rodopi, 1998).

Schuster, Marilyn R., *Marguerite Duras Revisited* (New York: Twayne, 1993).

Selous, Trista, *The Other Woman: Feminism and Femininity in the Work of Marguerite Duras* (London: Yale University Press, 1988).

Seylaz, Jean-Luc, *Les Romans de Marguerite Duras: Essai sur une thématique de la durée* (Paris: Archives des Lettres Modernes, 1963).

Skutta, Franciska, *Aspects de la narration dans les romans de Marguerite Duras* (Debrecen: Kossuth Lajos Tudományegyetem, 1981).

Steinmetz-Schünemann, Helga, *Die Bedeutung der Zeit in den Romanen von Marguerite Duras* (Amsterdam: Rodopi, 1976).

Tison-Braun, Micheline, *Marguerite Duras* (Amsterdam: Rodopi, 1985).

Udris, Raynalle, *Welcome Unreason* (Amsterdam: Rodopi, 1993).

Vircondelet, Alain, *Marguerite Duras ou le temps de détruire* (Paris: Seghers, 1972).

—— *Duras* (Paris: Éditions François Bourin, 1991).

—— (ed.), *Marguerite Duras: Rencontres de Cerisy* (Paris: Éditions Écriture, 1994).

—— *Pour Duras* (Paris: Calmann-Lévy, 1995).

—— (ed.), *Duras, Dieu et l'écrit* (Monaco: Éditions du Rocher, 1998).

Williams, James S., *The Erotics of Passage: Pleasure, Politics and Form in the Later Work of Marguerite Duras* (Liverpool: Liverpool University Press, 1997).

Willis, Sharon, *Marguerite Duras: Writing on the Body* (Urbana and Chicago: University of Illinois Press, 1987).

3.ii Chapters in Collections Devoted to Duras

Alazet, Bernard, 'La Tentation du sublime', in Vircondelet (ed.), *Duras, Dieu et l'écrit*, 85–101.

Ames, Stanford S., 'Edging the Shadow', in Ames (ed.), *Remains to be Seen*, 3–30.

—— 'Dead Letters, Impossible Witness', in Ames (ed.), *Remains to be Seen*, 279–85.

Armel, Aliette, 'Marguerite Duras et l'absence de Dieu', in Vircondelet (ed.), *Duras, Dieu et l'écrit*, 13–45.

Bajomée, Danielle, 'La Nuit, l'effacement, la nuit', in Bajomée and Heyndels (eds.), *Écrire, dit-elle*, 85–98.

—— 'C'est par ce chat maigre et fou que je vous atteins, ou la compassion chez Marguerite Duras', in Vircondelet (ed.), *Duras, Dieu et l'écrit*, 103–23.

Blot-Labarrère, Christiane, 'Dieu, un "mot" chez Marguerite Duras?', in Vircondelet (ed.), *Duras, Dieu et l'écrit*, 177–99.

Borgomano, Madeleine, 'Le Corps et le texte', in Bajomée and Heyndels (eds.), *Écrire, dit-elle*, 49–62.

—— 'Que sont les oiseaux devenus . . . ?: Étude sémio-analytique des écrits de Marguerite Duras depuis *L'Amant*', in Rodgers and Udris (eds.), *Marguerite Duras: Lectures plurielles*, 151–67.

Chawaf, Chantal, 'Puissance de la langue dans la langue de l'impuissance', in Vircondelet (ed.), *Marguerite Duras: Rencontres de Cerisy*, 241–8.

Cohen, Susan D., 'From Omniscience to Ignorance', in Ames (ed.), *Remains to be Seen*, 51–78.

—— 'The Beast and the Jungle: Longing, Learning, Love, and Luck in Marguerite Duras's "Le Boa"', in Rodgers and Udris (eds.), *Marguerite Duras: Lectures plurielles*, 35–55.

De Certeau, Michel, 'Marguerite Duras: On dit', in Bajomée and Heyndels (eds.), *Écrire, dit-elle*, 257–65.

Denes, Dominique, 'Marguerite Duras par-delà le bien et le mal', in Vircondelet (ed.), *Duras, Dieu et l'écrit*, 201–17.

Didier, Béatrice, 'Thèmes et structures de l'absence dans *Le Ravissement de Lol V. Stein*', in Bajomée and Heyndels (eds.), *Écrire, dit-elle*, 63–84.

Diet, Aurora, *et al.* (Collectif d'étudiants), '*L'Amant*, intertexte sacré', in Vircondelet (ed.), *Duras, Dieu et l'écrit*, 163–75.

Fabien, Michel, 'Auschwitz, mon amour', in Bajomée and Heyndels (eds.), *Écrire, dit-elle*, 249–56.

Grivel, Charles, 'EUX. Remarques sur les personnages de l'au-delà', in Bajomée and Heyndels (eds.), *Écrire, dit-elle*, 217–34.

Guers-Villate, Yvonne, 'Dérive poétique et glissements métaphoriques dans *Aurélia Steiner* de Duras', in Bajomée and Heyndels (eds.), *Écrire, dit-elle*, 179–88.

—— 'Marguerite Duras's *La Maladie de la mort*: Feminist Indictment or Allegory?', in Ames (ed.), *Remains to be Seen*, 127–35.

Harvey, Robert, 'La Communauté par le rire', in Vircondelet (ed.), *Marguerite Duras: Rencontres de Cerisy*, 197–216.

Ince, Kate, 'Woman, Lover, Daughter, Mother: Female Genealogies in *Le Navire Night and Savannah Bay*', in Rodgers and Udris (eds.), *Marguerite Duras: Lectures plurielles*, 133–49.

Jacquot, Benoît, 'Comment elle fait', in Barat and Farges (eds.), *Marguerite Duras*, 123–8.

Lacan, Jacques, 'Hommage fait à Marguerite Duras, du ravissement de Lol V. Stein', in Barat and Farges (eds.), *Marguerite Duras*, 93–9. (Originally in *Cahiers Renaud-Barrault*, 52 (1965), 7–15).

Le Dantel, Denise, 'Le Malheur merveilleux', in Vircondelet (ed.), *Marguerite Duras: Rencontres de Cerisy*, 217–24.

Lydon, Mary, '*La Maladie de la mort*: Love in Marguerite Duras', in Ames (ed.), *Remains to be Seen*, 113–24.

Marini, Marcelle, 'L'Autre Corps', in Bajomée and Heyndels (eds.), *Écrire, dit-elle*, 21–48.

—— 'Transgressions', in Vircondelet (ed.), *Duras, Dieu et l'écrit*, 71–84.

—— 'Fortune et infortune de l'œuvre durassienne', in Rodgers and Udris (eds.), *Marguerite Duras: Lectures plurielles*, 169–83.

Martin, Bronwen, 'Spatial Figurativity in Marguerite Duras', in Rodgers and Udris (eds.), *Marguerite Duras: Lectures plurielles*, 95–113.

Mascolo, Dionys, 'Naissance de la tragédie', in Barat and Farges (eds.), *Marguerite Duras*, 104–17.

Mertens, Pierre, 'Pour en finir avec "l'année Duras" . . . ', in Bajomée and Heyndels (eds.), *Écrire, dit-elle*, 9–20.

Rodgers, Catherine, 'Déconstruction de la masculinité dans l'œuvre durassienne', in Vircondelet (ed.), *Marguerite Duras: Rencontres de Cerisy*, 47–68.

—— 'Lectures de la sorcière, ensorcellement de l'écriture', in Rodgers and Udris (eds.), *Marguerite Duras: Lectures plurielles*, 17–34.

Safranek, Ingrid, 'L'Écriture absolue, ou la dernière des romantiques', in Vircondelet (ed.), *Duras, Dieu et l'écrit*, 243–76.

—— 'Texte des origines, origines du texte', in Rodgers and Udris (eds.), *Marguerite Duras: Lectures plurielles*, 57–75.

Saint-Amand, Pierre, 'La Photographie de famille dans *L'Amant*', in Vircondelet (ed.), *Marguerite Duras: Rencontres de Cerisy*, 225–40.

—— 'L'Abîme et le secret', in Vircondelet (ed.), *Duras, Dieu et l'écrit*, 219–41.

Sheringham, Michael, ' "Là où se fait notre histoire . . .": L'Autobiographique et la quotidienneté chez Marguerite Duras', in Rodgers and Udris (eds.), *Marguerite Duras: Lectures plurielles*, 115–32.

Vircondelet, Alain, 'Avant-propos', in Vircondelet (ed.), *Marguerite Duras: Rencontres de Cerisy*, 9–10.

—— 'Marguerite Duras "condamnée à écrire" ', in Vircondelet (ed.), *Marguerite Duras: Rencontres de Cerisy*, 273–88.

Vircondelet, Alain, 'Introduction', in Vircondelet (ed.), *Duras, Dieu et l'écrit*, 9–12.

—— 'Marguerite Duras, libre et captive: des voix de l'écriture à la voie fatale', in Vircondelet (ed.), *Duras, Dieu et l'écrit*, 125–46.

—— 'Conclusion', in Vircondelet (ed.), *Duras, Dieu et l'écrit*, 297–9.

Williams, James S., 'The Point of No Return: Chiastic Adventures Between Self and Other in *Les Mains négatives* and *Au-delà des pages*', in Rodgers and Udris (eds.), *Marguerite Duras: Lectures plurielles*, 77–94.

3.iii Chapters in Books Devoted to Other Subjects

Bajomée, Danielle, 'Amour spéculaire et inceste dans l'œuvre de Marguerite Duras', in Coste, Didier, and Zerrafa, Michel (ed.), *Le Récit amoureux* (Seyssel: Éditions du Champ Vallon, 1984), 235–53.

Blanchot, Maurice, 'La Douleur du dialogue', in *Le Livre à venir* (Paris: Gallimard, 1959; coll. 'Idées', 1986), 207–18.

—— 'Détruire', in *L'Amitié* (Paris: Gallimard, 1971), 132–6.

Calle-Gruber, Mireille, 'L'Amour fou femme fatale Marguerite Duras: une récriture sublime des archétypes les mieux établis en littérature', in Allemand, Roger-Michel, *Le Nouveau Roman en questions, I: nouveau roman et archétypes* (Paris: Lettres modernes, 1992), 13–59.

Coward, David, 'Marguerite Duras', in Tilby, Michael (ed.), *Beyond the Nouveau Roman* (Oxford: Berg, 1990), 39–63.

Crowley, Martin, ' "Il n'y a qu'une espèce humaine": Between Duras and Antelme', in Leak, Andrew, and Paizis, George (eds.), *The Holocaust and the Text: Speaking the Unspeakable* (London: Macmillan, 2000), 174–92.

Evans, Martha Noel, 'Marguerite Duras: The Whore', in *Masks of Tradition* (London: Cornell University Press, 1987), 123–56.

Günther, Renate, 'Alcohol and Writing: Patterns of Obsession in the Work of Marguerite Duras', in Vice, Sue, Campbell, Matthew, and Armstrong, Tim (eds.), *Beyond the Pleasure Dome: Writing and Addiction from the Romantics* (Sheffield: Sheffield Academic Press, 1994), 200–5.

Hewitt, Leah D., *Autobiographical Tightropes* (London: University of Nebraska Press, 1990), 93–126.

Ince, Kate, 'L'Amour la mort: The Eroticism of Marguerite Duras', in Hughes, Alex, and Ince, Kate (eds.), *French Erotic Fiction: Women's Desiring Writing, 1880–1990* (Oxford: Berg, 1996), 147–73.

Jardine, Alice A., *Gynesis: Configurations of Woman and Modernity* (London: Cornell University Press, 1985), 172–7.

Kristeva, Julia, 'La Maladie de la douleur', in *Soleil noir: Dépression et mélancolie* (Paris: Gallimard, 1987), 227–65.

Montrelay, Michèle, 'Sur *Le Ravissement de Lol V. Stein*', in *L'Ombre et le nom* (Paris: Minuit, 1977), 7–23.

Moraud, Yves, 'Le Personnage dans l'œuvre romanesque de Marguerite Duras', in *Cahiers du CERF XX*, 3 (Brest: Université de Bretagne occidentale, 1987), 57–75.

Porter, Dennis, 'Marguerite Duras: Autobiographical Acts, Celebrity Status', in *Rousseau's Legacy* (Oxford: Oxford University Press, 1995), 217–37.

Ramsey, Raylene, 'Through a Textual Glass, Darkly: The Masochistic in the Feminine Self in Marguerite Duras's *Emily L.*', in *The French New Autobiographies* (Gainesville: University Press of Florida, 1996), 165–88.

—— '(Re)Writing Power in Duras's *L'Amant de la Chine du Nord*', in *The New French Autobiographies* (Gainesville: University Press of Florida, 1996), 189–214.

Rykner, Arnaud, *Théâtres du nouveau roman* (Paris: José Corti, 1988), 139–201.

Sheringham, Michael, *French Autobiography: Devices and Desires* (Oxford: Oxford University Press, 1993), 316–20.

Suleiman, Susan Rubin, 'Nadja, Dora, Lol V. Stein: Women, Madness, and Narrative', in Rimmon-Kenan, Shlomith (ed.), *Discourse in Psychoanalysis and Literature* (London: Methuen, 1987), 124–51.

Willis: Sharon A., 'Staging Sexual Difference: Reading, Recitation, and Repetition in Duras's *Malady of Death*', in Brater, Enoch (ed.), *Feminine Focus: The New Women Playwrights* (Oxford: Oxford University Press, 1989), 109–25.

Wilson, Emma, ' "Mon histoire de Lol V. Stein": Duras, Reading, and Amnesia', in *Sexuality and the Reading Encounter: Identity and Desire in Proust, Duras, Tournier, and Cixous* (Oxford: Clarendon, 1996), 163–91.

3.iv Articles in Journals

Alazet, Bernard, 'Les Traces noires de la douleur', *Revue des Sciences humaines*, 202 (avril–juin 1986), 37–51.

—— 'L'Embrasement, les cendres', *Revue des Sciences humaines*, 204 (octobre–décembre 1986), 147–60.

Amar, David, and Yana, Pierre, ' "Sublime, forcément sublime": A propos d'un article paru dans *Libération*', *Revue des Sciences humaines*, 202 (avril–juin 1986), 153–76.

Bajomée, Danielle, 'La Nuit battue à mort: description fragmentaire de l'écriture du désastre chez Marguerite Duras', *Revue des Sciences humaines*, 202 (avril–juin 1986), 5–35.

Bal, Mieke, 'Un Roman dans le roman: encadrement ou enchâssement? Quelques aspects du *Vice-Consul*', *Neophilologus*, 58/1 (January 1974), 2–21.

Barrault, Jean-Louis, 'Vers Marguerite Duras', *Cahiers Renaud-Barrault*, 52 (1965), 48–50.

—— 'Silence et solitude', *Cahiers Renaud-Barrault*, 89 (1975), 4–7.

—— 'Un Enfant obstiné', *L'Arc*, 98 (1985), 56–7.

Bashoff, Bruce, 'Death and Desire in Marguerite Duras's *Moderato cantabile*', *Modern Language Notes*, 94/4 (May 1979), 720–30.

Besnard-Coursodon, Micheline, 'Significations du méta-récit dans *Le Vice-Consul* de Marguerite Duras', *French Forum*, 3/1 (January 1978), 72–83.

Bishop, Lloyd, 'The Banquet Scene in *Moderato cantabile*: A Stylistic Analysis', *Romanic Review*, 69/3 (May 1978), 222–35.

Borgomano, Madeleine, 'Histoire de la mendiante indienne', *Poétique*, 48 (novembre 1981), 479–93.

—— 'L'Écriture féminine? A propos de Marguerite Duras', *Littérature*, 53 (février 1984), 59–68.

—— 'Romans: la fascination du vide', *L'Arc*, 98 (1985), 40–8.

—— 'Cinéma-écriture', *L'Arc*, 98 (1985), 76–80.

—— '*L'Amant*: une hypertextualité illimitée', *Revue des Sciences humaines*, 202 (avril–juin 1986), 67–77.

Bosch, Elisabeth, 'Bataille-Duras', *Neophilologus*, 67/3 (July 1983), 377–84.

Brée, Germaine, 'Quatre romans de Marguerite Duras', *Cahiers Renaud-Barrault*, 52 (1965), 23–39.

—— 'A Singular Adventure: The Writings of Marguerite Duras', *L'Esprit Créateur*, 30/1 (Spring 1990), 8–14.

Cagnon, Maurice, 'Marguerite Duras: Willed Imagination as Release and Obstacle', *Nottingham French Studies*, 16/1 (May 1977), 55–64.

Calle-Gruber, Mireille, 'Pourquoi n'a-t-on plus peur de Marguerite Duras?', *Littérature*, 63 (octobre 1986), 104–19.

Cixous, Hélène, and Foucault, Michel, 'A propos de Marguerite Duras', *Cahiers Renaud-Barrault*, 89 (1975), 8–22.

Clerk, Jeanne-Marie, 'Marguerite Duras, collaboratrice d'A. Resnais', *Revue des Sciences humaines*, 202 (avril–juin 1986), 103–16.

Cohen, Susan D., 'La Présence de rien', *Cahiers Renaud-Barrault*, 106 (1983), 17–36.

—— 'Fiction and the Photographic Image in Duras' *The Lover*', *L'Esprit Créateur*, 30/1 (Spring 1990), 56–68.

Conley, Verena Andermatt, 'Rodomontages of *Le Ravissement de Lol V. Stein*', *Yale French Studies*, 57 (1979), 23–35.

—— 'Signs of Love: Duras's Minimal Ways', *L'Esprit Créateur*, 29/3 (Fall 1989), 101–9.

—— '"L'Affaire Grégory" and Duras's Textual Feminism', *L'Esprit Créateur*, 30/1 (Spring 1990), 69–75.

Damiens, Claude, 'Marguerite Duras ou le silence au théâtre', *Paris-Théâtre*, 198 (14 septembre 1963), 38.

Davis, Colin, 'Duras, Antelme, and the Ethics of Writing', *Comparative Literature Studies*, 34/2 (1997), 170–83.

Delanoë, Nelcya, 'Ascenseur pour l'échafaud', *Esprit*, 116 (juillet 1986), 85–6.

Demers, Jeanne, 'De la sornette à *L'Amante anglaise*: le récit au degré zéro', *Études françaises*, 14/1–2 (avril 1978), 3–20.

Didier, Jacqueline, 'L'Écrivain mène l'enquête', *Critique*, 240 (mai 1967), 433–7.

Duvignaud, Jean, 'Le Clair-obscur de la vie quotidienne', *Cahiers Renaud-Barrault*, 52 (1965), 16–22.

Edson, Laurie, 'Knowing Lol: Duras, Epistemology and Gendered Mediation', *Substance*, 21/2 (1992), 17–31.

Etienne, Marie-France, 'L'Oubli et la répétition: *Hiroshima mon amour*', *Romanic Review*, 78/4 (November 1987), 508–14.

Fauvel, Maryse, '*Le Marin de Gibraltar* et *Détruire dit-elle* de Duras: sous le signe de Dionysos', *The French Review*, 65/2 (December 1991), 226–35.

Gaensbauer, Deborah B., 'Revolutionary Writing in Marguerite Duras' *L'Amour*', *The French Review*, 55/5 (April 1982), 633–9.

Gans, Eric, 'The Last French Novels', *Romanic Review*, 83/4 (November 1992), 501–16.

Golopentia, Sanda, 'De Versailles aux Yvelines', *Romanic Review*, 80/1 (January 1989), 30–49.

Gorrara, Claire, 'Bearing Witness in Robert Antelme's *L'Espèce humaine* and Marguerite Duras's *La Douleur*', *Women in French Studies*, 5 (October–November 1997), 243–51.

Greene, Robert W., 'Words for Love in Marguerite Duras: *L'Après-midi de Monsieur Andesmas* (1962) and *Le Ravissement de Lol V. Stein* (1964)', *Romanic Review*, 53/1 (January 1989), 131–48. (Reprinted in Greene, *Just Words: Moralism and Metalanguage in Twentieth-Century French Fiction*, 115–36).

Guers-Villate, Yvonne, 'L'Imaginaire et son efficacité chez Marguerite Duras', *Les Lettres romanes*, 29 (1975), 207–17.

—— 'Les Personnages durassiens et le temps', *Neophilologus*, 66/3 (July 1982), 360–6.

—— 'De l'implicite à l'explicite: de *Moderato cantabile* à *L'Homme assis dans le couloir*', *The French Review*, 58/3 (February 1985), 377–81.

Guicharnaud, Jacques, 'Woman's Fate: Marguerite Duras', *Yale French Studies*, 27 (1965), 106–13.

—— 'The Terrorist Marivaudage of Marguerite Duras', *Yale French Studies*, 46 (1971), 113–24.

Heathcote, Owen, 'Masochism, Sadism and Women's Writing: The Examples of Marguerite Duras and Monique Wittig', *Nottingham French Studies*, 32/2 (Autumn 1993), 71–84.

Hill, Leslie, 'Marguerite Duras and the Limits of Fiction', *Paragraph*, 12/1 (March 1989), 1–22.

—— 'Marguerite Duras: Sexual Difference and Tales of Apocalypse', *Modern Language Review*, 84/3 (July 1989), 601–14.

Hoog, Armand, 'The Itinerary of Marguerite Duras', *Yale French Studies*, 24 (Summer 1959), 68–73.

—— 'Today's Woman: Has She a Heart?', *Yale French Studies*, 27 (1961), 66–73.

Huston, Nancy, 'Les Limites de l'absolu', *Nouvelle Revue Française*, 542 (mars 1998), 10–20.

Kneller, John W., 'Elective Empathies and Musical Affinities', *Yale French Studies*, 27 (1961), 114–20.

Kristeva, Julia, 'Une Étrangère', *Nouvelle Revue Française*, 542 (mars 1998), 3–9.

Kritzman, Lawrence D., 'Duras' War', *L'Esprit Créateur*, 33/1 (Spring 1993), 63–73.

Liscia, Claude, 'La Place du pauvre', *Esprit*, 116 (juillet 1986), 87–96.

Luccioni, Gennie, 'Marguerite Duras et le "roman abstrait"', *Esprit*, 263–4 (juillet-août 1958), 73–6.

McLure, Roger, 'Duras *contra* Bergson: Time in *Moderato cantabile*', *Forum for Modern Language Studies*, 25 (1989), 62–76.

Makward, Christiane P., 'For a Stylistics of Marguerite Duras', *L'Esprit Créateur*, 30/1 (Spring 1990), 28–39.

Manceaux, Michèle, 'Tuer, dit-elle', *Nouvelle Revue Française*, 542 (mars 1998), 101–6.

Marini, Marcelle, 'La Mort d'une érotique', *Cahiers Renaud-Barrault*, 106 (1983), 37–57.

—— 'Une Femme sans aveu', *L'Arc*, 98 (1985), 6–16.

Michalski, Elaine, and Cagnon, Maurice, 'Marguerite Duras: vers un roman de l'ambivalence', *The French Review*, 51/3 (February 1978), 368–76.

Mistacco, Vicki, '*Plus ça change* . . . : The Critical Reception of *Emily L.*', *The French Review*, 66/1 (October 1992), 77–88.

Moskos, George, 'Child's Play: Repetition and Death in Duras's *Savannah Bay*', *Neophilologus*, 77/2 (April 1993), 215–22.

Murphy, Carol J., 'Thematic and Textual Violence in Duras' *Dix heures et demi du soir en été*', *L'Esprit Créateur*, 19/2 (Summer 1979), 75–84.

Noguez, Dominique, 'La Gloire des mots', *L'Arc*, 98 (1985), 25–39.

—— 'Notes sur Marguerite Duras (1975–1983)', *Nouvelle Revue Française*, 542 (mars 1998), 41–53.

O'Brien, John, 'Metaphor Between Lacan and Duras: Narrative Knots and the Plot of Seeing', *Forum for Modern Language Studies*, 29/3 (July 1993), 232–45.

Peraldi, François, 'The Passion of Death: A Free Associative Reading of Freud and Marguerite Duras', *L'Esprit Créateur*, 30/1 (Spring 1990), 19–27.

Pierrot, Jean, 'Histoire d'un fantôme', *Revue des Sciences humaines*, 202 (avril–juin 1986), 117–38.

Plottel, Jeanine Parisier, 'Memory, Fiction, History', *L'Esprit Créateur*, 30/1 (Spring 1990), 47–55.

Portuges, Catherine, 'Love and Mourning in Duras' *Aurélia Steiner*', *L'Esprit Créateur*, 30/1 (Spring 1990), 40–6.

Rosello, Mireille, 'L'Amertume: l'eau chez Marguerite Duras', *Romanic Review*, 78/4 (November 1987), 515–24.

Saporta, Marc, 'Les Possibles parallèles', *L'Arc*, 98 (1985), 3–5.

—— 'L'Existence inévitable de Marguerite D.', *L'Arc*, 98 (1985), 17–24.

—— 'Le Regard et l'école', *L'Arc*, 98 (1985), 49–50.

—— 'Les Yeux fermés', *L'Arc*, 98 (1985), 68–70.

Schulz-Jander, Eva-Maria, 'Marguerite Duras's *Le Ravissement de Lol V. Stein*: A Woman's Long Search for Absence', *Symposium*, 40/3 (Fall 1986), 223–33.

Schuster, Marilyn R., 'Reading and Writing as a Woman: The Retold Tales of Marguerite Duras', *The French Review*, 53/1 (October 1984), 48–57.

Sevilla, Miguel Angel, 'Duras et le nom des autres', *Esprit*, 116 (juillet 1986), 79–84.

Sheringham, Michael, 'Knowledge and Repetition in *Le Ravissement de Lol V. Stein*', *Romance Studies*, 2 (Summer 1983), 124–40.

Thibaud, Paul, 'Marguerite Duras: Les Ambiguïtés de la compassion', *Esprit*, 116 (juillet 1986), 75–7.

Tomiche, Anne, 'Repetition: Memory and Oblivion', *Revue de Littérature comparée*, 65 (1991), 261–76.

Williams, James, '*Le Système D.—le malheur merveilleux*. Duras and the Erotic Crimes of Montage in *Le Camion and Aurélia Steiner*', *Paragraph*, 15/1 (March 1992), 38–72.

Williams, James S., 'A Beast of a Closet: The Sexual Difference of a Literary Collaboration in the Work of Marguerite Duras and Yann Andréa', *Modern Language Review*, 87/3 (July 1992), 576–84.

Zepp, Evelyn H., 'Language as Ritual in Marguerite Duras's *Moderato cantabile*', *Symposium*, 30/3 (Fall 1976), 236–59.

3.v Articles in Newspapers, Periodicals

Amette, Jacques-Pierre, 'La Duras qui nous touche', *Le Point*, 9 mars 1996, 63.

Andréa, Yann, 'Duras mon amour', *Le Nouvel Observateur*, 26 août–1 septembre 1999, 4–12. (Extracts from Andréa, "*Cet amour-là . . .*").

Armel, Aliette, 'Le Jeu autobiographique', *Le Magazine littéraire*, 278 (juin 1990), 28–31.

Bajomée, Danielle, 'Veiller sur le sens absent', *Le Magazine littéraire*, 278 (juin 1990), 32–4.

Benichou, Paul, 'Ses Mots à elle . . .', *Le Nouvel Observateur*, 7–13 mars 1996, 46–7.

Calder, John, 'Marguerite Duras', *The Independent*, 4 March 1996, 14 (Obituary).

'Contre Duras', *L'Express*, 7–13 mars 1996, 46.

Coward, David, 'Passion into Prose', *The Guardian*, 4 March 1996, 12 (Obituary).

—— 'Light from a Dying Star', *Times Literary Supplement*, 21 May 1999, 6–7.

Damiens, Claude, 'Marguerite Duras ou le silence au théâtre', *Paris-Théâtre*, 198 (14 septembre 1963), 38.

Del-Bono, Jean-Laurent, 'L'Idole des jeunes', *Le Nouvel Observateur*, 3–9 février 1994, 18.

Desanti, Dominique, 'Cellule Marguerite', *Le Nouvel Observateur*, 7–13 mars 1996, 48–9.

Devarrieux, Claire, 'Morte, je peux encore écrire', *Libération*, 4 mars 1996, 31–4.

Dobbels, Daniel, 'L'Écriture du corps', *Le Magazine littéraire*, 278 (juin 1990), 35.

Eribon, Didier, 'La Maladie de la mort', *Le Nouvel Observateur*, 26 août–1 septembre 1999, 13.

Farges, Joël, 'Tourner le désastre du film', *Le Magazine littéraire*, 158 (mars 1980), 20.

Fernandez, Dominique, 'Rue Saint-Benoît', *Le Nouvel Observateur*, 7–13 mars 1996, 46.

Forrester, Viviane, 'Voir. Être vue', *Le Magazine littéraire*, no. 158 (mars 1980), 11–13.

—— 'L'Exactitude de l'excès', *Le Magazine littéraire*, 278 (juin 1990), 44–5.

Garcin, Jérôme, 'Quand Marguerite Duras scandalise ses consœurs . . .', *L'Événement du jeudi*, 25–31 juillet 1985, 28–30.

Gauthier, Xavière, 'Marguerite Duras et la lutte des femmes', *Le Magazine littéraire*, 158 (mars 1980), 16–19.

Hefez, Serge, 'Coups de foudre', *Gai pied*, 20 (novembre 1980), 17.

Josselin, Jean-François, 'M.D. la terrible', *Le Nouvel Observateur*, 7–13 mars 1996, 48.

—— 'Duras: La Vérité', *Le Nouvel Observateur*, 20–6 août 1998, 4–7.

—— 'Le Dernier Amant', *Le Nouvel Observateur*, 26 août–1 septembre 1999, 6.

—— 'Elle était d'une jalousie atroce', *Le Nouvel Observateur*, 26 août–1 septembre 1999, 8 (Interview with Yann Andréa).

Lamy, Jean-Claude, 'Marguerite Duras, l'éternelle rebelle', *Le Figaro*, 4 mars 1996, 26.

Lançon, Philippe, 'Le Survivant', *Libération*, 18 mars 1996, 44 (Interview with Yann Andréa).

Lefort, Gérard, 'Un Cinéma à voir entre les lignes', *Libération*, 4 mars 1996, 34.

—— ' "Sa pente paysanne" ', *Libération*, 4 mars 1996, 34 (Interview with Gérard Depardieu).

Le Naire, Olivier, 'Les Éclats de Marguerite', *L'Express*, 7–13 mars 1996, 49.

Marsan, Hugo, 'Cri et dépouillement', *Gai pied*, 20 (novembre 1980), 17.

Philipponnat, Véronique, 'Parlez-vous Duras?', *Elle*, 11 mars 1996, 79.

Poirot-Delpech, Bertrand, 'Marguerite Duras ou l'écriture mise à nu', *Le Monde*, 5 mars 1996, 1, 15.

—— ' "Blue Moon", ou le triomphe, enfin, du "subjectivisme" ', *Le Monde*, 5 mars 1996, 26.

Rouart, Jean-Marie, 'Une Exploratrice des abîmes', *Le Figaro*, 4 mars 1996, 26.

Roy, Claude, 'Celle qui écrivait les voix', *Le Nouvel Observateur*, 7–13 mars 1996, 49.

Salino, Brigitte, 'Marguerite Duras: pas forcément', *Le Monde*, 19 mars 1996, 29.

Sigaud, Marie, 'Duras est morte, forcément', *France-Soir*, 4 mars 1996, 5.

Sollers, Philippe, 'Duras "Telle Quelle" ', *Le Nouvel Observateur*, 12–16 janvier 1970, 36.

—— 'Comment elle est devenue Duras', *Le Nouvel Observateur*, 3–9 février 1994, 20–2.

Trétiack, Philippe, 'Son dernier livre', *Elle*, 11 mars 1996, 81.

—— 'Le Look Marguerite', *Elle*, 11 mars 1996, 82.

Tytell, Pamela, 'Lacan, Freud et Duras', *Le Magazine littéraire*, 158 (mars 1980), 14–15.

Vircondelet, Alain, 'L'Actualité imaginaire', *Le Magazine littéraire*, 278 (juin 1990), 54–6.

—— 'Marguerite Duras: L'écriture, c'est moi', *L'Express*, 7–13 mars 1996, 94–7.

Wajsbrot, Cecile, 'Traduire, dit-elle . . .', *Le Journal littéraire*, 2 (décembre 1987–janvier 1988), 114.

Webster, Paul, 'Row over Duras Biography Muddies Fact and Fiction', *The Guardian*, 28 July 1998, 13.

Weinzaepflen, Catherine, 'Un Itinéraire de raréfaction', *Le Magazine littéraire*, 158 (mars 1980), 10.

3.vi Special Numbers Devoted to Duras

Cahiers Renaud-Barrault, 52 (1965).

Cahiers Renaud-Barrault, 89 (1975).

Le Magazine littéraire, 158 (mars 1980).

L'Arc, 98 (1985).

Revue des Sciences humaines, 202 (avril–juin 1986).

L'Esprit Créateur, 30/1 (Spring 1990).

Le Magazine littéraire, 278 (juin 1990).

Nouvelle Revue Française, 542 (mars 1998).

4. GENERAL WORKS

Adorno, Theodor W., *Negative Dialectics* (1966), trans. E. B. Ashton (London: Routledge and Kegan Paul, 1973).

Andréa, Yann, *M.D.* (Paris: Minuit, 1983).

Antelme, Robert, *L'Espèce humaine* (1947) (Paris: Gallimard, 1957; édition revue et corrigée, coll. 'Tel', 1978).

—— *Textes inédits/ Sur* L'Espèce humaine/ *Essais et témoignages* (Paris: Gallimard, 1996).

Armel, Aliette, 'Un Itinéraire politique', *Le Magazine littéraire*, 278 (juin 1990), 36–40.

Atack, Margaret, *Literature and the French Resistance* (Manchester: Manchester University Press, 1989).

Bakhtin, Mikhail, 'Discourse in the Novel' (1934–5), in Holquist, Michael (ed.), *The Dialogic Imagination*, trans. Caryl Emerson and Michael Holquist (Austin: University of Texas Press, 1981).

Barthes, Roland, *Mythologies* (Paris: Seuil, 1957; coll. 'Points', 1970).

—— 'La Métaphore de l'œil', in *Essais critiques* (Paris: Seuil, 1964; coll. 'folio', 1981), 238–45.

—— *Sade, Fourier, Loyola* (Paris: Seuil, coll. 'Tel Quel', 1971).

—— *Fragments d'un discours amoureux* (Paris: Seuil, coll. 'Tel Quel', 1977).

Bataille, Georges, *L'Expérience intérieure* (Paris: Gallimard, 1943; texte revu et corrigé, 1954; coll. 'Tel', 1994).

—— 'Réflexions sur le bourreau et la victime', in *Œuvres complètes*, xi (Paris: Gallimard, 1988), 262–7.

Bataille, Georges, *Madame Edwarda* (Paris: Jean-Jacques Pauvert, 1956).

—— *L'Érotisme* (Paris: Minuit, 1957; coll. 'Arguments', 1970).

—— *Œuvres complètes*, v (Paris: Gallimard, 1973).

Bauman, Zygmunt, *Modernity and the Holocaust* (Cambridge: Polity, 1989).

—— *Postmodern Ethics* (Oxford: Blackwell, 1993).

Beardsmore, R.W., *Art and Morality* (London: Macmillan, 1971).

Beckett, Samuel, and Duthuit, Georges, *Proust* and *Three Dialogues* (London: John Calder, 1965).

Benjamin, Andrew (ed.), *The Lyotard Reader* (Oxford: Blackwell, 1989).

Bennington, Geoffrey, 'Frontier', *Paragraph*, 17/3 (November 1994), 224–6.

Bernasconi, Robert, 'Deconstruction and the Possibility of Ethics', in Sallis, J. (ed.), *Deconstruction and Philosophy* (London: University of Chicago Press, 1987), 122–39.

Bersani, Leo, *The Culture of Redemption* (Cambridge, Mass.: Harvard University Press, 1990).

Blanchot, Maurice, *L'Entretien infini* (Paris: Gallimard, 1969).

—— 'Le Refus', in *L'Amitié* (Paris: Gallimard, 1971), 130–1.

—— *Le Pas au-delà* (Paris: Gallimard, 1973).

—— *L'Écriture du désastre* (Paris: Gallimard, 1980).

—— *La Communauté inavouable* (Paris: Minuit, 1983).

—— 'Énigme', *Yale French Studies*, 79 (1991), 5–7.

Booth, Wayne C., *The Company We Keep* (London: University of California Press, 1988).

Bowie, Malcolm, *The Morality of Proust* (Oxford: Oxford University Press, 1994).

Caputo, John D., *Against Ethics* (Bloomington: Indiana University Press, 1993).

—— *The Prayers and Tears of Jacques Derrida* (Bloomington: Indiana University Press, 1997).

Cixous, Hélène, 'Le Rire de la Méduse', *L'Arc*, 61 (1975), 39–54.

Cohn-Bendit, Daniel, 'Notre commune du 10 mai', *Le Nouvel Observateur*, 15 mai 1968, 32–4.

Combes, Patrick, *La Littérature et le mouvement de mai 1968* (Paris: Seghers, 1984).

Connor, Steven, 'Honour Bound?', *Times Literary Supplement*, 5 January 1996, 24–6.

Cornell, Drucilla, *The Philosophy of the Limit* (London: Routledge, 1992).

Critchley, Simon, *The Ethics of Deconstruction* (Oxford: Blackwell, 1992).

—— *Very Little . . . Almost Nothing* (London: Routledge, 1997).

—— 'The Original Traumatism: Levinas and Psychoanalysis', in Rainsford and Woods (eds.), *Critical Ethics*, 88–104.

Crowther, Paul, *The Kantian Sublime* (Oxford: Oxford University Press, 1989).

Dardigna, Anne-Marie, *Les Châteaux d'Éros ou les infortunes du sexe des femmes* (Paris: François Maspero, 1981).

Davis, Colin, *Elie Wiesel's Secretive Texts* (Gainesville, Florida: University Press of Florida, 1994).

—— *Levinas* (Cambridge: Polity, 1996).

De Certeau, Michel, *La Prise de parole et autres écrits politiques* (Paris: Seuil, coll. 'Points', 1994).

De Man, Paul, 'Autobiography as De-Facement', in *The Rhetoric of Romanticism* (New York: Columbia University Press, 1984), 67–81.

Derrida, Jacques, 'Violence et métaphysique', in *L'Écriture et la différence* (Paris: Seuil, 1967; coll. 'Points', 1979), 117–228.

—— 'Hors livre', in *La Dissémination* (Paris: Seuil, coll. 'Tel Quel', 1972), 7–67.

—— 'La Double Séance', in *La Dissémination* (Paris: Seuil, coll. 'Tel Quel', 1972), 199–317.

—— *Glas* (Paris: Galilée, 1974; Denoël/Gonthier, 1981).

—— 'En ce moment même dans cet ouvrage me voici', in Laruelle, François (ed.), *Textes pour Emmanuel Levinas* (Paris: J.-M. Place, 1980), 21–60.

—— *Feu la cendre* (Paris: des femmes, 1987).

—— *Spectres de Marx* (Paris: Galilée, 1993).

Derrida, Jacques, and Labarrière, Pierre-Jean, *Altérités* (Paris: Osiris, 1986).

'Duraille, Marguerite', *Virginie Q.*, Texte présenté par Patrick Rambaud (Paris: Balland, 1988).

Eaglestone, Robert, 'Flaws: James, Nussbaum, Miller, Levinas', in Rainsford and Woods (eds.), *Critical Ethics*, 77–87.

Eichenberg, Ingrid, *Mai 68 im französischen Roman* (Marburg: Hitzeroth, 1987).

Ezrahi, Sidra Dekoven, *By Words Alone: The Holocaust in Literature* (London: University of Chicago Press, 1980).

Felman, Shoshana, and Laub, Dori, *Testimony: Crises of Witnessing in Literature, Psychoanalysis, and History* (London: Routledge, 1992).

Foucault, Michel, 'Préface à la transgression', in *Dits et écrits, 1954–1988*, i (1954–1969) (Paris: Gallimard, 1994), 233–50.

Genet, Jean, *L'Ennemi déclaré* (*Œuvres complètes*, vi) (Paris: Gallimard, 1991).

Grand Larousse de la langue française, 7 vols. (Paris: Larousse, 1977).

Greene, Robert W., *Just Words: Moralism and Metalanguage in Twentieth-Century French Fiction* (Pennsylvania: Pennsylvania University Press, 1993).

Gregg, John, *Maurice Blanchot and the Literature of Transgression* (Princeton: Princeton University Press, 1994).

Hadfield, Andrew, Rainsford, Dominic, and Woods, Tim (eds.), *The Ethics in Literature* (Basingstoke: Macmillan, 1999).

—— 'Introduction: Literature and the Return to Ethics', in Hadfield, Rainsford, and Woods (eds.), *The Ethics in Literature*, 1–14.

Hand, Seán (ed.), *The Levinas Reader* (Oxford: Blackwell, 1989).

Harpham, Geoffrey Galt, *Getting It Right: Language, Literature, and Ethics* (London: University Press of Chicago, 1992).

Heaney, Seamus, *The Redress of Poetry* (London: Faber and Faber, 1995).

Hill, Leslie, *Blanchot: Extreme Contemporary* (London: Routledge, 1997).

Holland, Michael (ed.), *The Blanchot Reader* (Oxford: Blackwell, 1995).

Irigaray, Luce, *Éthique de la différence sexuelle* (Paris: Minuit, 1984).

Jefferson, Ann, 'Autobiography as Intertext', in Still, Judith, and Worton, Michael (eds.), *Intertextuality: Theory and Practices* (Manchester: Manchester University Press, 1990), 108–29.

Josebury, Simon, 'Sublime: Hurts So Good', *Paragraph*, 17/3 (November 1994), 266–9.

Kearney, Richard, *Dialogues With Contemporary Thinkers* (Manchester: Manchester University Press, 1984).

Kierkegaard, Søren, *Fear and Trembling* and *Repetition*, ed. and trans. Howard V. Hong and Edna H. Hong (Princeton: Princeton University Press, 1983).

—— *Either/Or*, ed. and trans. Howard H. Hong and Edna V. Hong (Princeton: Princeton University Press, 1987).

Kolb, Philippe (ed.), *Correspondance de Marcel Proust*, v (1905) (Paris: Plon, 1979).

Kristeva, Julia, 'Éthique de la linguistique', *Critique*, 322 (mars 1974), 206–16.

—— 'Un Nouveau Type d'intellectuel: Le Dissident', *Tel Quel*, 74 (Hiver 1977), 3–8.

Lacan, Jacques, *Le Séminaire, livre VII: l'éthique de la psychanalyse* (Paris: Seuil, coll. 'Le Champ freudien', 1986).

Lacoue-Labarthe, Philippe, and Nancy, Jean-Luc, *L'Absolu littéraire* (Paris: Seuil, coll. 'Poétique', 1978).

Land, Nick, *The Thirst for Annihilation: Georges Bataille and Virulent Nihilism (An Essay in Atheistic Religion)* (London: Routledge, 1992).

Laplanche, Jean, and Pontalis, Jean-Baptiste, *Vocabulaire de la psychanalyse* (Paris: PUF, 1967).

Lechte, John, *Fifty Key Contemporary Thinkers* (London: Routledge, 1994).

Lejeune, Philippe, *Le Pacte autobiographique* (Paris: Seuil, 1975).

Levi, Primo, *If This Is A Man* and *The Truce*, trans. Stuart Woolf (London: Sphere, 1987).

Levinas, Emmanuel, *De Dieu qui vient à l'idée* (Paris: Vrin, 1982).

—— *Éthique et infini* (Paris: Fayard, 1982).

Lignes, 33 (Paris: Hazan, 1998).

'Longinus', *On Sublimity*, trans. D. A. Russell (Oxford: Clarendon Press, 1965).

Lyotard, Jean-François, *Le Différend* (Paris: Minuit, 1984).

Macey, David, *The Lives of Michel Foucault* (London: Vintage, 1994).

MacIntyre, Alisdair, *A Short History of Ethics* (1987) (London: Routledge, 1993).

McNab, Chris, 'Derrida, Rushdie, and the Ethics of Mortality', in Hadfield, Rainsford, and Woods (eds.), *The Ethics in Literature*, 136–51.

Marks, Elaine, and Stambolian, George (eds.), *Homosexualities and French Literature* (London: Cornell University Press, 1979).

Mascolo, Dionys, *Autour d'un effort de mémoire* (Paris: Maurice Nadeau, 1987).

—— *A la recherche d'un communisme de pensée* (Paris: Fourbis, 1993).

Massey, Irving, *Find You the Virtue* (Fairfax: George Mason University Press, 1987).

Miller, J. Hillis, *The Ethics of Reading* (New York: Columbia University Press, 1987).

Nancy, Jean-Luc, 'Les Iris', *Yale French Studies*, 81 (1992), 46–63.

—— *Les Muses* (Paris: Galilée, 1994).

The New Encyclopaedia Britannica (London: University of Chicago Press, 1993).

Newton, Adam Zachary, *Narrative Ethics* (London: Harvard University Press, 1995).

Norris, Christopher, *Truth and the Ethics of Criticism* (Manchester: Manchester University Press, 1994).

Noys, Benjamin, 'Transgressing Transgression: The Limits of Bataille's Fiction', in Duffy, Larry, and Tudor, Adrian (eds.), *Les Lieux interdits: Transgression and French Literature* (Hull: University of Hull Press, 1998), 307–21.

Nussbaum, Martha C., *Love's Knowledge* (Oxford: Oxford University Press, 1990).

Oxford English Dictionary, Second Edition (Oxford: Clarendon Press, 1989).

Parker, David, *Ethics, Theory and the Novel* (Cambridge: Cambridge University Press, 1994).

Price, Martin, *Forms of Life: Character and Moral Imagination in the Novel* (London: Yale University Press, 1983).

Rainsford, Dominic, and Woods, Tim (eds.), *Critical Ethics: Text, Theory, and Responsibility* (Basingstoke: Macmillan, 1999).

Ravvin, Norman, 'Have You Reread Levinas Lately? Transformations of the Face in Post-Holocaust Fiction', in Hadfield, Rainsford, and Woods (eds.), *The Ethics in Literature*, 52–69.

Reader, Keith, and Wadia, Khursheed, *The May 1968 Events in France* (Basingstoke: Macmillan, 1993).

Readings, Bill, *Introducing Lyotard* (London: Routledge, 1991).

'La Révolution ici maintenant', *Tel Quel*, 34 (1968), 3–4.

Richards, I. A., *Principles of Literary Criticism* (1925) (London: Routledge and Kegan Paul, 1983).

Roques, Philippe, and Donnadieu, Marguerite, *L'Empire français* (Paris: Gallimard, 1940).

Rose, Gillian, *The Broken Middle* (Oxford: Blackwell, 1992).

Roy, Claude, *Nous* (Paris: Gallimard, 1972).

Royle, Nicholas, *After Derrida* (Manchester: Manchester University Press, 1995).

Rudd, Anthony, *Kierkegaard and the Limits of the Ethical* (Oxford: Clarendon Press, 1993).

Sartre, Jean-Paul, *L'Imaginaire* (Paris: Gallimard, 1940).

—— *Réflexions sur la question juive* (Paris: Gallimard, 1954).

Schiach, Morag, *Hélène Cixous: A Politics of Writing* (London: Routledge, 1991).

Seale, Patrick, and McConville, Maureen, *French Revolution 1968* (London and Harmondsworth: Heinemann and Penguin, 1968).

Sedgwick, Eve Kosofsky, *Between Men: English Literature and Male Homosocial Desire* (New York: Columbia University Press, 1985).

Siebers, Tobin, *The Ethics of Criticism* (London: Cornell University Press, 1988).

Smith, Robert, *Derrida and Autobiography* (Cambridge: Cambridge University Press, 1995).

Sontag, Susan, 'On Style', in *Against Interpretation* (London: Vintage, 1994), 15–36.

Steiner, George, *Antigones* (Oxford: Clarendon Press, 1984).

—— *Real Presences* (London: Faber and Faber, 1990).

Du Sublime (Paris: Belin, coll. 'l'extrême contemporain', 1988).

Suleiman, Susan Rubin, 'Transgression and the Avant-Garde', in *Subversive Intent* (Cambridge, Mass.: Harvard University Press, 1990), 72–87.

Surya, Michel (ed.), *Georges Bataille: Choix de lettres, 1917–1962* (Paris: Gallimard, 1997).

Tolstoy, Leo, *What Is Art?* (1898) (Harmondsworth: Penguin, 1995).

Touraine, Alain, *Le Communisme utopique* (Paris: Seuil, coll. 'L'histoire immédiate', 1972).

Wardi, Charlotte, 'L'Oubli du génocide dans le roman français de 1945 à 1970', *Les Nouveaux Cahiers*, 58 (Automne 1979), 4–9.

West, Lori Branch, 'The Benefit of Doubt: The Ethics of Reading', in Rainsford and Woods (eds.), *Critical Ethics*, 187–202.

Whitford, Margaret, *Luce Irigaray: Philosophy in the Feminine* (London: Routledge, 1991).

Williams, Bernard, *Ethics and the Limits of Philosophy* (London: Fontana, 1987).

Williams, Linda, *Hard Core* (London: Pandora, 1990).

Winterson, Jeanette, 'The Poetics of Sex', in Reynolds, Margaret (ed.), *The Penguin Book of Lesbian Short Stories* (Harmondsworth: Penguin, 1993), 412–22.

Wittgenstein, Ludwig, *Tractatus Logico-Philosophicus* (London: Routledge and Kegan Paul, 1949).

Yale French Studies, 79 (1991): *Literature and the Ethical Question.*

INDEX